The
Church
on the
Margins

The
Church
on the
Margins

LIVING
CHRISTIAN
COMMUNITY

Mary R. Sawyer

TRINITY PRESS INTERNATIONAL
A Continuum imprint
HARRISBURG • LONDON • NEW YORK

In loving memory of my mother
Polly Kentfield Sawyer

Trinity Press International
P.O. Box 1321
Harrisburg, PA 17105

Trinity Press International is a member of the Continuum International Publishing Group.

Design: Corey Kent

Library of Congress Cataloging-in-Publication Data
Sawyer, Mary R.
  The church on the margins : living christian community / Mary R. Sawyer
    p. cm.
Includes bibliographical references and index.
  ISBN 1-56338-366-7 (pbk.)
  1. United States--Church history. I. Title.
  BR515.S26 2003
  277.3'08'08--dc21

                    2003008310

Printed in the United States of America

03 04 05 06 07 08   10 9 8 7 6 5 4 3 2 1

Contents

Preface

Some time ago, my friend's Uncle Art, who lived in a glass house on a mountainside near Eden, Vermont, declared that, "Except for the Religious Right, the churches are dying." In saying this, he was not throwing stones, but simply harvesting his tree of knowledge. I countered that while many institutional churches were indeed struggling,[1] another model of "church"—namely, Christian community—appeared to be growing and perhaps held promise as the church of the future. This model, I hastened to add, was emphatically not the model of the Religious Right.

The Christian Church in the United States is a complex entity—a mosaic of churches of the privileged and churches of the oppressed; churches of Euro-Americans and churches of people of color; churches of individual salvation and churches of social action. They all count themselves Christian, but they all present an understanding of Christianity as it has been filtered through the respective social experiences of their leaders and members. The United States, with its great diversity of peoples, has been the seedbed for a garden of varieties of Christianity. Some varieties, however, have garnered more attention than others.

The common exclusion of Christians who are Native American, African American, Latina\o, Asian American, feminist, gay, and lesbian from majority discussions of the status of Christianity in the United States is itself testimony to their continued marginalized status in our society. This exclusion is testimony as well to the paucity of Christian community, at least as it is defined in this book, in mainstream American Christianity. The characteristic absence of Christian community in white churches, however, is not a new or recent phenomenon, but dates to the Protestant colonization of what became the United States of America. Anti-community, discussed at length in part 1, was solidified as colonial Christianity's first principle in the genocide, slavery, and patriarchy practiced by the representatives of Western Christendom who settled the New World and determined the majority values of a new society.

The experiences of being colonized, exterminated, enslaved, and otherwise marginalized did not preclude those deemed to be "other" from embracing Christianity. But these experiences did cause many of them to make Christianity something different than the colonizers' version. Marginalized converts came to Christianity with indigenous systems of cultural values that preceded the experience of oppression at the hands of the colonizers. Prominent among these values was that of community. This value was only reinforced as people were assigned subordinate social status based on their membership in a given group. Members of the racial and ethnic groups that were subjected to cultural imperialism by European and Euro-American Christians—that is, that were forbidden their own indigenous rituals, traditions, and languages—nonetheless discerned in the religion of Christianity, if not in the practices of Christians, further support for the centrality of community.

Conversely, the dominant values of white colonizers, with notable exceptions, became individualism, dominance, and control, all of which were and are antithetical to "community." Among the central features of Christian community are inclusiveness, spirituality, and just relations. What resulted in white establishment Christianity was less a community-oriented church and more an Imperial Church. While many mainstream churches over the past century have sought to become something other than colonizing churches, they have achieved only partial success. In most of them, the numbers of ethnic minority members are relatively few. The continuation of repressive and exclusive practices, in both mainline and sectarian churches, is the source of the discomfiture felt by many heterosexual women and gay, lesbian, bisexual, and transgendered persons who, in recent decades, have publicly claimed membership in the Church on the Margins.

Members of these groups have pursued their own constructions of Christian community. Among the examples discussed in part 2 are the community-building efforts of African American churches, Latina/o base Christian communities, Asian American traditions of community, feminist movements such as Women-Church and Re-Imagining, and the Welcoming movement of gays and lesbians.

Always there have been prophetic exceptions among the ranks of the privileged classes; always there are those among the proverbial blind who are "made to see" and in the "seeing" become alienated from the paradigm in which they had been socialized. Thus, the story of Christian community-building includes descendants of the colonizers who by virtue of this alienation are themselves among the marginalized. Some of these individuals, men as well as women, are working to renew or transform their churches—some of them by creating alternative "churches" within or parallel to the traditional established churches. These efforts, which range from intentional Christian communities, to Catholic extra-church organizations, to Protestant networks of progressive, justice-seeking groups are explored in part 3.

My interest in these developments is inextricably tied to my own life journey, and so I would be remiss not to speak of my particular experiences with community. Reflecting on decades past, it becomes apparent to me that the central issue of my life has been community—or more precisely, the pursuit and loss of community.

For some years now, I have expressed to my students the sentiment that a large part of the difficulty white Protestants in this country experience is due to the lack of a "tribal" identity. The values of materialism, consumerism, individualism, and competition make it difficult for persons socialized in such a culture to know who they otherwise are. White Protestants define themselves in contrast to "others." Most everyone in the United States, except for white Protestants, belongs to a socio-psychological "tribe": Jews, African Americans, Muslims, Korean Americans, gays and lesbians, Cuban Americans, and even non-Hispanic Catholics. This doesn't mean there are not also marginalized individuals with membership in one or another of these groups. But relatively few white Protestants, except to the extent that fundamentalism provides an identity for Protestants on the right, any longer experience a connection to a distinct heritage or cultural tradition other than being generically "American."

On an occasion when I was present at a women's Celtic spirituality gathering, the participants, most of whom were Catholic and all of whom were Americans, were asked to identify themselves. With but one or two exceptions, they said that they were "all Irish." I identified myself as being "all Nebraskan." I was born a white Protestant in St. Mary's Catholic Hospital where my earliest caregivers were Catholic nuns; I have never been sure if this circumstance was the origin of my lifelong quest for tribal membership.

I grew up in a racially homogeneous farming community in south-central Nebraska. My first contact with people of other colors, which occurred at about the age of five, was with members of a black gospel quartet who, through circumstances unknown to me, were invited to perform at our local Presbyterian church. From that time on I recall seeing no other people of color in person until, as a high school student, I attended an International Girl Scout Jamboree where the occupants of the tents neighboring mine were southern and black. It is an understatement of substantial proportions to say that this was an enlightening experience, as were my first encounters with African American students when I began college.

I do not recall hearing overt statements of bigotry in my growing up years. There was no need: Difference was not a significant part of our day-to-day living. At the same time, as I later came to realize, lessons of racial stereotyping and prejudice were subtly embedded in the songs we sang, in our storybooks, and in the taken-for-grantedness that the real world was white. These are the messages that so many of us spend much of our lives working to excise.

The arrival of television in our corner of the world coincided with the early events of the civil rights movement. My first memory of these televised events is of the Little Rock, Arkansas, school desegregation conflict. Exactly what impact this made I do not know, but the images assuredly were imprinted on my subconscious mind and no doubt fused with the turmoil in my own young life at that time.

The world changed when my parents divorced and my mother, my sisters, and I left the farm to move into town. The relational, supportive features that we associate with community were not a part of my growing up years beyond the age of ten. As a 1950s child of a low-income, single, working mother in conservative, rural Nebraska, I felt very much outside the local community norms of acceptability and certainly outside the social circles of the economically "elite." For the most part I experienced the world as a hazardous, often threatening place. How astonished I was to learn, upon leaving home, that whole populations of people experience the world as a hazardous, often threatening place. Fortuitously, this was the decade of the sixties, which afforded me the opportunity to become a social activist in pursuit of racial justice.

The motivation for my activism came not solely from the fact that my own spirit had been violated; it came as well from the tenets of the faith as I had come to understand them: All people were equal in the eyes of God and all people were to be treated accordingly. It turned out that ministers both in my hometown and in my college town disagreed with me. In the face of their condemnation of my associating with blacks, I left the organized church, rejecting on principle an institution that was decidedly racist. At the same time, I was confirmed by the preaching of the Reverend Dr. Martin Luther King Jr., and his fellow black clergy.

This book has its origins in these experiences—in the tension between an imperial church on the one hand and an embodied theology of justice on the other. This tension, in turn, is tied to issues of community.

My earliest experience of spirit-community was the civil rights movement. Indeed, engagement in this movement proved to be the most profound, most formative religious experience of my life. Dr. King's social gospel theology resonated with my own sense of how the world was meant to be, while the black liberation theology later given voice by James Cone and others contributed the concept of empowerment that was so essential for building such a world.

The sense of community that we experienced in the civil rights movement was never complete, in part because it was so idealized. But it was substantial. And it was shattered in 1968 with the deaths of Martin Luther King Jr. and Robert Kennedy. My heroes in the sixties were the Kennedys, King, and Pope John XXIII—three Catholics and a Baptist preacher. Many of us who had been involved in the civil rights movement, however peripherally, found our lives thereafter defined by a great longing for the re-creation of that extraordinary moment of purpose and possibility.

After working in a municipal human relations department in the Midwest for several years, the mid-1970s found me living in northern California and working for one of the two black lieutenant governors to have been elected since Reconstruction. Black political development, at that time, was understood to be an extension of the civil rights movement. In addition to being a speechwriter for Governor (later Congressman) Mervyn Dymally, I served as his liaison with social justice movements, among which were the United Farm Workers, the American Indian Movement, and the Rainbow Coalition. I also had the opportunity to work with the Democratic Minority Coalition, an organization started by Dymally that constituted the first political coalition in California to include the gay and lesbian community overtly.

In addition, I reconnected with the spirit of the civil rights movement by way of a politically progressive, interracial movement in San Francisco known as Peoples Temple. While I was neither a member of Peoples Temple, nor a regular participant in either its worship activity or political events, I was emotionally and spiritually nurtured by this movement. Peoples Temple became a sanctuary—a primary source of encouragement and support for the social justice work in which I was then engaged. In 1978, that community—my community—died in the mass homicides and suicides that we know as "Jonestown."[2]

I spent a good part of the next decade in seminary and in graduate school, studying liberation theology, black religion, and social change movements. Throughout those years, I also experienced a profound aversion to anything that evoked the feeling of community. The one exception was my experience at the Howard University School of Divinity, where I was enfolded in the pastoral care of Dean Lawrence Jones, as well as faculty members and classmates.

In the late 1980s, I began, finally, the emotional work of coming to terms with Jonestown. In the process, I experienced the church in which I was then a member—a black Methodist congregation—as the one place I could go to sit and weep and, in the midst of a community well acquainted with suffering, be welcomed with no requirement of explanation or justification. At the same time, I began to engage feminist spirituality and theology more systematically and, in doing so, found the *concept* of community gradually, gingerly, moving to center stage in my life and work.

In the mid-1990s, I was invited by a religious community—the Dubuque Sisters of St. Francis—to test their trustworthiness; I accepted, though not without a degree of apprehension. Following a prolonged absence from the institutional church (the better to avoid its racism), I had subsequently become a member of various African American congregations. But at this point in my journey, I was drawn to the diversity, spirituality, and social teachings of the Catholic tradition, in which I found certain parallels with the black religious tradition. For a time, I felt as if I had ended up where I had always been.

I quickly learned that the Franciscan community, which was then engaged in a four-year study/action program on racism, was one face of the Catholic Church while the local parish was quite another. Even in the exceptional "peace and justice" parishes there remained the nonnegotiable realities of patriarchal authority, exclusive language, and heterosexism. I retained my association with the Franciscans,[3] joined an ecumenical Christian community, and connected with a nearby Women-Church group. I also began hanging out at the Unitarian-Universalist Fellowship, which I think of as a tribe of tribeless people, while simultaneously journeying with a local United Methodist church as it became a Reconciling congregation, welcoming gays and lesbians.

These experiential engagements with community prompted me—nudged me—to begin this book project, but the work was interrupted when significant individuals in my life—a dear friend of twenty-three years, my closest colleague, and then my mother—became ill. Between October 1996 and October 1999, each of them died of cancer. I have returned to this project as a way of honoring and remembering Leanna Bell, JoDee Rottler, and my mother, Polly Kentfield Sawyer, to whom this book is dedicated. They continue to be part of my spirit community.

In my professional capacity, my objective in this book is to examine manifestations of Christian community on the margins of our society. As a survivor of community experimentation gone wrong, I am concerned about the pitfalls associated with the process of community-building. As a social, spiritual being with my own needs of relationship, I write in order to understand "community" more fully. There is thus a creative tension in this work between my scholarship and my personal story. So, too, a theme throughout the book is the perpetual tension between seeking Christian community and falling short, between the ideal and human fallibility.

I mean for this book to be of use to practicing Christians, both professionals in ministry and lay activists, and students of religion in America. At the same time, I hope it will not be of disinterest to professional theologians, social historians, and sociologists of religion. It will be of greater interest to scholars who affirm the interrelationship of these fields.

I start from the premise that all theologies arise out of particular social contexts and all theologies have social consequences, for good or for ill. My sociological affinity is with that school that acknowledges an ethical dimension and affirms practical application. I have much empathy with what Dr. Marie Augusta Neal, S.N.D., calls "socio-theology." In my own work, I have taken to heart her insight that "one aspect of the link between religion and society that needs careful study is the difference in people's ideas about God and where God is to be found, depending on whether they are bent on liberation or on repressing movements of liberation."[4]

I come to this task variously as insider, outsider, and engaged observer, readily acknowledging that I cannot be as experientially grounded in groups other than my own as are the members of these respective groups. My intent is to enable the voices of different particularities to be heard. At the outset, however, I propose a working definition of "Christian community" as a backdrop against which to view the varied understandings of Christian community in their respective contexts.

For myself, and I would hope for the reader as well, this entire project is an exercise in entering into the experience of the "other." "Otherness" changes, of course, depending on where one stands. For those on the margins, the established church may be "other." Those whom the established church defines as "other" often define themselves—"we, the people"—as "we, the church." It is also the case that one marginalized group may regard another marginalized group as "other." A part of my experience has been that while African Americans, to use one example, know their own experience, they may know little of the experiences of Asian Americans or Latina/o Americans. And so it is for each group in turn. It follows that members of respective particularities are not always aware of one another's approaches to Christian community. (Of course, for reasons of survival, it is historically the case that people of color know more about white folk than white folk know about people of color.)

This is by no means an exhaustive account of Christian community; rather, it is but a window through which to glimpse significant historical and contemporary expressions. At the end of each chapter, I have provided suggestions for further reading.

If it is possible to build Christian community within the faltering church institutions of white America—and that is a matter of some question—some essential building blocks may be found among the very people whom the mainstream church and society have alternately despised, patronized, and proselytized. At the same time, contemporary community-building efforts by disaffected white Christians could potentially lead to the final extinguishment of the Imperial Church in America. Certainly there are committed Christians from all racial, ethnic, economic, and gendered populations who have much to contribute in the way of community-building, both within the boundaries of their respective cultures and cross-culturally, and even across religions.

It has been my privilege and delight to experience a sense of community in the process of writing this book. Numerous friends and colleagues served as readers and friendly critics: My thanks to Hector Avalos, Nikki Bado-Fralick, Larry Gross, Gary Guthrie, Nancy Guthrie, Kathy Hickok, David Hunter, Adela Licona, Cindy McCalmont, Eugenio Matibag, Anthony Pinn, Tony Smith, and Nancy Warner—each of whom made this work better. I am especially grateful to Brian Eslinger, for hours of wonderfully helpful discussions of chapter drafts; Mary Lenz, OSF, for her literary talents and spiritual support; Rita Marinko, reference librarian at Iowa State University's Parks Library; and Michele Svatos, for her computer skills. Special thanks to Anne Recker for her affirmations and enthusiasm and to Margaret Hanson for research assistance at a critical juncture. Both the book and I would be poorer without the contributions of each of these individuals.

I am deeply indebted to John L. Kater Jr. for his generosity in permitting me to include in an appendix of this book a selection of previously unpublished case studies of Christian communities, which he researched and wrote. They add a dimension that significantly enhances the book as a whole. All book authors should be so fortunate as to have Henry Carrigan as their editor. His commitment to this project and his empathetic encouragement made all the difference.

My family is my "first community." To Beverly Reddick, Polly and Dennis Richter, Kathy and Don Tegtman, Bess "Bea" Turner, and my two generations of nieces and nephews—I cherish each of you. So, too, I cherish the memory of our Louise. To all the members of my support network, my heartfelt appreciation for your interest and care.

I am indebted to my students whose concerns and commitments both challenge and sustain me. My hope always is to pass on to them a measure of what was given me by my circle of mentors, including Dr. C. Eric Lincoln, who welcomed me on the journey of redressing "the continuing American dilemma." Lincoln died while this work was in process; his dictionary, which he bequeathed to me some years ago, was an ever-present help and a poignant reminder of his respect for the power of the word. Silence is indeed the voice of complicity.

I take this opportunity to express my appreciation as well to Rosemary Radford Ruether. Working on this project has only further impressed upon me the extraordinary contributions that she has made to our understanding of the world and to the cause of justice.

Finally, I acknowledge the companionship of my cat, Luke, who slept in my mother's chair nearby while I fashioned these words. He, most of all, will be forgiving of the imperfections of this book, for which I alone am responsible.

NOTES

1. Most mainline Protestant churches steadily grew in the first half of the twentieth century, then leveled off and began to decline in the 1960s. According to Winthrop Hudson, the United Methodist Church lost over half a million members between 1968 and 1972. The losses continued in the 1970s and 1980s. Hudson cites these loss percentages over the fifteen-year period from 1970 to 1985: Christian Churches (Disciples of Christ), 27.8 percent; Episcopal Church, 14 percent; Presbyterian Church (U.S.A.), 15.4 percent; United Church of Christ, 16.3 percent; United Methodist Church, 14.5 percent. The two largest mainline Lutheran groups together lost 10 percent during these years. In contrast, during the same time period, evangelical and pentecostal churches—not all of which are part of the Religious Right—enjoyed substantial growth. The Southern Baptist Convention grew by 25 percent, the Church of the Nazarene grew by 40 percent, and the Assemblies of God tripled their membership. Winthrop Hudson and John Corrigan, eds., *Religion in America* (6th ed., Upper Saddle River, N.J.: Prentice-Hall, 1999), 385–86. According to David Roozen and Kirk Hadaway, eight leading mainline Protestant churches lost 6.4 million of their 29 million members between 1965 and 1990, a decline of 22 percent. See their *Church and Denominational Growth* (Nashville: Abingdon Press, 1993.) This decline continued in the 1990s, but at a slower rate. The membership losses are accompanied by financial losses that have their own implications for agency and church support. For an overview of mainline churches, see William McKinney, "Mainline Protestantism, 2000," in *Americans and Religions in the Twenty-First Century,* edited by Wade Clark Roof, The Annals of the American Academy of Political and Social Science 558 (July 1998): 57–66. Also see chapters 3 and 10 of this book.

2. For a contextual treatment of the Peoples Temple movement, see Rebecca Moore, Anthony B. Pinn, and Mary R. Sawyer, eds., *Peoples Temple and Black Religion in America* (Indiana: Indiana University Press, 2003).

3. Associate membership does not involve taking vows, but does admit one to many of the activities of community life.

4. Marie August Neal, S.N.D., *The Just Demands of the Poor: Essays in Socio-Theology* (New York: Paulist Press, 1987), 82.

—INTRODUCTION—
Models of Christianity

"The extraordinary genius of the Christian religion," observed historian and sociologist C. Eric Lincoln, "is exemplified in the fact that it has always managed to survive its distortions."[1] For some thirty years, Lincoln devoted his scholarly attention to the distortions in white American Christianity[2] and, conversely, to the survival of Christianity in the Black Church. The frame of reference for his work was the concept of the "American dilemma," a phrase coined by Swedish sociologist Gunnar Myrdal in 1944 to describe the bedrock contradiction between this nation's creed of freedom and equality and its code of conduct where race was concerned.[3] Lincoln emphasized the role that American Christianity played in creating and sustaining this contradiction. The very fact of playing this role, he said, was itself the biggest and most damaging distortion.

Lincoln's work on African American Christianity has been ignored for the most part by mainstream sociologists of religion. Where Christianity is concerned, establishment theologians and sociologists of religion alike typically limit their inquiries to white, institutional Christianity. Few of them write about Christianity as it is being lived by the people, particularly the people on the margins of society.[4] What this means is that few of them write about Christian community, for Christian community is lived community.

Much has been written in recent years about the status of predominantly white Christian churches in the United States. Scholars of religion report that mainline denominations have declined in the past forty years, while evangelical churches have enjoyed unprecedented growth. Both mainline and evangelical Christians, they say, have become more individualistic, leading the former to discount church authority and construct their own belief systems, and the latter to reject denominational structures altogether in favor of Bible authority alone. Others have become more dogmatic in asserting the salvific necessity of being "born again" and in upholding traditional, conservative doctrine. These accounts take note that some mainline churches are exploring reform and spiritual renewal but, on balance,

1

American Christianity has moved decidedly to the right, with a political orientation that fosters hierarchy and exclusiveness rather than equality and inclusiveness.

These patterns are indeed reflective of religious changes in certain quarters of America. The problem is that generalizations are made from these segments to the entire population of the country, while departures from majority patterns among other segments go undetected or unnoted. Especially given that Asian Americans are the fastest growing immigrant group and that Latinas/os[5] and African Americans each now constitute close to 13 percent of the population of the United States—together, over a quarter of the population—sociological studies must attend more precisely to the religious characteristics of these groups. Their experiences are markedly different—their experiences with *Christianity* are markedly different—and cannot ipso facto be generalized from the majority population.

One of these differences is the relative emphasis on individualism versus community. In the dominant culture of this country, "community" is the contested value, while "individualism" is the privileged value. Community is the subordinate component of our national psyche, the exception rather than the norm. For some, the primacy of individualism is a matter of pride—a triumph of Western, rationalistic liberalism. For others, it is a source of dismay—a judgment on a system of values that exalts competitive success and achievement over enhancement of the common good.

The latter was the lament of the 1985 book, *Habits of the Heart: Individualism and Commitment in American Life*, written by a team of sociologists of religion headed by Robert Bellah. Bellah and his associates contend that it has not always been so; that historically, the type of individualism that prevailed in American society was a civic (republican) and biblical individualism that together provided for a communitarian balance of the individual and society. In recent decades, they say, a different individualism—a utilitarian and self-actualizing type—has become the "first language" of Americans.[6] Their lament might have been tempered had they extended their search to other quarters of American society. What they were really saying was that self-actualizing individualism had become rampant among *white Protestant* Americans, for while they acknowledged that their study excluded midwesterners, Catholics, and blacks, they proceeded to present their conclusions as if they characterized America as a whole.

The issues of individualism and community play differently among feminists, African Americans, Latinas/os, Native peoples, and Asian Americans. They, too, are America. No claim is made here that members of these groups are unaffected by the individualism of the dominant culture. However, Native Americans, African Americans, most Latinas/os, and many

Asian Americans came into the American mosaic with a worldview that privileged community over individualism, and in varying degrees this community emphasis has been retained in their respective cultures and religious systems.

Individualism and community have historically played differently among white Catholics than among white Protestants—which is to say, differently among Irish, Italian, German, and Polish Catholics in the days of the Immigrant Church than among Anglo Protestants in the post-Puritan, evangelical era. Roman Catholic immigrants of the nineteenth and early twentieth centuries brought with them a strong orientation to community. This proclivity was reinforced during a century and more of being regarded as "other" by their fellow Protestant citizens. Their assimilation into Protestant-dominated American culture proved to be swifter and more complete than for peoples of color and, in part, this meant internalizing the values and behaviors of individualism. During the Second Vatican Council of the mid-1960s, however, an emphasis on community was restored, which has influenced many contemporary Catholics—and, indeed, is even beginning to influence some Protestants.

Robert Wuthnow, one of today's most prolific sociologists of religion, much like Bellah and his associates, treats white Christianity as if it were the whole of Christianity. His book, *The Restructuring of American Religion*,[7] described when it was written in 1988 as "a major survey of the last four decades of American religious life," includes one paragraph on black denominations—using data from 1946—and makes only brief reference to new religious organizations of blacks, women, and gays and lesbians, which he describes as "special purpose groups." Five years later, his *Christianity in the 21st Century: Reflections on the Challenges Ahead*,[8] briefly acknowledges the religious motives and contributions of Martin Luther King Jr., but omits any discussion of the contribution African Americans might make to twenty-first-century Christianity. African American Christianity, according to Wuthnow, has an insignificant past and no future at all. Based on Wuthnow's model, Latina/o, Asian American, and Native American Christianity would appear to be in the same situation.

While the information provided by these establishment scholars of religion offers us insight into real and important trends, the information does not tell the whole story. In ignoring the Church on the Margins, their work tells us of the status of American Christianity, but not of Christianity in America. The objective of this book is to point to other expressions of the Christian religion—expressions that have survived or are struggling to survive the "distortions" of Christianity and, particularly, to expressions that are more community-oriented.

Christian community points to a particular way of being Christian—a way that is in contrast, and often in opposition, to establishment churches. In theory, the two are not mutually exclusive, but in historical and contemporary practice they usually have been and are. The tasks of this introduction are first to examine briefly and historically these different models of Christianity, and second, to weave together a working definition of Christian community as it is used in this book. The reality, however, is that this project in its entirety constitutes a process of discerning how different populations understand and express Christian community. Accordingly, the various expressions encountered throughout the book may supplement or modify the core elements of community described here.

Historical Models of Christianity

Many scholars have pointed out that the Christian Church as it developed institutionally in the third and fourth centuries favored and fostered a version of Christianity that contradicted what many Christians of the time understood to be Jesus' vision and intent. Speaking from a contemporary perspective, James Evans remarks:

> One might say that the ministry and mission of Jesus was driven by his eschatological consciousness. This consciousness was concretized in Jesus' proclamation of God's "reign" or *basileia*. A central metaphor for this reality is that of the *beloved community*. Eschatology became a central concern for the Christian community early in its existence. The delayed *parousia* or return of Jesus and its implications for the faith had to be dealt with while preserving the promissory foundation of the gospel. Yet the early church managed to maintain its self-understanding as a beloved community in Christ.[9]

This "self-understanding" was undermined when the Emperor Constantine converted and established Christianity as the religion of the Roman Empire. Thereafter, the organized church evolved as a hierarchical, patriarchal, and episcopal institution in which the charismatic, or spiritual, expression of Christianity was suppressed. Christianity became not only the "state" religion but an imperial religion.[10] This development was intensified, according to Evans, by "Augustine's redefinition of the church from 'beloved community' to 'the City of God.' This move from *communitas* to *polis* introduced radically different notions of social organization within the church."[11]

The "church's self-concept," Evans argues, was then further modified by "the emergence of feudal society and Thomas Aquinas' intellectual reconstruction of the medieval church along those lines. Within the emergent hierarchical structure of the church certain class distinctions became codified and identified with normative church order. As a result of these events, the communal eschatological consciousness so evident in the early church went underground."[12] Consequently, as Rosemary Radford Ruether puts it, "The history of Christianity is a history of continual tension and conflict between two models of church: church as spirit-filled community and church as historical institution."[13]

Jung Young Lee goes even further in describing the new form of Christianity that developed as "a pseudo-Christianity." And, says Lee, "We are still promoting the central ideology of dominance in church today. This pseudo-Christianity has become a partner with the capitalist society. Pseudo-Christianity became the handmaid of early European colonial policy and penetrated deeply into the third-world countries."[14]

Creation spirituality theologians such as Thomas Berry and Matthew Fox concur with this characterization of the official church, but assert the historic presence of a second, albeit minority, Christian tradition emphasizing spirituality, community, equality, and, to use Fox's phrase, "original blessing." This tradition, Fox claims, stands in opposition to the theology privileged by the official church, which emphasized original sin and sacrificial redemption. One version of Christianity, he says, became preoccupied with the question of life after death, while the other was preeminently concerned with the quality of life in this world.[15]

The problem is not solely that fall/redemption theology led to escapism and other-worldliness, to which the corollary was neglect of human conditions in this world, but that in the church's involvement in this world, fall/redemption theology—who was saved and who was savable—often provided justification for political dominance, elitism, and exploitation, while issues of equity, justice, and quality of life for the disinherited and disenfranchised were dismissed.[16]

These traditions are not always so dichotomous as creation spirituality theologians suggest. Rather, they represent the extremes of a continuum of models in which one tradition or the other may be emphasized more by particular groups of believers in specific times and places. It is the case, however, that one's station in life, or in the Church, historically has tipped the emphasis in one direction or the other: In practice, spirit-community is more often the province of sociopolitically marginalized Christians and their allies, while imperialism, which precludes community, has been the hallmark of official, establishment Christianity. As Ruether puts it, the Western Christian tradition "is a culture that has shaped and continues to shape the rest of the world, through imperialist colonialism and neo-colonialism. It is the major culture and system of domination that has pressed humans and the earth into the crises of ecological unsustainability, poverty, and militarism we now experience."[17]

Howard Thurman, whose prophetic book, *Jesus and the Disinherited*, was a source of inspiration to Martin Luther King Jr. and other leaders of the black freedom movement of the 1950s and 1960s, makes the same point as he speaks on behalf of the dominated. "Many and varied," his book begins, "are the interpretations dealing with the teachings and the life of Jesus of Nazareth. But few of these interpretations deal with what the teachings and the life of Jesus have to say to those who stand, at a moment in human history, with their backs against the wall."[18]

> To those who need profound succor and strength to enable them to live in the present with dignity and creativity, Christianity often has been sterile and of little avail. The conventional Christian world is muffled, confused, and vague. Too often the price exacted by society for security and respectability is that the Christian movement in its formal expression must be on the side of the strong against the weak. This is a matter of tremendous significance, for it reveals to what extent a religion that was born of a people acquainted with persecution and suffering has become the cornerstone of a civilization and of nations whose very position in modern life has too often been secured by a ruthless use of power applied to weak and defenseless peoples.[19]

Thurman, who bore in his soul the suffering of a people enslaved and segregated for reasons of economic profit and white racism, continued:

> I do not ignore the theological and metaphysical interpretation of the Christian doctrine of salvation. But the underprivileged everywhere have long since abandoned any hope that this type of salvation deals with the crucial issues by which their days are turned into despair without consolation. The basic fact is that Christianity as it was born in the mind of this Jewish teacher and thinker appears as a technique of survival for the oppressed. That it became, through the intervening years, a religion of the powerful and the dominant, used sometimes as an instrument of oppression, must not tempt us into believing that it was thus in the mind and life of Jesus. I belong to a generation that finds very little that is meaningful or intelligent in the teachings of the Church concerning Jesus Christ.[20]

Thurman is representative of a long line of prophetic believers, both inside and outside the established church, who have spoken and acted on behalf of a spirit-community model of Christianity. In important respects, the monastic movement that developed from the fifth and sixth centuries into the medieval period constituted such a model. The Franciscans and Dominicans were later examples of those seeking to reassert a spirit-community model, though they did so imperfectly. The fact that members of both communities were active participants in the Inquisition attests to the difference between ideal models and human reality.[21]

In the 1500s and 1600s, still others registered "protest" at the practices and teachings of the historic church, though their focus was more "reform" of internal imperialistic practices of the historic church than dismissal of its sociopolitical actions. The reforms of John Calvin and his followers were scarcely in the spirit-community tradition; Martin Luther's movement moved further in that direction, though not nearly so much as the Pietist wing of the Reformation—the Mennonites, Amish, and Universalists—which explicitly affirmed spirituality in opposition to harsh and dogmatic doctrine and which privileged communal expressions of Christian living. While the Protestant bodies that separated from the Roman Catholic Church sought to avoid the excesses of episcopal autocracy, those that became state churches—Anglican, Lutheran, and Presbyterian—retained hierarchical and exclusivist features of establishment churches.

The Puritan Reform movement in England, producing Congregationalists, Quakers, and Baptists, sought to go a step further in ridding the church of imperial characteristics. In part to avoid the persecution imposed upon them for their deviant religious views, these English reform groups, along with Anglicans, transplanted themselves to the New World of North America in the seventeenth and eighteenth centuries. With the exception of the Quakers and the descendants of the Pietist movement, however, as these sectarian bodies became the established denominations of the United States they, too, functioned imperialistically. Spanish Catholics, of course, had preceded the English Protestants, bringing their own forms of colonization. Representatives of both branches of the Christian Church abused and exploited the Native peoples who occupied the land before the colonizers arrived. Protestants, while aided by Catholic slave traders, worked alone in the English colonies to create a system in which the free labor of Africans was put into service to work the land taken from the Indians. Methodists, a delayed expression of Puritan reform, initially functioned more in the spirit-community camp, as had some of the Baptists, but over time both of these groups also took on imperial features of historic churches.[22]

Countercultural Christians

The history of the Imperial Church in the United States is told in more detail in part 1 of this book, while parts 2 and 3 tell stories of community-oriented Christianity in America today. Suffice it to say at this juncture that in the United States, as in Europe in earlier times, the community model of Christianity has been asserted repeatedly—sometimes by believers seeking to transform or renew established churches, and other times by adherents of the faith creating "church" outside of established institutions. Whichever the case may be, Christian community is invariably countercultural, opposing one aspect or another of the status quo of society, and of established churches insofar as they sanction and embody the secular status quo. As Ruether reminds us,

> The church as historical institution tends to sacralize the established social order. The polity of the church tends to reflect the social and political hierarchy of the established society, whether that be the political hierarchies of the Roman imperial ruling class over the plebeians, or the feudal nobility over the peasantry, or the managerial class over the consumers in modern times.... By contrast, the concept of the church as spirit-filled community tends to break down these social hierarchies.... The church as spirit-filled community thus believes itself called into an exodus from the established social order and its religious agents of sacralization. It is engaged in witnessing to an alternative social order demanded by obedience to God.... [Spirit-community] Christianity thus sets itself in tension with established society and tends to see the traditional religion of those societies, including established Christian churches, as false or fallen religions. These religions or churches worship the idols of oppressive power rather than the living God.[23]

Practically speaking, Ruether sees a dialectical relationship of spirit-filled community and historical church, for community rarely sustains itself without institutional form. At their best, she asserts, "Historical institutions create the occasion for the experience of the Spirit. But they cannot cause the presence of the Spirit, which always breaks in from a direct encounter of living persons and the divine. Historic institutions also transmit a culture of interpretation around such spiritual encounters, but this culture of interpretation cannot be closed and finalized. Thus what must be rejected is not institutionalization as such, but the myth that some particular form of historical institution is the only legitimate one."[24]

These three features of established churches when they are at less than their best—the tendency to sacralize the status quo, the attendant proneness to act imperialistically in its relationships with subordinate populations, and the failure to "create occasions for the experience of the Spirit" or to adequately interpret accounts of spiritual experience—are all factors in the rejection of traditional mainline Christianity, not only historically but in recent decades. Dissenting Christians are nothing new in the history of the religion; but contemporary times have brought new forms and new expressions of dissent.

There are those who attribute the decline of the historic churches to the fact of the Western world's having entered into a postmodern era in which modernist assumptions about rationality, organization, and authority are uniformly challenged. The argument is that the church, like other social institutions, is a feature of modernity, and that in the "deconstruction" of that world, the pursuit of meaning must take place outside of conventional religious structures—indeed, outside of religion altogether.

Sociologist of religion Nancy Ammerman offers a more benevolent understanding of postmodernism as "a time when we begin to look at the fact that there is no longer a center and that difference is important"; it is "a time that is about new ways of knowing—that is, moving beyond rationality"; it is "a time when we have to privilege 'outsiders'—the old 'other'—a time when we have to create a space for them to tell their stories"; it is "a time for listening to people who trust both spirit and mind."[25] Accepting these understandings of postmodernism, one may consider that if the church is disassembling, it is also reassembling—that it is being reconstructed on the foundation of gospel values that point not only to spiritual experience as a way of knowing, but to a pluralistic world in which hierarchies of gender, race, class, and heterosexism are abolished.

Christian Particularities

The diversity of Christians in America calls forth the proposition that Christian community arises out of the particular sociopolitical experiences of particular groups of people. As C. Eric Lincoln puts it, "Every authentic religion is a precipitate of the peculiar cultural experiences that shape [a people's] sense of identity and self-awareness as these relate to some ultimate presence beyond the self and other selves cast from the same clay but fired in a different furnace."[26] The same is true of varied expressions of a given religion. Peoples who have been colonized or otherwise marginalized have different worldviews and epistemologies; they may have different understandings of what constitutes wisdom and knowledge and religion—and specifically, what constitutes Christianity.

In short, there is no top-down, universal mold for Christian community. Community-building is a creative process that emerges from the grassroots of a people who share a common history and social experience. Workable community models connect to people's stories; they arise out of the experiences of the people—out of the experiences of *peoples*. This is precisely what has occurred among those Christian particularities that have been marginalized on the basis of color, or gender, or economic status. Their experiences and histories in this society are different from those of privileged classes, and different from one another. Since, however, particularities may be defined not only by race, ethnicity, or gender, but also by economics, sexual orientation, disability, and age, the experiences of white Christians are no more monolithic than the experiences of members of other groups. Their stories vary by locale, by lifestyle, by relationship to the land or to the city, by exaltation of the rational or the experiential. Not all white Christians are wealthy or enjoy the exercise of power, and not all share the values or condone the practices of imperial churches or colonial society.

That said, it remains the case that the experiences of the historically dominant class (white, moneyed, patriarchal Protestants) are different in significant ways from the experiences of particularities that are regarded as "other" by the dominant group—for example, members of racial and ethnic minorities, members of the working class, non-heterosexual Christians, and, at times, Catholics. At the same time, the experiences of particularities differ from one another by virtue of being regarded as "other" for different reasons. There is, to reiterate, no single model of Christian community.

One of the gifts of the liberation theology movements of the 1960s and 1970s was to clarify emphatically that what was touted as universal Christian theology was in fact the theology of a patriarchal European/Euro-American version of Christianity that failed to take into account the experiences of people of the Two-Thirds World and the other-gendered world. Just as there are different understandings of Christian theology, so there are different understandings of the meaning of "church" and of "Christian community." One understanding of these terms is that they are synonymous: no community, no church.

The word "community" is itself an elusive term. As one person has put it, "Community is a many *splendored* and many *splintered* thing. Like most of our ordinary discourse, its meaning varies with context and usage."[27] The term "community" will in fact be used in multiple ways in this book. It may refer to a group of people who count themselves part of a community by virtue of common interests and activity, as in the "community of artists" or the "community of scholars" or the "community of believers." "Community" may be used to denote a particular people, as in "the black community" or "the Jewish community"—meaning that members within their respective cultural groups, their heterogeneity notwithstanding, are bonded together by virtue of the common heritage and historical memory they share. At the micro-level, community commonly denotes a gathering that provides nurture and mutual support, as depicted in this poignant reflection:

> We are all longing to go home to some place we have never been— a place, half-remembered, and half-envisioned we can only catch glimpses of from time to time. Community. Somewhere, there are people to whom we can speak with passion without having the words catch in our throats. Somewhere a circle of hands will open to receive us, eyes will light up as we enter, voices will celebrate with us whenever we come into our own power. Community means strength that joins our strength to do the work that needs to be done. Arms to hold us when we falter. A circle of healing. A circle of friends. Someplace where we can be free.[28]

Christian community is the fulfillment of this longing, and more. The "more" comes in various forms, as divergent experiences and understandings give rise to diverse models of Christian community and Christian community-building. The range of Christian community as the term is used in this work may include Catholic religious orders, alternative denominations such as the Metropolitan Community Church, the "black sacred cosmos," spiritually-grounded social action organizations, and theological reflection groups in local parishes. Today, Christians in the United States, and for that matter, worldwide, variously use the language of "base Christian communities, "or "small Christian communities," or "intentional Christian communities." Others speak of "communities of resistance" or "communities of renegotiated discipleship." For some, community-building refers to efforts to improve the quality of life for all members of a given particularity in a given locale. For some, Christian community is an orientation, a way of living one's life, while for others it means an organization, however formally or loosely constructed. Some Christian communities are located within or on the periphery of institutional churches; others are not connected at all.

In short, Christian communities differ both in form and in content. But whatever their relation to the official church, all Christian communities, as defined here, are "anti-establishment" either theologically or structurally or politically or in some combination of these dimensions.

While the form and content of different communities vary, many of them hold in common a simple understanding of the faith: They consider community to be the essence of Jesus' teachings and so the essence of Christianity. That is not to say that the accumulated wisdom of the tradition is cast aside, or that meaningful rituals, sacraments, and liturgies are not retained. But it is to say that Christian community is more than the accoutrements of the institution—and it is more than doctrines, rules, and creeds. As one person put it, "The church is not something we go to. The church is something *we are*—an organism, not an organization."[29]

Jesus is understood to have been neither a churchman nor a professional theologian, but one who spoke of spiritual matters, concerning himself with ecclesiology and dogma primarily in his capacity as a critic of established religion. Further, the understanding is that Jesus commended, and modeled in his actions, a particular spirituality in which *relationship*, to the Divine Presence *and* to one another, is foundational and preeminent. The scriptural sources for such an understanding include the Beatitudes (Matt 5:1–11), the Great Commandment (Mark 12:28–31; Matt 22:36–40), the New Commandment (John 14:34; 15:12, 17), the Golden Rule (Matt 7:12), the reading in the temple from the book of Isaiah (Luke 4:16–21), the condemnation of the Pharisees (Luke 10:42), and the Great Judgment (Matt 25:31–46). *Love your neighbor, welcome the stranger, liberate the oppressed*— not just in thought or rhetoric, but in deed. What one "does unto others" is done in recognition of fundamental interdependence and in a mode of compassion, justice-seeking, and both personal and systemic transformation. *Love, hospitality, justice.* Members of Christian communities take as their referent these values as they understand Jesus to have applied them to the marginalized of his day: to children, women, the poor, ethnic minorities, and all peoples excluded from the power centers of society and religion. What is inhospitable, what is unjust, what is unloving must be challenged.

Thus, their diversity notwithstanding, those who find these values to be authoritative, and even salvific, do share a common understanding of the elements and characteristics of Christian community.

Voices of Community

It is, of course, easier to say what is *not* meant by Christian community than what is. Often, in traditional church circles, the word community is used simply to refer to a gathering for food and fellowship, or to the people assembled for worship, or to self-selected membership in a Bible study class or adult forum, or to the collegiality of choir members, or even to the response of the bereavement committee to a family's loss. All of these potentially may be aspects of church-related community. But this level of community does not necessarily involve more than social contact or friendly association.

Nor does Christian community mean merely charity or service to the needy. Providing charity and/or referring those in need to social service agencies can easily lead to paternalism and disempowerment. Food pantries and agency referrals do not constitute welcoming the stranger; they do not constitute hospitality. Financial aid may pay the rent or the light bill, and this may be vital in meeting people's survival needs, but it does not go the next step of creating community.[30]

In contrast to these activities, "community" as the heart of the Christian faith, as the very essence of living a Christian life, is a concept that lies dormant in more institutional churches than not. For many members and ex-members of these churches, it is precisely the elements and practices of traditional Christianity that *are* emphasized that impede the construction and experience of Christian community. Among these stumbling blocks of church life are creeds that make no mention of the teachings and ministry of Jesus; dogma that is experienced as archaic and irrational; exclusivist claims on "truth"; racial and life-style discrimination; subordination of women; rule-bound congregations of "dos" and "don'ts"; biblical literalism and judgmentalism; excessive bureaucracy and the prioritizing of fundraising to sustain the bureaucracy. Time and again throughout history, the prophetic lament is that in the land of churchdom, institutional forms and theological constructs have passed as Christianity, while spirituality and relationality, which go hand in hand, have slipped into oblivion. The present time is no exception. A deeper sense of what is meant by Christian community may be cultivated by listening to a few of these prophetic voices.

In 1994, a group called Priests for Equality published an inclusive-language translation of the New Testament, called *The Inclusive New Testament*. Priests for Equality is a Catholic group that defines itself as a "movement of women and men—lay, religious and clergy—that works for the full participation of women and men in the church and society." Its New Testament translation was prepared, according to the editors, "for lay people and clergy alike who thirst for reform in establishment Christianity, and for those who, having despaired of change, are striking out on their own, both individually and through intentional communities." They continue,

> We direct the translation especially to those who will be initially exploring scripture while searching for broader goals in their spiritual life. One does not need a course on pain in order to understand it. Nor does every sin need to be experienced in order to teach morality. By the same token, neither young people nor inquirers into the faith need to experience the sin of sexist language at such an early stage in their spiritual lives. There is ample time to learn the more painful lessons of the hierarchical church once they are firmly established in the faith community.[31]

On the subject of community, the editors write, "In the belief that the Spirit encourages truly communal, egalitarian *koinonia* among Christian believers, we have modified terms of community. We replace the sexist 'kingdom,' which defines a group of people by its (male) ruler, with the more communal (albeit coined) term kindom, which defines a group by the ties that unite it. We use the terms *kindom of God* and *kindom of heaven* as the heart of Jesus' proclamation."[32]

Christian community calls forth new exegesis, new hermeneutics, and new language—that is to say, discernment of deeper textual meanings and inspired application to the issues of today's world. Where old terms and symbols have lost meaning and contextual significance, new definitions and representations are refreshing and life-giving.

In 1987, in anticipation of a national United Methodist Convocation on Racism, *e/sa* (*engage/social action*) published a forum entitled "Our Task: Anti-Racism." In one of the articles, Joe Agne wrote, "The present reality of our world and the future reality of our country is that whites will no longer be in a majority. God is fashioning a new truly inclusive church. Those of us who are white must decide if we want to be a part of God's church. Many of us who are white like institutions that are colorful, but that give up only token amounts of white power."[33]

Christian community admits of no racial superiority. It is inclusive and pluralistic in that it welcomes everyone in—but also in that it reaches outward.

Lawrence Jones, dean emeritus of Howard University School of Divinity and preeminent historian of the Black Church, writes,

> Faithfulness to the Christian gospel requires gathered communities of faith to be involved in the changing panorama of political, economic, social, demographic, educational, and cultural realities in which persons live out their lives. Though often cloaked in secular jargon, the ever-increasing involvement of [black] churches in the world is rooted in the Gospel's requirement that believers must care for "the least of these." One thing is clear: Any institution that hopes to survive must take account of the dynamism that characterizes the life of its community. It must have grasped the truth that "concern for those God loves is worship."[34]

The editors of a collection of statements from the radical discipleship movement write in their introduction,

> The Christian community is not immune from sin and failure—no purity of groups is required or evidenced here—but at its best, the church knows itself as called to be different. We think that God intends the church to be an ongoing human experiment—infused with grace and Spirit—in the world, a continuous trial-and-error of fellowship built on love, reconciliation, and sacrifice. To do so, it

must stay true to the Way of Jesus and others who have set their hearts on the [Kindom] of God before all else. To be that kind of church, it must be countercultural, an alternative community, in the midst of cultures and powers that operate on assumptions and priorities not centered on the [Kindom]. The church is faithful to its origins when it views itself as a community distinct from larger social forces [and] draws on the "politics of Jesus" … as an alternative to Christian theology and practices cut to fit the needs of imperial power.[35]

Christian community is radically critical of the status quo to the extent that the latter diminishes instead of enhances human life.

A leader of a New York congregation elaborates on this notion, while adding emphatically that politics is not enough:

We're an inclusive community where people know each other, increasingly through small groups. We don't check at the door to see if you're rich or poor, gay or straight, have religious background or not. Second, because religion can't stay within the sanctuary, we're dedicated to action and justice. God doesn't need our prayers, but our partnership in changing the world. Most importantly, we're spiritual. We look beyond the material life of paychecks and security to some echo of the truth that lasts and is meaningful when everything we take for granted crumbles around us. We believe in liturgy done with passion. Whether painful or joyful, life must be lived intensely, especially when standing before God.[36]

The congregation described here is B'nai Jeshurun; the leader is Rabbi Rolando Matalon who, perhaps not incidentally, is Argentinian. Their congregation worships in a Methodist church building and shares with the congregation of St. Paul and St. Andrew not only sacred space, but neighborhood social ministry as well.[37]

Like this Jewish congregation, Christian community is experiential and passionate. It makes no claim to exclusive truths, but acknowledges values shared by other religions of the world; it affirms Jesus' Jewishness. And it affirms the worth and dignity of all individuals.

It goes without saying that community cannot abide excessive egocentrism. But neither does it disallow individual identity and rights. Indeed, the preservation of the sanctity of the individual becomes one of the major challenges in the building of community. Self-actualization need not be a negative thing. Insofar as self-actualization is an end in itself, it certainly is antithetical to community-building. At the same time, effective community-building seems unlikely absent mature, self-actualized members. For many individuals, psychological and spiritual healing are but a way station on the road to community. Community in turn fosters healing and wholeness; to live community is to be engaged in an ongoing process of conversion. Individualism and community are not necessarily mutually exclusive, but may be constructively dialectical. It is also apparent from the foregoing discussion that community is not merely the opposite of individualism.

Nor, it should be noted, is individualism the same thing as the "personal." Feminists have contributed to our collective consciousness the insight that "the personal is political" and vice versa. Our personal lives are intertwined with the folkways, principalities, and powers of our larger world. Christianity is not a religion of individualism, but it is both a personal and social religion. Community is its essence, many are saying, but community consists of individuals who are engaged with one another and the larger world. This excerpt, written a quarter of a century ago, makes the point well:

> The Gospel is personal in the sense that it addresses our individual integrity as responsible to and for human community. The call to preach the [Kindom] of God invites personal enlistment in a community whose faith in practice produces systemic change affecting all areas of life. It creates parallel institutions over against the old order, and is not to be confused with self-serving reforms that prop up sagging church rolls or other social institutions whose base is individualistic western capitalism. In short, Christian evangelism calls the individual person to responsibility for the social matrix according to the visions of the [Kindom] of God and after the mind of Christ. This commitment is not to be confused or equated with membership in the institutional church. Evangelism is the antithesis of saving your soul and letting the world go to hell, or of attempting to reform what can only be recreated.[38]

Christian Community: A Working Definition

Christian community may be defined as *a group of people coming together with intentionality to live the gospel values of inclusiveness, justice, and caring in order to create a transformed world.* Ultimately, the process and purpose of Christian community is healing the woundedness of the world; its task is peacemaking. But Christian community acknowledges that there is no healing, no wholeness, no peace without justice. In ideal terms, Christian community rejects no one, reaches out to all, and values differences. Christian community cares for the earth and cares for the earth's disenfranchised people, being co-creators with the one and agents of empowerment with the other. Members of Christian community who come from privileged classes are in solidarity with the oppressed, rather than penalizing, suppressing, or ignoring them; being "in solidarity with" is more than offering charity. Members who themselves are among the oppressed seek self-empowerment rather than accepting victim status.

Christian community seeks transformation—the creation of new structures and systems and modes of relating to one another predicated on these countercultural values—as opposed to reform, which is merely the rearranging and adjusting of old structures and patterns. Transformation is radical by its very nature; it goes to the root of what is oppressive and dehumanizing. It therefore involves risk-taking; Christian community is not for the faint of heart. Furthermore, Christian community is dynamic: it is ever changing, ever cognizant of changing times, changing power relationships, and changing needs. If it becomes static, it dies.

Christian community is emphatically not social action alone; it engages in social action that issues from spiritual centeredness. Internally, Christian community is experiential; it invites and honors and depends on experiences of Spirit. Christian community is relational; it is characterized by empathy, compassion, patience, forgiveness. Christian community is nonhierarchical, insisting on participatory decision making and using a process of consensus rather than competition. Christian community is not imposed from the top, but arises from the grassroots and out of the specific sociopolitical experiences of community members. Christian community is protected space where no one need fear ridicule or reprisal. Christian community is contemplative, fostering self-reflection; it values and validates constructive criticism. Christian community respects reason and knowledge, while invoking wisdom and trusting the intuitive.

Finally, Christian community is intrinsically loving, "for love is the spirit that breathes through relationships of care."[39] Love and crucifixion, however, often go hand in hand: "People are crucified for living out a love that disrupts the social order, that calls forth a new world."[40] But people who live out such a love also get to live in that new world—in community.

NOTES

1. C. Eric Lincoln, *Race, Religion, and the Continuing American Dilemma* (New York: Hill & Wang, 1984), 58.

2. The term "America" properly includes both the Northern and Southern continents of America. For the sake of convenience, unless otherwise stated I follow the practice of using the term to refer to the United States, but the reader should be mindful, as am I, that it is technically a misnomer.

3. Gunnar Myrdal, *The American Dilemma: The Negro Problem and American Democracy* (New York: Harper, 1944).

4. Among the exceptions is sociologist of religion Wade Clark Roof. See, for example, the July 1998 issue of The Annals of the American Academy of Political and Social Science,

entitled *Americans and Religions in the Twenty-First Century*, which Roof edited. At the same time, Roof's writings on religion and the baby boomer generation fail to separate out different populations by race or ethnicity, although they are included in his sample. See Roof, *Spiritual Marketplace: Baby Boomers and the Remaking of American Religion* (Princeton, N.J.: Princeton University Press, 1999), 192.

5. The terms "Latina" and "Latino" (Latina/o for short) in present-day usage refer to women and men living in the United States who trace their origins to the Spanish-speaking countries of the Americas and who share a common culture and language. The terms are sometimes used interchangeably with "Hispanic." The designations include Mexican Americans, Puerto Ricans, and Cuban Americans, as well as individuals from Central and South America. The definition has its limitations. Not all persons who self-identify as Hispanic or Latina/o speak Spanish. Many who self-identify as Latina/o regard themselves as "persons of color," while others regard themselves as "white." The U.S. Census Bureau now uses the description "non-Latino whites." To avoid the awkwardness of this phrase, when I refer to whites, I am meaning non-Latina/o whites; when I include Latina/os in the category of "peoples of color," it is with the awareness that there are exceptions. The terms Chicana and Chicano are also sometimes used to designate Mexican Americans.

6. Robert N. Bellah et al., *Habits of the Heart: Individualism and Commitment in American Life* (Berkeley: University of California Press, 1985). For an excellent interpretation of *Habits* as it relates to small Christian communities, see Bernard J. Lee and Michael Cowan, "U.S. Culture and Christian Communities," in *Dangerous Memories: House Churches and Our American Story* (Kansas City, Mo.: Sheed & Ward, 1986).

7. Robert Wuthnow, *The Restructuring of American Religion* (Princeton, N.J.: Princeton University Press, 1988).

8. Robert Wuthnow, *Christianity in the 21st Century: Reflections on the Challenges Ahead* (New York: Oxford University Press, 1993).

9. James H. Evans Jr., *We Shall All Be Changed: Social Problems and Theological Renewal* (Minneapolis: Fortress Press, 1996), 69.

10. Rosemary Radford Ruether, *Women-Church: Theology and Practice* (San Francisco: Harper & Row, 1986), 13.

11. Evans, *We Shall All Be Changed*, 69.

12. Ibid.

13. Ruether, *Women-Church*, 11.

14. Jung Young Lee, *Marginality: The Key to Multicultural Theology* (Minneapolis: Fortress Press, 1995), 15.

15. Matthew Fox, *Original Blessing: A Primer in Creation Spirituality* (Santa Fe, N.Mex.: Bear & Co., 1983), 11.

16. Ibid., 12.

17 Rosemary Radford Ruether, *Gaia and God: An Ecofeminist Theology of Earth Healing* (San Francisco: HarperSanFrancisco, 1992), 10.

18. Howard Thurman, *Jesus and the Disinherited* (Nashville: Abingdon Press, 1949), 11.

19. Ibid., 11–12.

20. Ibid., 29.

21. Two members of the Dominican community were the authors of *Malleus Maleficarum*, otherwise known as *The Hammer of the Witches*, which was the guide book for the Inquisition conducted under Pope Innocent VIII. Many Franciscan brothers functioned as traveling inquisitors and served as consultants in the courts of inquisition.

22. In sociological terms, this dynamic is known as sectarianism. It refers to the tendency for groups (sects) to break away from established churches or denominations for reasons of dissatisfaction or protest, but then over two or three generations to take on the characteristics of the established church or denomination, which may in turn precipitate new sectarian movements. Thus, technically, all the Protestant groups that came out of the Reformation began life as sects. In the New World, Congregationalists, Anglicans/ Episcopalians, and Presbyterians became the established denominations, joined later by Methodists and Baptists, Lutherans and Reformed Churches, and so forth. For an elaboration of the dynamic, see Steve Bruce, *Religion in the Modern World: From Cathedrals to Cults* (New York: Oxford University Press, 1997), chap. 4.

23. Ruether, *Women-Church*, 22–23.

24. Ibid., 33, 35. Ruether explores these themes further in an earlier book entitled *The Church Against Itself* (New York: Herder & Herder, 1967).

25. Nancy Ammerman, "Reforming the Center Conference" (remarks made at Messiah College, Grantham, Pennsylvania, June 1995).

26. C. Eric Lincoln, introduction to *Mighty Like a River: The Black Church and Social Reform,* by Andrew Billingsley (New York: Oxford University Press, 1999), xx.

27. Walter E. Fluker, *They Looked for a City: A Comparative Analysis of the Ideal of Community in the Thought of Howard Thurman and Martin Luther King Jr.* (Lanham, Md.: University Press of America, 1989), xi.

28. Starhawk, *Dreaming the Dark* (Boston: Beacon Press, 1982), 92.

29. Shane Claiborne, "Downward Mobility in an Upscale World," *The Other Side* (November/December 2000): 13.

30. John Knight, "Why Servanthood Is Bad," *The Other Side* (November 1995): 56–59.

31. *The Inclusive New Testament* (W. Hyattsville, Md.: Priests for Equality, 1994), i, xx.

32. Ibid., xix.

33. Joe Agne, "The Vocation of White Anti-Racism," *e/sa* (July-August 1987): 12.

34. Lawrence N. Jones, foreword to *Mighty Like a River: The Black Church and Social Reform,* by Andrew Billingsley (New York: Oxford University Press, 1999), xiv.

35. Michael L. Budde and Robert W. Brimlow, eds., *The Church as Counter Culture* (Albany, N.Y.: State University of New York Press, 2000), 7–8.

36. Winifred Gallagher, *Working on God* (New York: The Modern Library, 1999), 23.

37. Ibid., 21–22.

38. Iowa Conference Chapter of the Methodist Federation for Social Action, Discussion Paper, "What Kind of Evangelism?" circa 1978.

39. Rita Nakashima Brock and Rebecca Ann Parker, *Proverbs of Ashes: Violence, Redemptive Suffering, and the Search for What Saves Us* (Boston: Beacon Press, 2001), 4.

40. Claiborne, "Downward Mobility," 13–14.

PART 1:
The Imperial Church in the United States

The religion of Christianity has always been about community. People who speak and act in the name of Christianity, however, have not always placed community at the center of their faith life. On the contrary, Christian theologizing, which after all is a human enterprise, has all too often been placed in the service of precluding or destroying community.

The contemporary status of Christian community is illuminated when located in historical context. As a primary agent of colonialism in the West, the Christian Church, in all its present-day manifestations, is unavoidably affected by the legacy of colonialism. The limitations placed on inclusiveness in the colonial and constitutional eras generated multiple dimensions of marginality that were variously mitigated and reinforced by developments in the nineteenth and twentieth centuries. One way of telling both the American story and the story of American Christianity is to tell of compromises to inclusive community, and of the responses of those who were excluded.

The chapters in part 1 present highlights of compromises made in the colonial and postcolonial periods that were initiated or condoned by the established churches. This is not a comprehensive history of white Christianity in the United States; such a treatment is beyond the scope of this work. Nor are the patterns presented here descriptive of every white congregation or of all white religious leaders. Always there are exceptions; always there are visionaries, prophets, and renegades who depart from the established norm. But from the perspective of the marginalized, the profile presented in chapters 1 through 3 is the profile of the Imperial Church in the United States.

—CHAPTER 1—
Religious Roots of a New Nation

The role of religion in the founding of the United States of America is a complex and convoluted story. Whatever their positive contributions may have been, from the beginning the churches of the colonies and of the newly created nation were imperialistic. Sometimes the imperialism was intentional; other times it was unwitting. But the consequences were the same. The multiple manifestations of imperialism can be summarized in a word: inequality. Inequality is inherently anti-community; imperialism is inherently anti-community. In large part, the story of America is the story of the creation of inequality by the dominant class, on the one hand, and of the efforts by the marginalized classes to secure equality on the other. The struggles of the latter variously have been to become partners in the national community and/or church community, or to be permitted to preserve community within the boundaries of their own groups, or both.

In fact, before there were imperial churches in the United States—indeed, before there were any states to unite—there were imperial actions by the thrones and churches of Spain and England. Spanish Catholics, English Anglicans, and English dissenters alike, as they established themselves and their churches in the New World, engaged in practices that were both politically and culturally imperialistic. To a substantial degree, the values and worldviews of these Christians determined the character of colonists' relationships with the original inhabitants of the conquered territories and with the residents brought to these shores involuntarily.

The motives of both English and Spanish colonizers were mixed. The mythology of American history is that English colonizers came seeking religious liberty for themselves—as indeed many of them did. But the acquisition of resources to expand the emerging economic system of capitalism was an equal if not more powerful incentive. The Spanish came seeking wealth first and foremost. At the same time, they considered that "the state had the duty to evangelize. The crown appointed bishops and religious superiors, decided what priests would come to the New World, paid the salaries of the clergy, and created new dioceses. Moreover, evangelization was part of the process of conquest. The Spaniards saw religion as an interminable conflict between the kingdom of God and the dominion of the Devil. They had no compunction about using force to impose Catholicism."[1]

Thus, in contrast to the British, the objective of Spanish colonizers was not religious freedom for themselves, but rather expansion of the reaches of the Catholic Church: the whole of the New World was viewed as a mission field.[2]

Conversion by Coercion

The Spanish colonizers brought with them both Catholic orthodoxy and expressions of popular religion that facilitated the "conversion" of Native peoples to Catholicism—sometimes genuinely but often only superficially. However, the consequences for Indians, as they came to be called, of failing to at least appear to be devout were dire, for the Inquisition that sought out heretics in Spain was extended to the New World.[3] The charge to convert the inhabitants of this land was not given to missionaries alone. It was an official responsibility of all Spanish explorers who, upon encountering Native leaders, were required to read to them a policy statement of the Spanish crown called the *Requerimiento*.

> This document claimed that Christ had been made absolute ruler over the entire world, that he had given his authority to the pope as his representative on earth, and that the pope in turn had given these lands to the Spanish crown. Those who heard the *Requerimiento* were invited to accept these facts and submit to their new masters. If they refused—or if they simply did not understand what was being said, usually in Spanish—they became rebellious subjects, and therefore those reading the document to them were free to take military action against them, to take their lands and to enslave them.[4]

Thus, if the representatives of Native peoples did not become Christian, they did become landless—if they were fortunate enough to survive.

The earliest missionaries to be commissioned to convert Native Americans in what would become the United States arrived in Florida in 1527. These Franciscans and their Dominican successors only met with ill fortune and a permanent mission was not established until 1565, as part of the settlement of St. Augustine. For the next one hundred years, additional Florida missions were funded with gold, silver, and other wealth taken from the New World by Spanish *conquistadores*. During this time, the labors of Florida-based missionaries "occasionally were rewarded by dramatic mass conversions, but were plagued by equally dramatic mass defections."[5]

Missionary efforts in "New Spain," as the Southwest territory was called, likewise produced mixed results.[6]

The first task of the Spanish was not to convert, but to vanquish the Mayans and Aztecs who controlled vast areas of land in what came to be known as Mexico. As early as the 1540s, missionaries accompanied explorers northward from Mexico City into areas later known as New Mexico, Arizona, Oklahoma, and Kansas. A hiatus of forty years followed before explorations resumed. Missionaries were a part of the first settlement in New Mexico, established in 1598, and throughout the 1600s oversaw a proliferation of missions, churches, and chapels. Nearly a century later, beginning in the 1690s, missions were established in Texas and Arizona. Throughout the 1700s and early 1800s, numerous missions were established in California as well.

> The basic mission structure was the reduction, usually encompassing villages and surrounding cultivated areas where the Indians were obliged to live and work. The reductions were common in Florida, California, Arizona, and Texas. In New Mexico, where the missionaries dealt with sedentary peoples, they usually placed the mission compound within or just outside the pueblos. The Indians were forced to work at various tasks in the mission compound, from building the churches to caring for livestock to cultivating the soil and raising the crops. Moreover, they had to give up their religion for Christianity. Instruments of worship such as masks, prayer sticks and prayer feathers were confiscated. Indian places of worship, such as the kivas of the Pueblos, were destroyed or closed.[7]

The numbers of Indian converts reported by missionaries to church officials are highly suspect. But if the numbers are inflated, the harsh treatment of Indians in the pursuit of their souls is not.

In addition to the mission reductions, a system of *encomiendas* based on the feudal system in Europe was instituted.[8] "The word *encomendar*," writes Justo González, "means 'to entrust.' Therefore, an *encomienda* was a group of natives who were 'entrusted' to a Spanish settler in order to be taught the rudiments of Christianity. In exchange for that service, which they had not requested, and for their keep, which they could easily earn in their traditional occupations with much less work, the natives were to work for the settler—the *encomendero*."[9]

González ascribes a benevolent intent to these policies of the Spanish crown, but in practice they served as instruments of exploitation and servitude. He acknowledges, too, the benevolence of some of the religious order missionaries—Dominicans, Franciscans, and Jesuits—who worked more closely with Native people than did the conquistadors and so were inclined to treat them more humanely. Franciscans, especially, emphasized aspects of

Christianity that resonated with indigenous rituals and concepts. Some missionaries protested the harsh treatment of Native people by speaking on their behalf in the court of Spain, or by denying communion to Spanish settlers who had taken Native lands. Not a few of these missionaries were in turn the victims of reprisal.[10] Nonetheless, the mission settlements that resulted from their work often became exploitative outposts of imperial authority. "Thus," González writes,

> The Christianity that came to Spanish America was marked by contrasts that today we find striking. It was intolerant and authoritarian. It found ways to justify wanton war, cruelty, and exploitation. Yet many within it raised voices of protest and criticized the entire colonial enterprise with a firmness that had no parallels in the British colonial enterprise—or, later, in the United States' continued conquest of Native Americans' lands, which destroyed and uprooted entire tribes.[11]

Otherness

The behavior of Spanish and English colonizers alike was shaped by understandings of "the other" that were part and parcel of the Old World mindset. Traditionally in Europe, peoples who were not of European stock—who were "foreign, strange, and different"—were consigned to the categories of "savage," "slave," or "subhuman." Native and African peoples were deemed to be all three. They were regarded as savages for failing to exhibit the virtues and refinements of "civilized" society. "Savages" were human in some degree, or else there could have been no project to save their souls. But they were not *fully* human. Europeans had adopted the hierarchical classification of humans based on skin color, emotional disposition, and body posture offered by Linnaeus in his *Systema Naturae*. The four classes of humans, based on color, were *Europeas* (whites), *Asiaticus* (sallow or yellow), *Afer* (black), and *Americanus* (reddish). Humans who had color were considered an aberration; in the ethnocentric minds of Europeans, people were supposed to be white.[12]

Secondly, non-Europeans, in accordance with a doctrine first established by Aristotle, were considered to be "natural slaves." That is, slavery was construed to be "the natural condition for 'persons of both inborn rudeness and of inhuman and barbarous customs.' Civilized men were regarded as the natural masters of such 'barbarians.' If the 'barbarians' would not recognize their natural conditions of slavery, then they could be compelled to come under the rule of civilization."[13] So it was that Columbus was moved to write, in one of his reports to the Crown, "From here, in the name of the blessed Trinity, we can send all the slaves that can be sold."[14]

Repatriation of Indians to Europe did not work out; nor did attempts to exact slave labor from Native peoples in the New World, for they resisted accommodation to the European work style and deftly disappeared into the woodlands. But appropriation of their land was another matter.

Since Native peoples, and Africans as well, were regarded as less than fully human, it followed that they did not have human rights. Most particularly, so far as the British were concerned, they did not have the right to own property; indeed, both populations were considered to *be* property. Nor did Native peoples, for the most part, perceive themselves to be landowners. Rather, the land was regarded as the source of life power, as the mother of the living and the repose of the dead, all of whom coexisted in harmonic interdependence to sustain community. The land was sacred space. British colonizers, in contrast, who were guided by the biblical theology of Adam and Eve, understood that God had given them the land for dominion and cultivation.

David Chidester writes that, for Europeans, the land "could be sanctified only by imposing a strict human design upon its inherent disorder. Land was made sacred only when it was converted to human patterns, intentions, and uses. Its religious and political value resided solely in human efforts to mold, shape, and conform it to European ideals. In this sense, the Native Americans were perceived as not using the land properly and, therefore, as ultimately having forfeited their right to occupy it."[15]

Some English colonizers of the 1600s did make efforts to convert Native peoples, a task requiring that they first be "civilized."

> It was felt that an essential part of the conversion process was a dramatic change in Indian modes of clothing, hair styles, and appearance. The wild and colorful attire of the Indians, the animal skins, bird feather, and bright paint had to be replaced by the civilized clothing of English society. Likewise, the long hair of the males, which stood as a symbol of the sin of pride in Puritan eyes, had to be shorn in order for these "proud savages" to enter into the regimen of Christian humility. As James Axtell observed, "the infallible mark of a Protestant 'praying' Indian was his English appearance: short hair, cobbled shoes, and working-class suit." An Indian's progress toward Christian civilization could be read in his appearance.[16]

When insufficient numbers of Indians obliged the colonists, they resorted to other means of control. The Pequot War, for example, which was initiated by Puritan John Winthrop and resulted in the deaths of nearly a thousand Native Americans, led a fellow Puritan leader to remark, "Thus was God pleased to smite our enemies and to give us their land as an inheritance."[17]

This event was followed by successive militaristic actions that displaced Indians completely from the colonies of Massachusetts, Connecticut, and Rhode Island, and, ultimately, from nearly all the eastern seaboard.

The Sin of Slavery

Land acquisition did not itself satisfy the English colonizers' objective of acquiring wealth. Participation in the emerging economic system of capitalism depended on the availability of laborers to work the land. The dilemma of labor shortages was resolved by importing people who were captured from the lands of western Africa and, against their will, shipped to the New World under the most inhumane conditions.

The European slave trade that had been initiated by the Portuguese in 1441 and taken up by the Spanish shortly thereafter was expanded during the 1500s as the Dutch, French, and English joined these two nations in this profit-making enterprise. By the middle of the sixteenth century, England dominated the trade. The practice of slavery reached its height, particularly where the colonies of North America were concerned, under the leadership of England between 1713 and 1804.[18]

The specific practices involved in slavery were not uniform throughout the colonies. "In New England and New York the Negroes were merely [sic] house servants or farm hands, and were treated neither better nor worse than servants in general in those days." At the other extreme, in the deep South where the largest numbers of slaves were concentrated, "crucifixion, burning and starvation were legal modes of punishment. Between these two extremes, the system of slavery varied from a mild serfdom in Pennsylvania and New Jersey to an aristocratic caste system in Maryland and Virginia."[19]

These variations notwithstanding, the very fact of slave status served to divest Africans of all humanity insofar as most of their captors were concerned. For the European slave dealers, they were but a commodity, while colonial plantation owners regarded them as chattel even before their status was officially defined as such by the passage of law. As dark-skinned "barbarians" captured from "primitive" Africa, the slaves were located outside the "civilized" social hierarchy. In time, religious justifications of the practice of slavery required the admittance of blacks to the category of "human," but blackness persisted in symbolizing "otherness." Shorn of their language, rituals, and kinship ties, survival in the New World was contingent on the wit of the slaves and the whims of their owners. Subject to sale, mutilation, sexual exploitation, and murder, whites exercised total power over and reaped absolute profits from the labor of these human beings whose presence and condition served to affirm Anglo-Saxon Protestants in their convictions of superiority.

The slave trade was formally abolished in Great Britain in 1805, and in the United States in 1808, though it continued informally into the 1860s. In contrast to the experience of many Native Americans, the Christianizing of Africans was not initially deemed a matter of urgency. During the 1600s, their numbers were nonthreatening, and while their status during this period was somewhat ambiguous, legal rulings gradually made clear that they were not free beings. By 1700, their perpetual enslavement for life, as well as perpetual enslavement of their offspring, was well established. To the extent that they were regarded as chattel and not as persons, the salvation of their souls, if such they possessed, was a matter of little concern. The very forms of enslavement provided sufficient control to obviate the need for domestication through religious evangelizing. Furthermore, conversion of slaves and attendant rituals of baptism raised questions as to what would then be their legal status and whether blacks might have to be treated as equals.

This ambiguity was eliminated through actions such as the Virginia law of 1667, which stipulated that conversion did not alter the slave's status, and the 1727 ruling by the bishop of London that "Christianity does not make the least alteration in civil property." With these assurances, some few missionaries and slave owners assumed the task of taking the gospel to the slaves, but with careful selectivity so as to foster an understanding of the Scriptures emphasizing docility and obedience. In order that blacks not acquire misguided notions of justice and equality from their reading of the Bible, literacy was widely discouraged and in many places prohibited by law.

Theological justification for the treatment of African slaves, and of Native peoples as well, was found in the biblical story of the "curse" of Ham, from whom the darker races were allegedly descended and who in turn were consigned to serve their light-skinned cousins in perpetuity. The teachings of Paul with regard to the mandated obedience of slaves to their masters (Eph 6:5; 1 Pet 2:18) were selectively enjoined to give legitimacy to this socioeconomic arrangement. Even the New Testament directive to carry the good news to the ends of the earth was invoked—except that the directive was inverted and Africans, for the alleged privilege of being "saved," were instead brought to the New World.

There was, of course, nothing redemptive in these actions—either in genocide or in slavery. On the contrary, many have come to regard the racism inherent in both as America's original sin.

From Puritan Chosenness to Imperial Republic

"Otherness" was defined by the colonists not only on the basis of skin color, but of religion. Religious convictions, in turn, were closely associated with the colonists' understanding of proper church-state relations. Of the thirteen English colonies, nine established a theocracy as their form of governance—Anglicans in the southern colonies, Presbyterians in the middle colonies, and Congregationalists, or Puritans, in the northern colonies. These theocracies were something less than the state churches of Europe; however, they required the civic unit to be governed by representatives of God and mandated an assessment of taxes to support the churches. Even in the four colonies that did not have a formal theocracy, "political leaders assumed that Christianity was the bedrock of civil virtue. In 1701, for example, Pennsylvania's Charter of Privileges required all officeholders to affirm their belief in Christ."[20]

Among these colonists, none were more strict in their religious requirements or more influential in shaping the character of what became the United States than the Puritans who settled the colonies of Massachusetts, Connecticut, and New Hampshire. Theologically, the Puritans appropriated the Old Testament imagery of the Israelites, considering themselves to be a "chosen people" who had a special "covenant" with God; the New World was envisioned as the "promised land." Accordingly, they believed themselves to be charged with a divine mission—namely, to create and model for the rest of the world a moral, Christian society. As an elect group with a common destiny, the Puritans were strongly communal. But the corollary of "chosenness" is exclusiveness. All who were not a part of their community were regarded as the "other," and "the other" invariably was regarded as "less than." For the Puritans, "other" included all people of divergent religious sentiments. Baptists, Quakers, and Catholics, as well as Jews, were among those excluded from the Puritan realm—and among those who suffered at the hands of their righteous brothers in the faith.

In the theocracies of the Puritans, citizenship rights were conjoined with church standing and property ownership. Only church members in good standing who were among the landed gentry in the mode of European aristocracy were eligible to vote and to serve as God's elected representatives on Earth. Thus, not only Native Americans, Africans, and members of unacceptable religious sects were excluded from the *sanctum sanctorum,* but white Puritan women as well, for by custom, gentry meant men only.

Strongly influenced by John Calvin's doctrine of predestination, the Puritans understood that even among white men, some were worthy and others were not. There were the "saints," the elect of God who would know salvation, and there were the "damned." In the world of the Puritans, the "saved" were understood to be the property owners. Thus, to race, gender, and religion was added class as a component of "otherness."

In short, the orientation of the Puritans was at once both communal and anti-community. The promise of the "promised land" was that it served the Puritans's interests, which they held first to be God's interests. Ultimately, this worldview—that they were a special class of people who were heeding the will of God in their relations with "other" people, both domestically and internationally—became a part of the hegemonic worldview of the new nation that was to be.

The eighteenth-century revival preaching that characterized what came to be known as the First Great Awakening (1730–1760) gravely weakened the structures of theocracy. Agrarian and illiterate residents, who constituted the overwhelming majority of the white colonial population, readily embraced the anti-establishment ideas that one could have a personal one-on-one relationship with God unmediated by the church and that salvation adhered not in catechetical instruction, but in heartfelt spiritual experience—in being "born again." The authority of the older, established colonial churches and their representatives was thus substantially undermined, a development that had far-reaching consequences.

First, while evangelicalism resulted in a leveling of all believers, it also preserved a hierarchy of "saved" and "not saved." Second, the "democratization of religion" ultimately led to a "free market" of religious choice, which in turn enabled phenomenal growth in the newer Methodist and Baptist sects. Third, the ideas of chosenness and divine mission were no longer reserved to the Puritan elite but became the cultural theology of all the colonies, helping to create a sense of a national community. Fourth, both the ideas of spiritual freedom and independence and the notions of being a special people covenanted with God fueled the growing sentiment for political independence from Britain.

All these factors contributed to the creation of the American republic, which in turn included elements of both civil religion and biblical religion. Describing the nature of republics in the ideal, Robert Bellah writes:

> A republic will have republican customs—public participation in the exercise of power, political equality of citizens, a wide distribution of small and medium property with few very rich or very poor—customs that will lead to a public spiritedness, a willingness of the citizen to sacrifice his own interests for the common good, in a word a citizen motivated by republican virtue. Since republics go against "gravity," it is essential if a republic is to survive that it actively concern itself with the nurturing of its citizens, that it root out corruption and encourage virtue. The republican state has an ethical, educational, even spiritual role, and it will survive only so long as it reproduces republican customs and republican citizens.[21]

Implicit in the structure of a republic, in other words, is a communal orientation, which in turn leads to a civil religion. "A republic must attempt to be ethical in a positive sense and to elicit the ethical commitment of its citizens. For this reason it inevitably pushes toward the symbolization of an ultimate order of existence in which republican values and virtues make sense. Such symbolization may be nothing more than the worship of the republic itself as the highest good, or it may be, as in the American case, the worship of a higher reality which upholds the standards that the republic attempts to embody."[22]

In this particular historical instance, the "religious superstructure" of the republic consisted not only of civil religion but of the "providential religious meaning of the American colonies in world history."[23] Thus, the "public theology" of the new republic privileged a particular understanding of Christianity that lent itself to imperialism. This theology persisted notwithstanding the subsequent constitutional mandate of separation of church and state, for the First Amendment mandated only that—separation of church and state—and not separation of religion and politics, which was to become a crucial distinction.

In fact, the established churches were not even dissolved immediately:

Older attitudes about church and state died slowly. Ever since the fourth century, when Constantine had established Christianity as the Roman Empire's official religion, most Westerners had assumed that governments could not exist without strong religious foundations. Even though Americans knew they were too pluralistic to ever agree on a single national church, they also believed that the republic would collapse if it ever lost its distinctive Christian identity. Many Americans demanded that state legislatures follow a different course from the federal government. In Pennsylvania, officeholders were forced to "acknowledge the Scriptures of the old and new testaments to be given by inspiration," and in New Jersey, they were required to be Protestant. In the Puritan strongholds, state legislatures did not begin disestablishing the churches until more than twenty years after the Bill of Rights. Despite the new rhetoric of religious freedom, most Americans still assumed that Protestantism should be the religion of the republic.[24]

Eventually, legally established churches were eliminated, but the public theology of the republic endured, with the primary agencies of its transmission being voluntary churches and, for a century and more, the public schools.[25] Public theology, as Bellah points out, has provided the undergirdings for many of the actions of the country and its citizens, both positive and negative, since revolutionary times. "Every movement to make America more fully realize its professed values has grown out of some form of public theology, from the abolitionists, to the social gospel and the early socialist party, to the civil rights movement under Martin Luther King, and the farm workers movement under César Chávez. But," he adds, "so has every expansionist war and every form of oppression of racial minorities and immigrant groups."[26] The public theology that sanctions the latter types of actions is an extension of the theology of Protestant colonists of the 1700s.

The new nation of the United States, as Martin Marty aptly puts it, became a "Righteous Empire" which understood itself as having both a moral obligation and a moral right to evangelize the world, not only with Christian tenets but with cultural, political, and economic values. This presumption would infuse both domestic and foreign policy in the form of the doctrine of manifest destiny,[27] of which more will be said in chapter 2. Furthermore, from the beginning of the revolutionary era, the rhetoric of independence and concern for the common good rarely extended to the status of Indians, slaves, or white women. Consequently, the republic that emerged was a seriously compromised republic, for its citizenry consisted only of white males—primarily white, Anglo-Saxon, Protestant males. Republicanism, then, was further challenged by the choices of the founding fathers, who opted for what Bellah terms "liberal constitutionalism."

Property versus People

In contrast to the Declaration of Independence, the Constitution of the new nation overtly embraced the Enlightenment political philosophy of liberalism that had been given impetus by the rise of capitalism. Liberalism prescribed a form of government based on self-interest and the "social contract." Social contracts, in turn, were based on "natural rights," which replaced Christianity as the framework of the republic.

> [Liberalism] gave rise to the most wildly utopian idea in the history of political thought, namely that a good society can result from the actions of citizens motivated by self-interest alone, when those actions are organized through the proper mechanisms. A caretaker state, with proper legal restraints so that it does not interfere with the freedom of citizens, need do little more than maintain public order and allow the economic market mechanisms and the free market in ideas to produce wealth and wisdom.
>
> Not only are these political ideas—republicanism and liberalism—different, they are profoundly antithetical. Exclusive concern for self-interest is the very definition of the corruption of republican virtue. The tendency to emphasize the private, particularly the economic side of life in the liberal state, undermines the public participation essential to a republic. The wealth that the liberal society generates is fatal to the basic political equality of a republic.[28]

Liberalism was framed in a religious orientation called Deism, which, in contrast to orthodox Christianity, taught that God had created the world, established natural laws, and then withdrawn from the world. Rather than biblical or personal knowledge of God, the "mind" of God could be understood only through discernment of these natural laws, which in turn defined natural rights.

> The basis of all political authority obviously required reconsideration by men [Deists] who no longer believed that God personally intervened in human affairs. Without Divine Providence, divine-right monarchy became mere usurpation. An alternative basis for legitimizing government was found in the notion of a social contract. [Furthermore], John Locke and Jean-Jacques Rousseau both justified revolution by appropriate redefinition of the contract's terms. Rousseau's *Social Contract* was a thoroughly revolutionary book, for it advanced a democratic theory of sovereignty and held that rebellion was justified whenever a government failed to satisfy the people it ruled.[29]

The perceived violations by the British of the colonists' natural rights, defined by Locke as "life, liberty, and estate," were deemed just such grounds for rebellion. In the colonists' Declaration of Independence, these "natural rights" were paraphrased by Thomas Jefferson as "life, liberty, and the pursuit of happiness." In specifying "estate" as a natural right, Locke was functioning as an advocate of the emerging middle class whose interests were served by the assertion that society's sole purpose was to protect the property of the individual members of society.[30] So far as Locke was concerned, self-interest was the one and only basis for the establishment of the state.[31]

These ideas, in turn, converged with the Calvinist beliefs about salvation held by New World Protestants. Since wealth was the sign of election, for any given white Protestant male, "the only way of assuring himself that he had been chosen for passage to the other world was to keep on producing in this one. The more he produced the more he was able to overcome his anxiety about election, and the more he was able to develop a sense of confidence and faith in the Reformation's worldview." As "capitalism in turn provided the institutional mechanisms for translating these truths into the secular world,"[32] Calvinist theology and Enlightenment philosophy combined to foster an indigenous social philosophy predicated on self-interest and property.[33]

Self-interest was the only legitimate grounds for the social contract and property the basis of natural rights. The Puritans' two-tiered system of the saints and the damned and Enlightenment Deism, having sprung from common roots, found ready compatibility and a mutuality in continuing to exclude blacks and others from the civil privileges that were dependent on the demonstration of acceptable signs of election, namely, prosperity and possession of wealth. It was the law of the natural world that men (white "civilized" men) had a right to own property and it was in the discerning and actualizing of this right that men might be regarded as equal.

The Constitution thus legalized a three-tiered "republic" in which those who were represented were those who owned property, for only those who owned property were permitted to vote. Property-less white men, women, Native Americans, free blacks, and children occupied the second tier. To this configuration of social and civic class was added a third and bottom tier of caste, for if the property-less were excluded, the more so were those beings regarded themselves *as* property. "It was obvious that compulsory manumission would violate the right of masters to their own property. Insofar as slaves were property, their masters possessed an inherent right to dispose of them as they wished."[34]

Lest there be any doubt on the matter, the Constitution of this new country stated that "Representatives and direct taxes shall be apportioned among the several States which may be included within this Union, according to their respective numbers, which shall be determined by adding to the whole number of *free* persons, including those bound to service for a term of years, *and excluding Indians not taxed, three fifths of all other persons*," which was to say, slaves (emphasis added). The Constitution in effect modified the meaning of the literal words of the Declaration of Independence, so that it might have read: "We hold these truths to be self-evident, that all men [who own property] are created equal, that they are endowed by their Creator with certain unalienable rights, that among these are life, liberty, and the pursuit of happiness [which consists in the holding of property].... And for the support of this Declaration, with a firm reliance on [natural law rather than Divine Providence], we mutually pledge to each other [who own property] our lives, our fortunes, and our sacred honor."

This tension between republicanism and liberalism has endured throughout the entire history of the United States. Of course, the connotations of the words have been reversed insofar as political parties are concerned, with the Republican Party being the party of wealth and private interest, and the Democratic Party more the party of equality. Indeed, in common usage, the term "liberal" refers to those who seek social reform to create a society more in accord with the preamble to the Declaration of Independence as it was actually written. But the American creed of equality and justice that derives from the Declaration of Independence has always been in conflict with America's code of conduct, which gives primacy to property rights over human rights. While at times this code has been vigorously contested by America's established churches, more often it has been condoned and sustained by them.

The legacy of Enlightenment philosophy and religion was not only a hierarchy of rights, but a privileging of individual rights over the common good. On the one hand, the emphasis on individual rights, at least in theory, moved the country in the direction of democracy (the more so when African American men and, later, women, through constitutional amendments, were granted the right to vote). On the other hand, the extreme focus on individual rights that developed is inherently anti-communal. The two approaches make opposite assumptions about the nature of human associations. "Contractual [individualistic] thinkers bring people into unity with each other through various kinds of agreements, negotiations, conventions, and arbitrations—labor contracts, for example, or premarital property agreements, or constitutions. Communal thinkers take people to be in some kind of unity with each other by nature, prior to any choices or negotiations. Negotiations and agreements then merely ratify and specify what is already the case, bringing about various associations between people that reflect bonds that are already there, bonds that are right and good because such is the nature of the human person."[35]

In short, the choices made in the constitutional era served to impede both a community-oriented society and community-oriented expressions of Christianity, which already had been discounted by the colonial activity of the church, by Calvinist theology, by Puritan exclusiveness, and finally by the evangelical emphasis on the salvation of individual souls. Constitutional liberalism and establishment Protestantism were thus able to coexist and jointly legitimate an economic system built on exploitation and the pursuit of profit. Marginalized populations, whose availability for exploitation made capitalism possible, were buffeted throughout the first century of the new nation's existence by the ramifications of these religious, political, and economic developments.

For Further Reading

Chidester, David. *Patterns of Power: Religion and Politics in American Culture.* Englewood Cliffs, N.J.: Prentice-Hall, 1988.

Dolan, Jay P. *The American Catholic Experience: A History from Colonial Times to the Present.* Garden City, N.Y.: Doubleday & Co., 1985.

Lindley, Susan Hill. *"You Have Stept Out of Your Place": A History of Women and Religion in America.* Louisville, Ky.: Westminster John Knox Press, 1996.

Marty, Martin. *Righteous Empire: The Protestant Experience in America.* New York: Harper Torchbooks, 1970.

Wood, Forrest G. *The Arrogance of Faith: Christianity and Race in America from the Colonial Era to the Twentieth Century.* Boston: Northeastern University Press, 1990.

NOTES

1. Moisés Sandoval, *On the Move: A History of the Hispanic Church in the United States* (Maryknoll, N.Y.: Orbis Books, 1990), 8.

2. Octavio Paz, *Sor Juana* (Cambridge, Mass.: Harvard Press, 1988). On page 15, Paz writes: "Religious motives also inspired the Spanish, but whereas the English founded their communities to escape an orthodoxy, the Spanish established theirs to expand one. For one group the founding principle was religious freedom; for the other, the conversion of the natives to an orthodoxy of the church."

3. Winthrop Hudson and John Corrigan, *Religion in America* (6th ed.; Upper Saddle River, N.J.: Prentice Hall, 1999), 24–25.

4. Justo González, "The Religious World of Hispanic Americans," in *World Religions in America* (ed. Jacob Neusner; rev. and exp. ed.; Louisville, Ky.: Westminster John Knox Press, 2000), 82.

5. Hudson and Corrigan, *Religion in America*, 27.

6. Ibid., 29.

7. Sandoval, *On the Move*, 12.

8. Ibid.

9. González, "Hispanic Americans," 83.

10. Ibid., 83–84.

11. Ibid., 84.

12. David Chidester, *Patterns of Power: Religion and Politics in American Culture* (Englewood Cliffs, N.J.: Prentice-Hall, 1988), 113–14. Even some Europeans were regarded by other Europeans to not be white. See Theodore W. Allen, *The Invention of the White Race* (London: Verso, 1994). Charles Orser, in "The Challenge of Race to American Historical Archaeology," notes that Jews and some of the Irish were considered by some Europeans to be other than "white" (*American Anthropologist* 100, no. 3 [1998], 661–68).

13. Lewis Hanke, *Aristotle and the American Indians: A Study of Race Prejudice in the Modern World* (Bloomington: Indiana University Press, 1959), 19, cited in Chidester, *Patterns of Power*, 114.

14. H. Konig, *Columbus: His Enterprise* (New York: Monthly Review Press, 1976), 53, cited in Chidester, *Patterns of Power*, 113. Konig references Alfred W. Crosby Jr., *The Columbian Exchange: Biological and Cultural Consequences of 1492* (Westport, Conn.: Greenwood Press, 1972).

15. Chidester, *Patterns of Power*, 112.

16. Chidester, *Patterns of Power*, 118, is here citing James Axtell, "The Invasion Within: The Contest of Cultures in Colonial North America," in *The Frontier in History: North America and Southern Africa Compared* (eds. Howard Lamar and Leonard Thompson; New Haven and London: Yale University Press, 1981), 240.

17. Richard Drinnon, *Facing West: The Metaphysics of Indian-Hating and Empire-Building* (Minneapolis: University of Minnesota Press, 1980), 19, cited in Chidester, *Patterns of Power*, 119. The Puritan who uttered these words was John Mason.

18. W. E. B. DuBois, *The Suppression of the African Slave Trade* (Baton Rouge: Louisiana State University Press, 1896), 2.

19. Ibid., 6.

20. Catherine A. Brekus, "The Revolution in the Churches: Women's Religious Activism in the Early American Republic," in *Religion and the New Republic: Faith in the Founding of America* (ed. James H. Hutson; Lanham, Md.: Rowman & Littlefield, 2000), 117–18.

21. Robert N. Bellah, "Religion and Legitimation in the American Republic," in *In Gods We Trust: New Patterns of Religious Pluralism in America* (eds. Thomas Robbins and Dick Anthony; 2d ed., rev. and exp.; New Brunswick, N.J.: Transaction Publishers, 1990), 416.

22. Ibid., 418.

23. Ibid., 418–19.

24. Brekus, "Revolution in the Churches," 122.

25. Bellah, "Religion and Legitimation," 421.

26. Ibid., 420.

27. Martin Marty, *Righteous Empire: The Protestant Experience in America* (New York: Harper Torchbooks, 1970).

28. Bellah, "Religion and Legitimation," 416.

29. William McNeill, *The Rise of the West* (Chicago: University of Chicago Press, 1963), 687.

30. "Middle class," from Locke's perspective, meant large-scale capitalist agricultural estates and large-scale merchant enterprises, as distinct from the old aristocracy.

31. Jeremy Rifkin with Ted Howard, *The Emerging Order: God in the Age of Scarcity* (New York: G. P. Putnam's Sons, 1979), 30.

32. Ibid., 223, 218.

33. Marxist philosopher Tony Smith argues that it is as much the case that the development of capitalist property relations in the first place "gave rise to a social world in which Calvinist theology and Enlightenment philosophy could become significant intellectual movements." Personal memo, September 2001.

34. Winthrop Jordan, *White Over Black* (Baltimore: Penguin Books, 1968), 80.

35. Mary F. Rousseau, *Community: The Tie That Binds* (Lanham, Md.: University Press of America, 1991), 2.

−CHAPTER 2−
The First
One Hundred Years

The nineteenth century was a time of great social and religious ferment. Protestant theologies and actions variously shaped and were shaped by matters of race, ethnicity, and gender, as well as industrialization, the immigration of large numbers of Catholics and Jews, and westward expansion. The "Righteous Empire" suffered multiple internal fractures in addition to the Civil War that threatened to rend the nation in two. The 1800s produced a high degree of religious dissent, with alternative Christian expressions appearing in the form of utopian communities such as the Shakers and the Oneida Community and in sectarian movements such as the Church of Jesus Christ of Latter-day Saints; Church of Christ, Scientist; Seventh-Day Adventists; and Jehovah's Witnesses. But by the end of the century, traditional white Protestants had settled into what Martin Marty has called a "two party system": conservative evangelicals in the South, and modernist Christians in the North.[1] The former had no inclination toward community-oriented expressions of Christianity, while any such inclinations on the part of the latter were betrayed by their inability to come to terms with systemic racism and sexism.

Class and Caste
Following the War for Independence and the constitutional era of the 1780s, Protestant evangelical fervor resumed in what is known as the Second Great Awakening. This movement of spiritual renewal, which produced tremendous growth in Methodist and Baptist memberships, differed from the First Great Awakening both in character and in consequences.

One of the most significant consequences was that large numbers of slaves were introduced to Christianity through the Awakening's revivals and camp meetings and the ministry of itinerant Methodist preachers. The slaves' religious conversions in fact did not alter their status as property. Because their freedom to worship was severely circumscribed, they were compelled to gather secretly in small clusters away from the plantation under the cover of darkness. Here, biblical theology conjoined with African worldviews and cultural forms. Participation in this "invisible institution," involved great risk if discovered, but great reward in terms of keeping intact a sense of community and self-worth.[2]

At the same time, free blacks in the North initiated a process of separating from white churches in which some had held membership to form their own churches. This separation from white churches was prompted not by doctrinal or organizational disagreements, but by racially discriminatory practices on the part of white church leaders. The result was the formation of separate black Methodist and Baptist congregations and even denominations.[3]

In the antebellum period, black ministers constituted a large portion of black political leadership. Along with significant numbers of white Christians who were influenced by reform-oriented evangelicalism, black ministers were key players in the abolitionist movement. This movement became divisive for several Protestant denominations as northern churches and southern churches quarreled over the issue of holding slaves. Shortly before the Civil War, three groups—Baptist, Methodist Episcopal, and Presbyterian—each split along regional lines. Not until the 1930s did Methodists reunite, and then with a segregated black jurisdiction. Presbyterians reunited in the 1980s; Baptists have yet to do so. White southerners, of course, had greater vested economic interests in the preservation of slavery, as much of their wealth consisted of the slave population and the land on which the slaves toiled. But even northern Christians, while less committed to a system of slavery, continued to discriminate against people who were not white Anglo-Saxon Protestants.

Abolitionism was but one expression of the social reform dimension added to Protestant evangelicalism in the first half of the 1800s. Various regions of the country were affected differently by this second wave of religious fervor. The so-called "Bible Belt" of the South embraced a conservative, apolitical form of evangelicalism that stressed preservation of the racial caste system while focusing on individual salvation and individual sins such as smoking, drinking, dancing, and swearing. In the North, where evangelicals were influenced by new currents of religious thought, the idea of "reform" had somewhat broader social implications, including implications for community.

First, concerned that the theology preached by his famous evangelical mentor, Jonathan Edwards, might foster an extreme Christian individualism, the Reverend Samuel Hopkins, in the latter years of the 1700s, countered with his "New Light" theology, which emphasized benevolence and community. Hopkins defined the very essence of God as "benevolence" and by extension, true Christianity as sacrifice for the well-being of others. Second, the evangelical requirement of securing salvation by being "born again" displaced the Calvinist doctrine of predestination. Believers found a meaningful alternative in "Arminianism," a theological approach formulated by Jacob Arminius in the Reformation years that, in opposition to Calvin's deterministic notion of "election," emphasized "free will." People were free to make choices, Arminius had argued, and the choices they made entered into their spiritual destiny. Third, John Wesley appeared on the scene with his ideas of holiness and perfection. One might never achieve spiritual perfection, he allowed, but one was obliged to work toward the highest degree of perfection possible, not only in terms of one's individual life, but in terms of the condition of society. Change was possible, and change was a moral responsibility.[4]

These theological currents combined to shape an evangelicalism that mandated societal involvement for the sake of the good of the people. But, as theological ideas often do, these notions took on a life of their own, ending up in the service of objectives that were not originally intended.

The renewed evangelicalism of the North converged with the beginnings of industrialization. Gradually, the agrarian "moral economy," which was founded on cooperation and interdependence and which stressed fair wages and the dignity of all work, was replaced by a "market economy" in which the prominent features were competition, consumerism, and labor exploitation. The alienation fostered by this market economy fed the revivalist spirit. But at the same time, revivalism cultivated the Protestant work ethic of industriousness, diligence, and thrift. The dialectic that developed contributed to the growth of the middle class, whose members in turn condoned the developing industrial, capitalist economy. Revivalists, as Donald Swift puts it, were caught in a "lovers' quarrel," resisting the exploitative dimensions of the market economy on the one hand, but on the other, welcoming the opportunity to improve one's personal status by participating in it.[5]

In short order another theology emerged that, in appropriating Hopkins's concept of benevolence, helped resolve this conflict. According to the "Gospel of Wealth" that was preached by ministers of large upper-class churches, whose memberships often included the captains of industry, accumulation of wealth was morally justifiable, so long as it was shared through acts of benevolence. Mostly the resulting benevolence benefited the middle and upper classes in the form of artistic projects, libraries, and museums, some of which continue to dot the American landscape.[6] In the post–Civil War period, when both the population and wealth grew at unprecedented rates, individual prosperity, "regardless of the condition of the nation's masses, became equated with private virtue and integrity in the sense of being its reward. Many Americans considered this era to be the actual realization of the fruits of their having kept their covenant with God to preserve the union."[7]

Once again, the tension of community and individualism surfaced. The nation might be intact, but acts of benevolence did not modify the elitist theology of powerful, upper-class white Protestants; indeed, the well-intentioned fostering of benevolence ultimately nurtured the churches' substitutionary understanding of charitable giving as fulfillment of the gospel mandates for social justice. Nor did the emphasis on benevolence moderate the nation's public theology of Manifest Destiny.

Manifest Destiny, Manifest Theft

At the same time that regional conflicts of North and South were being worked out, the white American populace was moving westward. The frontier settlement movements of the nineteenth century represented freedom and opportunity for some, but quite the opposite for others. The Homestead Act of 1862—which ironically took effect on January 1, 1863, the same day the Emancipation Proclamation was issued—authorized settlement on, and ultimately ownership of, up to 160 acres of public land by "any person who is the head of a family, or who has arrived at the age of twenty-one years, and is a citizen of the United States, or who shall have filed his declaration of intention to become such, ... and who has never borne arms against the United States Government or given aid and comfort to its enemies."[8]

Significantly, the act specifically acknowledged that women might be heads of households, which allowed them to exercise the right of settlement. Similarly, naturalized citizens or immigrants in the process of seeking citizenship were granted these opportunities. African Americans and Native Americans were excluded, for in the year 1863, none of these persons were regarded as citizens. Indeed, Native Americans and Mexican Americans might have been excluded by virtue of having taken up arms against the United States. From where they stood, of course, the "public land" offered to white settlers by the government in fact was their land; they were the original and rightful "homesteaders." The Homestead Act in effect was a plan for massive land redistribution that greatly empowered white Americans and assured economic privilege for generations of their descendants. Meanwhile, the "forty acres and a mule" promised to newly freed slaves both by Union generals and the United States Congress never materialized.

For those who were in the West to receive the white settlers, the theologically derived doctrine of Manifest Destiny was but a fancy phrase for imperialism. Both the North and the South were complicit in the policy of expansionism that was regarded by whites as "simply the natural growth process of a superior nation," but that involved the domination of some eight million people of color.⁹ Put another way, this expansionism, of which the Homestead Act was but one expression, was seen by WASP political and church leaders as implementation of the divine mandate to disseminate Western values and life-styles. Manifest destiny was part of the legacy of the original Puritan theology of chosenness and was an integral aspect of the self-understanding of the "Righteous Empire." Expansionism was deemed to be God's will and America's obligation.

Native Americans were the immediate victims. In 1830, passage of the federal Indian Removal Act required all Native peoples in eastern states to move west of the Mississippi. In the infamous relocation project that the Cherokee call *nuna dat shun'yi,* "the Place Where They Cried," or the Trail of Tears, five Indian nations in the Southeast—the Cherokee, Creek, Choctaw, Chickasaw, and Seminole—were marched to the so-called "Indian Territory" in Oklahoma. Thousands died on the way, and many more died of smallpox upon their arrival. While the area that included Georgia, Alabama, Tennessee, Kentucky, South Carolina, and North Carolina had once all been Cherokee land, only one thousand Cherokees who had hidden out in western North Carolina remained.¹⁰

In the 1850s, the United States government implemented a plan to confine Plains Indians of the Midwest and Upper Midwest to reservations. White settlers and soldiers were sent west to defend the new treaties, take possession of the land, and further extend "God's kingdom." By 1865, nearly one million whites had settled west of the Mississippi River to build railroads, cattle ranches, and farms. By 1890, the Lakotas' primary source of livelihood and important symbol of spirituality, the buffalo, had all but been exterminated.¹¹ The Lakota Sioux who survived massacre, starvation, and disease were confined to reservations and denied access to sacred lands, which included the Black Hills. Their children were ordered to attend government schools, which were often administered by churches, where they were forbidden to speak, dress, or worship in their own cultural traditions.

Whereas ten million Native people are estimated to have resided in North America in the mid-1500s, in the 1840s only one million remained in the United States and by 1900 the numbers had been reduced to around three hundred thousand.¹² Each Indian nation has its own story to tell of lies, deceit, and betrayal, but there are common villains and they include both government agents and missionaries. The thousands of Catholic and Protestant missionaries who were a presence on virtually every Indian reservation not only preached a Western interpretation of the gospel and Western secular values, but were complicit in enforcing destructive government policies. In the estimation of one commentator,

More devastating to Indian communities than the imposition of new cultural standards was the missionaries' tendency to act consistently, sometimes self-consciously and sometimes implicitly, in the best interests of the economic and political structures of their Western cultural world. Thus, it was almost natural for the missionaries to participate in the political process of subjugation and to support the repressive efforts of their own government in whatever program had been devised at the time to serve that interest. It was just as natural for them to support the economic enterprises that manipulated and exploited Indian labor and resources. What finally must be realized is that the missionaries were deeply involved in symbiotic relationships with the very structures of power that crushed Indian resistance to the European invasion every step of the way, as Manifest Destiny moved "From California to the New York Island, from the redwood forest to the gulf stream waters...."[13]

In the Southwest, not only Native peoples but Hispanics, the new people that had been created by the mixing of Spanish settlers and Indians, found themselves at the mercy of the government's expansionist policy.[14] Under Spanish rule, the territory of Mexico, which included areas that later became the states of California, New Mexico, Arizona, Utah, Colorado, and Texas, was closed to North American trappers, traders, and settlers. When Mexico gained its independence from Spain in 1821, the new nation not only welcomed the "Anglos" but allowed them to acquire land. By the 1830s, however, the greed and sentiments of superiority of white settlers led them to begin organizing to take control of the Southwest.[15]

In 1836, the settlers in Texas declared their independence; in 1845, the United States granted Texas statehood. When Mexico refused to sell California, the United States declared war, an event that prompted an eastern newspaper editor to write: "It is our manifest destiny to overspread the continent Providence has provided."[16] Upon defeating Mexico in 1848, the United States annexed the northern half of that country. According to Moisés Sandoval,

These territories contained, in addition to 180,000 to 250,000 Indians, between 75,000 and 100,000 inhabitants with at least partial Hispanic heritage. Most of them, about 60,000, lived in New Mexico. Of the remainder, about 8,000 lived in California, 2,000 in Arizona and the rest of them in Texas. Through the Treaty of Guadalupe Hidalgo, signed in 1848, they became citizens of the United States, with specific guarantees of their civil rights and land titles. It soon became evident, however, that the provisions of the treaty would not be honored.

Anglo Americans refused to accept the Hispanics as equals. Many agreed with the political philosopher John C. Calhoun that only the "free white race" should be added to the union. Many also agreed with Anglo Americans in California who were willing to allow non-whites to live there "but only if they had few or no human rights and they could be considered without argument to be born inferior."[17]

As the number of white settlers in the Southwest increased, Mexican Americans for all practical purposes were reduced, if not to legal slavery, to membership in a caste system that was not so different from the racially segregated Southeast. Hispanics were routinely subjected to both personal and institutional violence and were regularly deprived of the protection of the law. In fact, Sandoval reports that "between 1865 and 1920, more Mexicans were lynched in the Southwest than blacks in the old South."[18] Furthermore,

In the courts, they were sometimes disqualified from being witnesses because they were not white. Through legal and illegal means, they were denied the right to vote. Squatters who seized their lands were not prosecuted; neither were persons who assaulted them. But if the victims defended themselves, they were punished severely. Real estate taxes were raised until Hispanic owners lost their properties for being delinquent; then the rates were lowered for the new Anglo American owners. Others were dispossessed by means of a statute that required validation of all land titles issued by Mexico.[19]

As Hispanics were deprived of productive land holdings and excluded from all but the most menial work, they were reduced to poverty. Some left their homes of many years to relocate to what remained of Mexico. Those who stayed were often accused of being outlaws, a result of their taking measures to protect themselves from lawlessness, or of being uninterested in improving their lives, the appearance of which stemmed from profound hopelessness. Sandoval observes that "the absolute subjugation of the Hispanic population became possible because Anglo Americans controlled the armed forces, the police, the courts, the legislatures, and the economy"—in the world that once belonged to Native peoples and Mexicans.[20] The partial exceptions to this subjugation were the Mexican Americans who lived in New Mexico or in large cities in Texas where sheer numbers afforded them protection and power. However, even these persons were never exempt from prejudice and discrimination.

The imperialism of the Roman Catholic Church paralleled the imperialism of the United States government. In the 1800s, the European Catholic hierarchy saw its task as restoring the churches that they perceived had lapsed after Mexico gained independence. In doing so, the plan was to extend the European church into this part of the world that they defined as a "region of the infidels"—this, notwithstanding that New Mexico, as Sandoval points out, had been Catholic for 250 years.[21]

The Status and Role of Women

The 1800s were a critical period for American women of all colors. Native and Hispanic women were challenged to invent means of coping with dislocation, cultural imperialism, and coerced changes in life-styles. Southern black women, as they experienced the transition from slavery to emancipation, were called upon to reassemble family units, support newly organized churches, and educate themselves and their children. For the overwhelming majority of women of color, as well as low-income white women, the challenge was sheer survival. The courage and resilience of these women was largely invisible and little noted.

Unburdened as they were by oppression based on color, the experiences of most white women, and certainly upper-class white women, were qualitatively different. But while the status of white women differed dramatically from that of women of color—in part because they *were* white; in part because they enjoyed the benefits of having fathers and husbands and sons who were white—they nonetheless knew the oppression of patriarchal assumptions that infused Judaism, Christianity, and American culture.

Even older than the imperialism of race is the imperialism of gender. Sexism, as much as racism, involves ideas of superiority and inferiority, dominance and subordination. Long before the colonizing of the New World, long before the Reformation, European women were caught in the web of a Church-condoned arrangement that regarded women as evil, sexual beings to be controlled and contained—unless they joined religious orders to live a life of celibacy, in which case saintly qualities were attributed to them. Women who did not take vows in the Church were to take vows to a husband; in either case, they were to be silent, obedient, and subservient—though not all respected these restrictions. Allegedly lacking in redeeming spiritual graces, women leading secular lives were always suspect with regard to their faithfulness to the teachings of the church. In greatly disproportionate numbers, they became targets of the Inquisition, which was prone to see in them heretical proclivities for which they were routinely apprehended, imprisoned, and even burned at the stake as witches, without benefit of defense or trial.

These prevailing views about women were little changed by the Protestant Reformation and so accompanied the colonists to the New World.

In the colonial theocracies, women were regarded as spiritually inferior and politically incompetent; accordingly, their roles in both religious and political arenas were circumscribed. During the Second Great Awakening, women became conspicuously the majority of church members, at which time some ministers began expressing the radical notion that women were in fact more pious than men; at the same time, women were described as being "sinfully weak and passionate." They were not allowed to be ordained or to occupy any positions of religious leadership. Indeed, in establishment churches, they were not even allowed to speak publicly and could not vote in church elections. Women who challenged these conventions were subject to censure and even severe punishment.[22]

In the non-established churches—the "dissenting" churches of Moravians, Quakers, Separate Baptists, Unitarians, and Universalists—the situation was somewhat different:

> In contrast to the established churches, which saw themselves as virtually a branch of the government, sects such as the Moravians, Quakers, and Separate Baptists were opposed to the principle of religious establishment, and they thought it was possible to defend women's *gospel* liberty without raising questions about their *political* liberty as well. On the negative side, none of these churches treated women as the full equals of men, and despite their egalitarian rhetoric, they never questioned women's legal, economic, and political subordination. Despite their hostility to established churches, dissenters shared the popular disdain for women who tried to "rule" over men. More positively, however, they also gave women unprecedented freedom to vote in church meetings, serve on disciplinary committees, choose new ministers, and speak as evangelists. Because they severed the connection between religion and politics, they saw no reason why women could not participate in the public life of the church.[23]

Among these groups, Quakers and Unitarian Christians (wealthy, intellectual Calvinist Congregationalists who came out of those churches in the late 1700s to form their own denomination) were the most open to the leadership of women. By 1800, according to Catherine Brekus, "almost half of the Quaker ministers in the Philadelphia Yearly Meeting were female."[24] In the early 1800s, Unitarians and Universalists were in the forefront of ordaining women and ultimately became the first national bodies to achieve parity of men and women ministers.

In contrast, Catholics, who in the eastern United States were also a minority, non-established church, joined establishment Protestants in forbidding women to vote on church matters or to speak publicly during worship. For many Catholics, private homes were the only places available for meetings, and in these settings, Catholic women apparently did exercise considerable influence. According to Brekus, however, they were never given as much authority as men.[25]

With the official disestablishment of churches and the growth of evangelicalism came more opportunities for white Protestant women. Under the legally protected system of religious voluntarism, congregations and church leaders depended more and more on women not only to perform church work but to preserve the religious character of the new nation. During the 1800s, women became increasingly involved in missionary work, reform movements, and charitable activity. The coming of industrialization served to expand their roles and responsibilities further, if largely by default.

Especially in the North, as factory work drew men, as well as some young single women, away from the farms, women's responsibilities for the home and the church increased proportionately. Gradually men came to perceive church work as the domain of women. This "feminization of religion" turned the equation of spiritual superiority and inferiority on its head as women were declared to be in fact the spiritual *superiors* of men. It became the duty of women to Christianize their children and to steer their husbands away from the sordid temptations of city life. The ordained ministry continued to be the nearly exclusive province of men, but the content of their sermons shifted to address women's concerns and to praise women's virtues.

These changes, however, did not by any means alter society's notion of "true womanhood." White women, if exalted for their spiritual sensitivities, were still expected to be deferential and obedient, both to their husbands and to the state, and to function preeminently as wife and mother. Many black women, of course, would have rejoiced to experience such liberating restrictions.

Not all women wore the yoke of subservience lightly, and a number of them found outlets for their talents in the reform movements of the day. Through volunteer activity, some women, black as well as white, found a voice and grew experienced in speaking out on matters of public policy including, in the mid-1800s, the abolition of slavery. Ultimately, the praising of women's piety and the asserting of their moral authority by unwitting churchmen helped lay a foundation for the suffragette movement that in the second decade of the next century gained women the right to vote.[26]

Even then, in both church and society, the expectation was that women were to be subordinate to men; women who challenged this cultural and theological arrangement were the exception rather than the rule. At the same time, out of their common experiences many women developed a sense of sisterhood with one another. Public activists, especially, bonded as members of a select community, or more aptly, as members of one of two such communities—one black, one white—with only occasional, genuine merging of the two.

The attitudes and actions of most white Protestant women reflected the values of the larger society, not only with regard to race but to religious diversity. When large numbers of Catholic immigrants arrived during the early to mid-1800s, the responsibility for meeting their social and educational needs was assumed to a large degree by Catholic sisters. While Catholic lay women had even less status in their churches than did Protestant women, members of Catholic religious orders were another matter. These were women who had rejected marriage, which itself was suspect, and who appeared to enjoy an extraordinary degree of independence. At the same time, "they were decried [by white Protestant women] as submissive, obedient dupes who mindlessly followed the orders of their bishops and the pope."[27]

But the disparagement cut both ways. "While Protestant women urged impressionable 'young ladies' not to be seduced by the illusion of sisters' religious independence, Catholic sisters waged a smear campaign of their own: one Catholic woman denigrated Protestantism as 'mere chaos; dark and void, and shapeless like the original nothing from which the world was founded.' These public disputes raged throughout the rest of the century, bringing Catholic and Protestant women into the public sphere to promote their own distinctive understandings of Christianity."[28] The reality, however, was that Protestants held the political and cultural power, so that Catholics were far from equals even in a war of words.

Conflict between Protestants and Catholics was not new to the nineteenth century and not restricted to women. Among the thirteen colonies, Maryland alone was originally designated as a place of welcome and safety for the relatively few Roman Catholics among the population of eastern colonists. Before the seventeenth century ended, however, Anglicans took over the colony and prohibited Catholics from voting, holding office, or worshipping anywhere but in their private homes. In a petition of protest, a group of Catholics wrote, "They deprive us of all the Advantages promised our Ancestors on their Coming into this Province."[29]

A century and some years later, the state of Maryland would emerge as a stronghold of Catholicism within the new nation, but its influence would not be sufficient to protect new waves of Catholic immigrants from indignities and outright hatred much as *their* colonial ancestors had known. Nor were Catholic immigrants alone in suffering from WASP sentiments that came to be known as "nativism."

An Anti-immigrant Ideology

The ideology of "nativism," the idea that the nation belonged to native citizens—by which was meant not Indians, but WASPS—grew apace with Catholic and Jewish immigration and became widespread among white Protestants in the second half of the 1800s. While the Catholic Church was dominant in the Southwest in these decades, Catholic immigrants in the East were among the dominated. The millions of Catholic immigrants who arrived on the eastern seaboard from the 1820s through the 1920s failed one crucial test: they did not have the Protestant credentials to be certified as WASPs.

At the time, they were not just "Catholic immigrants," but "Irish Catholics" and "German Catholics" and later "Italian Catholics" and "Polish Catholics." The ethnic designations constituted a privilege that had been denied Africans, who as slaves were forced to abandon their original ethnic identities and take on a common racial identity that served to obliterate distinctive tribes, traditions, and heritages. Ethnic Catholics, at least for a generation and often more, kept their languages, their feast days, their cultural idiosyncrasies. This was at once both an asset and a deficit—fostering internal community on the one hand, but generating conflict with the larger Protestant society on the other. The bigger sources of conflict, however, had to do with economics and the question of loyalty. While some Catholic immigrants were skilled in the trades or took up farming, the majority of them were unskilled laborers who settled in northern cities where they were perceived to be as great a threat to wage scales as were black laborers.

Beyond that, Protestants often wondered whether Catholics could and would be loyal to their adopted country because they were members of a centralized church under the jurisdiction of a pope who was located in another country. The anti-Catholic movement known as "Popery" took various forms, from libelous name calling to physical terrorism to the organizing in the mid-1850s of an anti-Catholic political party, formally the "American Party," but better known as the "Know Nothing Party." The Know Nothings, so called because when asked about their agenda members replied that they "knew nothing," were devoted to passing legislation hostile to European Catholic immigrants as well as to Mexican residents living in lands in the Southwest that had been annexed by the United States.[30] In later decades, a secret society known as the American Protective Association was organized to eliminate "foreign despots," as Catholics were frequently alleged to be.

The response was for ethnic Catholics to build power bases in the form of political machines in northern, urban cities such as New York as a means of protecting their interests. They also built their own health and welfare institutions, creating, to a significant degree, a parallel society that included parochial schools, hospitals, orphanages, and other social service agencies. First and foremost, of course, their society included churches—Catholic parishes that retained ethnic identities, but collectively came to be referred to as the "Immigrant Church."

In 1924, the National Origins Act established restrictive quotas to prevent further immigration of non-WASPs, including Eastern Europeans, who were mostly Catholic or Jewish. Nativist sentiment was further reinforced in the 1920s by the inclusion of Catholics in the hate agenda of the Ku Klux Klan, which had been originally organized in the 1860s as an anti-black terrorist organization. This demonic underside of American Protestantism— for it did identify itself as being Christian—like the National Origins Act, included in its purview not only Catholics but Jews. The large numbers of Jews who had immigrated to the United States during roughly the same decades as Catholics were as much the victims of nativism as were Catholics; indeed, they were regarded as even further beyond the pale for not being Christian at all.

Chinese and Japanese immigrants who arrived in California during the 1800s were subjected to similar attitudes. Much like Africans, Indians, and Mexican Americans, they were thought of as inferior and thus fair game for exploitation. Chinese immigrants were conscripted into slave labor to build the railroad that joined the nation from West to East in 1869. Citizenship was officially denied them in California after a delegate to the constitutional convention declared, "This state should be a state for white men. We want no other race here." After federal anti-immigrant legislation was passed prohibiting others from their countries of origin from coming to the United States, Chinese and Japanese individuals already here became the targets of virulent hatred and violence. Discrimination against Chinese Americans was legalized; they were segregated in areas designated as "Chinatowns" and neither corporations nor governmental units were permitted to hire them.[31]

Jim Crow Segregation

The experiences of African Americans in the 1800s were qualitatively different from those of other non-WASPS, for they were neither a colonized people, as were Native Americans and Mexican Americans, nor immigrants targeted by nativist sentiments. They were the descendants of people taken from their own lands and brought to this country involuntarily for purposes of enslavement. Emancipation in the 1860s brought only momentary change in their status. During the twelve brief years of Reconstruction that followed the Civil War, Southern black men were able to vote and hundreds of black representatives were elected to public offices—from local boards of education to state legislatures to the United States Congress. But this brief venture into citizenship was brought to a close with the withdrawal of federal troops from the South in 1878. Very soon, southern states instituted "black codes" that for all practical purposes returned African Americans to a state of bondage.

The system of Jim Crow segregation that developed during the latter decades of the 1800s effectively created two separate societies in which African Americans were required to attend segregated schools, prohibited from using public transportation and facilities, prevented from voting, and forbidden to engage in everyday social intercourse with whites. Violence and terrorism reigned as black boys and men, for the least perceived offense, were subject to mutilation, burning, and lynching.

The religious factors involved in maintaining this racial caste system were multiple. The evangelicalism of the 1800s, northern and southern, ended up justifying the pursuit of self-interest rather than the common good. John Wesley's "method" of breaking congregations down into cells or small groups, the better to exercise spiritual care for one another and social responsibility for the less fortunate, succumbed to a more individualistic focus on perfectionism, while the Arminian idea of "free will" devolved into the notion of "every man for himself." Individualism, competition, materialism, and white supremacy became the hegemonic cultural values of Protestant America. Members of groups that held to other constellations of values continued to be regarded as the "other."

In their discriminatory stances, white churches were following the norms of the larger society. Notwithstanding the successful creation of independent black churches, schools, and businesses in both the North and South, the tenacious dogma asserting physical and cultural inferiority of blacks, as well as Indians, was refurbished in the mid-1800s by leading ethnologists as pseudo-scientific "truth." These claims were given further credence by the Social Darwinism of the late 1800s and early 1900s, which borrowed the concepts of biological evolution—natural selection, struggle for existence, and survival of the fittest—to account for differences in cultures and races. Perhaps not coincidentally, the last decade of the nineteenth century saw the institution of the "separate but equal" doctrine by the United States Supreme Court in *Plessy v. Ferguson*—a ruling that came little short of reinstating the 1857 *Dred Scott* decision declaring that blacks "had no rights the white man was bound to respect." The finding that separate black and white facilities were constitutional so long as they were "equal," which of course they never were, prevailed until the 1954 Supreme Court decision in *Brown v. Topeka Board of Education.*

These pernicious ideas reinforced the racism that had been introduced to the New World by European colonists over two centuries earlier. Over that period, racism was conjoined with sexism—particularly with the notion that white women, at the same time they were to be subordinate to men, were to be kept pure and chaste for the exclusive pleasure of white men. Especially in the South, white women were placed on a pedestal where they were regarded as virtuous but vulnerable beings in need of the protection of white men— and from what? From the attributed bestiality of black men. Strict segregation and acts of violence were means of assuring that the egos of Southern white men and the "safety" of Southern white women would be preserved. Meanwhile, African American women knew no such protection, as they remained vulnerable to sexual assault by white men who saw them as undeserving of the respect and consideration extended to white women.

Not that white Americans, including white Christians, did not seek in various ways to temper these anti-Christian attitudes and behaviors. Following Emancipation, for example, New England Congregationalists redeemed themselves in some measure by sending missionary teachers to the South to establish and staff schools for the newly freed African Americans. Northern black churches did likewise and these collective efforts greatly enhanced the opportunities of impoverished and illiterate Southern blacks. Inevitably, white missionaries and teachers also imparted the values of middle-class white culture and, for that matter, so did black missionaries who believed that emulation of white manners and customs was the path to acceptability. Nonetheless, the contributions they made at some sacrifice and with substantial sincerity were a welcome contrast to the recalcitrance of most church bodies.

The so-called "Social Gospel" theology that developed within mainline Protestantism in the new century implied a commitment to building inclusive Christian community, but not, it turned out, if community meant transcending racial and gender divides. Consequently, the system of Jim Crow segregation remained intact for another fifty years and more. When it was finally dismantled, it was not at the initiative of white churches.

For Further Reading

Dolan, Jay P. *The American Catholic Experience: A History from the Colonial Times to the Present.* Garden City, N. Y.: Doubleday & Co., 1985.

Lincoln, C. Eric. *Race, Religion, and the Continuing American Dilemma.* New York: Hill & Wang, 1984.

Lindley, Susan Hill. *"You Have Stept out of Your Place": A History of Women and Religion in America.* Louisville, Ky.: Westminster John Knox Press, 1996.

Marty, Martin E. *Righteous Empire: The Protestant Experience in America*. New York: Harper Torchbooks, 1970.

Swift, Donald C. *Religion and the American Experience: A Social and Cultural History, 1765-1997*. Armonk, N.Y.: M. E. Sharpe, 1998.

Takaki, Ronald. *Iron Cages: Race and Culture in 19th Century America*. New York: Oxford University Press, 1990.

NOTES

1. See chapter 17 of Martin E. Marty, *Righteous Empire: The Protestant Experience in America* (New York: Harper Torchbooks, 1970). A later edition of this book inverts the title and subtitle.

2. Albert J. Raboteau, *Slave Religion: The "Invisible Institution" in the Antebellum South* (New York: Oxford University Press, 1978).

3. The African Methodist Episcopal Church was organized in 1816, the African Methodist Episcopal Zion Church in 1821, the Colored Methodist Episcopal Church (now Christian Methodist Episcopal, or CME) in 1870, and the National Baptist Convention in 1895.

4. For a more extended discussion of these ideas, see chapter 4 in Donald C. Swift, *Religion and the American Experience* (Armonk, N.Y.: M. E. Sharpe, 1998).

5. Ibid.

6. Ibid.

7. David G. Bromley and Anson Shupe, "Rebottling the Elixir: The Gospel of Prosperity in America's Religioeconomic Corporations," in *In Gods We Trust: New Patterns of Religious Pluralism in America* (eds. Thomas Robbins and Dick Anthony; 2d ed., rev. and exp.; New Brunswick, N.J.: Transaction Publishers, 1990), 235.

8. The *Homestead Act,* 37th Cong., sess. 11, chapter 75 of 1862: Chapter LXXV – An act to Secure Homesteads to actual Settlers on the Public Domain.

9. Louis Knowles and Kenneth Prewitt, eds., *Institutional Racism in America* (Englewood Cliffs, N.J.: Prentice-Hall, 1969), 10–13.

10. Joseph Bruchac, *The Trail of Tears* (New York: Random House, 1999).

11. From the PBS Film, *The American Experience: The Way West*, prod. Ric Burns and Lisa Ades, 90 min., 1994, videocassette.

12. Ibid. Statistics for the Native population in 1900 range from less than 250,000 to as many as 360,000.

13. George E. Tinker, *Missionary Conquest: The Gospel and Native American Cultural Genocide* (Minneapolis: Fortress Press, 1993), 17.

14. Another term for persons whose parentage is a mixture of Spanish and Indian is *mestizo.* This term is less commonly used than Hispanic or Latina/o which, as indicated in a note in the introduction, encompass not only Mexican Americans but Puerto Ricans, Cuban Americans, and persons from Central and South America. In this chapter, the discussion is limited to Mexican Americans, whose experiences historically are quite different from other Latinas/os. For a more inclusive discussion, see chapter 6.

15. Moisés Sandoval, *On the Move: A History of the Hispanic Church in the United States* (Maryknoll, N.Y.: Orbis Books, 1990), 25–26.

16. Cited in *The American Experience: The Way West.*

17. Sandoval, *On the Move,* 26.

18. Ibid.

19. Ibid., 27.

20. Ibid., 28.

21. Ibid., 31.

22. Catherine A. Brekus, "The Revolution in the Churches: Women's Religious Activism in the Early American Republic," in James H. Hutson, ed., *Religion and the New Republic: Faith in the Founding of America* (Lanham, Md.: Rowman & Littlefield Publishers, Inc., 2000), 118.

23. Ibid., 119–20.

24. Ibid., 120.

25. Ibid., 121.

26. This discussion draws on chapter 5 of Swift, *Religion and the American Experience,* "Women, the Churches, and Empowerment," and chapter 4 of Elisabeth Fox-Genovese, "Religion and Women in America," in *World Religions in America* (ed. Jacob Neusner; rev. and exp. ed.; Louisville, Ky.: Westminster John Knox Press, 2000).

27. Brekus, "Revolution in the Churches," 126.

28. Ibid., 127. Brekus is here quoting Mary Sadlier, *Con O'Regan; or, Emigrant Life in the New World,* cited in *American Catholic Women: A Historical Exploration* (ed. Karen Kennelley; New York: Macmillan, 1989), 27.

29. Ibid., 118.

30. LW, "Immigrant Bashing Long a Part of U.S. History," *National Catholic Reporter,* November 1, 1996, 5.

31. Ibid.

—CHAPTER 3—
The Twentieth Century

The most significant story of the first half of the twentieth century, where white Christians are concerned, was the development of "social Christianity." Subplots of the story include the narrow understanding of this concept by mainline Protestants, ambivalence on the part of Catholics, and resistance by conservative evangelicals. These expressions of Christianity differed from one another in a multitude of ways, not least being their respective stances with regard to the centrality of community. While Pentecostals[1] were preeminently concerned with spirituality, mainline Protestants turned to social conscience, and Catholics divided over whether to preserve a separatist stance or embrace modernist worldviews and values. For fundamentalists, there was no question of which side of the fence to be on, which in turn meant that Christian community was evident the least in their ranks. But each of their stories contributed scaffolding for the shape that American Christianity would take in the second half of the century.

Social and Unsocial Gospels

Among the mainline churches at the turn of the century were Episcopalians, Congregationalists, and Northern Presbyterians, Methodists, and Baptists. These were the churches that ultimately became the "social gospel" churches, or what were also termed "liberal" or "postmillennial" churches. The "liberal" moniker referred to these churches being open to methods of biblical criticism and interpretation; to scientific theories, including Darwin's ideas of evolution; to an understanding of history that embraced the idea of "progress"; and to involvement in progressive politics. Their positions stood in opposition to conservative evangelicals who rejected science, were apolitical and otherworldly, emphasized fate and "providence" and, as fundamentalists, believed in inerrancy and a literal reading of the Bible.

The "postmillennial" designation referred to the conviction held by liberal Protestants that salvation adhered in whole or in part in working to establish the "kingdom of God" on earth, while conservative evangelicals held strictly to a doctrine of salvation centered on Jesus' death and resurrection as God's sacrifice for their sins. These premillennialists, as they were called, were highly individualistic, stressing piety and personal virtue. "Social Christianity," or the "Social Gospel," in contrast, essentially meant "the attempt to move beyond individual piety to address broad social problems."[2]

The Social Gospel movement began in the latter part of the 1800s as a reaction against the Gospel of Wealth. Formalized by a handful of Protestant theologians, Walter Rausenbusch prominent among them, this social justice interpretation of Christianity was spread initially by a small number of ministers who believed that churches ought to be on the side of the laboring class rather than the managerial class. The Christianity of the wealthy, they declared, was no Christianity at all, for true Christianity was a religion concerned for the poor; it followed that the proper responsibility of the churches was advocacy on behalf of workers and, particularly, advocacy for labor legislation to protect the rights of workers. Regrettably, the movement's most prominent spokespersons, including Josiah Strong, were blatantly racist. Their concern for laborers did not extend to people of color.

Throughout the first half of the twentieth century, nearly all established churches were racially discriminatory. Especially in the South, blacks were not allowed to worship in white congregations. Even in the North, few blacks were appointed as ministers to white churches; indeed, few black ministers or priests were available for such assignments, for most seminaries were racially exclusive as well. Catholics were no exception, for in the process of seeking to be accepted as "true Americans," they had adopted means that were less than meritorious. Catholics in the United States became anti-black, supporting first slavery and then racial segregation, both inside and outside the Church. Not surprisingly, the numbers of black Catholics remained small until after the 1960s. In contrast, the numbers of Hispanic Catholics were substantial. On account of aggressive missionary efforts, so were the numbers of Native Americans who were at least nominally Catholic. But the Church was little more attentive to their issues and needs than to those of African Americans.

For the first several decades of the 1900s, Catholic parishes continued to be ethnic-based. As the Catholic population grew, so did ethnic clubs, lodges, orders, and fraternities. Along side these grassroots institutions were the service institutions—hospitals, charities, and orphanages—that were typically founded, staffed, and administered by communities of religious women, though ultimately with male oversight. These institutions, along with the separate Catholic school system that had been mandated by the American bishops in 1884, reinforced the cultural identity of Catholics, sustaining the cosmos of Roman Catholicism.

At the same time, divisions developed within Catholic ranks over whether they should embrace American culture or whether they should maintain the Church's official anti-modernist stance of separation from the world. This "Americanism controversy," as it was known, would not be fully resolved until the Second Vatican Council of the 1960s. Gradually, however, as the children of immigrants became better educated and were more gainfully employed, they achieved middle-class status. At the halfway point of the century, Catholics, by these measures, were approaching parity with white Protestants. Concomitantly, anti-Catholic bias began to decline in the larger society.

During these decades, social justice teachings in the Catholic Church, as in mainline Protestantism, were concerned primarily with the rights of the working class. For Catholics, these ideas represented the official position of the Catholic hierarchy, while among Protestants, social gospel tenets were initially a grassroots development. In time, however, these teachings permeated mainline Protestant seminaries and through their graduates were widely disseminated to local church congregations. Once the national church bodies embraced the Social Gospel movement and its labor concerns, these ideas fostered the development of what became known as the ecumenical movement, with its focus on interdenominational dialogue and action. The ecumenical movement was a strictly Protestant movement in which Roman Catholics did not participate, although Eastern Orthodox groups ultimately did; nor did all Protestants participate.

The exclusivist claims to truth on the part of conservative evangelicals prohibited their participating in the ecumenical venture. Not until the 1940s did they form their own ecumenical group, the National Association of Evangelicals, whereas mainline Protestants first came together in 1908 in the Federal Council of Churches of Christ in America (FCC), one of the forerunners of today's National Council of Churches of Christ in the U.S.A. (NCC).

Social Creeds versus Social Practices

Black denominations were invited to become members of the FCC, which created a Commission on Race Relations that was headed by an African American for twenty-five years. While the commission laid important groundwork for the ultimate receptivity of white mainline churches to civil rights, the council as a whole, in its first thirty years, steadfastly refused to address such issues as the lynching of black men. Not until 1946 did the FCC pass a resolution officially and publicly opposing racial segregation. By then, the discrepancy within the FCC between black expectations and white intentions had long since prompted the formation of a separate black ecumenical body, the Fraternal Council of Negro Churches.[3]

White Protestant women fared little better than African Americans in the early decades of the century; in fact, women activists in the church lost ground. A number of Protestant women were involved in the abolitionist and temperance reform movements of the nineteenth century. Toward the end of the 1800s, women's clubs and societies often were more politically engaged than churches in general. One historian suggests that women leaders "articulated a 'social gospel' to a broader spectrum of Christians than those affected by the later, male liberals more identified with the term."[4] Women's success, unfortunately, proved to be their undoing.

> By the beginning of the twentieth century, women's organizations had become so successful as promoters of Protestant churches that they were perceived as a threat by male church leaders. With membership far outnumbering that of denominational counterparts led by men, women's missionary societies pursued a distinctive agenda based on women's values, support for women missionaries, and social services for women in the mission field. Because women's missionary societies were organized on a national level, they offered a female alternative to the exclusively male hierarchies of their denominations. Denominations occasionally acknowledged that these groups represented the disenfranchised majority of members by turning to missionary societies when they wanted to communicate with the women of the church. In the early decades of the twentieth century, male church hierarchies moved to take control by subsuming women's organizations into "general" missionary societies. Although this change was touted as a move toward equality, the result for the most powerful women's groups was a loss of control of their organizations, budgets, and programs.[5]

In 1912, the Federal Council of Churches adopted a "social creed" that, while addressing labor matters, addressed neither racial nor gender inequities. This creed was based on a social creed that had been adopted four years earlier by the Methodist Episcopal Church (North). FCC's social creed, in turn, became the model for statements on issues related to industrialization that were adopted by a number of mainline denominations, including those that ultimately merged to become the United Church of Christ and the United Methodist Church. In the 1920s, these statements were expanded to address such issues as "family life, children's development, liquor traffic, conservation of health, and prevention of poverty."[6]

In part, these social creeds of middle-class Christians were intended as evangelical strategies to bring members of the working class into their churches. "The assumption," writes Winthrop Hudson, "was that the gap between the churches and the wokingmen would be closed if the churches would only exhibit an interest in their plight and support them in their struggle for justice."[7] But as Hudson points out,

> Middle-class Protestants were mistaken in assuming that there was such an alienation of workingmen. They simply did not belong to middle-class churches. Overlooked had been the existence of "a working-class social Christianity" running parallel to "the more widely known and well-studied social gospel" of middle-class critics of society. A study of labor periodicals makes it clear that Christian rhetoric, imagery, and motivation were characteristic of labor leadership and that workingmen found religious sanction for their discontent and union activities in the evangelicalism of traditional American Protestantism.[8]

On the one hand, Christian liberalism failed in this mission; on the other, it precipitated the reactionary fundamentalist movement that was anti-modernism, anti-blacks and Jews, anti-historical, and anti-intellectual.

The social creeds nonetheless laid the issue of social consciousness at the feet of mainline churches. Following the Great Depression, these churches experienced a mild resurgence of social gospel thinking, with a few prophetic voices openly advocating socialism, charging that "capitalism was essentially incompatible with the Christian gospel" and that "churches need to challenge the profit motive effectively and espouse the cause of the oppressed and underprivileged."[9] But for the most part, in the 1940s and 1950s, middle-class white Protestants went their own way, which was the way of freeways and suburbia.

People of color, however, took an entirely different path, and before the century was over, whites had also sketched alternative routes on the map of religion in America. Key developments in the second half of the 1900s included the freedom movements of oppressed and marginalized populations; the responses to these movements by white mainline Protestants and Catholics; the rejection, most notably by liberal white baby boomers, of denominationalism in favor of spirituality;[10] the emergence of conservative "new paradigm" or "seeker" churches and of the Religious Right; and, finally, a new interest on the part of some believers in Christian community-building. In fact, each development made its own statement about Christian community.

White Retreats, Black and Brown Advances

White Catholics who had the means to move to suburbia initially returned to their parish churches for worship and community gatherings. White Protestants were more disposed to building close to home. Following World War II, church memberships increased as baby boomers were enrolled and by the end of the 1950s the numbers of white Americans affiliated with churches had reached an all-time high.

The reasons for moving to the suburbs were in large part political; specifically, they had to do with the politics of race. From the late 1890s into the 1940s, black Americans took part in what is known as the "Great Migration," leaving the rural South in order to escape racial terrorism and to seek out opportunities in the cities of the North and West. The suburbs became white preserves, while the tax bases of central cities were eroded, allowing the quality of life for those left behind to deteriorate dramatically. In the suburbs, the churches were white and prejudiced but in other respects, typically apolitical. "Social Christianity" in this context meant social pleasantries and social status.

In contrast, black Protestant churches were entering into an era of political activism for the express purpose of combating racial segregation and racial bigotry. With impetus provided by the 1954 Supreme Court decision in *Brown v. Topeka Board of Education,* which declared racially segregated schools to be inherently unequal and therefore unconstitutional, black churches began mobilizing across the South to dismantle Jim Crow segregation and to secure protection for voting rights. As the civil rights movement advanced, white churches began a slow divide between their national offices and their local congregations. The National Council of Churches (NCC) was initially reluctant to become involved in civil rights activism. Faced with the persuasion of the Reverend Dr. Martin Luther King Jr., its own black staff members, and stunning television coverage of racial violence, however, the council finally came on board in the early 1960s. Northern ministers, priests, and sisters were among those who journeyed south to participate in the boycotts and demonstrations organized by black churches and local affiliates of King's organization, the Southern Christian Leadership Conference.

Ultimately the NCC played a critical role in lobbying for the passage of the 1964 Civil Rights Act and the 1965 Voting Rights Act. But the ordinary white congregation in suburbia and in small towns of rural white America wanted no part of it. Gradually they began their own protest, withholding funds from the national offices and chastising the national staff for carrying out a "political" agenda antithetical to their understanding of the "proper" role of the church. Even national denominational bodies faltered when younger black activists expressed their impatience with the Christian "turn the other cheek" theology of nonviolence and, in the language of "black power," began to speak out for more swift and radical change. Failing to understand this younger generation's intentions, and feeling somewhat betrayed, representatives of mainline denominations began to rethink their support of the more radical activity of social change movements.

Ethnic minority staff members within the national offices, however, seized the moment to develop creative theological statements of liberation and to organize or revitalize ethnic caucuses and commissions within the denominational structures. Acknowledging that many white officials of these churches had taken earnest steps toward seeking justice, African American, Latina/o, Native American, and Asian American members nonetheless asserted the need to organize separately in order to speak more effectively with regard to their own interests and concerns, among which was the persistent racism in denominational policies and programs.

In comparison to the black consciousness and civil rights movements of the 1960s, far less notice was given by the media and by mainstream white society to the parallel movement of Mexican Americans known as *La Raza* ("the people"). This movement addressed similar issues of segregation, disenfranchisement, prejudice, and discrimination that were directed against Mexican Americans. *La Raza*, then, found a counterpart in the American Indian Movement (AIM). Like the movements of African Americans, both these movements were instrumental in developing cultural awareness, pride in history and heritage, and legitimacy of indigenous religious traditions.

Each of these groups, along with Asian Americans, sought greater representation in the power structures of mainline denominations. Catholic and Protestant churches, in turn, formed commissions and agencies to address the needs of these constituent members. Mission activity among disenfranchised groups continued, but with greater sensitivity and respect with regard to each group's own history and culture.

In short, mainline churches that up until the 1960s were scarcely concerned with race and racism added these issues to their institutional agendas in the 1970s. With the advent of the contemporary women's movement, yet another accommodation was made, if reluctantly, in mainline Protestant churches. As women protested their exclusion from ordination, from theological and liturgical language, and from positions of leadership, and as more and more women enrolled in seminary, mainline churches were compelled to revise some of their procedures and practices. Following the Second Vatican Council of the 1960s, even Catholic women were empowered to assume liturgical and governance roles, short of ordination, that previously were closed to them.

The Decline of Mainline Christianity

Gradually, these changes were accepted by middle-of-the-road, rank-and-file members. But to some members, the changes had gone too far and to others not far enough. Some protested that their churches had become too political. Some opposed outright the empowerment of ethnic minorities and women and sought to preserve patriarchical and racially hierarchical arrangements in their churches and in society at large. To others, the reforms of the 1960s and 1970s, while positive as far as they went, had fallen short of bringing the traditional church into conformance with the requirements of justice. If they emphasized community in form, they were insufficiently so in content.

From 1970 to 1985, respective mainline Protestant denominations lost from 10 to 28 percent of their members, with the norm being around 15 percent.[11] The Catholic Church would have experienced comparable loss had it not been for the influx of large numbers of immigrants, notably Asian Americans and Latinas/os.

In his studies of the baby boomer generation—defined as those born between 1946 and 1966—Wade Clark Roof identifies five major categories of religious inclination as of the mid-1990s: mainstream believers (26 percent); born-again Christians (33 percent); dogmatists, or fundamentalists (15 percent); metaphysical believers and spiritual seekers (14 percent); and secularists, who count themselves neither religious nor spiritual (12 percent). These numbers themselves tell a story about the changing status of mainline Christianity. Roof breaks down the 26 percent who are mainstream believers as follows: 50 percent Catholic; 35 percent old-line (mainline) Protestants; and 15 percent "other." Included in the "other" group are "ex-Fundamentalists and burned-out Evangelicals, blacks, Jews, and assorted religious others," including Muslims. Roof goes on to say that Catholics and Protestants, presumably white Catholics and Protestants, set the tone for the mainstream category.[12] But life for both groups was qualitatively as well as quantitatively different after the 1960s.

The Second Vatican Council was without question the most significant event in the life of the Catholic Church in the twentieth century. Convened by Pope John XXIII in 1962 and concluding in 1965, Vatican II took place in the midst of the social turmoil already underway in the United States. While the First Vatican Council, occurring in the 1870s, had been a strongly anti-modernist event, the Second Vatican Council had the opposite agenda, to bring the Catholic Church into full participation in the modern world. Vatican II resulted in dramatic liturgical changes, including the use of indigenous languages rather than the universal use of Latin and the affirmation of indigenous cultural worship styles. It resulted in a diminishment of the authority of clergy, on the one hand, and an increase in the roles of laity, in the authority of individual conscience, and in the possibility of dissent on the other. In the United States, the Catholic Church became more open to ecumenism, allowing for unprecedented dialogue with Protestants.

It also became more supportive of the social struggles of disempowered peoples. Finally, there was a renewed emphasis on Christianity as a religion of communalism and community.

With regard to communalism, Andrew Greeley writes that Catholics "picture society as organized into families, local groups, and communities, and they picture humankind as relating to God as members of such clusters of people. Therefore they have a strong inclination to identify [with efforts that support] human and community well-being over against rugged individualism."[13] By the 1960s, Euro-American Catholics had experienced a decline in ethnic-based community as they became mainstream white Americans. But the new Catholic immigrants brought their own emphases on community to American society and to the American Catholic Church. In addition, influenced both by the community emphasis of Vatican II and by the liberation theology that developed in Latin America in the late 1960s and 1970s, many non-Hispanic white Catholics turned to community-building with the goal of transforming the Catholic Church.

Since the early 1980s, however, the Catholic Church in the United States has found itself in an increasingly schizophrenic dilemma, in large part because of the pope who has presided over the Roman Catholic Church for the past two decades and more. In what is almost a caricature of Rosemary Radford Ruether's dialectic of the two models of church, the pope and the bishops of the Catholic Church in America alternate between advocating "spirit-community church" and behaving as "imperial church." Among the actions of the institutional church perceived by many Catholics to be imperial in character are the silencing of progressive Catholic theologians; the excommunication in at least one diocese of members of progressive lay movements such as Call to Action; the continued requirement for priests to be male and celibate; the injunction against sexual activity on the part of gay and lesbian Catholics; the resistance to inclusive language liturgy; and diminished support for liberation theologies. No actions, however, have been more revelatory of the anti-community dimensions of the Catholic Church than the pattern of sexual abuses perpetrated against children by its priests and the Church hierarchy's decades-long cover-up.

Among Christians of color, imperialism is still experienced as a feature of both Protestant and Catholic churches. While establishment churches made significant changes in the 1960s and 1970s, solidarity with the oppressed has always been partial and often ambivalent. Tensions continue to be manifested within the institutions and among their members with regard to what kind of churches to be. In the 1980s and 1990s, white churches attended far less to matters of social justice than in the two preceding decades. While a relatively few white members worked to keep this issue in the forefront, others were more concerned with a perceived absence of spirituality in their churches than with matters of social equity.

Spirituality Movements

The expanded interest in spirituality in the last decades of the twentieth century had its roots in the predominantly white countercultural movements of the 1960s. Social activism was not the only way to protest the values and practices of mainstream society: so was "dropping out" and "turning on"; so was exploration of Eastern religions and a plethora of so-called "new religious movements." At the heart of these alternative forms of protest was a disaffection with the excessive reliance on scientific materialism and rationalism in Western culture, to the exclusion of spiritual experience as a source of meaning and a mode of understanding and explaining the world. The values of individualism, consumerism, and militarism were rejected by a generation of middle-class, white youth, many of whom opted to explore communal living arrangements.

In the 1960s and 1970s, significant numbers of those on the advance edge of the baby boomer generation expressed their anti–status quo sentiments by rejecting traditional institutions of all sorts, including established churches. While many in this cohort had rejoined establishment society by the 1980s and 1990s, some of them continued to seek richer spiritual grounds than were offered by traditional congregations.

Roof's category of "metaphysical believers and seekers" (not to be confused with conservative seeker churches), which he says constitutes 14 percent of baby boomers, is, as he himself acknowledges, an imprecise and eclectic grouping.[14] But what it points to is the recognition on the part of many individuals that religion, as Julia Corbett puts it, "is more than an empty husk." Rather, religion consists of the "enduring artifacts that come out of spiritual experience and that in turn channel spiritual experience." But channels do dry up, at which point believers seek to reform their religion, or abandon it and begin anew; they become "seekers" and "questers."[15] In the case of Christianity, the organized church has presumed to function as that channel. What many middle-class Christians—predominantly, but not exclusively, white—have acknowledged, often with great pain and sorrow, is that their channel has indeed dried up. The naming of this reality, which is occurring among both Protestants and Catholics, leads to a variety of responses.

Some have left the church to live a totally secular life unconcerned with matters of religion or spirituality. Roof points out that while "ninety percent of Americans claim an institutionally based religious identity, ... the salience, or significance, of that participation and belonging varies enormously over the individual's life-course. At any given moment a sizable proportion of those identifying with any of the historic religious communities can more appropriately be described as 'cultural' (as opposed to religious), as 'nominal,' as 'unchurched,' as 'nonobservant,' as 'nonpracticing,' as 'inactive.'"[16] In other words, when people are asked their religious affiliation, they may answer "Catholic," or "Protestant," or "Baptist" because that was their family and/or childhood affiliation, and not because they have any active connection with the group at the present time.

Others, who emphatically identify themselves as Christian, leave the church to wander in the proverbial wilderness, becoming, in the language of Episcopal bishop John Spong, "believers in exile."[17] Some believers in exile continue to sit in the pew on Sunday morning, tuning out or inwardly translating the words that are spoken into a language more sensical and meaningful. Some of the believers in exile are in the pulpit, preaching a doctrinal theology that no longer has meaning even for them. In the process, a conspiracy of silence is perpetuated that keeps parishioners and congregants closeted in their personal belief systems, thereby precluding the possibilities for building community.

Still others despair of what they perceive as charade or institutional rigor mortis and embark upon a search for spiritual fulfillment in venues of a non-Christian nature, be that Buddhist meditation, earth-based religions, therapeutic and self-help groups, or some combination of these and other choices on today's spirituality menu. Even for those who do not leave the church, spirituality has replaced organized religion insofar as a source of meaningfulness for their lives is concerned. A 1996 poll found that "of the 89 percent of those who considered religion important, only 29 percent saw it as primarily about a tradition's beliefs and teachings. Sixty-nine percent regard their religion as their 'direct experience with God.'"[18] In other words, a great number of people who say religion is important are actually talking about spirituality.

Conservative Christians

Conversely, some who say they are religious are speaking of doctrinal absolutes or charismatic experiences within a church context. Between 1970 and 1985, as mainline denominations were losing members, evangelical churches, including fundamentalist and pentecostal churches, were growing. The Southern Baptist Convention grew by 25 percent and the Church of the Nazarene by 40 percent, while the Assemblies of God tripled their membership.[19] Furthermore, not all those who remain in "liberal" churches are themselves liberal; since the early 1990s, steadily expanding conservative factions in the historic mainline churches have aggressively sought to refashion these denominations in their own image.

Roof's finding that, in the 1990s, 33 percent of the baby boomer generation considered themselves to be "born-again" Christians and another 15 percent identified themselves as "dogmatists or fundamentalists" represents a striking change since the 1960s. Of the born-again Christians, some 50 percent were to be found in conservative Protestant churches, but 25 percent were Catholic and 20 percent were members of mainline Protestant groups—that is, Episcopalian, Presbyterian, United Methodist, United Church of Christ, Evangelical Lutheran Church of America, Christian/Disciples of Christ, and American Baptist. In terms of the backgrounds of born-again Christians, "38 percent grew up as conservative Protestants (including fundamentalist backgrounds), 27 percent as mainline Protestants, 28 percent as Roman Catholics, and the remaining 7 percent as Jews, some other faith, or nothing."[20]

Intersecting with these categories of conservative Christians since the 1980s is a newer category variously termed "seeker" or "new paradigm" or "postdenominational" churches. Among these churches are the exceptionally large congregations also known as "megachurches," the majority of which are independent, although some have nominal denominational affiliations. As of 1993, there were more than five thousand megachurches in the United States, each with a membership of more than five thousand individuals.[21]

One hallmark of these churches is the minimizing of Enlightenment rationalism, philosophical theology, and doctrine in favor of neo-pentecostal, New Testament experiences—healing, miracles, exorcism, visions, and speaking in tongues. Another is the rejection of traditional church culture in favor of contemporary music, drama, and multimedia presentations, although this is less characteristic of black congregations than white. These new congregations, most of which are suburban and middle class and consist of younger adults and families, prefer to meet in non-church-like buildings such as auditoriums or clublike settings where traditional symbols of Christianity are conspicuously absent. Rather than sin and damnation, the message is one of love and self-fulfillment. While these congregations reject the trappings of conventional denominations, they do develop networks through which they share liturgical resources, literature, and strategies with one another. Most notable among these is the Willow Creek Association, which is credited with having fostered the seeker church movement.[22]

The initial objective of these churches was to evangelize the secular, unchurched, or what is sometimes called the "pre-Christian," population of American society. However, George Hunter III, one of the leaders of the seeker or apostolic movement, as he calls it, points out that they have also attracted "many churched non-Christians" as well as dissatisfied, unchurched Christians.[23] Hunter departs from most of his colleagues in the movement in arguing for a radical indigenization of Christianity among populations commonly excluded from middle-class churches. The objective, however, is strictly evangelization and not remediation of factors that cause other populations to be marginalized.

Megachurches, especially, are organized on a model of small groups that focus variously on Bible study, twelve-step recovery, family and marriage issues, and emotional support for people in personal crisis. The emphasis is on personal transformation, not systemic change. Notwithstanding the configuration of small groups, these congregations are highly individualistic and little disposed to engage in social justice efforts. On the contrary, their literalism and exclusivism cause them to reserve the designator "community"—and, indeed, the designator "Christian"—for those who meet their exacting criteria.

At the same time that seeker churches are criticized for offering more "entertainment" than substance, increasing numbers of mainline churches are adding a "contemporary" service based on the seeker model to their Sunday schedules in hopes of drawing more youth to their congregations. Meanwhile, some postdenominational churches are rejecting the extremes of contemporary worship and moving to what are called "blended" services in which older liturgical forms and symbols are combined with contemporary presentations.[24] It remains to be seen whether either of these approaches will join the new styles of worship with socially inclusive and transformative spiritual experience and theology.

The more public and vocal movement to emerge from the ranks of conservative Christians since the 1970s is the fundamentalist movement known as the Religious Right. The purpose of this movement is less evangelism than it is the reassertion of patriarchical and imperialistic stances of chosenness and manifest destiny. The Religious Right emerged in the context of the political backlash of the 1970s. During that decade, Jerry Falwell and his "Moral Majority" movement became the "Christian" voice of so-called white "middle Americans" who resented and feared the gains that were being made by African Americans and women. In the 1980s and 1990s, the reactionary agenda of the Religious Right was asserted through such organizations as the Christian Coalition, Focus on the Family, and the Promise Keepers, which drew members not only from independent churches and evangelical denominations, but also from mainline denominations, including the Catholic Church.

A consequence of mainline churches now having born-again and fundamentalist Christians within their ranks is the building up of tensions and conflicts that threaten the very unity of some of these denominations. Certainly not all members or congregations within mainline Protestant churches can any longer be counted as social gospel Christians, and not a few Catholics would return to a pre–Vatican II church.

While white fundamentalists undoubtedly see themselves as creating and living Christian community, the validity of that claim is highly contestable. In this movement, the overt "others"—feminist women; so-called secular humanists; and members of the gay, lesbian, bisexual, and transgendered community—are held responsible for the alleged moral decline in society as a whole. Public rhetoric notwithstanding, people of color are also covertly counted among the offenders. One suspects that outreach to African Americans, Latinas/os, and non-Hispanic Catholics has more to do with building political strength than with building Christian community.

In the 1970s a gap developed between denominational offices and local churches with regard to the appropriateness of political engagements. The complaint by local members was that national staff had become excessively, if not exclusively, political as they occupied themselves with such "secular" matters as civil rights, women's rights, and environmental rights. This perception was one reason some of the members of mainline denominations turned to a theologically and socially conservative platform, where they found a larger measure of theological certainty and security. The irony is that they have now become part of the Religious Right, the agenda of which is to reinstate and "protect" white patriarchal America against the encroachments of people of color, feminist women, and gays and lesbians. In short, they have become ultra-imperial, anti-community, and emphatically political.

On the other hand, many postmillennial Christians have left their churches precisely because they believe their churches do not go far enough in challenging the status quo: they venture neither radical social restructuring nor life-enhancing spirituality. In light of the increasing disaffection with postmillennial churches by Christians both on the right and on the left, it is appropriate to speak of at least five divisions of white Catholics and Protestants in the United States today: mainline traditionalists or liberals, born-again believers, fundamentalists, believers in exile, and builders of Christian community.

Community Christians

Disaffected mainline Christians who seek a more substantive experience of community take diverse paths to their goal. Some among the faithful "leave" by "defecting in place,"[25] endeavoring valiantly to build Christian community while remaining in the institutional church. Others, motivated by tension and futility on the one hand and hopefulness on the other, seek to create communities external to established churches to function as channels of Christian spirituality and, to varying degrees, of social activism.

In the 1960s and 1970s, one manifestation of community-oriented Christianity was the predominantly Catholic "underground church" of the Berrigan brothers and other radically prophetic persons who opposed the Viet Nam War and supported the freedom movements of black Americans and other disenfranchised ethnic and racial minorities. Another manifestation was the freedom movements themselves. While these movements, with the exception of the civil rights movement and the United Farm Workers movement, were not overtly religious, they had spiritual dimensions and religious implications. The predominantly white women's movement, which developed both secular and religious/spiritual expressions, was joined by movements of African American women, Latinas, and more recently, Asian American women.

Out of these movements came an array of liberationist theologies—black, Latino, feminist, womanist, and *mujerista*—which by definition were opposed to historic, colonial churches.[26] These liberation theologies were qualitatively different from traditional, dogmatic theologies because they subordinated "correct belief" to the imperative of seeking justice and to the dialectic of action and reflection. Theology was understood to be something that was *lived*, not merely an intellectual construction. For liberationist Christians, spirituality—that is, the experience or awareness of the sacred or divine in everyday life—combined with a nonhierarchical, nonexploitative vision of "church" and of the world, is the essence of Christian community. In the 1980s and 1990s, these theologies gave impetus to various programs and organizations that sought to embody Christian community; the efforts continue into the present century.

In a few instances, entire congregations have committed themselves to being Christian community. These so-called "open churches" are highly democratic and participatory, rejecting top-down, denominational authority. They are on the progressive end of the continuum, both in theology and in social involvements.[27] They are also a very small, though perhaps growing, minority of congregations.

The growth of conservatism in American Christianity has to some extent energized these and other white Christians to be builders of spirit-community church—again, sometimes within mainline churches, both Catholic and Protestant, and sometimes outside institutional church structures. In other words, life-diminishing features of the Christian Church in the United States increasingly coexist with life-enhancing features.

But while progress has been made, issues regarding the status of women and the patriarchal—and therefore inherently oppressive—structures of even mainline churches have not been fully resolved. That these predominantly white denominations have not completely relinquished their racism is evidenced in the continuing need for ethnic caucuses. Heterosexism and homophobia are today's lightning rods for church strife even in what have been counted as "liberal" churches, while issues of economic inequity and militarism remain on the agenda of radical and social gospel Christians. In short, both "liberal" and "conservative" churches continue to sacralize the status quo in ways that violate and preclude community.

Consequently, progressive church members, former church members, and colonized church members all continue to speak of the experienced "imperial" church. At the same time, the people's church—the Church on the Margins—persists determinedly. Notwithstanding the limitations placed on community by establishment churches in the colonial and constitutional eras and throughout the nineteenth and twentieth centuries, the value of community has been preserved among those who have been marginalized and disempowered and among those who were and are their allies.

The targets of imperial activity were never solely victims; on the contrary, they brought dimensions to the American experience and character without which the nation would be qualitatively different and ever so much the poorer. They continue to do so today, not least in their ongoing challenges to the imperial and supremacist traits embedded in the psyche of white American culture and white American churches. It is, of course, also the case that the oppressed have sometimes internalized and reproduced the oppression dealt to them by the dominant society; indeed, they have at times devised their own internal modes of oppression. Thus, marginalized peoples themselves experience a tension between the ideal of Christian community and its imperfect realization. Accordingly, spirit-community efforts invite and require ongoing critique as much as do established churches.

For Further Reading

Dolan, Jay P. *The American Catholic Experience: A History from Colonial Times to the Present.* Garden City, N. Y.: Doubleday & Co., 1985.

Lippy, Charles H. *Pluralism Comes of Age: American Religious Culture in the Twentieth Century.* Armonk, N. Y.: M. E. Sharpe, 2000.

Porterfield, Amanda. *The Transformation of American Religion.* Oxford: Oxford University Press, 2001.

Roof, Wade Clark. *Spiritual Marketplace: Baby Boomers and the Remaking of American Religion.* Princeton, N.J.: Princeton University Press, 1999.

Swift, Donald C. *Religion and the American Experience: A Social and Cultural History, 1765–1997.* Armonk, N. Y.: M. E. Sharpe, 1998.

NOTES

1. Pentecostalism started in the 1890s as an interracial movement with predominantly black leadership. Following the Azusa Street Revival in Los Angeles in the first decade of

the 1900s, the movement split along color lines, with black pentecostalism retaining a more communal character than white pentecostalism. Fundamentalism, as a distinctive movement, was a white movement that began in the 1920s.

2. "Social Witness for the New Century: Ethics in Our Time," *Christian Century* (September 27–October 4, 2000): 952.

3. The Fraternal Council of Negro Churches was organized in 1934 under the leadership of Reverdy C. Ransom, an AME bishop. See Mary R. Sawyer, *Black Ecumenism: Implementing the Demands of Justice* (Valley Forge, Penn.: Trinity Press International, 1994), chap. 1.

4. Ann Braude, "Women's History IS American Religious History," in *Retelling U.S. Religious History* (ed. Thomas A. Tweed; Berkeley: University of California Press, 1997), 101.

5. Ibid., 102.

6. Margaret Lamberts Bendroth, Lawrence N. Jones, and Robert A. Schneider, eds., *The Living Theological Heritage of the United Church of Christ, Volume 5: Outreach and Diversity* (Cleveland, Ohio: The Pilgrim Press, 2000), 434–35.

7. Winthrop S. Hudson and John Corrigan, *Religion in America,* (6th ed.; Upper Saddle River, N.J.: Prentice Hall, 1999), 305.

8. Ibid.

9. One such person was Elmer Arndt, professor at Eden Theological Seminary and member of the pre-UCC Evangelical and Reformed Church. Bendroth, Jones, and Schneider, *Living Theological Heritage,* 444–45.

10. African American baby boomers also left churches in significant numbers, but they were as inclined to become politically involved as they were to participate in the range of spiritual activities that appealed to white baby boomers. See chap. 4.

11. Hudson and Corrigan, *Religion in America,* 385–86. See note 1 of the preface for more detailed statistics.

12. Wade Clark Roof, *Spiritual Marketplace: Baby Boomers and the Remaking of American Religion* (Princeton, N. J.: Princeton University Press, 1999), 192.

13. Andrew Greeley, "Religion and Politics," in *World Religions in America: An Introduction* (ed. Jacob Neusner; rev. and exp. ed.; Louisville, Ky.: Westminster John Knox Press, 2000), 239.

14. The category of "metaphysical believers and seekers" includes individuals who self-identify as "Neo-Pagans, Wiccans, goddess worshippers, Zen Buddhists, Theosophists, nature-lovers, feminists, holistic people, New Agers, spiritual people, 'followers' of various spiritual masters, 'seekers,' and many without a name for themselves, or who in some instances shift from one name to another so frequently it depends on which day you ask." See Roof, *Spiritual Marketplace,* 203. The inclusion of feminists here is not to say there are not feminists in the categories that include large numbers of Christians, but merely to acknowledge that some in this category of spiritual seekers identify themselves only by that name. Furthermore, this category and the category of mainstream believers overlap in that many Christians and Jews supplement their traditional religious engagement with various metaphysical perspectives and practices.

15. Julia Corbett, Address to the Upper Midwest Regional Meeting of the American Academy of Religion, St. Paul, Minn., April 29, 2000.

16. Roof, *Spiritual Marketplace,* 36–37.

17. This phrase was popularized by John Spong, an Episcopal bishop. See his book, *Why Christianity Must Change or Die: A Bishop Speaks to Believers in Exile: A New Reformation of the Church's Faith and Practice* (San Francisco: HarperSanFrancisco, 1998).

18. Cited in Winifred Gallagher, *Working on God* (New York: The Modern Library, 1999), xix.

19. Hudson and Corrigan, *Religion in America,* 385–86.

20. Roof, *Spiritual Marketplace,* 182–83.

21. Barry A. Kosmin and Seymour P. Lachman, *One Nation Under God: Religion in Contemporary American Society* (New York: Harmony Books, 1993), 238. While many of the megachurches are independent, some are loosely affiliated with a denomination, including the Southern Baptist Convention and Assemblies of God. In more recent years, even the United Methodist Church and the United Church of Christ have produced megachurches, as has the African Methodist Episcopal Church.

22. See Donald E. Miller, *Reinventing American Protestantism: Christianity in the New Millennium* (Berkeley: University of California Press, 1997) and Simon H. Sargeant, *Seeker Churches: Promoting Traditional Religion in a Nontraditional Way* (New Brunswick, N.J.: Rutgers University Press, 2000).

23. George G. Hunter III, *Church for the Unchurched* (Nashville, Tenn.: Abingdon Press, 1996), 27–28.

24. Ellen T. Charry, "Consider Christian Worship," *Theology Today* (October 2001): 286.

25. This concept originates with a book by Miriam Therese Winter, Adair Lummis, and Allison Stokes entitled *Defecting in Place: Women Claiming Responsibility for Their Own Spiritual Lives* (New York: Crossroad, 1994).

26. Womanist theology is the liberation theology of black feminist women, while *Mujerista* theology is the liberation theology of feminist Latina women. See chapter 8 for further discussion.

27. Roof, *Spiritual Marketplace,* 198. Roof here cites James L. Kelley, *Skeptic in the House of God* (New Brunswick, N.J.: Rutgers University Press, 1997).

PART 2:
The Church
on the Margins

As of the year 2000, racial and ethnic minorities constituted nearly 30 percent of the total United States population of 281 million. African Americans and Latinas/os each accounted for about 12.5 percent; 4 percent were Asian Americans and Pacific Islanders, while about 1 percent were American Indians and Alaskan Natives.[1] Many different religions are represented in these collective groups, but Christianity is prominent in each of them. Exactly how many are Christian is difficult to ascertain, especially where Native Americans and Hispanics are concerned. The criteria for what constitutes being Catholic are not always the same among Hispanic practitioners as they are within the official church, while Native Americans who have blended Christian elements with traditional religions may be less disposed to name themselves Christian than are organized churches.

The great risk in speaking of Christians among marginalized populations is to homogenize them, as if they all share the same history and experience and manner of being Christian. What racial/ethnic minorities, white women and women of color, and gay/lesbian/bisexual/transgendered (GLBT) individuals have in common are experiences of oppression. But the particular experiences vary and, consequently, so, too, do cultural priorities, theological formulations, spiritual expressions, and strategies for change. For example, African Americans, whose foreparents were brought here as slaves, have fought to secure their freedom and their civil rights. Mexican Americans of the Southwest, in contrast, contend with living on land that from their perspective is their own but that is occupied by an alien population. The issues of Native Americans have to do with treaty violations, sovereignty, and the return of sacred lands. Asian Americans are voluntary immigrants, but existentially feel excluded from mainstream American society. Women in each of these groups have suffered not only by virtue of being members of the group and from the patriarchy of the larger society, but often from the patriarchy of their own group as well. GLBT individuals may be doubly or triply oppressed by virtue of ethnicity, gender, and sexual orientation. While heterosexual white women enjoy privileges unavailable to others, they nonetheless know the crushing impact of sexism.

As their defining historical experiences vary, so, too, do the manner and method in which members of these populations were converted to the Christian faith and in turn adapted Christianity to meet their particular needs and circumstances. Indeed, variations exist not only among the different racial, ethnic, and gender groups, but within them as well. Native

Americans are not just Native American, but Hopi, Lakota, Navajo, Cherokee, Apache, Anishinaabe, and more. Asian Americans are not just Asian American but Japanese American, Korean American, Chinese American, Filipino American, Vietnamese American, Asian Indian, and more. Latinas/os are not just Latinas/os but Mexican American, Puerto Rican, Cuban American, Guatemalan, Honduran, El Salvadoran, and more. Blacks are not just black, but African American, African, Jamaican, Trinidadian, Haitian and more.

To address the specific character of Christianity within each of these subgroups is well beyond the scope of this book. The accounts in part 2 and the case studies in appendix 2 can only suggest the variety of expression, but nonetheless demonstrate that the Church on the Margins is emphatically different from the Church of the Center.

Members of the Church on the Margins are distributed among predominantly white denominations and sects, nondenominational/independent congregations, historic black denominations and sects, Native American Churches, and popular religious movements. Mainline Protestant denominations account for relatively few ethnic minority Christians. Indeed, they account for relatively few white Christians, for the six largest of these denominations together represent only 7.8 percent of the total U.S. population. In contrast, the Catholic Church alone accounts for 28 percent of the U.S. population and 42 percent of all reported church members. Over a third of Catholics are members of ethnic minority groups, with the overwhelming majority of these being Latina/o. (See appendix 1.)

Upwards of 80 percent of African American Christians are to be found in historic black Protestant denominations. In recent years, the most significant growth among black Christians has occurred in megachurches, some of which are independent while others are affiliated with the traditional black denominations and yet others with predominantly white denominations. While the majority of Latinas/os are Catholic, a growing number are Protestant and, among these, the greatest numbers are Pentecostal. The majority of Latina/o Catholics practice a nonofficial version of Catholicism so that the religious character of Latinas/os as a whole is more to be discerned in popular religiosity than in the culture of white Catholicism. Just as Asian Americans are diverse in their national origins and sociopolitical histories, so are their Christian expressions. The majority of those who are Christian, however, are evangelical, while more than a third are Catholic.

These variations among ethnic minorities are examined more closely in the next four chapters. In general, however, the meanings of certain terms— "megachurch" and "evangelical" and "fundamentalist"—when used in relation to peoples of color, cannot simply be extrapolated from these categories as discussed in part 1. Numerous references were made in part 1 to conservative white evangelicals, but conservative white evangelicals do not exhaust the range of those who name themselves evangelical. Even among white Christians, there is a continuum from ultra-conservative to moderate to radically left evangelicals; members of the Sojourners Community, for example, which publishes the politically left *Sojourners* magazine, count themselves as evangelicals.

Today's theologically conservative movement of independent white evangelicals is proselytizing people of all colors with some success, although their churches still account for only a small percent of racial and ethnic minority Christians. But Christians of color in America have been evangelical for decades and even centuries. Among African Americans, in particular, the evangelical mission often has been understood to be the conversion of whites, Christian and otherwise, who by virtue of their racist actions are in need of redemption. No differently from ethnic, racial, and tribal members of mainline churches, evangelical Christians come to the faith through the prism of their respective experiences of exclusion and discrimination in this country. Consequently, evangelicalism within these groups often has dimensions not found in conservative white evangelicalism, particularly with regard to matters of freedom, justice, and outreach. (See Table 1.) Correspondingly, the pronounced individualism found in white evangelicalism is more or less tempered among evangelicals of color.

Table 1. Percent of Congregations with Justice and Organizing Programs

	Social Issue Advocacy	Community Organizing Projects
Liberal Protestants	23%	44%
Moderate Protestants	18	29
Evangelical Protestants	14	19
African American Protestants	68	46
Catholic/Orthodox	33	32

Source: Faith Communities Today: A Report on Religion in the U.S. Today, Hartford Institute for Religion Research, Hartford Seminary, March 2001.

A similar claim, though perhaps to a lesser degree, may be made for gay, lesbian, bisexual, and transgendered Christians who have found a church home in the Metropolitan Community Church (MCC) denomination. While MCC congregations are commonly more in the evangelical camp in terms of theology and worship style, the ethos of these churches clearly is shaped by the experience of being an excluded and even despised people insofar as establishment Christianity is concerned.

Along with these qualitatively different expressions of evangelicalism, each of these marginalized groups has produced overtly liberationist expressions of Christianity, as have feminist women. Various of these movements of the past thirty years gave life to forms of Christian community ranging from Latina/o base Christian communities to black ecumenical organizations to the feminist Women-Church movement. It is helpful, before entering into discussions in part 2 and part 3 of particular expressions of liberationist Christianity, to point out some general features as described by Rosemary Radford Ruether:

> Liberation Christianity judges truth by orthopraxis, rather than orthodoxy. Not the person who is able to pronounce the correct theological formulas, but the person who is really living the work of justice and peace, is the true believer. Christianity is not a unique truth and divine grace available only through its historical institutional channels. Rather, it is a historic culture for naming and reflecting on this same truth available through God's redeeming presence everywhere.

> Liberation eschatology belongs to the tradition of the quest for the [kindom] of God, rather than the eschatology of "eternal life." The goal of redemption is a redeemed and reconciled world, where all oppression and violence has ceased, where doing justice has become the fullest expression of love. Liberation theology has often been accused of reducing redemption to the "political" level. But this accusation comes from a dissociation of the political and the spiritual which liberation theology rejects.

> Liberation theology interconnects prayer and political struggle, contemplation and resistance. Cultivation of a profound inward spirituality grounds the person who is able to risk torture and death in the struggle for justice. It enables that person to maintain loving concern even for those who are torturers and killers. To love one's enemies, in such a spirituality, is not a pious abstraction, but a concrete demand to leap beyond the barriers of dehumanization.[2]

Marginalized Christians in the United States have regularly leapt "beyond the barriers of dehumanization," whether they called their lived theologies liberation theology or not.

NOTES

1 United States Census Bureau, 2000.

2 Rosemary Radford Ruether, "Christian Quest for Redemptive Community," *Cross Currents* 28 (spring 1988): 11. In this essay, Ruether remarks in a footnote that "I will use

the word 'Kingdom' in this paper to identify this traditional biblical symbol, but there is need for an inclusive and non-monarchical way of expressing it." The term "kindom" came into usage after this essay was published.

—CHAPTER 4—
African American Communalism

From the beginning, the religions of Africans in the Americas were communal in nature. As Africans became African Americans, their religious expressions, including Christianity, maintained a communal character. The reasons for this were threefold: first, the retention of an African worldview; second, the discernment of community as the essence of Christianity; and third, the common experience of oppression as a subjugated people in the colonies and subsequently in the United States.

That Africans brought to these shores as slaves remained religious at all is testimony both to the universality of the need to find meaning in the face of horrific life circumstances and to the spiritual creativity of those sold into bondage. Subjected not only to the holocaust of the Middle Passage, in which some 10 million Africans perished;[1] the terror of the auction block, which divided family and kinship groups; and forced labor in which one's status was that of a nonhuman, the foreparents of African Americans also knew the brutality of religious intolerance.

Failing to understand that Africans brought with them their own religious systems and fearing the sounds and rituals that were decidedly not Christian, colonists and plantation owners forbade their expression—in spite of which African slaves retained aspects of their indigenous religions for upward of two centuries. More to the point, what slave owners *did* comprehend was the threat implicit in cultural coherence and cohesion. In the interests of forestalling organized rebellion and resistance, slaves were stripped of their indigenous languages, deprived of cultural rituals, and prohibited from learning to read and write. For the same reasons, slave owners were reluctant to introduce slaves to Christianity. Belying their declaration of Africans' inferior intelligence was a fear that Africans might discern in this religion the values of equality and justice—notwithstanding the corrupted use to which white Christians had put the faith.[2]

Only when legal assurances were obtained in the early 1700s that slaves baptized in the Holy Spirit would not thereby gain earthly liberty were episodic endeavors made to introduce slaves to the Christian faith, and then only in a selective fashion designed to further docility and obedience. Nonetheless, by the mid-1700s, a handful of southern blacks, both slave and free, had managed to organize the first black Baptist churches. Throughout the 1700s, religious instruction in the North was somewhat less censured than in the South. Only about 10 percent of blacks lived in the North, but here, a larger proportion were free—had always been free, or were declared free, or escaped from the South to be free—and among these, some became members of white churches.

The Christianity that was received by Africans, however, was qualitatively different from the Christianity imparted to them. In the words of C. Eric Lincoln, "The strategy of American Christianity failed in its effort to make black Christians a class of spiritual subordinates. For, in accepting Christianity in America, the Africans were not necessarily accepting American Christianity. The God they addressed and the faith they knew transcended the American experience. If the white man's religion sacrificed its moral and spiritual validity to the Baal of white supremacy, the Black Church was born of the firm conviction that the racial Baal was a no-god."[3]

White Christian hegemony, in short, failed to produce Christian homogenization. As Lawrence Jones puts it, "Black Americans have always had a high concept of the church as an inclusive community. When they were discriminated against in the church, blacks were able to rationalize the ubiquitous racism by making a distinction between 'white Christianity' and the real thing."[4]

The Rise of Black Churches

In the second half of the 1700s, Christian blacks in the North created organizations, called Free African Societies, whose initial purpose was to provide protection and care for widows and orphans. These Societies were actually proto-churches, providing sanctuary and spiritual nurture for local groups of men, women, and children. Functionally, they were small Christian communities. As such, they heralded the model of Christianity that would develop among African Americans and that continues to characterize many black churches today. As the Free African Societies were transformed into formal black congregations, they added to their agendas the causes of social reform and particularly the abolition of slavery.

Large numbers of southern slaves were introduced to Christianity in the late 1700s and early 1800s through the evangelical revivals of the Second Great Awakening and the ministries of itinerant Methodist and Baptist ministers. When the conversion of slaves confirmed the fears of slave owners by giving impetus to biblically inspired slave revolts—for Christian slaves understood that God willed them to be free—the religious liberty of blacks was circumscribed by legal statutes restricting the size and times of slave gatherings and mandating white chaperones. The response was to assemble secretively in proto-churches that collectively are referred to as the Invisible Institution.[5] These informal clusters of Christian worshipers scattered across the southern landscape retained an African cosmological orientation, as did many of the organized black congregations into which they evolved following Emancipation.

In those instances where blacks—slave or free, South or North—were admitted to white churches, it was commonly to a segregated loft or bench in the rear of the building or, in the case of northern free blacks, to separately scheduled communion services. It was circumstances such as these, and the inherent violation of the Christian tenets of equality and justice, that caused the seeds of the independent black church movement to begin to germinate.

Black churches in the North date from the latter part of the 1700s, when many black members of white Methodist and Baptist bodies withdrew from fellowship—not for reasons of doctrine or polity, but on account of racial discrimination and disparate theological understandings about human relationships. In the first two decades of the nineteenth century, black Methodist congregations were in turn organized into denominations, the two most prominent being the African Methodist Episcopal (AME) Church and the African Methodist Episcopal Zion (AMEZ) Church. These were joined shortly after the Civil War by another Methodist body, the Colored (now Christian) Methodist Episcopal (CME) Church, which separated from the Methodist Episcopal Church (South).

After decades of forming regional and short-lived national conventions, an enduring black Baptist convention was organized in the 1890s. From 1915 to the 1960s, a series of schisms, prompted by disagreements ranging from property ownership to civil rights strategies, produced the National Baptist Convention, U.S.A., Inc., the National Baptist Convention of America, Inc., and the Progressive National Baptist Convention, Inc. These three conventions collectively represent the overwhelming majority of black Baptists, overshadowing an assortment of smaller black Baptist sects as well as black membership in predominantly white conventions.

At the turn of the twentieth century, the order of development was reversed as black pentecostalism gave rise to a host of movements and churches, some black and some white. The Church of God in Christ is by far the largest black Pentecostal denomination among an array of holiness and pentecostal bodies collectively known in black religious circles as the Sanctified Church.

These seven historic black denominations—three Methodist, three Baptist, and one Pentecostal—account for over 75 percent of all black Christians, or about 62 percent of the 35 million African Americans in the Unites States. The remaining 20 percent or so are members of smaller black denominations and sects, independent congregations, or predominantly white denominations, including the Catholic Church. (See Tables 2 and 3.) That so many are Baptist and Methodist is in part a legacy of the evangelical activity of those particular Christian families during the Second Great Awakening. The large number of Baptists is also attributable in part to the congregational polity of Baptist churches, which afforded black clergy and congregants maximum independence and autonomy. Both the Baptist and Sanctified Churches allowed for a freedom of expression that accommodated African cultural forms; even the Methodist style was less formal than other white Christian denominations.

Table 2. Reported Memberships in Historic Black Denominations

National Baptist Convention, U.S.A., Inc.	5.0 m
Church of God in Christ	5.5 m
National Baptist Convention of America, Inc.	3.5 m
Progressive National Baptist Convention, Inc.	2.5 m
African Methodist Episcopal Church	2.5 m
African Methodist Episcopal Zion Church	1.3 m
Christian Methodist Episcopal (CME) Church.	.8 m

Source: *Yearbook of American and Canadian Churches*, 2002[6]

Table 3. Reported Black Memberships in Predominantly White Denominations

Catholic Church	2,000,000
American Baptist Churches	586,000*
Southern Baptist Convention	575,000*
United Methodist Church	393,000
Presbyterian Church (U.S.A.)	94,000
United Church of Christ	64,000*
Evangelical Lutheran Church of America	52,000

Source: Offices of the respective denominations. Figures are for 2000.
*These figures represent the number of members in predominantly black congregations, rather than the actual number of black members.

Not all blacks who were members of white churches in the 1700s and 1800s left to become part of the newly formed black denominations. On the contrary, blacks have been a continuous presence in mainstream white churches, at least in the North, since the colonial period. Throughout the 1800s, both in the antebellum period and the post-Emancipation decades,

Episcopal and Presbyterian ministers were well represented among the politically active black ministers who worked for the abolition of slavery or participated in nationalistic movements to build ties with Africa.

Since World War II, the number of African Americans in white Protestant denominations, as well as in the Catholic Church, has increased, although most of these members are in predominately black parishes and congregations that in worship style and church culture share much in common with congregations of the historic black churches. Collectively, these denominations and congregations constitute what is termed the "Black Church."

Structurally, there is no Black Church in the same sense that there is a Catholic Church or an Anglican Church. Rather, the Black Church denotes the body of African American Christian believers. It also denotes a particular African American expression of Christianity.

Elements of African Cosmology

Theologian Gayraud Wilmore speaks of the Black Church as encompassing persons who share a certain "cultural affinity." Specifically, he argues that,

> An attenuated but continuing nexus to an African past has stamped a distinctive mood and mode upon the spirituality, music and forms of worship of this segment of American Christians. A common participation in what was originally a blend of diasporic African culture with a culture of poverty in rural slums and urban ghettos has given these Black Christians an awareness of mutual lifestyles and group identity. An experience of racial prejudice and oppression has given them a sense of solidarity in suffering and struggle for more than 375 years.
>
> These characteristics and others have convinced many scholars that it is accurate to speak of a Black or Afro-American Church in North America, even though there may be considerable diversity among its constituent parts.[7]

The extent of the "continuing nexus to an African past" to which Wilmore refers has been a subject of debate among scholars over the years. Few would contest the persistence of two primary aspects of African traditional religions in African American religion—namely, communalism and spirituality. The degree to which these features are manifested today in institutional black churches, however, generates less agreement.

Peter J. Paris, in his book, *The Spirituality of African Peoples,* argues that African Americans have a syncretized cosmology—that is, a worldview that differs from both traditional cosmology and Western cosmology, but represents a blending of the two. That part of their cosmology that connects to an African worldview, he asserts, continues to be the source of common moral and ethical values. Paris identifies four interrelated dimensions of African cosmological understanding: first, spirit, which is "the source and preserver of life"; second, community, which "constitutes the paramount goal of human life"; third, family, which "constitutes the principal guiding force for personal development"; and fourth, "the individual person who strives to integrate the three realms in his or her soul."[8] Community, he asserts, is "the paramount moral and religious value among African peoples," and the African family is precisely "a large, closely knit community of blood relatives that is constitutive of the life and destiny of each of its members. In short, kinship constitutes the paramount social reality for all African peoples."[9] These elements of African cosmology, Paris contends, extend to African Americans. "Centuries of slavery, racial segregation, and disenfranchisement greatly enabled African Americans in retaining the most prominent elements of an African worldview that constituted their only reliable frame of meaning. Hence, all encounters with the world of their Western captors were interpreted through that frame of reference. Accordingly, they transmitted African meanings through a vast variety of Euro-American cultural forms."[10]

The Christian Church was one such form. But Christianity provided more than form; African Americans also discerned convergences of Christian meanings with African meanings, in spite of the distortions in the Western expressions of Christianity.

> Besides the spirituality of an imperial and materialistic culture, colonialism also brought with it the spirituality of Western Christianity. While in many ways the spirituality of Western Christianity resisted modern materialism and condemned traditional African culture, Africans found that resistance to be shallow and that condemnation to be unfounded. That is, Western Christian spirituality was too closely aligned with the interests of colonialism, [but] Christian spirituality stripped of its Western bias had much in common with traditional African spirituality.[11]

Paris elsewhere argues that the central principle in African American Christianity is the "parenthood of God and the kinship of all people."[12] Indeed, it was the experienced violation of this principle that caused African American Christians to separate from white churches in the first place and led black Methodist denominations to adopt formal policies of nondiscrimination. In both African spirituality and African American Christian spirituality, family and community were paramount.

To the dimensions of spirit, community, and family was added, as a result of the experience of bondage, the dimension of freedom. "Throughout black history," observes C. Eric Lincoln, "the term 'freedom' has found a deep religious resonance in the lives and hope of African Americans. Depending upon the time and the context, the implications of freedom were derived from the nature of the exigency. [But] from the very beginning of the black experience in America, one critical denotation of freedom has remained constant: freedom has always meant the absence of any restraint that might compromise one's responsibility to God. The notion has persisted that if God calls you to discipleship, God calls you to freedom."[13] But freedom is not preeminently an individualistic concern. Rather, "for African Americans freedom has always been communal in nature."

> In Africa the destiny of the individual was linked to that of the tribe or the community in an intensely interconnected security system. In America, black people have seldom been perceived or treated as individuals; they have usually been dealt with as "representatives" of their "race," an external projection. Hence, the communal sense of freedom has an internal African rootage curiously reinforced by hostile social convention imposed from outside on all African Americans as a caste. But Dr. Martin Luther King's jubilant cry of, "free at last, free at last, thank God Almighty, we are free at last," echoed the understanding black folk always had with the Almighty God whose impatience with unfreedom matched their own. In song, word, and deed, freedom has always been the superlative value of the black sacred cosmos.[14]

The communal orientation and commitment to this-worldly freedom—particularly racial freedom—are evident in the central roles the Black Church has assumed: from building the infrastructure of black society following Emancipation, to fighting to abolish Jim Crow segregation, to support for black political development, to contemporary community development efforts. "Community," for black churches, has never been restricted to internal relationships, but mandates outreach to the larger black community.

Freedom and Community

African American Christians identified themselves as a distinct people not only socially but theologically. America's self-understanding of being a chosen people covenanted with God to carry out a divine mission was appropriated and inverted by African Americans while still in slavery and then retained throughout a century of segregation that in practice approached the parameters of re-enslavement. The Exodus story became the preeminent biblical text for African Americans' interpretation of their life circumstances. Since, from their perspective, America was more akin to

Egypt than to the Promised Land, the firm belief was that God and God's agents would deliver them from bondage.

The necessary antecedent of freedom, however, was survival. In large measure, it was the ministerial leadership of the Black Church that secured the minimal requisites of life when some four million slaves were set free in 1863. Most of the freed men were manual laborers, lacking either professional or trade skills. Some of the women had domestic experience, having worked in the homes of the slave owners. But few women, men, or children could read or write, and fewer still had formal educations. Many black families were compelled to become sharecroppers, working the land of former slave owners for nominal pay, but rarely showing a profit because of the debt incurred as a result of having to borrow from the landowner in order to make it through the year.

Promptly on the heels of Emancipation, southern states adopted laws designed to control the black labor force—indeed, to control blacks generally.

> These laws, called Black Codes, bore a remarkable resemblance to the antebellum Slave Codes. Several of them undertook to limit the areas in which [blacks] could purchase or rent property. Vagrancy laws imposed heavy penalties that were designed to force all [blacks] to work whether they wanted to or not. The control of blacks by white employers was about as great as that which slaveholders had exercised. If a [black] quit his job, he could be arrested and imprisoned for breach of contract. [Blacks] were not allowed to testify in court except in cases involving their race. Numerous fines were imposed for seditious speeches, insulting gestures or acts, absence from work, violating curfew, and the possession of firearms.[15]

Thus was the foundation laid for the system of Jim Crow segregation that endured until 1964. Lest there be any misunderstanding, the Ku Klux Klan was founded to enforce the two separate spheres of existence.

In such circumstances, it fell to black churches to provide those essentials of society that were otherwise denied to black citizens. The churches built schools, provided job training, created insurance agencies, started financial institutions, and offered leisure activities—in addition to being the primary sources of moral guidance and spiritual nurture. During the brief period following Emancipation when black men were able to participate in electoral politics, many of those elected to public office were either ministers themselves or had received their political training in black churches. Under the auspices of the Black Church, black society became a theocracy of sorts, functioning as a "nation within a nation."[16]

When Reconstruction came to an end with the infamous compromise of 1877 that bought Rutherford B. Hayes the presidency and disenfranchised blacks once again, black clergy became a critical link between black residents and the white power structure. When tensions arose between blacks and whites, it was the minister who diffused the situation; if services were to be obtained for black residents, it was the minister who negotiated for them. When city hall, the sheriff's office, or the local board of education did not require his attention, there were ample pastoral functions to attend to. In the midst of a hostile and dangerous environment, ministers were challenged to create a self-contained world in which the talents of their flocks could be developed and members' self-worth affirmed.

Throughout the first half of the twentieth century, as the push-pull of white supremacist violence and potential economic opportunity prompted the mass migration of blacks from the rural South to urban areas, not a few ministers accompanied their congregations in the journey northward. Here, storefront Pentecostal churches re-created community for rural transplants to the hostile environs of industrialized cities, while larger and more affluent black churches offered a broad range of social services to members of the working class and the destitute.

Beginning in the mid-1950s, the entire world, by way of the communications media, became witness to the communal character of the Black Church as it provided the inspiration, resources, and leadership for combating legal segregation and disenfranchisement. Not that all black churches were engaged in the civil rights movement. In fact, one of Martin Luther King Jr.'s greatest challenges and greatest achievements was to draw "deradicalized" congregations and ministers out of their fatalistic acceptance of the status quo.[17] But from the Montgomery bus boycott of 1955 until Dr. King's assassination in 1968, black clergy staged rallies in black churches, recruited marchers from church ranks, used churches as their communications network, and raised funds from the people in the pews, all the while grounding the movement with their social justice preaching.

It was not by accident that the civil rights organization Dr. King headed was named the "Southern *Christian* Leadership Conference" (SCLC), or that it took as its motto and task, "To Redeem the Soul of America." The local affiliate chapters of SCLC constituted Christian communities that typically were led by black pastors, nurtured by prayers and spirituals, and committed to social activism carried out in the nonviolent tradition of Jesus as well as of Ghandi. Nor was it happenstance that Dr. King expressed his vision for a racially just America with the words "beloved community."

Historically, the beloved community has been a metaphor for the reign of God or kingdom of God in Christian writings. In the context of American society, the beloved community means, at minimum, "one which truly values diversity"; it is the antithesis of white supremacy.[18] Lawrence Jones writes that "ever since they have been in America, blacks have been in quest of the 'beloved community.'" Furthermore, "Blacks did not distinguish between sacred and secular in their quest for community. The issues of freedom from slavery, dignity as human beings, and [kinship] to God were too much intertwined to admit to this kind of division. As a consequence of this wholistic view of life every activity that enhanced any aspect of their lives was evaluated in terms of its contribution to the movement perceived as moving the race toward full membership in the beloved community."[19] King stood firmly in this historic tradition of black Christians. "All life is interrelated," he asserted. "We are caught in an inescapable network of mutuality; tied in a single garment of destiny. Whatever affects one directly, affects all indirectly." America's fate, he believed, hinged on the degree to which it was able to include fully all of its citizens.

In the latter years of his ministry, King's vision of what was required for community shifted from mere integration into the existing structures of American society to radical, systemic transformation of society.[20] King's earlier dream of equal opportunity, which was to be accomplished by way of moral appeal to the conscience of white America, was revised in the latter days of the movement as it became clearer that much of white America's conscience was stunted, that economics were what drove decision making, and that the securing of civil rights had done little to alleviate the devastation of poverty. King became skeptical of the premise that free-enterprise capitalism, through sustained economic growth, could solve critical social problems. While that approach might elevate all segments of the population to more affluent status, the disparity between those at the top and those at the bottom would remain unchanged. And that, to his theological mind, was decidedly un-Christian and anti-community.

King's reconstituted vision, with its shift to economic democracy, was no less anchored in biblical tradition than his earlier dream of the beloved community. If anything, it was a clearer and more comprehensive statement of the requirements of authentic Christian community. Responding to the black power movement of young activists in the mid-1960s who challenged the adequacy of the Christian ethic of love for bringing about social justice, King wrote, in *Where Do We Go from Here: Chaos or Community?*,

> Power, properly understood, is the ability to achieve purpose. It is the strength required to bring about social, political or economic changes. In this sense power is not only desirable but necessary in order to implement the demands of love and justice. One of the greatest problems of history is that the concepts of love and power are usually contrasted as polar opposites. Love is identified with a resignation of power and power with a denial of love. What is

needed is a realization that power without love is reckless and abusive and that love without power is sentimental and anemic. Power at its best is love implementing the demands of justice. Justice at its best is love correcting everything that stands against love.[21]

Both King's social justice preaching and the demands for empowerment on the part of younger activists were critical elements in the development of black liberation theology.

The Black Theology Movement

While the popular theology of black Christians had always had a liberative dimension, not until the 1960s and 1970s was it explicitly formulated, first by progressive black ministers from both black and white denominations and then by professional theologians. In 1967, a group called the National Conference of Black Churchmen or NCBC (later, the National Conference of Black Christians, in order to be inclusive of women) came into being with a threefold agenda: to seek rapprochement with the more radical activists who had parted ways with SCLC, to interpret "black power" to a white religious establishment angered by black rhetoric and demands, and to align more closely the institutional expression of the Black Church with the sentiments of its more progressive leaders. Both the interpretation and the alignment required a new language, and the language was called "black theology."

Black theology emerged at almost exactly the same time as Latin American liberation theology. Where the focus of the latter was classism and land redistribution, black theology was centrally concerned with redressing white racism. The first formal statement of black liberation theology was developed by the Theological Commission of NCBC, which was chaired by Gayraud Wilmore, a Presbyterian minister and dean of the New York Seminary. The first article on black liberation theology, written by James Cone, was published in 1968 and the first book, *Black Theology and Black Power*, also by Cone, appeared in 1969.[22] Cone subsequently joined the faculty of Union Theological Seminary in New York.

While NCBC did not preside over a mass movement as did SCLC, the two organizations were connected in important ways. Wilmore, for example, acknowledges, "As far as the modern history of black theology is concerned, I'm sure it could not have come into existence without Martin Luther King Jr., because we all stand on the shoulders of Martin Luther King Jr. as black theologians. I doubt very much whether … the articulation of a black theology could have occurred without Montgomery, 1955, and without the coming together of the affiliate groups to SCLC in the period between '55 and the end of the decade."[23]

Black empowerment was a concern of SCLC as much as of NCBC, though expressed in different ways. To a considerable degree, the two organizations had interlocking boards of directors. At King's direction, staff members of SCLC attended NCBC meetings and several of them became members. King called on NCBC for assistance in training urban black clergy as he prepared for the ill-fated Poor People's Campaign, which took place in Washington, D.C., shortly after King's assassination.

In other respects, however, the two movements were markedly different. One of these differences consisted of the language used by each. NCBC, for example, substituted the word "liberation" for the word "freedom," which was so prominent in the songs and sermons and slogans of the earlier movement. The difference, suggested one commentator, was a "reflection of middle-class academia" and its use of a different translation of the Bible than was read by grassroots clergy.[24] Dr. King's closest aide, the Reverend Ralph David Abernathy, had a reputation for speaking the language of impoverished southern black churchgoers. As Andrew Young put it, "You could go into Mississippi and tell people they needed to get themselves together and get organized. But if you started preaching to them about dry bones rising up, everybody had sung about dry bones. Everybody knew that language."[25] So SCLC leaders preached about dry bones and freedom; NCBC members talked about oppression and liberation.

To an extent, NCBC had a different audience than SCLC; its discourse, at least initially, was with the church establishment, black as well as white. But its purpose extended to social transformation. In black liberation theology, Jesus was understood as the liberator, blackness was understood as the preeminent symbol of the oppressed in the United States, and the mandate of Christians was considered to be active engagement in the pursuit of political and economic justice. Where whites were concerned, being Christian required being in solidarity with the oppressed; indeed, salvation for both blacks and whites came through resisting oppression.[26]

The transformation envisioned by black theologians was not only political, however, but also cultural. As Wilmore put it, "The controlling concept has to do with the whole gamut of human activity and involves a structural and dynamic renewal that goes beyond the pragmatic ends and shallow motivations of electoral politics. This does not, of course, mean a rejection of electoral politics. Far from it. But what is invoked here is a more profound vision and responsibility of the Church as 'custodian and interpreter' of the Afro-American religious and cultural heritage, not only on behalf of the black secular community but on behalf of the nation as a whole."[27] Thus, for Wilmore,

What Black Theology offers is more than a new Afro-American cultural nationalism afflicted with the same moralism, sexism, classism, and imperialism that afflict white civil religion. It builds upon a tradition that presents a counterculture to the American mainstream. An enumeration of some of the abiding characteristics of that black counterculture would have to include radical protest and agitation, Jesus as liberator of the oppressed, pragmatic spirituality, the dialectic of redemptive suffering and concrete victory in struggle, relativity and an openness on the question of violence, identification with the poor and victimized of all groups and cultures, a hermeneutical suspicion of racism as a constant in Western theology and church history, an openness to heterodoxy in dialogue with African traditional religions and independent churches, and an appreciation of and willingness to learn from other non-Western forms of spirituality.[28]

Toward the implementation of black theology's objectives, a variety of national and local black ecumenical organizations—that is, interdenominational, cooperative bodies committed to theological reflection and social action—came into existence from the late 1960s through the early 1980s. While limited in the numbers of lay participants, for many black ministers these movements and organizations became, in a sense, the ecclesial counterparts of Latin America's base Christian communities. They provided forums for biblical reflection on situations of social oppression and often led to activism directed toward the amelioration of inequitable power arrangements in local school districts, city governments, and police departments.[29]

Among these groups was the Black Theology Project, which was formed out of the larger "Theology in the Americas" effort. Based in the Northeast, its members included progressive black ministers, many of whom were also part of NCBC, and black theologians from various seminaries and universities. In part, the project was created because of the recognition that the vision of black theology was "woefully absent from the majority of Afro-American churches. Only here and there," pointed out Wilmore, were there black congregations that had "educational programs emphasizing black culture and the themes of Black Theology" and that were "engaged in a praxis demonstrating the coherence between spirituality and politics."[30]

In any given city, Wilmore observed, there were but a few individuals "struggling against the internal and external pressures in their situations that make for this grievous evaporation of the historic nature and purpose of the black church."[31] One of the intentions of the Black Theology Project, according to Wilmore, was "to identify these persons, build them into a national network of men and women of similar concern and commitment, and provide them with a variety of resources for reflection and action that are usually unavailable within their respective denominations. The work," he acknowledged, was "agonizingly slow and painful."[32]

In fact, neither King's radical prescriptions for realizing social justice nor the tenets of black liberation theology have been embraced in any significant way in local black churches. To the extent that black churches are change-oriented, they remain reformist in their approaches.[33] Around the country, only a handful of congregations are considered to be models of what it is to be "church" in the mode of black liberation theology. Among these are Allen Temple Baptist Church in Oakland, Trinity United Church of Christ in Chicago, and Payne Chapel AME in Nashville.[34] Short of fully embodying liberation theology, however, black churches display a considerable diversity, reflecting the multitude of social developments both within the black community and external to it that have shaped them since the 1970s.[35]

Changes and Challenges

Since the years of the civil rights movement, a portion of the African American population has rejected Christianity altogether. Estimates are that from one to three million African Americans now identify themselves as Muslim rather than Christian. Probably fewer than fifty thousand are members of the Nation of Islam; most African Americans who are Muslim are affiliated with groups recognized as being orthodox by the international Islamic community. Especially in large cities, significant numbers of African Americans have turned to quasi-African religions such as Santeria and Conjure, while others have embraced black humanism. Much of the black underclass, especially men and youth, has no institutional engagement with religion at all. The latter circumstance, in particular, is cited as part of the "crisis of the Black Church" as it seeks to clarify its function in the post–civil rights era.

Since the 1970s, conservative, evangelical black churches have identified with the anti-feminist, anti-gay rights movements of fundamentalist white churches, with some few of them becoming overt supporters of the Religious Right. These churches are an anomaly, representing the far end of the spectrum of diversity in black churches and, indeed, falling outside the parameters of the Black Church ethos as it has traditionally been defined. That black evangelicalism also can be and has been committed to community and to freedom is evident in the Voice of Calvary Ministries initiated by John Perkins in rural Mississippi in the 1960s[36] and in the organizing of the National Black Evangelical Association in the same decade for the express purpose of reconnecting social action to black evangelicalism.[37] But by and large, evangelical black churches are apolitical, at least in the conventional sense of the term.

In contrast to the ultra-conservative black congregations are the numerous churches, both Catholic and Protestant, that have become overtly Afrocentric, using black symbols and African worship styles, and intentionally fostering the communalism of African cosmology. Within Catholic churches, these developments were facilitated by the emphases of the Second Vatican Council on lay participation, cultural diversity, and community and by pastoral letters addressing issues of racism in the church and in the society at large.

The numbers of black Catholics began growing in the 1950s with the increased enrollment of African American children in parochial schools in the central cities of the urban North. The growth continued in the 1960s and 1970s as representatives of the Catholic Church became actively engaged in civil rights protests and demonstrations. Since the 1980s, membership has remained at about two million. While black Catholics emphasize community both among themselves and within the larger Catholic Church, the larger Church has often failed to respond in kind. There are but three hundred African American priests and eleven bishops. Not until 2001 was a black bishop elected president of the National Conference of Catholic Bishops.

The racial divide is manifested in various ways, most dramatically by the formation of a schismatic church, the African American Catholic Congregation, in 1989. In 1987, 1992, 1997, and again in 2002, lay Catholics convened a National Black Catholic Congress, resuming a tradition begun by black Catholics in 1889 that produced five such congresses in five years. In these forums for spiritual renewal and celebration of communal ties, black Catholics become a "church within the church," while at the same time affirming a commitment to transform the larger Church that they claim as their own.

Meanwhile, it is not uncommon for individual Catholics to divide their worship activity between parish masses and a black Protestant church, a circumstance that speaks not only to marginalization in predominantly white churches, but also to the unique experience of community that continues to be created by black churches. Writes one such believer,

> As a cradle Catholic used to hour-long masses, I'm occasionally drawn to a predominantly African American church, usually a Baptist one. It is here where the story of a people is sung and embraced over a two-hour time slot. It is here where one's spiritual grounding is rebuilt. It is here in the rich mosaic of a people used to seeing doors slammed shut where the doors to heart and heaven are open 24-7. It is here where people pull around you and say, "We love you, we believe in you, we will stand with you." There are times

when we all need to hear that, times when we all need to go back for some honest spiritual home cooking.[38]

A revitalization of black Protestant churches that began in the 1980s has paralleled the growth in the black middle class—from around 14 percent in the late 1950s to more than 37 percent in the early 1980s. Many middle class, professional African Americans, notably baby boomers, who had rejected traditional black churches in the 1970s have since been drawn to black, neo-pentecostal megachurches. These churches, according to Cheryl Townsend Gilkes, constitute as much as 25 percent of all megachurches in the United States.[39] While black megachurches, some of them new churches and others of them old churches that have been transformed, mirror such features of white seeker churches as the use of multimedia technology and the creation of support groups around different interests and life issues, they differ in other significant respects.

The neo-pentecostal style of worship strongly resembles the spirit-filled worship of historic black Sanctified churches. Gilkes observes that, "Their music is the best gospel music, and the preaching there is some of the best biblically-based preaching to be heard. Furthermore, most black megachurches offer a high degree of affirmation of a black identity in a hostile white society. The church reminds its members 'who they are and whose they are,' as a counterforce to oppressive social, economic, and cultural circumstances that may make them want to forget."[40]

Critics, however, have asserted a disjuncture between these churches and the black religious tradition. The issue has to do with the extent to which these "renewed" churches carry on the tradition of working for social justice and, specifically, whether they attend to the core task of community-building by maintaining ties with the black working class and underclass. A number of these churches, variously labeled "prosperity" or "word" churches, preach a theology of affluence that fosters individualism and self-enhancement, with scarcely a nod to the common good of the larger community. They represent, as Gilkes puts it, "a departure from more traditional liberationist and perseverance themes."[41] Other megachurches, however, retain the commitments to social justice and community-building that are characteristic of the black religious ethos.

In the words of one participant-observer, "We [black middle-class boomers] are returning, in part, because religion can provide a framework for basic questions regarding the origin, purpose and meaning of life. Passage into middle age and the new spirituality, therefore, account for some of this revival of interest by blacks, but there are also indications that many are returning to the church in hopes of reviving its role as a command center and strategic outpost in our community.... We [see ourselves as] part of a new generation of 'believers' seeking to revive the church as an instrument of change."[42]

A case in point is Bethel AME Church in Baltimore, Maryland, which has a membership of more than ten thousand with an average age of thirty-five. During the 1960s, Bethel's membership declined to only five hundred members. In 1975, a new pastor was appointed, the Reverend John Bryant, who was a product both of the charismatic movement and the black liberation theology movement. Under his leadership, Bethel became both an Afrocentric church and a "full gospel" church—that is, it was emphatically spiritual in the tradition of African religions as well as pentecostalism. As Beverly Lawrence points out, "Unlike many charismatic movements, which tend to be conservative, the full-gospel preachers like Bryant were aggressively liberal, politically and socially."[43] In 1988, Bryant was succeeded by the Reverend Frank Madison Reid III, who has continued these emphases while bringing his own creativity and commitments to the congregation and to the larger community. Under his leadership, the "Bethel model" represents "a synthesis of the Holy Spirit, African-American culture, and progressive social programs [with] the goals of salvation, empowerment, liberation, and peace."[44]

Socially engaged megachurches such as Bethel are joined by urban churches of various sizes and denominational affiliations that feature more mainstream worship services, but are similarly committed to community outreach and development.[45] Such activist churches—which are but a fraction of the totality of black churches—continue to express care and concern for local black communities through social service and community development programs that range from youth centers to teenage parenting classes to AIDS prevention on the one hand, to housing complexes, credit unions, and Afrocentric schools on the other.[46] The question here is the other side of the coin: To what extent have these churches retained the spirituality of African cosmology?

Christian Community Today and Tomorrow

Black liberation theologians have been critical of those black churches that fail to exhibit liberationist praxis. Although many of these churches continue to provide a place of refuge, spiritual renewal, and a sense of community, the concern is whether they have lost the cosmological commitment that compels action to redress dehumanizing social conditions. At the same time, some theologians have been criticized both for attending too little to the empowering role of spirituality in the black religious tradition and for conducting their theological activity apart from local churches and from the religious experiences of the people. In recent years, a number of black

ministers and scholars of religion have begun speaking of the need for a
more intentional fostering of Christian community that integrates theology,
spirituality, and liberationist activity.

One model that expresses this vision is the ChristAfrican Theological
Institute proposed by the Reverend Dr. Dennis Wiley and the Reverend Dr.
Christine Wiley at Covenant Baptist Church in Washington, D.C. The function of this church- and community-based institute is to "explore who God
is and how God applies to the everyday lives of persons of African descent."
The institute's objectives include bringing people together to do theology on
a grass-roots level; liberating African American people from oppressive theological ideas and sociopolitical structures; fostering personal, spiritual, social,
political, and economic changes for all age groups; engaging in African-cen-
tered studies; serving as a community-based "think tank;" and conducting an
ongoing critique of Christianity, the church, and Afrocentrism.[47]

The purpose of such efforts is not only to overcome external oppression, but also to address historic characteristics of black churches that
impede inclusive community. Even as it was advocating freedom from racial
oppression, black church culture has historically been patriarchal, auto-
cratic, and heterosexist.[48] In the past two decades, womanist (black feminist)
theologians have provided trenchant critiques of these shortcomings and
taken the lead in providing leadership on such matters as the ordination of
women; advocacy for black gay, lesbian, and bisexual Christians; and participatory decision making, all of which are critical to genuine community.[49]

Anthony Pinn has also pointed to the need for a "more communal model
of authority" and leadership in local churches.[50] Dwight Hopkins has proposed the creation of small Christian communities as one approach to this
task: "The second generation [of black liberation theologians] will have to
build and evaluate models of basic Christian communities in local areas.
Such an effort, whether centered around a particular church or house-hold
meetings of African American Christians, would teach, preach, and practice
a black theology of liberation for all to see and hear."[51] Forrest Harris, in
Ministry for Social Crisis, proposes an action-reflection model for social ministry in local congregations that is "relational, and contextual, and theologically grounded in the biblical vision of the community (reign of God)."[52]

> It is relational because its aim is to build community; it is contextual
> because it must make relevant contact with the human situation;
> and it is theological because it seeks unity between Christian social
> action and God's liberating purposes and activity in the world.
> Ministry is a mutual process grounded in relationality toward the
> end of accomplishing social transformation; it is ultimately commit-
> ted to the building of community. Communal power is relational in

character. In its relational quality, communal power cares for the total being of others; it is committed to empowering others to act.[53]

George Cummings, drawing on the example of Latin American base Christian communities, goes even further than Harris's model of shared power between pastors and congregants in pointing to the necessity for "the poor to evangelize and transform the community of faith." Black theologians, he argues, must "be converted to the thematic universe of the poor"; they must "deepen their understanding of the need to allow the church to be evangelized by the poor, who bear witness to the Spirit of the liberating Christ in their persistent struggle of faith and hope."[54] He continues:

> The inversion of the traditional approach of the church evangelizing the poor to a perspective of the poor evangelizing the church is not a rejection of the notion that the Christian church, in all situations, exists to bear witness to Jesus Christ. Churches exist in all classes and sectors of society, but this methodological shift establishes the priority of liberation theology, which places the witness to Jesus Christ among the poor in a position of providing prophetic and self-critical means of assessing the faithfulness or faithlessness of the churches to Jesus Christ.[55]

The point is that the resources for total church renewal are to be found not in the political prescriptions of formal liberation theologies alone, nor in the community development activities of middle-class churches alone, but also in the spiritual and survival experiences of those most in need of liberation. Only as these are conjoined will black churches fully embody the spiritual and liberative dimensions of Christian community.

For Further Reading

Cone, James H., and Gayraud S. Wilmore, eds. *Black Theology: A Documentary History, Volumes I and II.* 2d ed., rev. Maryknoll, N.Y.: Orbis Books, 1993.

Gilkes, Cheryl Townsend. "Plenty Good Room: Adaptation in a Changing Black Church." *Annals of the AAPSS* 558 (July 1998): 101–21.

Hayes, Diana L., and Cyprian Davis, O.S.B. *Taking Down Our Harps: Black Catholics in the United States.* Maryknoll, N.Y.: Orbis Books, 1998.

Hopkins, Dwight N. *Introducing Black Theology of Liberation.* Maryknoll, N.Y.: Orbis Books, 1999.

Lincoln, C. Eric, and Lawrence H. Mamiya. *The Black Church in the African American Experience.* Durham, N.C.: Duke University Press, 1990.

Paris, Peter J. *The Spirituality of African Peoples: The Search for a Common Moral Discourse.* Minneapolis: Fortress Press, 1995.

Pinn, Anthony H. *The Black Church in the Post-Civil Rights Era.* Maryknoll, N.Y.: Orbis Books, 2002.

Raboteau, Albert J. *Canaan Land: A Religious History of African Americans*. New York: Oxford University Press, 2001.

Wilmore, Gayraud. *Black Religion and Black Radicalism: An Interpretation of the Religious History of Afro-American People*. 3d ed. Maryknoll, N.Y.: Orbis Books, 1998.

NOTES

1. Estimates of the number who died in the process of transporting captured Africans to the New World between the mid-1600s and the early 1800s vary, but range as high as 17 million.

2. The justifications offered by white Christians for enslaving other human beings included the blessing it allegedly was for Africans to be brought to a land where they could be Christianized and their souls saved—if, in fact, they had souls, which was a matter of some conjecture. Various biblical texts were used to justify the practice as well, among the favorites being a perverse interpretation of the Hamitic story: that Ham's descendants had been "marked" with dark skin, and enslavement of Africans was a fulfillment of God's declaration that these descendants would be the servants of the descendants of Ham's brothers—the Europeans.

3. C. Eric Lincoln, *Race, Religion, and the Continuing American Dilemma* (New York: Hill and Wang, 1984), 58–59.

4. Lawrence N. Jones, "In Quest of the Beloved Community: Black Christians in Antebellum America" (unpublished paper presented to the Howard University School of Religion, December 12, 1978), 9.

5. See Albert J. Raboteau, *Slave Religion: The "Invisible Institution" in the Antebellum South* (New York: Oxford University Press, 1978).

6. Eileen W. Lindner, ed., *Yearbook of American and Canadian Churches, 2002* (Nashville, Tenn.: Abingdon Press, 2002). This yearbook was prepared and edited for the National Council of Churches of Christ in the U.S.A. Membership figures are reported by respective denominations; the years reported range from 1991 to 2000. The National Baptist Convention, U.S.A, Inc. was not included in the 2002 edition of the yearbook, as it was in the process of conducting a census, but it was reported in the 2003 edition as having 5.5 million members. Many black Baptists affiliate with both a historic black convention and a predominantly white convention, so that members may be double counted.

7. Gayraud S. Wilmore, "Black Christians, Church Unity, and One Common Expression of Apostolic Faith," *Mid-stream: An Ecumenical Journal* 24, no. 4 (October 1985): 357.

8. Peter J. Paris, *The Spirituality of African Peoples: The Search for a Common Moral Discourse* (Minneapolis: Fortress Press, 1995), 25.

9. Ibid., 72, 77.

10. Ibid., 162.

11. James H. Evans, Jr., *We Shall All Be Changed: Social Problems and Theological Renewal* (Minneapolis: Fortress Press, 1997), 97.

12. Peter J. Paris, *The Social Teaching of Black Churches* (Philadelphia: Fortress Press, 1985).

13. C. Eric Lincoln and Lawrence H. Mamiya, *The Black Church in the African American Experience* (Durham, N.C.: Duke University Press, 1990), 3.

14. Ibid., 5.

15. John Hope Franklin, *From Slavery to Freedom* (4th ed.; New York: Alfred A. Knopf, 1974), 241.

16. E. Franklin Frazier, *The Negro Church in America* (New York: Schocken Books, 1964), 36.

17. See chapter 7 of Gayraud Wilmore, "The Deradicalization of the Black Church," in *Black Religion and Black Radicalism: An Interpretation of the Religious History of Afro-American People* (3d ed.; Maryknoll, N.Y.: Orbis Books, 1998).

18. Evans, *We Shall All Be Changed*, 69, 86–87, and the complete chapter 4, entitled, "Hope, Racism, and Community." With regard to the metaphor of the beloved community, Evans specifically references the writings of Irenaeus and Jonathan Edwards.

19. Jones, "In Quest of the Beloved Community," 1, 7.

20. The address that perhaps best presents this change is King's "Beyond Vietnam" speech, delivered, ironically, at the Mother Church of American Protestantism, Riverside Church in New York City, exactly a year before his death, on April 4, 1967. The speech offered a brilliant and moving analysis of the immorality of the war, and an eloquent defense of his right to speak against it, despite any criticism that might result. (Theretofore, black prophets were only "supposed" to speak about "racial matters.") But it was also a forthright statement of an alternative course for the nation and, as such, represents the post-transformation counterpart of his original "I Have a Dream" speech. "We as a nation," King proclaimed in the later address, "must undergo a radical revolution of values. When machines and computers, profit and property rights are considered more important than people, the giant triplets of racism, materialism, and militarism are incapable of being conquered."

21. Martin Luther King Jr., *Where Do We Go from Here: Chaos or Community?* (New York: Harper & Row, 1967), 37.

22. The publication of both the article and the book was "mid-wifed" by C. Eric Lincoln, who, seeing the significance of the work, assisted Cone, as he did many young scholars, in finding a forum for its distribution.

23. Gayraud Wilmore, remarks at the Congress of National Black Churches Convocation, San Francisco, December 1979.

24. James Tinney, "A Theoretical and Historical Comparison of Black Political and Religious Movements" (Ph.D. diss., Howard University, 1978), 128, n. 42.

25. Charles V. Hamilton, *The Black Preacher in America* (New York: William Morrow, 1972), 133.

26. This is the formulation, particularly, of James H. Cone. See, for example, his book *A Black Theology of Liberation* (Maryknoll, N.Y.: Orbis Books, 1990). Other black theologians had somewhat different emphases. Albert Cleage, for example, developed what was termed "black Christian nationalism," while J. Deotis Roberts emphasized reconciliation.

27. Gayraud S. Wilmore, "Spirituality and Social Transformation as the Vocation of the Black Church," in *Churches in Struggle* (ed. William K. Tabb; New York: Monthly Review Press, 1986), 248.

28. Ibid., 249–50.

29. The National Conference of Black Churchmen/Christians was joined by the Black Theology Project, Partners in Ecumenism, the National Black Pastor's Conference, the Congress of National Black Churches, and an assortment of local and regional bodies from Boston and Philadelphia to Los Angeles and Oakland. For a full discussion of these groups, see Mary R. Sawyer, *Black Ecumenism: Implementing the Demands of Justice* (Valley Forge, Pa.: Trinity Press, 1994).

30. Wilmore, "Spirituality and Social Transformation," 250.

31. Ibid.

32. Ibid.

33. For an incisive critique of both black churches and black theologians, see Cornel West, *Prophesy Deliverance!: An Afro-American Revolutionary Christianity* (Philadelphia: Westminster Press, 1982), 112–21.

34. Kelly Miller Smith Institute, Inc., "What Does It Mean to Be Black and Christian?" in *Black Theology: A Documentary History, Vol. II: 1980–1992* (eds. James H. Cone and Gayraud S. Wilmore; Maryknoll, N.Y.: Orbis Books, 1993), 169–72. The two volumes of this title are an excellent resource for the history and development of black theology from 1966 to the early 1990s.

35. Lincoln and Mamiya, in *The Black Church*, provide a helpful typology characterizing this diversity. They posit six dialectical polarities, including priestly and prophetic functions, other-worldly and this-worldly, universalism and particularism, communal and privatistic, charismatic and bureaucratic, resistance and accommodation. See 10–16.

36. See John Perkins, *A Quiet Revolution* (Waco, Tex.: Word Books, 1976).

37. See Sawyer, *Black Ecumenism*, chap. 5.

38. Lovell Beaulieu, "The Angels Don't Just Touch the Few Who Believe They May Judge," *The Des Moines Register*, February 2, 2001, 13A.

39. Cheryl Townsend Gilkes, "Plenty Good Room: Adaptation in a Changing Black Church," *Annals of the AAPSS* 558 (July 1998): 102, 107.

40. Ibid., 104.

41. Ibid., 108.

42. Beverly Hall Lawrence, *Reviving the Spirit: A Generation of African Americans Goes Home to Church* (New York: Grove Press, 1996), 16, 18.

43. Ibid., 87–88.

44. Ibid., 97.

45. For a discussion of these trends, see chapter 3 in Robert M. Franklin, *Another Day's Journey: Black Churches Confronting the American Crisis* (Minneapolis: Fortress Press, 1997). Also see Lincoln and Mamiya, *The Black Church*, 385–91. For excellent case studies of the activity of urban black churches, see Nile Harper, *Urban Churches, Vital Signs: Beyond Charity Toward Justice* (Grand Rapids, Mich.: Wm. B. Eerdmans, 1999). Of the twenty-eight cases in the book, fourteen are African American churches and others are racially mixed.

46. See Billingsley, *Mighty Like a River*.

47. Kim Q. B. Leathers, "ChristAfrican Theological Institute Is 'Fresh,'" *Interlock*, n.d., 6.

48. Peter Paris draws connections between African and African American understandings of leadership, comparing black clergy to African monarchs. See Paris, *The Spirituality of African Peoples*, 59–60, 82, 97–98. Others have pointed to the severely circumscribed roles of black men during slavery and Jim Crow segregation, and the fact that black churches were for a long time the sole forum in which men were able to exercise leadership.

49. Among the influential writings are those of Katie Cannon, Kelly Brown Douglas, Cheryl Townsend Gilkes, Jacquelyn Grant, Marcia Riggs, Cheryl Sanders, Emilie Townes, Delores Williams, and Diana Hayes. See chapter 8 for an elaboration of womanist theology.

50. Anthony B. Pinn, *The Black Church in the Post–Civil Rights Era* (Maryknoll, N.Y.: Orbis Books, 2002), 30.

51. Dwight Hopkins, *Introducing Black Theology of Liberation* (Maryknoll, N.Y.: Orbis Books, 1999), 124.

52. Forrest E. Harris Sr., *Ministry for Social Crisis: Theology and Praxis in the Black Church Tradition* (Macon, Ga.: Mercer University Press, 1993), 74.

53. Ibid., 106–7.

54. George C. L. Cummings, *A Common Journey: Black Theology (USA) and Latin American Liberation Theology* (Maryknoll, N.Y.: Orbis Books, 1993), 145.

55. Ibid., 193, n. 50.

–CHAPTER 5–
Native American Indigenization

Native Americans[1] had their own unique experience of the colonization of the North American continent. Unlike Africans who were forcibly brought to this part of the world, stripped of their tribal identities, and compelled to create a new unifying identity, Native Americans retained their respective tribal identities and tribal sovereignty. They were many different nations representing many different cultures, each with its own religious and linguistic systems. These nations negotiated with the new white nation, signed treaties, accepted verbal promises, and protested when the negotiations and treaties and promises were not honored.

Of course, many died. And many today are among the living dead: homeless, unemployed, alcoholic, and hopeless. They are the product of what has been called the Native American apocalypse—the end time, the end of the world as Native peoples knew it before the white man came.[2] As Lawrence Gross (Anishinaabe) puts it, Native Americans today are suffering from Post Apocalypse Stress Syndrome (PASS).[3] But he affirms, too, that this is not the entire story. Native Americans, throughout their days of travail, have drawn on spiritual resources for survival and revitalization and they continue to do so today.

Community and Traditional Indian Values

The spirituality of Native peoples before the arrival of the colonizers centered around three elements: language, land, and community, or relationship. Although community is the focus of this discussion, the three elements are interrelated and all were diminished as a result of the encounters with European culture.

The cosmologies of Native Americans—the stories of creation, the roles of various spirits, the functions of rituals—differed in specifics from one nation to another. But all cosmologies were highly sacramental. That is, all of creation was sacred: humans, animals, plants, and the earth and sky that encompassed them. So, too, was the inner world of dreams and visions sacred. Time was cyclical and rhythmic, marked by seasons and life passages; place referred to one's location in relationship to the universe of spirits and relatives. The challenge of life was to learn the lessons that enabled living in harmony with other beings. The elders were respected as sources of wisdom and knowledge.

All of creation was interconnected. Everything was bound together by ties of kinship—that is to say, by community. "Peoplehood," the sense of being a people, was the norm, while individualism outside of the "people" meant spiritual, if not physical, death. Indeed, as Vine Deloria Jr., (Yankton Sioux) points out, "Almost all tribal names mean 'the people' or 'the first people.'"

> The foundation for the idea of being a "people" is found in the family and clan structures. The family/clan is not simply a nuclear, biological minimum as it is in non-Indian thought. Rather it includes all possible relationships by blood and law, all important lasting friendships, and all the special covenants established with plants, animals, and other forms of life through unique personal experiences. Each individual born into a tribe was also born into a clan, and a complex set of relationships between clans was organized so that social relations could be managed with a large population. Once could travel from one part of a tribe's territory to another and one would find some family belonging to one's clan. That family had a duty, strong as a blood tie, to welcome the stranger and care for him or her as their own.[4]

The reality of kinship and the relationship of the individual to community were preserved through tribal ritual ceremonies. Seasonal ceremonies were communal in nature while other ceremonies involved individuals and families. But even the individual rituals were for the ultimate well-being of the larger community. In a dialectical relationship, communal ceremonies created a sacred space in which individuals were given strength to participate in sweat lodge rituals and vision quests for the sake of the community as a whole. "Individual and group experiences were believed to be complementary halves of a sacred whole and, as experiences, were told and retold as stories and became part of the continuing oral tradition."[5]

Thus, for Native peoples, all of life was sacred, and all of life was organized around community. Still today, spirituality and community are intertwined, for survival itself depends on the mutually sustaining features of each. "Language, ceremony, songs, stories, and spiritual knowledge are precious to Native communities, and perhaps now more so than ever, as they negotiate a way to live as distinctive communities at the brink of the twenty-first century."[6] It follows that, for Native Americans who seek to preserve their identity, Christianity has meaning only insofar as it fosters community.

Native Americans' engagement with Christianity for most of the 450 years since Christian missionaries arrived has been shaped to a greater or lesser degree by these and other features of their traditional worldviews. Some aspects of Native religious traditions have been altered over the decades and centuries because of changing life circumstances and the widespread encounter with Christianity and other European cultural forms, but basic orientations have unquestionably survived. One characteristic is indicated in the fact that traditionally there was no word for religion. Even today, some Native Americans will assert, "We don't have a religion; we have a way of life." Contrary to Western perspectives, the sacred and the secular are not separate spheres. Rather, religion is integrated into the arts, economics, government, education, and all other aspects of society.[7]

When Christianity was introduced to Native Americans, they processed it through their extant worldviews and integrated systems of belief and action. As Catherine Albanese puts it, "Each Indian group that turns to Christianity does so in terms of prior beliefs and commitments that make the new religion plausible. Then, after conversion, the worshipers shape the Christianity to their own requirements."[8] Consequently, the Christianity that converts internalized commonly had a very different flavor than what was imparted to them. Certainly it was more spiritual and experiential than the Christianity of Europeans, and less preoccupied with doctrines and rules.

But Native Americans' experience with Christianity was external as well as internal. The role of Christianity overall in the experience of Native peoples—both in the travail and in the struggle for survival, both in the destruction of community and in the sustaining of community—is extremely complex and can only be intimated in this brief account. As the story unfolds, it moves from initial engagements with Christianity, to the consequential disassembling of community, to efforts to reconstitute community, and, finally, to contemporary ambivalence with regard to Christianity.

Historically, not all Indian nations accepted Christianity. If some were more receptive than others, some were also more coerced than others. Usually there was an inverse correlation. A few examples from the tribal traditions alive in the United States today, which by different counts number between five and six hundred, demonstrate the diversity of their engagements with Christianity.

Early Tribal Engagements with Christianity

The most brutal missionary activity took place in the Southwest in the 1600s at the hands of Spanish Catholics. Among the Rio Grande Pueblo,

Large chapels and mission compounds were built in the villages by forced Pueblo labor. The missionaries introduced Christianity in a manner similar to the way they built their chapels. Under punishment of whipping, they forced the native peoples to be baptized, to attend mass, and to make confession. Many were the occasions when native religious leaders were hanged as witches and when kivas were raided for the ceremonial paraphernalia and masks, which were collected and burned. The effect was to force the practice of Pueblo religion underground; to introduce a participation in Christian acts but with little internalized meaning; and to breed a deep resentment against the Spanish, including the Christian church.[9]

In 1630, Alonso De Benavides, the Spanish missionary responsible for missions in the area that became New Mexico, claimed that in just thirty years, "60,000 Pueblo Indians in ninety villages accepted the Catholic faith;" in 1834, Franciscan missionaries in California reported that 54,000 Indians had been converted over the previous sixty-five years.[10] Observes Moisés Sandoval, "These reports would give the impression that evangelization was accepted eagerly" by the Indians when "in fact, the number of willing converts was only a fraction of the statistics cited."[11]

The Hopi and Zuni tribes were also subjected to religious coercion and forced labor. But in the 1680s, after half a century of mistreatment, all three nations rose up, killing missionaries and settlers and driving the survivors out of their territory. Similar revolts took place in California and Georgia.[12]

Although a Spanish Catholic presence later returned to the Pueblo territory, from the late 1700s through the 1800s, the Pueblo people had little contact with Catholic priests. Over that century and more, Catholic rituals were modified to accommodate Native beliefs and practices. Saints' days became festive occasions, for example, and All Soul's Day a time to honor the ancestors. Holy Week and Christmas were not associated with Jesus, especially, but were special times of prayer.[13] Today, almost all Pueblo Indians are baptized in infancy in the Catholic Church and local churches may be found with representations of kachinas (Puebloan deities) alongside Catholic figures. At the same time, many neither practice Catholicism nor see a convergence of Pueblo and Christian spirituality.[14]

The Hopi initially rejected Christianity and missionaries altogether to return to their traditional practices. By the 1860s, Mormons, who told of Native descent from Hebrew tribes of Israel, were the most successful missionaries. Instead of blending the two religions, however, or discarding one, the Hopi participated in both at the same time.[15]

In the Northeast in the mid-1600s, after the elimination of most of the Nipmuc, Pennacook, and Massachusetts tribes, those few who survived were placed in planned Christian communities—or what were called "praying towns"—as a way of reinforcing religious identity. These communities were maintained for several decades, but ultimately were abandoned, whereupon the inhabitants returned to Native traditions. By 1700, there were few Indians to convert, for the Native population was a mere 5 percent of what it had been in 1500.[16]

The nations of the Southeast—Choctaw, Cherokee, Chickasaw, and the nations of the Creek (Muskogee) Confederacy—whom whites referred to as the "Five Civilized Tribes" on account of their greater willingness to embrace Euro-American culture, had a quite different experience. The Cherokee and Choctaw, especially, displayed an unusual openness to Christianity, no doubt in part because it was presented to them in a more civilized fashion. These circumstances, however, did not prevent the majority of members of these tribes from being forcibly relocated in the 1830s and 1840s to the federally defined "Indian Territory" in what later became the state of Oklahoma.[17] Recalls the Reverend Anita Phillips (Cherokee), "At the time of this event many Cherokees already embraced Jesus Christ as the son of Creator God. Native preachers had long witnessed to God's love through Christ. Preachers and missionaries walked the 'Trail of Tears' with us. Worship services and Cherokee hymns were also our companions."[18] Today, the Oklahoma Indian Missionary Conference—which includes not only Oklahoma, but Kansas and northern Texas—is a distinctively Indian component of the United Methodist Church.

The band of Cherokee who remained in North Carolina, in contrast, were missionized by fundamentalist, southern Baptists.

> Predominating themes were human sinfulness and the need to believe in salvation through Jesus Christ to escape the torments of hell. Still there was more to this Cherokee adherence to Christianity than first meets the eye. The Cherokee could relate to the Christian message of kinship and love because, in their own clans and extended families, they already felt they experienced both. Similarly, they could relate to the message of guilt and the need for atonement because, in their traditional religion, the quest for a rebalancing through purity had been an important theme. In fact, the ritual of baptism so central to the Baptist form of Christianity, echoed, for the Cherokee, their traditional cold baths in streams, the ceremony they knew as 'going to water.'"[19]

Following their forced relocation to Indian Territory, many Muskogee Creek Indians were also converted to evangelical Christianity. Today, some of their descendants constitute the congregations of twenty-seven Methodist and fifty-three Baptist churches. Enculturation is evident in these churches, as it is in many churches located on present day reservations and in urban centers. In this instance, the design of church sanctuaries reflects traditional ceremonial architecture and worshippers sit according to gender and age. In the Baptist churches, worship is conducted in the Muskogee language. The blending of Christianity and aspects of traditional religions, however, sometimes meets with strong opposition from fellow tribal members. Some Creeks adamantly reject Christianity, instead performing ancient ceremonies of their traditional religion. It is understood among Creeks that one can either participate in these rituals or go to church, but not both.[20]

The Cherokee were not the only nation who wrote their own hymns. Both the Seneca, one of the tribes of the eastern Iroquois Confederacy, and the Ojibwa, or Anishinaabe, of Minnesota are known still today for their singing of hymns in which Native terms and concepts are substituted for the original English, while biblical stories and expressions are paraphrased to reflect Native experiences.[21] Among the Ojibwa, such hymns were sung historically not only in missionary-run churches but in Anishinaabe space by groups of men and women known as "singing and praying bands." These singing groups became small Christian communities that met nightly to share food and prayer; they also shared their resources for use by all community members as needed. In addition, they functioned as singing missionaries and were often to be heard at the bedsides of community members who were ill or dying.[22]

Michael McNally suggests that in the context of reservation life in the later 1800s, the hymns assumed meanings beyond the literal meaning of the text.

> They drew on indigenous understandings of the power of song to transform, to restore right relations within a community torn by factionalism and disease, and to restore right relations between the people and the spiritual sources of life. If those Anishinaabe people who sang hymns were performing their accommodation to the Christian tradition, they were also performing their resolve to invest that religion with distinctively Anishinaabe ways of valuing land, community, and spirituality. The singing and praying bands were trying to integrate the old and the new as a spiritual foundation for the continuation of a viable Anishinaabe way of life.[23]

Today, says McNally, "The singing of those same hymns that were promoted by missionaries in order to eradicate what was distinctive about Ojibwa culture has become a profound expression of a distinctively Ojibwa value system."[24]

The experiences of the Plains Indians were notably different from those of other regions. Here, the spirituality that focused on relationship included a particularly meaningful relationship with the buffalo. When white settlers destroyed the buffalo, they came close to destroying the people. N. Scott Momaday (Kiowa) describes the loss of this relationship as creating a "great spiritual vacuum, a horrible existential hollow." According to Momaday, "Plenty Coups, a Crow chief, said, 'When the buffalo went away the hearts of my people fell to the ground, and they could not lift them up again. After this nothing happened. There was little singing anymore.' Sitting Bull, a great Lakota war chief and holy man, said, 'A cold wind blew across the prairie when the last buffalo fell—a death wind for my people.'"[25]

The tribes of the Sioux linguistic group, however, never completely lost their culture and tradition. According to William Powers, what developed among the Oglala Sioux, or Lakota, was a continuum of religious expression, with Christianity on the one end and traditional spirituality on the other, "with the majority of the people living in the mid range moving back and forth along the continuum situationally."[26]

Paul Steinmetz, S.J., suggests a multi-part model of Lakota religious identity comprised of three traditions symbolized by "Pipe, Bible, and Peyote." The pipe is the Sacred Pipe of traditional Lakota religion; peyote represents the Native American Church (of which more will be said shortly); and the Bible represents various denominational presences, including the Episcopal and Catholic churches, as well as the Body of Christ Independent Church, "a Pentecostal-type fundamentalist church whose members regard it as a Lakota church, in contrast to a white man's." Today, some tribal members practice their traditional religion and Christian religion completely separately, but perceive common religious forms in the two traditions, while others view Christianity as a fulfillment of the Lakota religion.[27]

Where the famous Lakota medicine man, Black Elk, fits in this scheme is a matter of ongoing controversy. Black Elk was initially introduced to Christianity by Episcopal missionaries between 1882 and 1887. In 1904, he was confirmed in the Catholic Church, given the name Nicholas, and thereafter known as Nick Black Elk. From 1907 to 1930, Nick Black Elk, according to Powers and others, was a devout lay minister who held prayer services in the absence of priests, worked as a missionary on reservations other than his own, and served as a godfather for the baptism of more than one hundred individuals.[28]

However, the book, *Black Elk Speaks*, by John G. Neihardt, whom Black Elk first met in 1930, tells only of his traditional Lakota experience, a circumstance that obscures Black Elk's perception of correspondence between the seven sacraments of the Catholic Church and the seven sacred ceremonials of traditional Lakota religion.[29] For much of his adult life, "Black Elk conducted a dialogue between his Roman Catholicism and his Lakota tradition, filtered through a life of continuous service to his community as a spiritual leader."[30]

In many respects, Black Elk's story mirrors the lives of countless individuals in the nineteenth century as they struggled to maintain a coherent meaning system—and to maintain community—in the face of governmental and church policies designed to conform Native people to European standards and customs.

Disassembling Community

An early and invidious policy involved the confinement of tribal members to restricted land areas known as reservations. This practice actually began on Long Island in 1666, but was most prevalent in the 1800s. During this century, motivated in part by the evangelism of the Second Great Awakening, the government also supported efforts to Christianize Native Americans. Beginning in 1802, Congress appropriated $15,000 annually to "promote civilization among the savages." After 1818, these funds were divided among Christian denominations that were similarly committed to "civilizing" Indians. These annual appropriations continued until 1973.[31]

With the westward movement of white settlers, intensified by the gold rush of 1848 and the completion of the transcontinental railroad in 1869, missionary activity increased dramatically. In 1869, reputedly to soften the harsh manner in which Indian affairs were being handled, President Ulysses S. Grant replaced military overseers of government-supported Indian agencies with Christian missionaries. These agencies, consisting of government houses, schools, blacksmith shops, warehouses, and Christian missions, were an intimidating factor in Native life by their sheer presence. Initially, reservations were divided up among twelve Christian denominations for purposes of oversight. After 1881, the assignments were no longer so methodical, but the church presence continued.[32]

Cultural imperialism inevitably accompanied mission work, even in instances where missionaries were well intentioned. George Tinker (Osage/Cherokee) points out that while many white missionaries made extraordinary sacrifices to carry out their work, they also operated out of the mindset and values of Euro-American society.[33] Embedded in these views were ethnocentrism and racism; central to their values were agricultural use of land, individualism, and private ownership of property. Thus, white Christian values were the polar opposite of Native values.

In Native traditions, community was understood to include not only the living, but those yet to be born, and those who had died. In part what this meant was that burial grounds were inviolable. Furthermore, not only humans, but animals and the environment required to sustain and protect them, were part of community. Land was not to be bartered or sold; it was not "owned," but was held in common by the people.[34] And the land was integrally tied to the spiritual world. Writes Deloria, "Since time immemorial, Indian tribal Holy Men have gone into the high places, lakes, and isolated sanctuaries to pray, receive guidance from the Spirits, and train younger people in the ceremonies that constitute the spiritual life of the tribal community. In these ceremonies, medicine men represented the whole web of cosmic life in the continuing search for balance and harmony, and through various rituals in which birds, animals, and plants were participants, harmony of life was achieved and maintained."[35]

Having neither understanding nor appreciation of these perspectives, church and government bodies joined forces in an effort to remake Native people in their image: culturally white and religiously Christian. This agenda inherently meant the destruction of community as Native Americans understood it and lived it.

In the mid-1850s, the government began allotting land to individual Indians, a practice that reached its zenith with the General Allotment Act of 1887, also known as the Dawes Act. This act represented "the most comprehensive attempt to break up tribal allegiances, communal ownership, and traditional associations. Parcels of 160 acres were given to heads of households; 80 acres to each unmarried male over eighteen. Any 'surplus' was sold to white settlers. By the time the allotment was ended in 1934, almost 90 million acres of Indian lands, amounting to over 60 percent of land held before 1887, had been transferred to the ownership of non-Natives."[36]

Even before this act was passed, in 1871 the United States ceased regarding Indian nations as sovereign entities, instead making Native people wards of the U.S. government. To further reinforce the ideology of individualism, U.S. citizenship was attached to land allocation. Indians who occupied their allotment for twenty-five years were made citizens. Then, under the Indian Citizenship Act of 1924, all those who had not yet become citizens were declared to be, whether they desired this status or not. The act provided that Indians would retain their tribal memberships, along with U.S. citizenship, but a number of nations opted not to accept citizenship in order to assure that their tribal memberships would remain primary.[37]

Beginning in 1885, largely on account of pressure from churches with reservation missions, the federal government prohibited the performance of important tribal ceremonies, including the Sun Dance of the Plains Indians and the practices of medicine men, who were also spiritual leaders. These restrictions continued through the 1920s.[38]

In yet another devastating blow to Native communities, by the end of the 1800s, all tribal schools had been closed and replaced by Bureau of Indian Affairs schools. These schools, in turn, were placed under the oversight of churches. "By 1887 there were 227 BIA and mission schools, with about 14,000 Indian children attending. Between 1880 and 1930 an estimated 50,000 Indian youths were taken, with force if necessary, to off-reservation schools." This was, as William Young observes, "simply the culmination of a long process which had begun in 1611 when native youngsters were forced to attend Jesuit boarding schools."[39]

The express intent of these schools was to strip Native children of all vestiges of their tribal cultures. They were dressed in military-like uniforms, forbidden to speak their own languages, required to cut their braids, and often permitted neither to go home nor to have visitors at their schools. Indeed, the children were often restrained in the summer and compelled to perform labor without pay. Severe corporal punishment was common, as was sexual abuse.[40] The one positive consequence of the boarding school experience was that Indians from different tribes became acquainted with one another and in the process became aware of common problems. As a result, Native identity began to transcend tribal boundaries.

Pan-Indian Identity: Reconstituting Community

Missionary activity by both Catholic and Protestant churches continued into the twentieth century. By 1921 a total of twenty-six Protestant churches were working among Native American tribes, unencumbered by competition with the forbidden Native rituals. In some instances, this involvement resulted in the creation of Native Christian churches with Native American leadership. According to Young, at this time there were "597 Indian churches and 268 Native American ministers serving congregations with a total membership of about 110,000. Approximately 336 Catholic churches, chapels, and schools served more than 61,000 communicants. Roughly half the Native Americans in North America were at least nominal Christians."[41]

Not until the appointment of a more sympathetic and knowledgeable Commissioner of Indian Affairs in 1934 were some of the more deleterious government policies modified. John Collier recognized that "the commitment to community in Native American cultures had served them well for centuries," and that conversely, "the individualism the government and churches had been trying to implant in native peoples in order to strengthen them had not produced the expected results."[42] In addition, he was committed to the principle of religious freedom. In 1934, the Indian Reorganization Act removed the restrictions on traditional ceremonies and at the same time prohibited forced attendance at Christian services in boarding schools.[43] The fact is, however, that a policy of assimilation remained intact, and the paternalism of white missionaries, with significant exceptions, continued into the 1960s.

Long before the Indian Reorganization Act was passed Native Americans had been asserting the necessity of preserving and practicing Native traditions in order to reconstitute and sustain community in the face of the apocalypse induced by white missionaries, agents, and settlers. Of special note are the prophetic, pan-Indian movements of the 1800s, including the Ghost Dance and the Peyote movement.

Among the prophetic, or messianic, movements that emerged in response to the devastation wrought by colonialism were those led by Handsome Lake (Seneca), Tenskwatawa (Shawnee and the brother of Tecumseh), Smohalla (Wanapum), and Wovoka (Paiute). Offering their own interpretations of Christian concepts of God, Jesus, sin, heaven, and hell, these messianic figures exhorted a return to Native ways and foretold the restoration of strong, vibrant Indian nations.

Wovoka is credited with starting the Ghost Dance (in Lakota, *wanagi wacipi*, the "spirit dance") of 1890, which became the largest pan-Indian movement to date, spreading from its origins in Nevada to California, Arizona, the Indian Territory of Oklahoma, Colorado, and the Dakotas, where it was especially strong among the Lakota. Coming to the Lakota at a time of death—the loss of the buffalo—the Ghost Dance "fueled hope of reunion with ancestors and promised to reverse a dreadful history."[44] Adapting the movement to their own circumstances, the Lakota "danced to bring back a lost land full of buffalo and devoid of white people." Alarmed by its popularity among the Lakota, military troops were mobilized to crush the movement, which led to the infamous massacre of Wounded Knee.[45]

While the Ghost Dance reemerges from time to time, the pan-Indian movement that has achieved continuity is the movement that started with an ancient native tradition of using peyote, a type of cactus that contains the mood-altering agent mescaline. In the 1880s, versions of the peyote religion were infused with Christian symbols and the use of peyote came to be regarded as a sacrament. As the movement spread through different Indian nations, it met with increasing opposition from both governmental and church agents. In an effort to legitimize the religion, beginning in 1918, Indians in various states founded Native American Churches. In 1944, the Native American Church of the United States (now the Native American Church of North America) was incorporated with its stated purpose being the promotion of "the Christian religion with the practice of the Peyote Sacrament."[46] Legal and social opposition to the church continued, however, throughout the twentieth century.

Two different versions of peyotism are practiced in the Native American Church, the Cross Fire way and the Half Moon way, with the former containing Christian elements to a greater degree than the latter. Because both versions preeminently involve traditional practices, scholars disagree as to whether members of the church are properly regarded as Christian or not. The Native American Church of Jesus Christ, in contrast, rejects traditional ways to embrace Christianity fully. At any rate, as Young, "Peyotism is an authentically pan-national Native American spiritual tradition."[47] In the 1990s, the Native American Church of North America was the largest Native American religious organization, with eighty chapters and a total member-ship of 250,000 from seventy different nations.[48] Peyotism as a whole is one of the most important influences in building community, focusing as it does on community groups, family, sobriety, education, and gainful employment.

The most recent pan-tribal movement unfolded in the 1960s and 1970s, inspired once again by misguided governmental policy. Following World War II, the federal government implemented a program of "reloca-tion" in which Indians were encouraged to leave the reservations and take up residence in urban areas. For many of those who did so, the move was disastrous. As promises of government support for the transition failed to materialize, individuals found themselves struggling to survive both poverty and the discrimination to which they were subjected. The loss of community and tribal support systems proved devastating and ultimately led many to return to the reservation.[49]

Some among those who remained in the city created cultural centers where members of different tribes congregated for support and celebration. Outside the cities, Indian events such as powwows and sun dances brought Native people together across tribal boundaries. Both circumstances helped foster what came to be referred to as "American Indian spirituality."[50] This countercultural movement, as Amanda Porterfield describes it, contrasts with earlier pan-Indian revitalization movements in that the latter "worked to preserve Indian cultures against destruction and assimilation," while "proponents of American Indian spirituality work for the transformation of American culture in terms of Indian values."[51]

Porterfield goes so far as to suggest that, "In certain hidden but never-theless important ways, American Indian spirituality is like a Christian reform movement within American society."

> As we have seen, the prophet religions that preceded American Indian spirituality appealed to Christian imagery and ethics as a means of criticizing Western culture and celebrating Indian culture. Spokespersons for American Indian spirituality build on this strat-egy in their representation of American Indian life to audiences that include persons of non-Indian descent. They call all Americans to a truer and purer understanding of God, to an ethic of peace and jus-tice, and to an aesthetic of natural simplicity. In attributing these characteristics to Indians, proponents of Indian spirituality make Indians exemplars of the Christian values cherished by many mem-bers of American society.[52]

Not everyone has seen the participation of whites in the Native American spirituality movement in quite the same light. As young, white spiritual seekers began embracing it, some Native spokespersons saw white involvement as only another form of cultural imperialism. At the least, they regard it as a corruption of Native tradition, because for many whites the "seeking" is an individual project and therefore anti-communal.[53]

During the "Red Power" movement of the 1960s, one of several change-oriented organizations to emerge was AIM—the American Indian Movement. AIM's purpose was to mobilize Native Americans to address historical grievances, including the reclamation of lost land. The movement strongly supported both the pan-tribal spirituality movement and the renewal of individual tribal traditions and languages, while opposing Christianity as a colonial religion. Among the more prominent voices of the times was that of Vine Deloria Jr. (Yankton Sioux), the son and grandson of Episcopal priests, graduate of the Lutheran School of Theology, lawyer, and prolific scholar of both religious and legal matters. Deloria, himself, rejected Christianity. His writings, especially his book, *God Is Red*, presented both an incisive critique of Christian imperialism and a contrasting theology of Native American religion.[54] They also brought into focus "the existential dilemma facing contemporary native Christians."[55] That dilemma has to do not only with how to relate to established Christian institutions, but whether one should relate at all.

Institutional Involvements

No population in the Western Hemisphere knows the bitter legacy of Christianity better than do Native peoples. For some, the memories of what was done in the name of Christianity are so repugnant and so hurtful as to be insurmountable; the religion cannot be redeemed. Among this population are those whose traditional religion fully meets their needs for spiritual and communal relationships and guidance. At the same time, it is not uncommon for Native Americans to participate earnestly in both religious systems—Christianity on Sunday and traditional spirituality during the week.[56] In yet other configurations, Christian symbols have long been incorporated into Native practices and, increasingly, Native symbols are included in Christian worship services. Some Indians practice a fundamentalist and exclusivist form of Christianity imparted by missionaries old and new. Others—sometimes consciously, sometimes unconsciously—live an indigenized Christianity in which the religion is interpreted through the lens of traditional tribal knowledge.

What the relative proportions of these different groupings might be is unknown. Of the nearly 2.5 million American Indians and Alaska Natives counted by the U.S. Census in 2000,[57] the Catholic Church claims 640,000 as members. The United Methodist Church reports 14,300 Native members; the Evangelical Lutheran Church of America, 7,400 members; and the Presbyterian Church (U.S.A.), approximately 7,200 members. The Assemblies of God estimates 9,000 to 10,000 regular church attendees, while the Southern Baptist Convention reports a mere 4,000 out of its nearly 16 million members. (See appendix I.) Extrapolating from these figures, perhaps a quarter to a third of Native Americans and Alaskan Natives are enrolled on denominational registers.

The Catholic Church works with Native Americans through the several Native American Ministry centers around the country and through programs in diocesan offices. Interactions take place day-by-day wherever there is a Catholic presence on reservations or in urban Indian parishes. Today, many of these contacts are mutually enriching; far fewer than in the past are patronizing or abusive.

At the beginning of the twenty-first century, however, in the entire Catholic Church there were only two Native American bishops, fifteen priests (at least one of whom calls himself a Native priest, rather than a Roman priest), fifty Catholic sisters, and some one hundred permanent deacons.[58] While some of the Native leadership is more Catholic-traditional than Native-traditional, at least one priest, who was initially dismissed from seminary for refusing to cut his hair, has been criticized by church officials for "espousing a Creation theology rather than one of Fall and Redemption."[59]

Not all Native Americans who are Protestant are mainstream by any means. Indeed, George Tinker points to the "conservative or even fundamentalist posture of many Indian-led congregations in nearly all Protestant denominations."[60] Tinker attributes this circumstance to the fact that "American Indian people have so internalized the missionary critique of Indian culture and religious traditions and so internalized our own concession to the superiority of Euroamerican social structures." Today, he says, "an Indian pastor is more likely than a white missionary to criticize the paganism of traditional spirituality."[61]

In short, not all Native Christians are communal or inclusive or sacramental in their religious orientation. The fundamentalist understanding of Christianity of which Tinker speaks has been extended since the 1970s with the growth of conservative evangelicalism generally. A multitude of organizations have come into being in recent decades, some led by whites and some by Native Americans, with the common agenda of evangelizing Native populations. Among these are Ethnic Harvest, which provides internet resources for evangelical churches engaged in cross-cultural ministry;

CHIEF (Christian Hope Indian Eskimo Fellowship), which reports having provided support for evangelism for three hundred tribes since 1975; and Network of Native Ministries, which includes a host of denominational and nondenominational groups such as AmeriTribes, Flagstaff Mission to the Navajo, Flame of Fire Ministries, Native Men for Christ, Center for Indian Ministries, and Indian Bible College.[62]

Not knowing how many Native Americans belong to independent congregations or how many consider themselves Christian but are not recognized by established denominations, there is no way of knowing how many Native Americans might be counted Christian.[63] As Tinker puts it, "The vast majority of our people today have or had some relationship with a Christian church—or two or four. Most have been baptized, at least once. Even those brothers and sisters who have rejected the church's teaching are indelibly marked by the missionary message, even in their disavowal. Yet many of us *are* Christian and have found life in the Gospel of Jesus Christ."[64] Within this body of believers, however, many are struggling with the question of whether Native and Christian identities are in fact compatible.[65]

Both Native and Christian?

Those who assert that it is possible to be both Native and Christian also assert that in order to be both, the gospel must be "decolonized." Thus, Marie Therese Archambault (Hunkpapa Lakota), a Franciscan sister, writes:

> When we read the Gospel, we must read it as *Native* people, for this is who we are. We have to go beyond the *white gospel* in order to perceive its truth.... When we do this, we shall meet Jesus as our brother and recognize him as one who has been with us all along as the quiet servant, the one who has strengthened us through these centuries. Then we will know that the cry of Jesus Christ from the cross was the cry of our people at Wounded Knee, Sand Creek and other places of the mass death of our people. He was our companion during these years of our invisibility in this society.... This is the heart and core meaning of the Gospel.[66]

Since the 1970s, Native theologians have been engaged in an ongoing project of de-colonization, or indigenization, to develop theologies that accommodate both heritage and conversion. These efforts are sometimes termed Native Christian theology and other times Native American theology.[67] The phrase "liberation theology" is generally not used. Much like black liberation theology, however, Native Christian theology emerged out of Native American activism and the Native American caucuses of mainline denominations, and its proponents have participated in dialogues with the theologies of liberation of other oppressed populations.[68]

One theologian, Jace Weaver (Cherokee), identifies what he regards as three essential components of Native theology: first, the combining of Christianity and indigenous religious traditions (as opposed to the dualistic practice of each separately); second, recognition of the importance of land for Native peoples and of their views regarding ownership; and third, assertion of the centrality of community. "A post-colonial hermeneutic for Natives," he says, "rejects the individualistic interpretations brought by assimilationist missions in favor of more communal and communitarian methods and understandings."[69]

Formal Native theologizing often occurs as a group process that includes both lay Christians and non-Christian representatives of Native traditions. As James Treat (Muskogee) puts it, "If native Christian 'theology' were to develop as nothing more than the elite intellectual culture of native Christian leaders, then it would promise only to reinforce colonial configurations by replicating the intellectual elitism that has characterized Western religious discourse since the Emperor Constantine I convened the Council of Nicaea in the year 325 C.E."[70] Volumes edited both by Treat (*Native and Christian*) and by Weaver (*Native American Religious Identity*) contain essays by Native writers from various avenues that explore the issue of being Native and Christian.

Aside from the more formal endeavors, indigenization, as has been noted throughout this chapter, takes place as well in the informal context of ordinary living. The result is what Weaver refers to as "the folk theology upon which Christianity at the ground level has always thrived as a living faith." As he puts it, "Native Christians give authority to scripture specifically because it resonates with their experience. They report relating to Moses trudging up Sinai to meet the divine as one about to embark on a vision quest. They recognize Mary, the mother of Jesus, because she is *la Virgen de Guadalupe*, or White Buffalo Calf Woman, or Corn Mother, or *La llorona* refusing to be consoled at the death of her child. They can chuckle knowingly at the exploits of Jacob because he is the trickster familiar to them as Coyote, or Raven, or Iktomi."[71]

And indigenization occurs in Catholic parishes and Protestant congregations in situations where Native Americans have leadership roles in designing worship services and outreach programs. Writes Tinker, "The old ways of tribal spirituality are beginning to be as much at home in Indian churches as they are in traditional ceremonies. The values that define Indian existence, Indian community, traditional spirituality and culture are being articulated in Indian preaching and Indian theology in our churches. Traditional forms of prayer … are making their way into the heart of our

Christian liturgies: the drum, the eagle feather, four direction symbolism, and rites of smudging."[72]

When the initiative for such changes as these comes from the denominational hierarchy, however, the term commonly used is "enculturation." Especially since the Second Vatican Council, the Catholic Church has been considerably more receptive to and respectful of Native spirituality. Thus, the 1996 annual Tekakwitha Conference of Native American Catholics found Archbishop Michael J. Sheehan declaring, "It is the same creator God who has breathed into all our ancestors, mine and yours, a love for the Great Spirit. The church affirms your culture, your language and your religious traditions. For the most part, these are all compatible with Christian teaching, which simply builds upon them. The Catholic church is not a white man's religion, it is a religion for everyone."[73]

It is not so clear from statements such as this who has converted whom. What is apparent from this overview of Native engagements with Christianity is that ultimately the time and place and means of the religion being presented to Native Americans is far less important than what Native people do with it. Where Christianity has been brought into traditional Indian frames of reference, Christianity has been brought to life. The shell of Christianity presented by European and Euro-American missionaries is filled with heart, power, and meaning. Christianity itself is resurrected. Perhaps the greatest gift of Native peoples to the Western world will be their demonstration of what it is to survive and transcend apocalypse. If freedom to worship in the sacred lands of old is yet denied, there is at least renewed hope for a vibrant and meaningful future.

For Further Reading

Deloria, Vine, Jr. *For This Land: Writings on Religion in America, with an Introduction by James Treat*. New York: Routledge, 1999.

Kidwell, Clara Sue, Homer Noley, and George E. Tinker. *A Native American Theology*. Maryknoll, N.Y.: Orbis Books, 2001.

Stewart, Omer C. *Peyote Religion: A History*. Norman: University of Oklahoma Press, 1987.

Tinker, George E. *Missionary Conquest: The Gospel and Native American Cultural Genocide*. Minneapolis: Fortress Press, 1993.

Treat, James, ed. *Native and Christian: Indigenous Voices on Religious Identity in the United States and Canada*. New York: Routledge, 1996.

Vecsey, Christopher. *Where the Two Roads Meet*. Vol. 3 of *American Indian Catholics*. Notre Dame, Ind.: University of Notre Dame Press, 1999.

———, ed. *Religion in Native North America*. Moscow: University of Idaho Press, 1990.

Weaver, Jace, ed. *Native American Religious Identity: Unforgotten Gods*. Maryknoll, N.Y.: Orbis Books, 1998.

NOTES

1 The terms Native American, American Indian, Indian, Native, and Native people are all in current usage. In this chapter, I use the terms interchangeably or follow the usage of respective authors cited. Similarly, the terms tribe and nation are used interchangeably to denote particular culture groups, in contrast to the terms pan-Indian or pan-tribal, which point to views, values, or practices that transcend tribal boundaries.

2 See, for example, Sidner Larson, *Captured in the Middle* (Seattle: University of Washington Press, 2000), 18.

3 Lawrence W. Gross, "The Comic Vision of Anishinaabe Culture and Religion," unpublished manuscript, 2002, 2. I am indebted to Dr. Gross for his assistance with this chapter.

4 Vine Deloria Jr., *For This Land: Writings on Religion in America* (ed. James Treat; New York: Routledge, 1999), 177–79.

5 Ibid., 183.

6 Michael D. McNally, "Religion and Culture Change in Native North America," in *Perspectives on American Religion and Culture*, (ed. Peter W. Williams; Malden, Mass.: Blackwell Publishers, 1999), 275.

7 McNally, "Religion and Culture Change," 272.

8 Catherine L. Albanese, *America: Religion and Religions* (3d ed.; Belmont, Calif.: Wadsworth Publishing Co., 1999), 44.

9 Sam Gill, *Native American Religions: An Introduction* (Belmont, Calif.: Wadsworth Publishing Company, 1982), 145.

10 Moises Sandoval, *On the Move: A History of the Hispanic Church in the United States* (Maryknoll, N. Y.: Orbis Books, 1990), 14–15.

11 Ibid.

12 Ibid., 15.

13 Albanese, *America*, 41.

14 Joel Martin, *Native American Religion* (New York: Oxford University Press, 1999), 81–83. See Martin's description of the paintings by Alex Seowtewa in Our Lady of Guadalupe Church.

15 Albanese, *America*, 40–41.

16 William Young, *Quest for Harmony: Native American Spiritual Traditions* (New York: Seven Bridges Press, 2002), 28–30.

17 The Relocation Act of 1830 required the removal of Native Americans in the East to the territory west of the Mississippi in order to make land available to white settlers.

18 Anita Phillips, "The Trail of Tears," in *Reflections on Singing a New Song*, the advance program of the 16th Assembly of United Methodist Women, held April 25–28, 2002 in Philadelphia, Pennsylvania, 16. The Reverend Phillips is a district superintendent in this conference.

19 Albanese, *America*, 44.

20 Martin, *Native American Religion*, 81–84.

21 Thomas McElwain, "'The Rainbow Will Carry Me': The Language of Seneca Iroquois Christianity as Reflected in Hymns," in *Religion in Native North America* (ed. Christopher Vecsey; Moscow: University of Idaho Press, 1990), 85, 91.

22 McNally, "Religion and Culture Change," 281.

23 Ibid., 282.

24 Ibid.

25 Cited in Martin, *Native American Religion*, 98.

26 William K. Powers, *Oglala Religion* (Lincoln: University of Nebraska Press, 1977), 205–6.

27 Paul B. Steinmetz, S.J., *Pipe, Bible, and Peyote Among the Oglala Lakota: A Study in Religious Identity* (Knoxville: University of Tennessee Press, 1990), ix, 4, 6.

28 William K. Powers, "When Black Elk Speaks, Everybody Listens," in *Religion in Native North America* (ed. Christopher Vecsey; Moscow: University of Idaho Press, 1990), 139–43, passim. Powers and Steinmetz disagree on the proper interpretation of Black Elk's religious identity, as do numerous scholars. Scholars also disagree as to the authenticity of Neihardt's representation of Black Elk's words. In addition to Power's essay, see Steinmetz, *Pipe, Bible, and Peyote*, 183–92.

29 Martin, *Native American Religion*, 104.

30 McNally, "Religion and Culture Change," 275.

31 Young, *Quest for Harmony*, 36.

32 Ibid., 40.

33 George E. Tinker, *Missionary Conquest: The Gospel and Native American Cultural Genocide* (Minneapolis, Minn.: Fortress Press, 1993), 8–11, 15–18. Tinker is more generous than some in allowing that missionaries were only operating out of their own worldviews. Others make the case that the missionaries might have preached the gospel without becoming involved in political and economic aspects of colonization. The latter position is expressed, for example, in Homer Noley, *First White Frost: Native Americans and United Methodism* (Nashville: Abingdon Press, 1991). For discussion of Tinker and Noley's views, see Jace Weaver, *Native American Religious Identity: Unforgotten Gods* (Maryknoll, N.Y.: Orbis Books, 1998), 3–5.

34 Weaver, *Native American Religious Identity*, 21.

35 Deloria, *For This Land*, 203.

36 David Chidester, *Patterns of Power: Religion and Politics in American Culture* (Englewood Cliffs, N.J.: Prentice Hall, 1988), 121.

37 Young, *Quest for Harmony*, 47.

38 Ibid., 44–45, 48.

39 Ibid., 43.

40 For autobiographical accounts of the boarding school experience, see Lanniko L. Lee, Florestine Kiyukanpi Renville, Karen Lone Hill, and Lydia Whirlwind Soldier, *Shaping Survival: Essays by Four American Indian Tribal Women* (eds. Jack W. Marken and Charles L. Woodard; Lanham, Md.: Scarecrow Press, 2001).

41 Young, *Quest for Harmony*, 47–48.

42 Ibid., 48–49.

43 Ibid.

44 Martin, *Native American Religion*, 99.

45 Ibid.

46 Ibid., 115.

47 Young, *Quest for Harmony*, 328.

48 Ibid., 324. The foregoing discussion draws on chapter 7.

49 Ibid., 51.

50 Ibid.

51 Amanda Porterfield, "American Indian Spirituality as a Countercultural Movement," in *Religion in Native North America* (ed. Christopher Vecsey; Moscow: University of Idaho Press, 1990), 155.

52 Ibid., 162.

53 Tinker, *Missionary Conquest*, 121–22.

54 See the introduction by James Treat and various essays in Deloria, *For This Land*.

55 James Treat, *Native and Christian?: Indigenous Voices on Religious Identity in the United States and Canada* (New York: Routledge, 1996), 17.

56 See chapter 5 in William K. Powers, *Beyond the Vision: Essays on American Indian Culture* (Norman: University of Oklahoma Press, 1987).

57 According to Young, in 1890 only 228,000 Native Americans remained in the United States. In 1950, the population had increased only to 343,000. "It then began a rapid rise, which has continued every census period since. The population increased to 523,000 by 1960, to 793,000 by 1970, to 1.6 million by 1980, to more than 2 million by 1990. The increase is due in part to a birthrate twice as high as that of the general population, but also to the heightened willingness of Indian people to identify themselves as Native Americans on census forms. Young, *Quest for Harmony*, 51.

58 The best source for information on Native Americans and the Catholic Church is Christopher Vescey, *American Indian Catholics* (3 vols.; Notre Dame, Ind.: University of Notre Dame Press, 1999). In the third volume, *Where the Two Roads Meet*, from which these statistics are taken, Vescey indicates the number of Native Catholics is 350,000—a little more than half of what is officially reported by the Church itself. See p. 229.

59 Vescey, *Where the Two Roads Meet*, 226. The priest at issue is Father Ed Savilla (Pueblo).

60 Tinker, *Missionary Conquest*, 118.

61 Ibid.

62 See <www.ethnicharvest.org and www.Chief.Org/network.html>.

63 Weaver suggests that "only between 10 and 25 percent of Natives consider themselves Christian, depending on what set of statistics one chooses to believe." Weaver, *Native American Religious Identity*, 6.

64 George E. Tinker, "Native Americans and the Land: 'The End of Living, and the Beginning of Survival,'" in *Lift Every Voice: Constructing Christian Theologies from the Underside* (eds. Susan Brooks Thistlethwaite and Mary Potter Engles; San Francisco: Harper & Row, 1990), 141.

65 See James Treat's discussion in the introduction to his edited volume, *Native and Christian*.

66 Marie Therese Archambault, "Native Americans and Evangelization," in *Native and Christian: Indigenous Voices on Religious Identity in the United States and Canada* (ed. James Treat; New York: Routledge, 1996), 135.

67 An example of the latter is the book by Clare Sue Kidwell, Homer Noley, and George E. Tinker entitled *A Native American Theology* (Maryknoll, N.Y: Orbis Books, 2001). For an overview of the history of Native theological endeavors, see the introduction in Treat, *Native and Christian*.

68 Treat, *Native and Christian*, 16–17.

69 Jace Weaver, "From I-Hermeneutics to We-Hermeneutics," in Weaver, *Native American Religious Identity*, 19–21.

70 Treat, *Native and Christian*, 12.

71 Ibid., 19.

72 Tinker, "Native Americans and the Land," 142–43.

73 *National Catholic Reporter*, August 1996, day and page unknown.

—CHAPTER 6—
Latina/Latino Ecclesiology

More so than for any other population, the ecclesiology of Latinas and Latinos—the form or structure that "church" takes—is small-scale community. The primacy of community, in turn, reflects the religiosity that permeates Latina/o culture, a religiosity that, in spite of the best efforts of the Constantinian church, has endured as an expression of the spirit-community tradition of Christianity. For the past forty years, the challenge for Latina/o Christians has been to create room for their religiosity and their ecclesiology within the Catholic Church of the United States—and, increasingly, within Protestant churches as well.[1]

In 1950, the total number of Hispanics in the United States was estimated to be only 4 million. In 1960, the estimate was 6.9 million and in 1970, 10.5 million. In 1980, for the first time, the Census Bureau conducted an actual count, arriving at 14.6 million. Between 1980 and 1990, owing both to high immigration and high birth rates, the figure increased to 22.4 million[2] and then reached 35 million in the year 2000. In 2002, Latinas/os actually surpassed African Americans as the largest minority group in the United States, a circumstance that has major implications for the country in general, and America's churches in particular.

"Latina/Latino" and "Hispanic" are terms used variously to designate the people of the United States who are descended from the colonial mix of Spanish settlers and Native peoples and/or African slaves, who share a common cultural tradition, and for whom Spanish is the first language of the home.[3] Traditionally, these terms have denoted an ethnic population rather than a racial category. That is, individual Latinas/os may self-identify as Indian or black or white (of Spanish descent) while claiming the more encompassing ethnic identity as well.[4]

The national origins of Hispanics are diverse: they include the United States, Mexico, Cuba, Puerto Rico, other countries of the Caribbean, and countries of Central and South America. Mexican Americans, or Chicanas/os, as some prefer, constitute by far the largest component of

Latinas/os, representing nearly 60 percent of the total population. Puerto Ricans account for nearly 10 percent, while Cuban Americans are third at 3.5 percent. The next three largest groups are Dominican Americans, Salvadorans, and Guatemalans. (See Table 4.) Latinas/os are diverse as well in the political circumstances of their becoming part of the United States.

Table 4. Distribution of Hispanics/Latinos by Origin, 2000

Mexican	58.5 %
Puerto Rican	9.6
Cuban	3.5
Central American	4.8
South American	3.8
Spaniard	.3
Other or non-specified	17.3

Source: U.S. Census Bureau, 2000.

Latina/o Diversity

Mexicans residing in the area that now encompasses Texas, New Mexico, Arizona, California, Utah, and Colorado became official citizens of the United States with the annexation of northern Mexico in 1848. The century and a half since has brought successive waves of immigration. As of 1990, two-thirds of all Mexican Americans had been born in the United States. In the last half-century, they have dispersed throughout the country, although the highest concentration remains in the Southwest and California. Today, more than a few fourth and fifth generation Mexican Americans in these states assert an issue of sovereignty that other Latinas/os do not, for many consider that they are living in occupied territory—that the land is theirs, while Anglo residents are illegal occupants.[5]

Both Cuba and Puerto Rico remained Spanish colonies until 1898 when, following the Spanish-American War, Cuba became an independent country. Puerto Rico, however, became a possession of the United States; residents were made U.S. citizens and granted the right to home rule. The most significant movement of Puerto Ricans to the U.S. mainland occurred in the twenty-year period following the Second World War in what is termed the Great Migration. In New York City, where most of them settled, they developed their own ethnic communities, keeping their Spanish identity and resisting assimilation into U.S. culture.[6] In recent decades, the Puerto Rican population, too, has become more dispersed, primarily throughout New England and into the Midwest.

Massive immigration of Cubans began in the early 1960s in the wake of the Cuban Revolution of 1959. In contrast to Puerto Rican and Mexican

American immigrants, most Cubans were well-educated, middle- to upper-class individuals. These immigrants quickly established their own institutions, creating a largely self-sustaining community in Miami. While Puerto Ricans and Mexican Americans were often the victims of discrimination, the initial waves of Cubans were welcomed as refugees fleeing from communism. Furthermore, because, as Jaime Vidal puts it, "class and color are connected in the Caribbean," they were received in this country as whites, rather than as "people of color."[7] A second wave of Cuban immigrants in the early 1980s, who were largely working class, experienced significantly more discrimination than did their predecessors.[8]

Their differences notwithstanding, Cubans hold in common with Puerto Ricans the expectation of one day returning home. Accordingly, they have resisted assimilation, working instead to keep their cultural identity and practices intact.

Immigrants from the Dominican Republic came to the United States in significant numbers after 1965, settling for the most part in New York City. They share with Puerto Ricans the practice, and opportunity, of frequent travel back and forth between their two countries in what is termed "revolving door immigration."[9] Most immigrants from El Salvador and Nicaragua have no such option, having fled their countries as refugees from the civil strife that tore their nations apart in the 1970s and 1980s. Salvadorans reside in Los Angeles and San Francisco for the most part, as do the majority of Guatemalans, while Nicaraguans have gravitated to Miami. These groups all have high rates of poverty and are disproportionately represented in the lowest rungs of the service economy. Like some Mexican immigrants, many Central American immigrants are undocumented, a circumstance that often deprives them of legal protection of basic human rights.

For all their diversity, Latinas/os have developed a consciousness of themselves as a people—that is, as a collective, marginalized population in the United States who share a common history of colonization and who share basic cultural features. Among these features, none is more salient than the religious ties to Catholicism.

More than 90 percent of Latinas/os identify as Christian and, because the form of Christianity presented by Spanish colonizers was Catholicism, the majority of Latinas/os today are Catholic. Just how many are Catholic depends on who is counting and who is included. The number officially registered in local parishes is 10.2 million. But the Secretariat for Hispanic Affairs of the United States Conference of Catholic Bishops estimates that 70 percent of the more than 35 million Latina/o residents of the United States, or 25 million, are Catholic.

This discrepancy points to the fact that being "Catholic" often means different things to the institutional church than it does to the people. For the former, being Catholic means being a formal member of a parish and conforming to the Euro-American expression of Catholicism. Some Hispanic individuals agree with these criteria. But for many Latinas/os, being Catholic primarily means participating in important liturgical events, observing the rituals of life passages, and practicing what scholars refer to as popular Catholicism. In fact, the Catholicism that binds diverse groups of Latinas/os together is preeminently the *religiosidad popular,* the popular religiosity, that emerged from *mestizaje,* which is not only the biological mixing that occurred during the period of colonialism, but the cultural mixing that occurred as well.

Hispanic Popular Religiosity

When Latinas/os speak of popular religion or religiosity, they are referring to the particular expression of Catholicism that developed out of the historic synthesis of Native spirituality and Spanish (Iberian) Catholicism, a form of Catholicism that predated the Counter Reformation (or Tridentine) Catholicism that was formulated during the time of the Protestant Reformation. This Spanish, medieval expression of Christianity emphasized "saints, shrines, relics, images, miracles, and religious storytelling." It was a religion of "symbols, stories, and dramas" rather than doctrine. Although it was the religion practiced at the local level under lay leadership, it was not without orthodox Christian content, for "the observance of the liturgical seasons and the arrival of occasional itinerant preachers gave the rural poor a necessary sense and knowledge of the fundamentals of Christianity."[10]

The popular Catholicism of Hispanics began when this version of Catholicism was brought to the New World in the 1500s and 1600s and imparted first to Native people, then subsequently to *mestizos,* through the interactions that occurred with peasant Spanish settlers.[11] This Catholicism of the common people, as contrasted with the Catholicism of religious order missionaries, mixed elements of the pagan religions that preceded Christianity with the official Christianity of the Church. In the New World, Iberian Catholicism joined with the traditional religions of Native peoples to form a distinctive religious expression that today is widely regarded as the defining characteristic of the Hispanic religious experience.

Speaking specifically of the Mexican experience, Virgilio Elizondo writes,

> The Christian word of God was inculturated deeply within the collective soul of Mexico not by the intention of the missioners, but by the process of symbolic interchange which took place in a very

natural way. The ordinary Spaniards were mostly illiterate and came from a Catholic culture which was rich in imagery, and the native world of the Americas communicated mainly through an image-language, as well. Thus it was much more at the level of the image-word than of the alphabetic spoken word that the new synthesis of Iberian Catholicism and the native religions took place and continue to take place today.[12]

Similar processes, which continued for three centuries and more, took place throughout Latin America and the Caribbean. The details of the popular Catholicism that developed varied somewhat from colony to colony and, after independence, from country to country, but the religious ethos and ambience were constants.

Not until the 1800s did Rome seek to gain more control over the Church of Latin America by imposing the European model of liturgy and theology. That influence, however, was felt primarily in the middle-class parishes of the larger towns and cities. The majority of the people lived in rural areas where a scarcity of priests fostered lay leadership and the continuation of popular practices.[13] And it was from these rural areas that most Mexican and Latin American immigrants to the United States came.

This social distance, it is argued, has been critical for the survival of popular religion; indeed, "popular" religion stands in contrast precisely to "clerical" religion.[14] Elizondo points out that the fiestas, processions, pilgrimages, and various popular celebrations that did not require clergy involvement "have been the deepest and most meaningful elements of our Iberoamerican religious tradition. The clergy have done their thing in the sanctuary, while the people of God have celebrated their faith in the homes, in the streets, and in the main plazas of their towns. Since," he adds, "the masses of our people were never allowed into the ranks of the clergy or religious, their clerical celebrations seemed more like the distant rites of foreigners than intimate celebrations of the faithful."[15]

Of the many symbols to be found in the various expressions of Hispanic popular religiosity, two are common to all: the crucified Christ and the Virgin Mary. In Latina/o culture, the representations of the crucified Christ invariably depict a figure of immense suffering and pain. One of the most important days of the liturgical calendar is Good Friday, when the procession of Christ to the cross is dramatically reenacted in the streets of local communities. "The Christ of Hispanic passion symbolism is a tortured, suffering human being," writes Orlando Espín. "This dying Jesus is so special because he is not just another human who suffers unfairly at the hands of evil humans. He is the divine Christ, and that makes his innocent suffering all the more dramatic. He is prayed to as one speaks with a living person, and not merely mourned or remembered as some dead hero of the past. His passion and death express his solidarity with all men and women throughout history who have also innocently suffered at the hands of evildoers."[16]

Of the numerous devotions to Mary found among different Latina/o groups, the most widespread is that of Our Lady of Guadalupe. The story of Our Lady involves the appearance of a figure to an Indian peasant in Mexico named Juan Diego who had recently converted to Christianity. Juan Diego was instructed by the apparition to convey to the bishop of Mexico that a temple was to be built on the site. He failed in his efforts to persuade the bishop, until the reappearing figure performed a miracle, producing an imprint of flowers on Juan Diego's apron.[17] Juan Diego, the story goes, knew this to be an appearance of the *Virgen de Guadalupe*, or the Virgin Mary.

As word spread of Juan Diego's visions, the Lady of Guadalupe quickly became an object of devotion, understood as the compassionate Mother who loves the poor and protects her children.

> By understanding Guadalupe, you understand Chicanos. In her poetry and songs one will find the history, the beauty, the spiritual role that the symbol of Guadalupe plays in the lives of Mexicans and Chicanos. As a symbol of faith she strengthens our belief in Jesus Christ; as a symbol of identity she is the essence of Chicano consciousness; as a symbol of hope she aids in our struggle to survive; as a symbol of the woman against *machismo* she beckons the *macho* to struggle at the side of women against oppression; as a symbol of liberation, in spite of her misuse by those in power, she is beside the poor as they fight oppression.[18]

Machismo notwithstanding, women play extremely important roles in popular religiosity on account of the cultural emphasis on the home and the extended family. Women make the preparations for the various fiestas. Ceremonies performed in the church are commonly followed by celebrations in the home of the honoree. Food is a major part of both. Home altars are an important aspect of popular religiosity, as well, providing a place for family and neighbors to gather to pray the rosary or novenas in times of crisis. Hispanic women, in particular, often approach their religion as a spiritual discipline to be practiced in the home, either exclusively or in conjunction with parish involvement. In the bringing up of children and the imparting of cultural traditions, women, to a large extent, have been the disseminators of popular religiosity.

Overall, as Elizondo makes clear, popular religiosity is a communal rather than an individual activity.

By popular expressions of the faith I do not refer to the private or individual devotion of a few people but to the ensemble of beliefs, rituals, ceremonies, devotions and prayers which are publicly practiced by the people at large. It is my contention that the deepest identity of the people is expressed in those expressions of faith which are celebrated voluntarily by the majority of the people, transmitted from generation to generation by the people themselves, and go on with the Church, without it, or even in spite of it. These religious practices are the ultimate foundation of the people's innermost being and the common expression of their collective souls.[19]

Elizondo also emphasizes the liberating dimension in popular religious expressions, asserting that, "for a colonized/oppressed/dominated group, they are the ultimate resistance to the attempts of the dominant culture to destroy them as a distinct group either through annihilation or through absorption and assimilation."[20] Others point out that Hispanic religiosity contains oppressive features as well, notably in its fostering of inequitable gender relations that are detrimental to the community as a whole.[21]

While this particular characteristic has not been a concern of the official Church, over the centuries most other characteristics of popular religiosity have been criticized or totally rejected. Consequently, what developed early on in the colonial experience was a "dual Catholicism." As Justo González puts it, "From its beginning, Spanish-American Roman Catholicism has been torn between a hierarchical church that has generally represented the powerful and stood by them and a more popular church, formed by the masses and led by pastors who have ministered at the very edge of disobedience."[22] That there would be tension between the two entities was inevitable, given that in the popular church, "authority does not reside in priesthood in the hierarchical sense but rather in Catholicism—in Catholicism understood as the faith of the people and not as the monopoly of the hierarchy."[23]

Institutional Catholicism in the United States

In the 1800s, European missionaries in the Southwest who were members of religious orders were gradually replaced by "secular" priests—that is, priests who were under the jurisdiction of American bishops. At the same time, permanent parishes began to replace the missions. In short order, the priests and their bishops were mostly French, English, and Irish. Fewer were Spanish, and hardly any Hispanic.[24]

Under their oversight, expressions of popular religion and lay Catholic organizations came under attack. Among the latter were the *Penitente* movements, which in some areas had preserved a folk version of

Catholicism for more than a century. Other *confradías,* or confraternities—small groups of lay Catholics organized originally within the mission structure to provide mutual aid and burial insurance, oversee sacramental life, and organize festivals—were brought under the jurisdiction of the parishes. Throughout Texas, California, and New Mexico, the explicit design of the Church was to replace Hispanic culture and identity with European forms. Very much the same agenda was pursued in Puerto Rico.[25]

As the numbers of white settlers in the Southwest increased, the American church devoted its resources and personnel disproportionately to this population. No provisions were made to train Hispanics as priests or as leaders in other capacities. Expressions of Hispanic culture were forbidden in local parishes, so that by 1900, parish worship had become Anglicized. After the turn of the century, as whites became increasingly averse to living or worshiping with Hispanics at all, the parishes were segregated, as were the schools in turn. In effect, a separate Hispanic church was created that preserved some of the values of Hispanic culture in spite of the fact that these parishes were staffed by Anglo priests and sisters.[26]

Beginning in the 1880s, dramatic changes in the life circumstances of Mexicans and Mexican Americans ultimately led to modifications in the stance of the official Catholic Church as well. Most significant were the changes in economic circumstances as Anglos came to view both Mexicans and Mexican Americans as important labor sources for farming, mining, and railroading. In part this change was prompted by federal passage of the Chinese Exclusion Act of 1882 and similar Japanese exclusion legislation a few years later.[27] The Mexican Revolution of 1910 resulted in more than a million Mexican immigrants becoming permanent residents of the United States, while thousands of temporary workers, called *braceros,* sought to take up residency without benefit of legal papers. Many of these workers were subsequently deported along with unknown numbers of Mexican American citizens.

In 1924, the National Origins Act that further restricted Asian immigration also closed the U.S./Mexico border. From this time until the mid-1960s, Mexican Americans were subjected to extreme violence and intimidation. Because of restrictions on immigrants from other parts of the world, their labor was in high demand, but the rate of exploitation was correspondingly high.[28]

Between 1920 and 1940, some Anglo priests and sisters, usually at their own initiative, though sometimes at the direction of bishops, began attending to the needs of Hispanic Catholics, particularly with regard to labor issues, immigration status, and social services. Not until 1945 were the first permanent units created in the American Church specifically for ministry to Hispanic members. In that year, a group of fourteen bishops meeting in

Oklahoma City formed the Bishops' Committee for the Spanish Speaking. They also established the regional Office for the Spanish Speaking and initiated the establishment of councils for the Spanish speaking in various dioceses of the Catholic Church, primarily to serve the needs of migrant workers.[29]

In the 1950s, dioceses began forming apostolate (service) offices to minister to the large numbers of Hispanics who were relocating to urban areas. Eventually, more than 100 such offices existed, out of a total of 176 dioceses in the United States.[30] By the mid-1960s, growing numbers of Hispanics—most of them laypersons, on account of the shortage of Hispanic priests and nuns—had assumed leadership of the diocesan councils for the Spanish speaking. In 1965, the Office for the Spanish Speaking became a national rather than regional office and in 1967 the first Hispanic layman was appointed director.[31] In 1970, the office was moved to Washington, D.C., to become the Division for the Spanish Speaking within the Department of Social Development. In 1974, this division became the Secretariat for Hispanic Affairs.

The initial motives on the part of Anglo church officials for establishing these units were mixed. Some officials were unquestionably sincere in wanting to attend to the needs of a growing component of the Church membership. To a large extent, however, these entities were created as a substitute for Hispanic parishes. At the time steps toward Hispanic ministry were being taken, support for national or ethnic Catholic parishes was waning in favor of "Americanizing" parishes—that is, parishes in which, as Allan Deck puts it, newcomers are required to adapt to "the way things have always been done." In short, the goal of the Church was assimilation. Many immigrant Latinas/os did end up in ethnic parishes by virtue of their residency in Hispanic barrios, and in these barrios the *confradías* and other expressions of popular religiosity persisted. But beginning in the mid-1940s, the official stance of the Church was to foster integrated parishes.[32]

One consequence of this policy was that local churches often failed to reach out to Hispanic residents. A second was that Hispanics who did go to predominately white parishes did not feel welcome. The language of assimilated parishes was English; even the clerical leadership most often did not speak Spanish. Consequently, rather than participate in the church of the parish in which they resided, Hispanics were inclined to travel to a distant parish that permitted and affirmed expressions of their culture.[33] In the parishes of large cities such as New York, Chicago, and Los Angeles where integration did occur, a phenomenon known as "basement churches" developed. In practice, two congregations shared the church building but functioned autonomously. Euro-Americans enjoyed the more privileged position in the parish while Hispanics were relegated to the basement. In effect, a "national" or ethnic-based parish was created within the larger parish, which had the consolation of extending to Hispanics considerable autonomy.[34]

During the 1950s, as Hispanics became more urbanized, Latina/o youth began attending parochial schools in far greater numbers. The number of Latinos who entered seminary to prepare for the priesthood increased as well.[35] But other Hispanics in these cities chose a different path, turning to Protestant, and especially Pentecostal churches, of which more will be said later.

Resisting the assimilation model and protesting the minimalist roles assigned to them, Latina/o Catholics began asserting their own vision of church. Corresponding with this development was the growth of a pan-Latino identity that transcended the identities of the respective Hispanic groups.

Latino Resistance and Religious Resurgence

The fostering of a pan-Latino identity in the 1960s and 1970s went hand in hand with what Ana María Díaz-Stevens and Anthony Stevens-Arroyo describe as "the Latino resurgence in U.S. religion" that occurred between 1967 and 1984. In this resurgence, they write, "a new role for Latino religion was proclaimed, elaborated, and implemented. Latino Catholic church leaders redefined their ecclesiastical roles. They announced a mission of restoring and redeveloping Latino religion because it was distinct and nonassimilable to the Euro-American experience."[36]

> The leadership produced many documents that, with considerable theological sophistication, explained the new trends. There was considerable emphasis on education and leadership formation so that the new vision of Latino religion was rapidly diffused through agencies, organizations, and institutions that had previously served an assimilationist function. In effect ..., Latino religion dissolved the last bonds to pious colonialism by subverting the very institutions that had been used for Americanization and reconfiguring them into vehicles for Latino reaffirmation.[37]

This religious resurgence was nurtured by a variety of movements that took place both inside and outside the Church.

The Second Vatican Council, which took place from 1962 to 1965, itself introduced far-reaching reforms. Multiculturalism was acknowledged and affirmed. Indigenous language masses were initiated. Much emphasis was put on lay leadership and parish governance. Provisions were made for greater participation of women. The overall emphasis of the Council was church renewal, but some of the emergent renewal movements were especially significant for Hispanics. Two of them, in fact, had their origins in Spain; one of them actually began even before the Council had been convened.

The movement known as *Cursillo de Cristianidad* was brought to the United States in 1957 and within two years was established among Hispanic Catholics. The *Cursillo* was an intense, experientially-based, three-day spiritual retreat utilizing personal testimony and Hispanic cultural forms. The retreats were led by lay Catholics, though both laity and clergy participated. Recruits came largely from the working class and the poor, drawing especially from the *confradías* and other traditional organizations of ethnic parishes. Participants often continued to meet together after their retreats, creating small ongoing communities that fostered a new sense of Catholic identity and belonging, as well as a consciousness of social issues and injustices. In time, the *Cursillo* movement created an important network of Hispanic Catholics, as well as an expanded class of lay leaders at all levels of the Church.[38]

A later movement, *Los Encuentros Matrimoniales*, or the Marriage Encounter, also began in Spain but was first introduced in the United States to English-speaking Catholics. In 1976, a Spanish-speaking component was developed for Hispanics that challenged the traditional gender roles in Hispanic marriages and had the effect of empowering Latinas while inviting Latinos to become less hierarchical and domineering.[39] In contrast to Marriage Encounter, the *Cursillo* movement moved from Hispanic Catholics into English-speaking populations. Both movements were supported by national offices of the Church, but had two different directorates—one Hispanic, and one primarily Anglo.[40]

A third movement, the *renovación carismática*, or charismatic renewal, in some respects countered the changes introduced by *Cursillo* and *Encuentros Matrimoniales*. This movement, too, started in the 1970s and took hold first among middle-class, white Catholics. It soon engaged both middle-class and lower-class Hispanics, however, for whom the emphases on emotion, prayer, family, and spirituality resonated with traditional piety and popular religiosity. The movement reinforced the community dimension of Hispanic religiosity with its emphasis on small prayer groups. But it also reinforced the subordination of women and rejected the appropriateness of social activism.[41]

In part, charismatic renewal, much like Protestant fundamentalism, was a reaction against the social change movements of the 1960s and 1970s. The civil rights and black consciousness movements of African Americans gave impetus to a Chicano movement that emphasized Hispanic culture and consciousness. The Chicano movement in turn produced a political party known as *La Raza Unida*, which fought for local community improvements and the protection of Chicana/o rights.

No individual was more influential in the emergence of these movements than the leader of the United Farm Workers Movement, César Chávez. Chávez, who grew up a migrant worker in the fields of California, became an organizer for social change in the early 1950s. In 1962, he organized the first union of Mexican American farm workers, which in 1966 became the United Farm Workers Organizing Committee. Adopting nonviolent tactics of social change, Chávez organized strikes and boycotts against grape growers, organized marches that were conducted under the banner of Our Lady of Guadalupe, and participated in hunger strikes to raise the awareness of the nation about the horrendous conditions suffered by migrant farm workers.

Chávez had been influenced by popular Catholicism as a youngster and was among those who had taken part in the *Cursillo* renewal movement. The indifference and apathy of the official Church, however, were the subject of many of his prophetic pronouncements. In its early days, the farm workers movement was supported primarily by Protestants, especially by the California Council of Churches. To the extent that the Catholic Church was supportive, it was largely due to the efforts of its "labor" priest, Monsignor George Higgins. In addition, many Hispanic priests and sisters who were inspired by Chávez's example and leadership mobilized support for the movement from Texas to California. Out of these involvements came two organizations, one of Mexican American priests called PADRES, formed in 1969, and another of Hispanic religious women called LAS HERMANAS, organized in 1971. Both groups became vocal advocates for the appointment of Hispanic bishops and for the allocation of more resources to Hispanic ministry.

High on the list of needs was training and Spanish-language instruction for lay religious leaders, as well as for priests and nuns engaged in ministry to Latina/o populations. In the early 1970s, regional and diocesan training programs were established around the country. The most influential of these was the Mexican American Cultural Center (MACC), organized in San Antonio, Texas, in 1972 by members of PADRES with the support of LAS HERMANAS. Virgilio Elizondo, a member of PADRES who served as the president of MACC for its first fifteen years, recalls the impetus for its formation:

> Church institutions had been so oppressive to us that when the radical Chicano movements started in the 1960s, the leaders often told priests and religious who tried to join them to get lost. They felt that the only way to help Hispanics get ahead was to get rid of

Catholicism. It was painful to hear their insults, but as painful as their accusations were, we had to admit that they were true—if not totally, at least 95 percent of what they were saying against the church was correct. The church had kept us out and had witnessed and by its silence approved the ongoing exploitation and oppression of the Hispanics in this country. The Chicano movements gave inspiration to the Chicano clergy and later on to all the Hispanic clergy in this country. We began to organize and to work for change within our own church.[42]

A significant forum for presenting the envisioned changes was created with the convening in 1972 of Hispanic religious leaders in the First National *Encuentro* (encounter), which brought the Hispanic "civil rights movement" within the Catholic Church. Subsequent *Encuentros* held in 1977 and 1985 were central to the issuance of the bishops's pastoral letter, entitled "The Hispanic Presence: Challenge and Commitment," in 1983 and the preparation of a National Pastoral Plan for Hispanic Ministry adopted by the bishops in 1987.

All of these developments, both inside and outside of church structures, had an impact not only on Mexican Americans, but on Puerto Ricans who developed their own forms of protest and cultural innovations. Many Cubans, in contrast, rejected the more radical aspects of Hispanic activism, finding in them reminders of the leftist politics that had led them to flee Cuba in the first place. Nonetheless, some individual Cuban leaders within and without the Church responded to the message of social justice and became a part of the growing pan-Latino identity.

The events of the 1960s and 1970s had an impact on individual bishops of the Church, as well, some of whom became strong advocates for Hispanic citizens and immigrants alike, and for the elevation of Hispanics within the Church hierarchy. In 1970, Patricio Flores was named the first Hispanic bishop in the American Church and subsequently became the archbishop of San Antonio. Moisés Sandoval writes that with Flores's appointment, "Symbolically, at least, the Hispanic Church was then complete; it had laity, women religious, brothers, priests, and a bishop, a man responsive to the needs of his times [and who] during the first few years following his elevation, functioned as the unofficial shepherd of the Hispanic people in the United States."[43]

By 1980, there were 12 Hispanic bishops out of a total of 360 U.S. bishops. Of the 1,400 Latino priests, which represented 2.4 percent of all Catholic priests in the country, about a third were from Spain, a third had been born in Latin America, and a third had been born in the United States.[44] By 1992, the number of bishops stood at 21—still a small minority, but large enough to constitute a Hispanic voice in the Conference of Bishops.[45]

But the emergent "Hispanic Church" was not just offices and officials; it was the church of the people, of lay leaders and activists, and of organizations outside the structures of the official Church. And it was strongly influenced by the liberation theology of Latin America.

The Impact of Latin American Liberation Theology

Liberation theology was widely embraced by activist religious leaders, both lay and clergy, a development that introduced a whole new dimension into relationships between the Hispanic Church and the official Church in the United States. MACC itself served as "the entry point for Latin America's liberation theology,"[46] which was readily accepted by the members of PADRES, including Elizondo, who saw their mission as the empowerment of poor and disenfranchised Hispanics in the United States. Many of these leaders embraced the *ecclesia* of the Latin American liberation theology movement as well, that is, the model of *comunidades eclesiales de base* (basic ecclesial communities) or base Christian communities (BCCs).

The defining characteristic of these communities, which continue to thrive in Brazil, El Salvador, and other parts of Central and South America, is the cyclical model of praxis involving biblical study, social analysis, experiential reflection, and social action. This reflection/action model was influenced by the pedagogy of the Brazilian educator Paulo Freire, the central concept of which was *conscienzaó* or conscientization.[47] Through Freire's process of developing self-awareness of one's personal and social world, illiterate peasants were encouraged and empowered to change dehumanizing social structures rather than passively accepting the status quo. In Central and South America, activist Catholic priests and sisters conjoined this pedagogy with Christianity to produce a liberative theology aimed at transforming oppressive social systems. They also helped organize base Christian communities in rural areas and then trained lay Catholics to assume leadership.

As Latin American religious scholars formalized liberation theology, they embraced the Second Vatican Council's image of church as "the people of God." In this model, "church" is effectively reinvented so as to place the focus on the everyday issues and needs of the people. The power of the church hierarchy is correspondingly moderated. Rather than having power over the people, leaders are to serve the people. Furthermore, this servant model of church emphatically sides with the poor, functioning as an instrument of liberation.

In liberation theology, the church is fundamentally communitarian; communitarianism, however, means not only providing support and social services, but working for structural change. As Leonardo Boff puts it,

> This process of liberation demands a much more detailed analysis of society: how the production of wealth functions, how wealth is distributed, the place of individuals in relation to capital, employment, and participation. The community that is awakened to this reality is already conscious of the violation of human rights, of structural poverty, of the social injustices that are the fruits of the organization of an entire system that is often presented as good, Christian, democratic, and so forth. Christian faith awakens one to social justice, to the true meaning of the global liberation of Jesus Christ that demands the transformation, the conversion, not only of the individual but also of the structures.[48]

In their activism, the people are guided as much or more by the Holy Spirit and the power of Jesus' love as by formal church teachings. Thus, spirituality has a central place in exercising a "preferential option for the poor." Furthermore, in a church that truly seeks justice, Boff maintains, women will be ordained, priests will have the choice of marrying, and the Eucharist will be celebrated by lay church leaders.[49] In short, the envisioned church of liberation theology, embodied in basic ecclesial communities, is inherently an anti-Constantinian church.

Elizondo remarks on the significance of Latin American liberation theology for Hispanic ministry: "Two great events took place in 1971 which have had a tremendous impact on Hispanic ministry in the United States: the birth of the Mexican-American Cultural Center (MACC) and the first publication in Lima, Peru, of Gustavo Gutiérrez's *Teología de Liberación*. Since then, Gustavo and the work of MACC have been intimately interrelated."[50]

It was the leaders of PADRES and members of MACC, influenced by liberation theology, who shaped the Second *Encuentro* that was held in 1977. Although the bishops had rejected the proposal of the First *Encuentro* to make base Christian communities a priority of the Church, the planners of this encounter stated, "The process leading to the Second *Encuentro* should serve to take the historic step from a mass Church to a Church of small ecclesial communities. It would therefore be an occasion for intensifying the creation and the renewal of these small communities throughout the country."[51] Furthermore, the planners stipulated that only those who had been involved in a base Christian community would be allowed to participate in this *Encuentro*.[52]

When the *Encuentro* concluded, five major directions for the emerging Hispanic Church had been stipulated: continuation of "a process of reflection and growth in Christ as a Hispanic community"; the correction of "injustices inside and outside the Church, especially those suffered by migrant farm workers and undocumented immigrants"; the inclusion of Hispanic culture and concerns in the activity of the Church as a whole; the development and recognition of lay ministry; and the formation of base Christian communities.[53]

Staff of the Secretariat for Hispanic Affairs pursued implementation of the *Encuentro*'s recommendations, preparing a guidebook called *Basic Ecclesial Communities: An Experience in the United States* (1980) that was published in both Spanish and English. By the third *Encuentro*, however, control had passed from the activist Hispanic leadership to the Church bishops. Over the next decade, while the bishops continued to endorse the *form* of small communities, the praxis component of the original base Christian community model was officially excised.

With the turn to political and social conservatism in the country as a whole, the liberationist voice in the Church was muted and priority given to pastoral matters such as increasing Hispanic staff and Hispanic ministry at the diocesan level.[54] The Latino religious resurgence had come to an end, but not the impact it had had in fostering the Hispanic Church.

The Hispanic Church

In the view of historian Jay Dolan, "A very vibrant Hispanic church has developed within the larger Catholic Church in the United States. This church has all the characteristics of an institution with the bureaucratic trademarks of national organizations, offices, conventions, and institutes. It is not centrally organized or controlled but is informally linked together by a common concern—the welfare of Hispanic Catholics. It is a Church within a Church, and its position within the Catholic Church somewhat resembles that of the Black Church within the Protestant ecclesiastical establishment."[55]

The Hispanic Church is a combination of the structures Dolan mentions, small Christian communities, and popular religiosity. The religious and political resurgences of Latinas/os had the overall effect of diminishing traditional configurations such as the *confradías*, but in other respects, they gave new life and affirmation to popular religion.[56] Politically, throughout the 1960s and 1970s, "meeting rooms at the local church became the assembly points for many neighborhood organizations and agencies, many of which received government funds. These new political roles were matched by effective—and sometimes spectacular—ritual celebration in Latino cultural idioms. In other words, the substantial and dramatic changes formulated by leadership were transmitted to Latino churchgoers in ways that were both pragmatically beneficial and culturally popular."[57]

The communal orientation of popular Catholicism was reinforced first by the group experiences of the *Cursillo* and then by the model of base ecclesial communities introduced from Latin America. As Edmundo Rodríguez, S.J., describes them, "Christian base communities are not a movement or an organization; rather, they are a different ecclesiology, a different way of thinking and of being Church which resurrects an intimate sense of community, trims the modern urban neighborhoods down to size, and affords ordinary people an opportunity to do ministry."[58]

Mexican Americans in the borderlands between the United States and Mexico, especially, were influenced by the action/reflection praxis of these communities. In the diocese of Brownsville, Texas, for example, more than five hundred such communities have come into being, as they have in other parts of the country from Rockford, Illinois, to Los Angeles, California.[59]

By the 1980s, several individuals had begun formulating a distinctive U.S. Latino theology, one that was explicitly based on social justice, but that, having developed in a different sociopolitical context, was not the same as the liberation theology of Latin America. For one thing, Latinos/as are in the minority in the United States. In addition, the issues here have more to do with social discrimination and cultural affirmation than with economic class and land distribution, as is the case in Latin America. Latino theology, in contrast to conventional Euro-American theology, supports more extensive lay ministry, affirms the legitimacy of popular religiosity, and places grassroots community-building at its center.[60] Apart from Latino theology, Latinas began writing what they termed *Mujerista* theology, which focused on the experiences of women.

While an extensive body of theological literature has been produced since the 1980s, these writings are not the only expressions of Hispanic theology.[61] Thus, Ada María Isasi-Díaz observes:

> Latino/Hispanic theology is a discourse, but it is also a praxis: we do not write theology; we do theology. Those of us who do theology are not just those academically trained but also grassroots people who are eminently capable of explaining our religious understandings and practices, people for whom religion is the spark enabling us to continue the daily struggle. Latino/Hispanic theology is elaborated in the books we publish, but it is also carefully laid out in the variety of prayers that our people are always willing to share aloud, prayers that identify what they value and how they see the divine participating in their lives.

Latino/Hispanic theology is a community theology, then, and not solely because of the commitment of academic theologians to the struggles of our people. It is a community theology because it is not only *for* the people but also *by* the people, by the grassroots people who are admirably capable of reflecting theologically. Furthermore, because of our understanding of the preferential option for the oppressed as an intrinsic element of the gospel message, we believe that it is the perspective of grassroots Latinas and Latinos that best can help us be a community committed to liberative praxis. The transformation that is the goal of our work involves a radical liberation that operates at the social and political level, at the psychological level, and at the spiritual-religious level.[62]

The Hispanic Church is envisioned by Latino/Hispanic theologians as preeminently a church of small communities. But the base Christian community model has been challenged in the past two decades by other Catholic renewal programs, most especially by the program known as RENEW, the Spanish version of which is *RENOVACIÓN.*

RENEW was started in the archdiocese of Newark, New Jersey, in the late 1970s as a program to promote the creation of small, short-term, faith-sharing groups within parish populations. It quickly became a national and even international program. Although these faith-sharing groups sometimes become permanent, they are not the same as base Christian communities. Their emphasis is typically spiritual renewal through Bible study and personal sharing. They do not, as a rule, emphasize social justice or call for social action, although there are exceptions. (See chapter 10 for a more extended discussion of RENEW generally.)

In the late 1990s, Bernard J. Lee, S.M., and William V. D'Antonio conducted a national survey of what they term "small Christian communities" (SCCs), in which they include the RENEW faith-sharing groups, as well as charismatic communities, base Christian communities, and various other types of small communities. They identified a total of 37,000 small Christian communities, about 20 percent of which (7,550) were Hispanic, with the remainder of the groups being predominately Anglo. In their published findings, the authors point out that "while the SCC is an important experience for the great majority of community members, it plays a far larger role in Hispanic/Latino life than it does elsewhere." They quote one Hispanic respondent as saying, "So if (at church) the homily is awful, the music is lousy, and the ushers are unfriendly … and that's all they get, how do they keep going? I'm not sure. But (when) you have your small communities, that's where church happens. You know that it is your church."[63]

While 26 percent of non-charismatic whites reported that their SCC was their primary source of spiritual nourishment, 87 percent of Hispanics so reported. From 56 to 74 percent of Hispanics said that participation in their SCC heightened their sense of social responsibility for parish, neighborhood, or the larger society; only 20 to 34 percent of non-Hispanics answered in like manner. When it came to engagement in social action, 8 percent of non-Hispanics said they were involved in social outreach, as compared to 19 percent of Hispanics.[64]

Important as these findings are for their documentation of significant differences between Hispanics and Anglos, they do not define the limits of Latina/o small Christian community. More and more, as the Hispanic population grows in small towns and cities around the country, small-scale Christian communities represent the fundamental process by which Latinas/os enter into predominantly white parishes. That is, wherever a local parish initiates a Spanish ministry to meet sacramental needs, a "small community" is invariably created. This Hispanic church community, in turn, may introduce aspects of popular religiosity, or form charismatic prayer groups, or generate outreach ministries that raise the consciousness of middle-class parishioners and motivate them to become involved in mission activity.[65] Even if Hispanics do not become the majority in these parishes, they nevertheless transform them to a greater or lesser degree. Thus, Justo González can write, "As the post-Constantinian era advances, Hispanic Catholics represent that segment of the church which is best prepared to face the new day."[66]

Hispanics now constitute upward of 40 percent of the total Catholic population in the United States. Along with Asian Americans, they have the highest rates of immigration and correspondingly are the fastest growing segments of the Catholic Church. In the not too distant future, the Catholic Church in the United States will be predominately Hispanic, the implications of which are far-reaching. Ultimately, the question is whether the Hispanic Church itself will become the Church of the center, rather than continuing to be a Church on the margins. But a corollary question is whether Hispanic Catholics will stay around to find out, or whether they will instead seek a home in Protestant churches, as many have already done.

Protestant Hispanics

Justo González is himself a Protestant theologian. He speaks comfortably of Catholic matters because Catholic and Protestant theologians have worked together, protested together, and developed their theology together—a circumstance made possible by the fact that Latino theology, in contrast to white Western theology, focuses on orthopraxis (right action) rather than orthodoxy (right belief). Latino theology is anchored in the experience of the people and gives attention to the symbols and rituals of popular religiosity—symbols and rituals that are as important to many Protestant Hispanics as they are to Catholic.

The relationships of Hispanic Catholics and Protestants have not always been so congenial. Protestantism was introduced into Latin America in the 1800s both by European and Euro-American missionaries and by northern European immigrants who settled in the southern part of the continent. In Cuba, exiles who had converted to Protestantism while living in Florida were instrumental in developing a Protestant presence either by sending missionaries or by returning as missionaries themselves. These churches of mainline Protestantism worked mostly among the poor, but imparted middle-class values from the United States. Even the fundamentalist movement that entered Latin America around the turn of the century imparted the same middle-class worldview and aspirations. But the fundamentalist impact was minor compared to the wave of pentecostalism that began to wash over the continent a few years later. By the end of the 1900s, pentecostalism was "the characteristic form of Latin American Protestantism."[67] All forms of Protestantism, however, were characterized by a strong anti-Catholic bias.

Protestantism has become a factor in Hispanic religion in the United States both through immigration and through conversion in this country. From the mid-1800s to the mid-1900s, the attraction for converts revolved to a large extent around personal access to the Scriptures, greater participation in the life of the church, and quicker access to ordained ministry. The anti-Catholic sentiments of Hispanic Protestants began to moderate in the 1960s, partly because of changes brought by the Second Vatican Council and partly because Protestants and Catholics found common cause in the social activism of the day.

According to a survey conducted by the Tomás Rivera Policy Institute, in the year 2000 about 71 percent of Hispanics were Catholic, while 21 percent were Protestant. About 3 percent were Jehovah's Witnesses or Mormons, while 5 percent had no religious affiliation. Of all Latinas/os, about 4.7 percent belong to mainline Protestant churches, 7.6 percent to evangelical churches, and around 7.9 percent to pentecostal churches.[68] The survey also revealed that 18 percent of Latinas/os who are immigrants identify themselves as Protestant, compared to 32 percent of third-generation Latinas/os,[69] suggesting that future generations may consist of an ever greater proportion of Protestants.

Hispanics who move from Catholicism to Protestantism generally fall in one of two camps. "The smaller camp," according to Edmundo Rodríquez, "is comprised of those with strong leadership potential who move up socially, economically, and educationally but identify Catholicism with a poorer and less enlightened life." Members of this group are more likely to join mainline Protestant churches. The larger camp, however, "is made up of those who have been at the margins of formal Catholic Church life and find themselves more comfortable in fundamentalist congregations. Often they have not followed or understood the changes which have taken place in the Catholic Church and feel betrayed by them, or they are motivated to change by their individual or family need for simple, clear, and Scripture-based solutions to their human problems."[70]

Díaz-Stevens and Stevens-Arroyo point out that the Latino religious resurgence affected mainline Protestant Hispanics in much the same way as it did Catholic Hispanic leaders; it also made an impact on mainline Protestant churches. In 1984, the United Methodist Church adopted a plan for Hispanic ministry that mirrored many of the changes spelled out in the Catholic bishops' 1983 pastoral letter. Other mainline denominations followed suit. The policy of Americanization was dropped, the legitimacy of Latino religion acknowledged,[71] and Hispanic caucuses given status and support.

In contrast to the first camp, most converts in the second come out of popular Catholic culture. Or as Allan Deck argues, "In a certain sense the movement of Hispanics to evangelical religion is a way to maintain a continuity with their popular Catholic faith," a faith whose main concerns, similarly to pentecostalism, are "an immediate experience of God, a strong orientation toward the transcendent, an implicit belief in miracles, a practical orientation toward healing, and a tendency to personalize or individualize one's relationship with the divine."[72]

Unlike many white Pentecostals, however, Hispanics continue to value both community and lay leadership. "Being relatively small, these evangelical/Pentecostal congregations come closer to the rural, small community context that is most familiar to the people. The small faith-sharing orientation of many evangelical churches affirms the communal thrust of Hispanic popular Catholicism."[73] Furthermore, fundamentalism does not necessarily have the same meaning for Hispanics as for non-Hispanics, largely because of the contradictions experienced between what white Protestants say and what they do. González offers the civil rights movement as a stark example:

> White Protestantism did not always show itself to be the force for progress and freedom that we had been told it was. Those whites who were constantly quoting the Bible were also contradicting it in their daily lives, and those who seemed to discount the authority of Scripture often seemed to have a clearer understanding of the

biblical demand for love and justice. This has made it very difficult for many in the Hispanic Protestant community to continue being fundamentalist in the traditional sense. The authority of Scripture is still held in high regard by that community. But there is also a growing awareness that there is a certain sort of fundamentalism that is grossly antibiblical. For this reason, many Protestants are seeking ways of interpreting Scripture that, while respecting the authority of the Bible, are different from what we were taught. The net result is that we find ourselves walking along the same path with Roman Catholics.[74]

Allan Deck suggests there are other potentials for walking a common path. Hispanic ecclesia in the form of base Christian communities and small evangelical/pentecostal congregations share their emphasis on communalism. Base Christian communities offer an emphasis on social justice that evangelicalism often lacks, while evangelical and pentecostal communities provide a spiritual focus that has waned in liberationist communities. One might conclude, muses Deck, that,

> A future path for Christianity in Latin America and among United States Hispanics can be found in a dialectical relationship, a dialogue, a give-and-take between the insights of liberation theology and the experiences of the base ecclesial communities on the one hand and, interestingly enough, the evangelical/pentecostal communities on the other. This path will perhaps be the fruit of a mature analysis and evaluation of the complex religious, social, economic, political, and cultural ferment experienced by Hispanics in North and South America. The path may become a new, vital form of ecumenism.... In the interplay between seemingly disparate religious traditions, a vision of Christianity, its possible future tone and texture, emerges to our surprise and wonderment.[75]

For Further Reading

Bañuelas, Arturo J., ed. *Mestizo Christianity: Theology from the Latino Perspective.* Maryknoll, N.Y.: Orbis Books, 1995.

Deck, Allan Figueroa, S.J. *The Second Wave: Hispanic Ministry and the Evangelization of Cultures.* New York: Paulist Press, 1989.

Dolan, Jay P., and Allan Figueroa Deck, S.J. *Hispanic Catholic Culture in the U.S.: Issues and Concerns.* Notre Dame: University of Notre Dame Press, 1994.

Elizondo, Virgilio. *Galilean Journey: The Mexican American Promise.* Rev. and exp. Maryknoll, N.Y.: Orbis Books, 2000.

González, Justo L. *Mañana: Christian Theology from a Hispanic Perspective.* Nashville: Abingdon Press, 1990.

Isasi-Díaz, Ada María, and Fernando F. Segovia, eds. *Hispanic/Latino Theology: Challenge and Promise*. Minneapolis: Fortress Press, 1996.

Maldonado, David Jr., ed. *Protestantes/Protestants: Hispanic Christianity within Mainline Traditions*. Nashville: Abingdon Press, 1999.

Sandoval, Moisés. *On the Move: A History of the Hispanic Church in the United States*. Maryknoll, N.Y.: Orbis Books, 1990.

NOTES

1. I am indebted to Dr. Hector Avalos for his support and assistance with this chapter, particularly for his bringing references to my attention of which I was unaware.

2. Moisés Sandoval, "The Organization of a Hispanic Church," in *Hispanic Catholic Culture in the U.S.: Issues and Concerns* (eds. Jay P. Dolan and Allan Figueroa Deck, S.J.; Notre Dame: University of Notre Dame Press, 1994), 132.

3. Although Spanish is the common language, many Hispanics are bilingual (English and Spanish), while others speak only English.

4. Many Latinas (women) and Latinos (men) who might otherwise self-identify as white include themselves in the designation "people of color" as an expression of identification with the ongoing struggle for liberation from the colonial legacy of oppression.

5. See Rodolfo Acuña, *Occupied America: A History of Chicanos* (4th ed., rev.; New York: Longman, 2000).

6. Jaime Vidal, "Citizens Yet Strangers: The Puerto Rican Experience," in *Puerto Rican and Cuban Catholics in the U.S., 1900–1965* (eds. Jay P. Dolan and Jaime Vidal; Notre Dame: University of Notre Dame Press, 1994), 55–56.

7. Jay P. Dolan and Jaime Vidal, *Puerto Rican and Cuban Catholics in the U.S., 1900–1965* (Notre Dame: University of Notre Dame Press, 1994), 4.

8. Isidro Lucas, *The Browning of America: The Hispanic Revolution in the American Church* (Chicago: Fides/Claretian, 1981), 34.

9. Ibid., 5.

10. Orlando Espín, "Tradition and Popular Religion: An Understanding of the Sensus Fidelium," in *Mestizo Christianity* (ed. Arturo J. Bañuelas; Maryknoll, N.Y.: Orbis Books, 1995), 155.

11. Ibid., 154–55.

12. Virgilio Elizondo, "Popular Religion as the Core of Cultural Identity Based on the Mexican American Experience in the United States," in *An Enduring Flame: Studies on Latino Popular Religiosity* (eds. Anthony M. Stevens-Arroyo and Ana María Díaz-Stevens; New York: Bildner Center for Western Hemisphere Studies, 1994), 115.

13. Allan Figueroa Deck, S.J., *The Second Wave: Hispanic Ministry and the Evangelization of Cultures* (New York: Paulist Press, 1989), 55–56.

14. Ana María Díaz-Stevens, "Analyzing Popular Religiosity for Socio-Religious Meaning," in *An Enduring Flame: Studies on Latino Popular Religiosity* (eds. Anthony M. Stevens-Arroyo and Ana María Díaz-Stevens; New York: Bildner Center for Western Hemisphere Studies, 1994), 21–22.

15. Virgilio P. Elizondo, foreword to *Mañana: Christian Theology from a Hispanic Perspective*, by Justo L. González (Nashville: Abingdon Press, 1990), 15. For the benefit of Protestant readers, the term "religious" as a noun in Catholic circles refers to vowed members of religious communities. So, for example, my Catholic students often ask me if I am "a religious."

16. Espín, "Tradition and Popular Religion," 157.

17. Ibid., 161. This story has been tied to a goddess of the religion of the Nahuatl Indians in Mexico. The goddess, Tonantzin, it was believed, dwelt on the hill known as Tepeyac. The religion was suppressed by the Spanish in the early decades of the 1500s, and it is during this time (1531), according to an older account, that the Lady of Guadalupe appeared. More recent scholarship, however, has contested this version, arguing that in fact no goddess was worshipped at Tepeyac; that the story of Juan Diego first appears in the mid-1600s, written for a Mexican-born Spanish audience; and that it was not popular among Indians and mestizos until the 1800s. See Stafford Poole, *Our Lady of Guadalupe: The Origins and Sources of a Mexican National Symbol, 1531–1797* (Tucson: University of Arizona Press, 1995) and Louise Burkhart, "The Cult of the Virgin of Guadalupe in Mexico," in *South and Meso-American Native Spirituality: From the Cult of the Feathered Serpent to the Theology of Liberation* (ed. Gary H. Gossen; New York: Crossroad, 1993). Whatever its origins, the fact remains that the story is central to popular religiosity and vitally important to many believers.

18. Andrés G. Guerrero, *A Chicano Theology* (Maryknoll, N.Y.: Orbis Books, 1987), 117.

19. Elizondo, "Popular Religion," 117.

20. Ibid.

21. See, for example, Anthony M. Stevens-Arroyo, introduction to *Discovering Latino Religion: A Comprehensive Social Science Bibliography* (ed. Anthony M. Stevens-Arroyo; New York: Bildner Center for Western Hemisphere Studies, 1995), 30.

22. Justo González, "Hispanics in the New Reformation," in *Mestizo Christianity* (ed. Arturo J. Bañuelas; Maryknoll, N.Y., 1995), 244–45.

23. Ibid.

24. Moisés Sandoval, *On the Move: A History of the Hispanic Church in the United States* (Maryknoll, N. Y.: Orbis Books, 1990), 30.

25. Stevens-Arroyo, introduction, *Discovering Latino Religion*, 17.

26. Ibid.

27. Ibid., 29.

28. The foregoing discussion draws on Sandoval, *On the Move*, chap. 4.

29. Sandoval, "Organization of a Hispanic Church," 134.

30. Ibid., 134–35, 141.

31. Ibid., 135, 137.

32. Deck, *The Second Wave*, 58–61.

33. Ibid.

34. Ana María Díaz-Stevens and Anthony M. Stevens-Arroyo, *Recognizing the Latino Resurgence in U.S. Religion* (Boulder, Colo.: Westview Press, 1998), 119.

35. Ibid., 120.

36. Ibid., 122.

37. Ibid.

38. See Díaz-Stevens and Stevens-Arroyo, *Recognizing the Latino Resurgence,* 133–35, and Edmundo Rodríguez, S.J., "The Hispanic Community and Church Movements: Schools of Leadership," in *Hispanic Catholic Culture in the U.S.: Issues and Concerns* (eds. Jay P. Dolan and Allan Figueroa Deck, S.J.; Notre Dame: University of Notre Dame Press, 1994), 215–16.

39. Rodríguez, "The Hispanic Community," 220–21.

40. Sandoval, "Organization of a Hispanic Church," 133.

41. Rodríguez, "The Hispanic Community," 224–25.

42. Virgilio Elizondo, "*Mestizaje* as a Locus of Theological Reflection," in *Mestizo Christianity: Theology from the Latino Perspective* (ed. Arturo J. Bañuelas; Maryknoll, N.Y.: Orbis Books, 1995), 8.

43. Sandoval, "Organization of a Hispanic Church," 149–50.

44. Lucas, *The Browning of America*, 39–40. See note 8 above. In the year 2000 there were approximately 2,200 Hispanic priests, representing about 3 percent of all priests in the United States. An estimated 4,500 priests were Spanish speaking. See *The Cara Report* 5, no. 3 (winter 2000): 4.

45. Sandoval, "Organization of a Hispanic Church," 150.

46. Ibid., 156.

47. See Paulo Freire's now classic book, *Pedagogy of the Oppressed* (New York: Seabury Press, 1974.) The book was translated from the original Portuguese manuscript in 1968.

48. Leonardo Boff, *Church: Charism and Power* (New York: Crossroad, 1985), cited in Dennis M. Doyle, *The Church Emerging from Vatican II* (Mystic, Conn.: Twenty-Third Publications, 1992), 179–80. This discussion draws from Doyle, *The Church*, 174–80. See also, Boff's *Ecclesiogenesis: The Base Communities Reinvent the Church* (Maryknoll, N.Y.: Orbis Books, 1986).

49. Doyle, *The Church*, 178–79.

50. Elizondo, "*Mestizaje*," 7.

51. Secretariat for Hispanic Affairs, *Pueblo Hispano—Voz Profética* (Washington, D.C.: National Catholic Conference, 1985), 77. Cited in González, "Hispanics in the New Reformation," 246.

52. González, "Hispanics in the New Reformation," 246–47.

53. Sandoval, "Organization of a Hispanic Church," 144–45.

54. See Díaz-Stevens and Stevens-Arroyo, *Recognizing the Latino Resurgence*, 199–201.

55. Jay Dolan, conclusion to *Hispanic Catholic Culture in the U.S.: Issues and Concerns* (eds. Jay P. Dolan and Allan Figueroa Deck, S.J.; Notre Dame: University of Notre Dame Press, 1994), 450–51.

56. See the discussion by Rodríguez, "The Hispanic Community," 209–15.

57. Díaz-Stevens and Stevens-Arroyo, *Recognizing the Latino Resurgence*, 122. This process is documented in Antonio M. Stevens-Arroyo, ed., *Prophets Denied Honor: An Anthology on the Hispanic Church in the United States* (Maryknoll, N.Y.: Orbis Books, 1980).

58. Rodríguez, "The Hispanic Community," 236–37.

59. Ibid., 237.

60. In this context, I am referring to formal, written theology.

61. *The Journal of Hispanic/Latino Catholic Theology* began publication in 1993. *Apuntes*, which is addressed more to Protestant Hispanic ministry, has been published since 1980. The Academy of Catholic Hispanic Theologians in the United States, with about fifty members, meets annually.

62. Ada María Isasi-Díaz, "Afterwords: Strangers No Longer," in *Hispanic/Latino Theology: Challenge and Promise* (eds. Ada María Isasi-Díaz and Fernando F. Segovia; Minneapolis: Fortress Press, 1996), 371–72. For an excellent discussion of U.S. Hispanic theology, as well as of the different emphases of individual theologians, see Arturo J. Bañuelas, "U.S. Hispanic Theology: An Initial Assessment," in *Mestizo Christianity* (ed. Arturo J. Bañuelas; Maryknoll, N.Y.: Orbis Books, 1995). For an earlier, but also excellent overview, see Allan Figueroa Deck, S.J., "Latino Theology: The Year of the 'Boom,'" *Journal of Hispanic/Latino Theology* 1, no. 2 (February 1994): 51–63.

63. Bernard J. Lee, S.M., with William V. D'Antonio et al., *The Catholic Experience of Small Christian Communities* (New York: Paulist Press, 2000), 58–59.

64. Ibid., 57, 94.

65. Conversation with Alejandro Aguilerá-Titus, Office of Hispanic Affairs, National Conference of Catholic Bishops, August 10, 2002.

66. González, "Hispanics in the New Reformation," 248.

67. See González, "Hispanics in the New Reformation," 248–51.

68. These preliminary findings were reported in an article by William Lobdell, "Latinos Slip Away from Catholicism," *Los Angeles Times,* May 12, 2001, B9, and by Gáston Espinosa, co-director of the Hispanic Churches in American Public Life Project, which sponsored the survey, at the project's national conference held in Washington, D.C., May 3, 2002.

69. Lobdell, "Latinos Slip Away."

70. Rodríguez, "The Hispanic Community," 207.

71. Díaz-Stevens and Stevens-Arroyo, *Recognizing the Latino Resurgence,* 111, 126.

72. Allan Figueroa Deck, S.J., "The Challenge of Evangelical/Pentecostal Christianity to Hispanic Catholicism," in *Hispanic Catholic Culture in the U.S.: Issues and Concerns* (eds. Jay P. Dolan and Allan Figueroa Deck, S.J.; Notre Dame: University of Notre Dame Press, 1994), 422.

73. Ibid., 425–26.

74. González, "Hispanics in the New Reformation," 254–55.

75. Deck, "The Challenge of Evangelical/Pentecosal Christianity," 432–33.

−CHAPTER 7−
Asian American Syncretism

Asian American Christians are among the least investigated of the major racial-religious groups in the United States, though they have come to be an important component of the story of Christianity in this country. Scholarly writings on this population, both social scientific and theological, have increased significantly since the mid-1990s, but the body of literature remains quite limited.

Asian Americans, like Native Americans and Latinas/os, suffer from the stereotype that they are a homogeneous population. Since the passage of the 1965 Immigration Act, fourth- and fifth-generation Japanese and Chinese Americans have been joined by ever growing numbers of Chinese, South Koreans, Vietnamese, Cambodians, and other Southeast Asians. Immigrants from India and Pakistan are to be counted among Asian Americans as well. From 1.5 million in 1970, the Asian American population increased to 3.5 million in 1980, 7.3 million in 1990,[1] and 10.2 million as of 2000. (See Table 5 for a breakdown by ethnic group.)

Table 5. Asian American Population by Ethnic Groups, 2000

Asian Indian	1,678,765
Chinese	2,432,585
Filipino	1,850,314
Japanese	796,700
Korean	1,076,872
Vietnamese	1,122,528
Other Asian (including mixed)	1,285,234
TOTAL	10,242,998

Source: U.S. Census Bureau. Hawaiians and other Pacific Islanders constitute an additional 398,835.

Asian Americans now constitute 3.6 percent of the population of the United States and there is every reason to think this figure will continue to increase. While the proportion of immigrants coming from Europe dramatically declined in the past four decades, the proportion of all immigrants who were Asian increased from 9 percent in 1960 to 25 percent in 1970 and 44 percent in 1980. Between 1980 and 1990, Asians made up close to 50 percent of all immigrants to the United States. The number one country in terms of origins of immigrants was Mexico, but the Philippines and South Korea were second and third respectively. Three other Asian countries— China, India, and Vietnam—were among the top ten sources of U.S. immigrants in the 1980s. As Asian immigrants have become naturalized citizens, many of them have brought nuclear and extended family members to the United States as well.[2]

Historical and Cultural Differences

Unlike other minority groups, Asian Americans have neither a common language nor a predominant religion. Most Korean immigrants are Christian, although many of them were not active in churches until coming to the United States. In contrast, only a few Chinese immigrants are Christians upon their arrival here. Many Chinese immigrants of recent decades arrived with no religious affiliation at all, although some practiced Buddhism, as do many Japanese Americans. Among the religions brought to the United States by Indian and Pakistani immigrants are Hinduism, Islam, Sikhism, Jainism, and Zoroastrianism, as well as various forms of Christianity. The Vietnamese were influenced by Confucianism and subsequently by French Catholicism, but Vietnam is predominantly Buddhist, as are Cambodia and Thailand.[3] Upward of 40 percent of the initial wave of Vietnamese immigrants, however, were Catholic,[4] as are the majority of Filipino immigrants.[5]

Nearly all Asian Indians and Pakistanis speak English, as do most Filipinos. The Filipino language of Tagalog, however, along with Chinese, Korean, and Vietnamese, was represented in the top ten non-English languages spoken in the United States as of 1990.[6]

In addition to their diversity in language and religion, Asian Americans have varied histories both in terms of their experiences with imperialism in their countries of origin and their experiences of segregation in the United States. Korea and certain provinces of China were at one time occupied by the Japanese. Vietnam was a Chinese colony for nearly a millennium. It was subsequently a French colony for almost a century and then was subjected to the military action of the United States in the 1960s. India gained its independence from Great Britain in 1947 after being a colony for nearly a century. The Philippines was a Spanish colony for more than 350 years, then became a colony of the United States following the Spanish-American War of 1898, and did not gain its independence until 1946. Chinese immigrants come not only from mainland China but Taiwan and Hong Kong.

Overlaying these histories is the long-term history of Western colonialism, which, as Stephen Kim puts it, came in the form of the "three Ms": merchants, the military, and missionaries. From the fifteenth to the nineteenth centuries, European trade interests led to economic exploitation. Intensive missionary activity that began in the fifteenth century with Catholic religious orders reached its zenith in the nineteenth century with both Catholic and Protestant missionaries. The military action was thought necessary, especially in the 1800s, to protect both missionaries and merchants.[7]

> The so-called civilized nations of the world felt a strong mission, expressed in terms of "bringing light to these dark countries of superstition and hideous pagan practices." The western nations intruded upon Asian ways, often with cannon. Even the well-intended missionaries dealt with the Asian peoples with an air of moral, cultural, and spiritual superiority, and they dared to undo and disgrace thousand-year-old venerated traditions such as ancestor worship, whose significance far surpassed the understanding of the self-righteous missionaries. These self-righteous ones were few in number but were enough to warrant the Asian feeling that they were intruders with moral, cultural, and spiritual arrogance imposing a legacy of imperialism and colonialism.[8]

Roy I. Sano, aUnited Methodist bishop, has suggested that a remnant of the colonial mindset, which he terms "internal colonialism," persists in the United States today and is manifested in ongoing prejudice and racism.[9] In spite of significant degrees of assimilation by descendants of the earlier generations of Asian immigrants, newer immigrants encounter stereotypes and discrimination that belie their full acceptance in American society. Considering that it was not until the 1950s that Asian immigrants were allowed to become naturalized citizens, even as all other immigrants enjoyed this privilege, the resistance to new Asian Americans is perhaps not surprising.[10]

Within the United States, "hostility against Asian immigrants can be divided into seven categories: prejudice, economic discrimination, political disenfranchisement, physical violence, immigration exclusion, social segregation, and incarceration."[11] Because Chinese individuals were the first Asian immigrants, their history of mistreatment is the longest and most encompassing. In the words of Sucheng Chan, new arrivals were viewed as "beasts of burden, depraved heathens, and opium addicts."[12] Chinese immigrants of the 1800s were confined to segregated areas of large cities and even today many Chinese immigrants and Chinese Americans continue to live in "Chinatowns." Japanese immigrants were the next to arrive and ultimately, as Japanese Americans, experienced the most severe form of segregation in their confinement to concentration camps during World War II.

In terms of more recent immigrants, Koreans and Southeast Asians typically live in ethnic enclaves in urban areas, partly by choice and partly because of limited options. Filipino and Asian Indian immigrants, however, are more likely to live in suburban areas, where they are distributed among the general population. These immigrants also tend to have professional backgrounds and to be more middle class in educational and economic terms. Vietnamese immigrants, in contrast, occupy the lowest rungs of the socioeconomic ladder among Asian Americans.[13]

Immigrant Religious Organization

For the sake of their own survival, both the Chinese and Japanese immigrants of the nineteenth century formed a variety of community organizations and mutual aid associations. Some of these performed a religious function. The Chinese, because of the strong emphasis on ancestral ties, placed priority on rites of passage and especially on funerals. According to Chan,

> It was possible for the district and family associations to serve religious or quasi-religious needs because popular Chinese religion is a syncretist amalgamation of Confucian, Taoist, Buddhist, and [spirit] beliefs. All that a believer requires is an altar with a deity and a metal pot for holding sticks of incense. There are no regularly scheduled worship services—although there are many festivals of religious significance—or much of an organized priesthood. Individuals can simply go to temples or pray in front of altars as their spiritual needs or particular occasions demand.[14]

Japanese immigrants, in contrast, were overwhelmingly Buddhist. In California, Young Men's Buddhist Associations and at least one Young Women's Buddhist Association were established in the 1890s. The North American Buddhist Mission was legally incorporated at this time, subsequently changing its name to the Buddhist Church of San Francisco, then the Buddhist Mission, and, finally, in 1944, to the Buddhist Churches of America. The term "church," however, was only an appropriated term to further acceptance in American society.[15]

Christian churches began competing with Chinese and Japanese religious groups in 1851 when a group of Presbyterians organized Bible classes in San Francisco for the Chinese population. A mission was opened in 1852, closed in 1857, and reopened in 1859. Shortly thereafter, Baptists, Methodists, and Congregationalists also began working among Asian immigrants. Only in Hawaii, however, were Asian Christians permitted to function as church pastors; in California, they could serve as assistants at most.[16]

Korean immigrants who arrived as Christians actively evangelized fellow immigrants who were not Christian and quickly moved to establishing churches. A Korean Methodist Church was organized in Los Angeles in 1905 and a Korean Presbyterian Church in 1906. In Hawaii, a Korean Episcopal Church was organized in 1905 and a Korean Christian Church in 1917.[17]

In the 1920s, Filipino immigrants formed numerous associations that, while not churches, had Christian overtones. In fact, one of the associations was named the Filipino-American Christian Fellowship. Although the majority of Filipinos were Catholic, they had developed a distinctive Catholicism that did not merge well with American Catholic churches. By and large, the immigrants' spiritual needs were met by their own organizations.[18]

Pan-Asian Unity, Christian Diversity

Their many differences notwithstanding, in recent decades a pan-Asian consciousness has developed among Asian Americans, giving rise to a sense of unity and common identity. Pyong Gap Min identifies three factors that have contributed to this development: "(a) commonalities in values; (b) similar treatment from both government agencies and the general public; and (c) the internal need for collective strategies to protect their economic, political, and other interests."[19]

With regard to common cultural values, Min points out that "Asian Americans are more or less group-oriented, in sharp contrast to the individualism that characterizes American values. Other Asian values include filial piety, respect for authority, self-control and restraint in emotional expression, emphasis on educational achievement, shame as a behavioral influence, high regard for the elderly, and the centrality of family relationships and responsibilities."[20] A premium is also placed on conformity and group harmony.

These values have relevance for Asian Americans' engagement with Christianity in the United States. One might predict that they would foster spiritual piety, congregational cohesion, deference to church leadership, and openness to charity and service. Religiously based social activism, however, would be less likely. And, indeed, this turns out to be the dominant profile. At the same time, community is a key value and practice of Asian American Christians.

Most Korean and Filipino immigrants bring their Christian faith to the United States, as do some Asian Indians and large numbers of Southeast Asians. Other immigrants convert after taking up residency here. Of the 10.2 million Asian Americans counted in the 2000 census, a substantial percent have no religious affiliation at all. Around 28 percent continue to practice Buddhism, Hinduism, Islam, or other non-Christian religions. Significantly, the proportion practicing these religions has nearly doubled since 1990, while the proportion of Asian Americans who are Christian has declined from 63 percent in 1990 to about 43 percent in 2001.[21] Still, approximately 4.6 million are Christian. Of the total population, at least 1,700,000 (17 percent) are Catholic; 2,663,000 (26 percent) are estimated to be evangelical Protestant, while only about 200,000 (2 percent) belong to the six largest mainline Protestant denominations.[22]

Asian Indian immigrants, who greatly outnumber immigrants from Pakistan and Bangladesh, are unusual in that many of those who are Christian join U.S. congregations that have ties with the Christian churches of India. As Raymond Brady observes, "During the late 1980s and the 1990s, congregations and parishes established their own American dioceses, synods, judicatories, and national fellowship groups and affiliated with churches in India: the Mar Thoma church, the Malankara Syrian Orthodox church, various pentecostal groups, the Brethren Assemblies, Syro-Malabar and Syro-Malankara Catholics, the Knanaya parishes, the Church of South India, and the Southern Asia Caucus of the United Methodist Church."[23]

Other Indian pastors and congregants affiliate with American denominations, especially Methodist, Episcopalian, and Catholic churches but, notes Brady, while "these Christians are finding their place in American Christianity, the process is fraught with complexity, disappointment, [and] misunderstanding," as well as "hope and potential."[24]

Approximately 37 percent of Asian American Christians are Catholic, with the largest number by far being Filipino, followed by Vietnamese, Indian, and Chinese, then Korean, and lastly Japanese. Although the Catholic Church established its first mission to Chinese immigrants in California in the 1880s, Asian Americans have largely been an invisible and unrepresented population in the Church at the national level. To date, no Asian American has been elevated to the rank of bishop. The Second Vatican Council's emphasis on multiculturalism, combined with the large numbers of new Catholic immigrants, has led to somewhat more attention being given to their presence in recent years, largely through the church's Office of Migration and Refugee Services. Some Asian American Catholics have challenged the appropriateness of being housed under this unit, however, given that many of them have been here for two generations or more.

In 2001, in what was a significant recognition of the growing numbers of Asian American Catholics, the United States Catholic Bishops issued a pastoral letter entitled "Asian Pacific Presence: Harmony in Faith." The letter proposed enhanced leadership roles for Asian American Catholics, called for a restructuring of the church to provide greater visibility, and affirmed the importance of enculturation, that is, the expression of aspects of indigenous cultures in Catholic worship.[25] Less acceptable to the church hierarchy, however, is the practice of popular or folk Catholicism, which is common especially among Filipinos. This popular Catholicism bears close resemblance to the popular Catholicism of Mexican Americans.[26] Other Asian Americans also draw on their cultural heritages, though not always with a conscious awareness of doing so.

Both Catholic Asian Americans and those who have become part of mainline Protestant denominations have experienced some of the same frustrations as African Americans, Latinas/os, and Native Americans. That is to say, Asian Americans are not unfamiliar with the imperial attitudes and practices of established, predominantly white churches. Accordingly, some members have become active in Asian American caucuses within these denominations, while others participate in extra-church organizations such as the Filipino Federation of America or the Hmong-American National Catholic Association. On the positive side, Protestant congregations and Catholic parishes alike have played an important role in sponsoring Southeast Asian immigrants in recent decades. For many such immigrants, their relationships with church-affiliated families are the primary avenue for entering into American society.

The majority of Chinese and Korean American Christians have opted for conservative Protestant congregations; most Chinese Americans prefer independent, nondenominational congregations, while most Korean Americans affiliate with conservative denominations and sects. Altogether, there are approximately 3,000 Korean, 700 Chinese, and 200 Japanese Christian congregations in the United States.[27] "Congregation" in this context does not necessarily imply ownership of a church building, for many Asian American congregations worship in the building of another congregation. To date, Korean churches are the most studied of Asian American congregations; other East Asian Protestants, however, appear to have many characteristics in common.

The evangelical and fundamentalist churches of East Asians perform important functions of identity formation and maintenance in a society in which members are minorities. Many congregations conduct worship in their first language. Many have adopted the evangelical "cell-group" structure in which the membership is divided into small groups, each of which meets on a regular basis in a member's home for food and fellowship. The cell groups also constitute a social service network in which needs and problems of members ranging from housing to legal issues to employment needs to child care are addressed. Women typically host these meetings, but otherwise are relegated to traditional roles of cooking, teaching Sunday school, and administering social services. Some congregations allow women to become deaconesses, but none permit ordination of women. For Korean men, especially, who as immigrants are often downwardly mobile, leadership roles in the church restore a degree of status.[28]

Religious Syncretism

Outward appearances notwithstanding, Asian American evangelicalism is shaped by sources different from those of white evangelicalism. The values of Confucianism influence Korean, Chinese, Japanese, and Vietnamese Christians alike. Shamanic indigenous religions have also influenced the cultures of China and Korea, as has Shintoism the culture of Japan. In addition to these traditions are Taoism and Buddhism. Jung Young Lee, for example, points to evidence of various traditions in the worship practices of Korean American Protestants:

> Our spontaneous prayers on almost every occasion and our cease-less meditation in every walk of life are deeply influenced by the Buddhist way of life. Our love of music and passionate desire for singing in the church and at other social gatherings comes from that part of our heritage rooted in indigenous religion, known as *mutang,* or shamanism.[29]
>
> The emphasis in Korean Christianity on healing, on charismatic appeals in preaching and prayers, on material blessings through spiritual power, and on the experience of ecstatic trance during worship are all results of shamanistic influence.... Shamanism as an internal character of the Korean ethos will never disappear, but will continue to reappear in different forms in contemporary life, for it is the native religion of the Korean people.[30]

David Ng suggests that the Confucian idea of *li* is central in Chinese culture and religious perspectives, as well as other East Asian cultures. Ng writes that, "Infused into this one word are two or more thousand years of understanding of what enables people to live in community. Much more than formal acts in social settings, *li* symbolizes a whole way of thinking about how people relate to each other and practice respect, reciprocity, mutuality and, ultimately, community."[31]

Not only *li,* but the Five Virtues of Confucianism, Ng asserts, are embedded in the worldviews of first- and second-generation Asian North

Americans. These virtues are: (1) being humane or benevolent, (2) acting righteously, (3) acting with propriety or observing rites, (4) exhibiting wisdom, and (5) being mutually faithful.

> Each of these virtues, when practiced properly, requires the individual to accomplish these in relation to other people, that is, in community. To be humane or to reach self-fulfillment is to become a person who is benevolent—one whose actions benefit others. Righteousness, doing the right thing, is to act justly toward others. Propriety comes from properly acting out one's principles. In other words, when one's principles are acted on, they become real. The original purpose of rites was to provide structures and forms for proper actions. Propriety or right rituals and actions are understood socially; propriety is performed in public and for the sake of right relationships. Similarly, wisdom and mutual faithfulness suggest virtues that an individual accomplishes for the sake of right relationships or the practice of community. The Five Virtues are not abstract principles existing for their own sake; they are done in community and they enhance relationship. To be a good person is to be a person in community acting for the sake of the community.[32]

To these enduring Eastern influences, note Ng and Heup Young Kim, may be added "the circular symbols of *tai chi* and *yin-yang*."

> These symbols depict very well the Asian outlook of the wholeness and unity of life, wherein all things coexist in harmony and balance. The basic elements of life are vitalized by the cosmic life force and function interdependently. Day and night together make up a full day; male and female make up a social relationship; good and bad, suffering and joy, and life and death exist in balance in one's life. Even so, religion/life/ethics/spirituality (how can these be considered separately and without relationship to each other?) combine to make up a full life. This is *Tao*, "the Way." This is life.[33]

What the continuing influence of these concepts points to, argues Ng, is that persons of Chinese, Korean, Japanese, and Vietnamese heritage embody a pluralistic approach to life and religion. "To an Asian, syncretism, or the incorporating of new or outside elements into one's beliefs, is both positive and creative. It is not heresy."[34]

Asian American Theology

The handful of Asian American theologians who in recent years have sought to construct a distinctive Asian American Christian theology have done much not only to bring these influences to light, but to encourage and cultivate them. However, their syncretism emphasizes early forms of indigenous traditions, for while the residual cultural heritages of Asian Americans are very real, they have also been corrupted. Ng acknowledges that while "Confucian and other Asian religious and social values are communal, in practice, power, authority, and relationships often are structured into hierarchies. Men and elders dominate; women and children suffer the consequences."[35]

> In many Asian North American congregations, the ideal of a community of diverse elements in harmonious relationship is not fully realized. Asian practices have been influenced by thousands of years of interpretation of Confucian and other social systems of relationships. What originally were benevolent principles of mutuality, reciprocity, respect, and good will demonstrated by the practice of rites and proprieties have evolved into codes and regulations directing young people to obey their elders and women to submit to men. In regard to women, the Asian North American church has a long, long path to travel toward the ideal community of mutual respect and acceptance.[36]

Because the goal of community is so central in Asian American theology, most theologians embrace the methodology of storytelling, that is, the use of narrative and autobiography as primary sources; theology comes out of one's experience. But while the theologizing is biographical and autobiographical, it is not individualist. "It is communal and of necessity includes the lives of other persons and [one's] own life-in-community. Theology begins with their stories from within their social and cultural contexts."[37]

Asian American theologizing, in short, eschews the rationalistic, systematic theologizing of the West, giving more emphasis to spirituality, the intuitive, and indigenous religious and philosophical resources. At the same time, it commends attention on the part of Asian American Christians to matters of social injustice. Asian American theologians, reflecting on Asian Americans' experience as marginalized and oppressed peoples in the United States, are increasingly speaking of the need to be prophetic. Eleazar Fernandez, for one, observes:

> Asian American preachers must choose, and many have decided to do so, marginalization as a site of resistance and transformation. I say "must choose," because there is strong pressure both from the congregation and from the wider society for Asian American

preachers not to touch issues that rock the boat. Actually, in numerous quarters of Asian American churches and in the wider Asian American populace there is this discouragement of prophetic critique, for doing so is construed as being ungrateful for the benefits that Uncle Sam has bestowed. Thus, Asian American preachers have a task not only of linking the community's faith to the wider society's challenges, but also of raising the prophetic consciousness of their congregation.[38]

Raising consciousness necessarily entails criticizing the fundamentalism and attendant biblical literalism of many Asian American churches. Speaking specifically of Korean American churches, Jung Young Lee observes:

> The distinctive character of the worshipping community of Korean Christians can be summed up by three emphases: prayer life, musical interest, and ultrafundamentalistic biblicism. Both our prayer life and musical interest are deeply rooted in our traditional culture and religions, but our ultraconservative fundamentalistic biblicism came from the West. In the past these three distinctive emphases made Korean worship vital and added a spiritual dimension to preaching. Today it is apparent that the Korean church must be liberated from the untraconservative fundamentalistic doctrine it adopted from the first Western missionaries.[39]

Lee acknowledges that in Korea, this fundamentalism served a positive function in that it provided a strong Christian identity and "certitude in times of crisis and uncertainty." Even in the United States, fundamentalism made a contribution in that its emphasis on Bible study was a major factor in church growth. But, he says, "The downside is that the idea of 'the Bible alone' and the so-called self-hermeneutic, or interpreting biblical texts through the Bible, has incapacitated the Korean preacher's ability to be prophetic about the injustices of the world, and makes him or her ineffectual in communicating the profound implications of the Word for a changing world. Today's crucial issues such as social justice, human rights, women's liberation, and so on, are almost completely missing from most Korean sermons."[40]

In contrast, common themes in the writings of Asian American theologians include racism, ethnocentrism, marginality, and oppression. Theologians invoke the concept of *han,* a Korean word pointing to the pain and suffering that comes of having been treated unjustly. Speaking of the "agonies of Asian American communities," Andrew Sung Park defines *han* as "the deep inner wounds of a victim that are at once conscious and unconscious, individual and collective. The deep pain of *han*, which is often indescribable, shapes our mode of thinking as well as our attitude." Theology must start, he argues, "from the perspective of victims," which requires "hearing the voice of the voiceless and the suffering."[41] Thus, Park embraces "the unity of theory and practice" in what he terms "theopraxis."

> Theopraxis is living out God in our lives. The goal of theopraxis is to embody God's life. This means that we have to bring forth social and political changes until our society is filled with God's presence. Even liberation as salvation is secondary; "living out God" is primary. In the process of embodying God, we will experience liberation as a gift.
>
> Liberation can mean different things to the oppressed and the oppressors. For the oppressed, theopraxis means moving toward God through restoring self-respect and self-confidence, healing oneself and one's fellow oppressed, confronting the oppressors, and transforming the evil structure of the social system which perpetuates injustice and oppression. For the oppressors, theopraxis implies turning toward God via self-negation, relinquishing power, redistributing wealth, converting fellow oppressors, and dismantling the evil social customs, traditions, and systems.[42]

For most Asian American theologians, the defining concept is not liberation, but marginality.

> A theology of marginality is different from most liberation theologies, which seek only to liberate the poor and the oppressed through reaction. According to a theology of marginality, the liberation of marginal people is not possible without the liberation of central-group people from their exclusive thinking. Liberation is, then, a mutual process. The goal of marginal people, however, is more than liberation from central-group people, rather it is a harmonious coexistence of all people in a genuinely pluralistic society.
>
> The power of new marginality is love, which is willing to suffer redemptively by accepting others unconditionally as Jesus did on the cross. If justice is more important than love in liberation theology, love is more important than justice in marginal theology. Justice reacts to injustice but love responds to it; justice often demands revenge but love forgives; justice is often given by the law, while law is fulfilled by love. Justice and love are inseparable, for love includes justice. Likewise, marginality and liberation belong together.[43]

As Jung Young Lee uses the term, marginality has both negative and positive manifestations. The marginality that is created by the presence of a dominant "center" in human society is the objectionable form. However, original marginality and plurality are "the essence of creative order and God's intention."[44] In creation, diverse peoples are all marginal to God. But the practice of one group of humans creating a dominant center and marginalizing other humans is in violation of God's creation plan.

> The center that we seek is our [human] creation; it is based on an idea of sameness and singularity.... The denial of difference by those who seek the center excludes different people from their right of existence, their right to freedom, and their right to have their own space to make their own history and civilization. [45]

> For example, white Americans marginalize ethnic minorities because they value their singularity, whiteness, more than a broader plurality. This is white supremacy. The more similar to white, the more valued by the white.[46]

> If racial and gender difference is the base of creative order, the denial of such difference is the most serious sin of humanity.... The hierarchical ideology of domination is perversive to the original order of creation.[47]

Such centrality, Lee asserts, is precisely the condition of most churches—"Roman Catholic, Protestant, Evangelical, or liberal.... The church is deeply embedded in centralist motivation. Most are based on a centralist ideology and a hierarchical structure of belief, which both exclude and control the poor, minorities, and the powerless. This is contrary to the essence of Jesus Christ's intent. As Jesus Christ was a marginal person, the norm of the church should be marginality. A church based on the norm of centrality contradicts the church of Jesus Christ. The contemporary church, based on centralist motives, is the fundamental Christian problem needing resolution."[48]

The ideal church, in contrast, "will move away from centrality and return to the marginality from which it sprang." For the authentic church, in the final analysis, is "the community of God's marginal people."[49]

For Further Reading

Kwon, Ho-Youn, Kwang Chung Kim, and R. Stephen Warner, eds. *Korean Americans and Their Religions: Pilgrims and Missionaries from a Different Shore.* University Park: Pennsylvania State University Press, 2001.

Lee, Jung Young. *Marginality: The Key to Multicultural Theology.* Minneapolis: Fortress Press, 1995.

Matsuoka, Fumitaka. *Out of Silence: Emerging Themes in Asian American Churches.* Cleveland: United Church Press, 1995.

Min, Pyong Gap, and Jung Ha Kim, eds. *Religions in Asian America: Building Faith Communities.* Walnut Creek, Calif.: Alta Mira Press, 2002.

Ng, David. *People on the Way: Asian North Americans Discovering Christ, Culture, and Community.* Valley Forge, Penn.: Judson Press, 1996.

Phan, Peter C., and Jung Young Lee, eds. *Journeys at the Margin: Toward an Autobiographical Theology in American-Asian Perspective.* Collegeville, Minn.: The Liturgical Press, 1999.

Yang, Fenggang. *Chinese Christians in America: Conversion, Assimilation, and Adhesive Identities.* University Park: Pennsylvania State University Press, 1999.

NOTES

1. Pyong Gap Min, ed., *Asian Americans: Contemporary Trends and Issues* (Thousand Oaks, Calif.: Sage Publications, 1995), 15.

2. Ibid., 12.

3. Ibid., 25–26.

4. Jeffrey M. Burns, Ellen Skerrett, and Joseph M. White, eds., *Keeping Faith: European and Asian Catholic Immigrants* (Maryknoll, N.Y..: Orbis Books, 2000), 231.

5. Min, *Asian Americans,* 26.

6. Helen Rose Ebaugh and Janet Saltzman Chafetz, eds. *Religion and the New Immigrants: Continuities and Adaptations in Immigrant Congregations* (Walnut Creek, Calif.: Alta Mira Press, 2000), 14.

7. Stephen S. Kim, "Seeking Home in North America: Colonialism in Asia, Confrontation in North America," in *People on the Way: Asian North Americans Discovering Christ, Culture, and Community* (ed. David Ng; Valley Forge, Penn.: Judson Press, 1996), 6–7.

8. Ibid.

9. Ibid., 5.

10. A federal naturalization law passed in 1790 provided that only "white" persons could become naturalized citizens. In 1922, the United States Supreme Court ruled that Asians were not Caucasian and therefore could not become citizens. With the revocation of the Chinese Exclusion Act in 1943, Chinese immigrants were allowed to become citizens upon demonstrating English competency and knowledge of American history and the Constitution. Not until 1952, however, with the passage of the McCarran-Walter Act, was the 1790 law overturned, allowing other Asians to become naturalized citizens. Ronald Takaki, *A Different Mirror: A History of Multicultural America* (Boston: Little, Brown 1993), 273, 387, 400.

11. Sucheng Chan, *Asian Americans: An Interpretive History* (Boston: Twayne Publishers, 1991), 45.

12. Ibid.

13. Min, *Asian Americans,* 22–24.

14. Ibid., 64.

15. Ibid., 72–73.

16. Ibid., 73.

17. Ibid.

18. Ibid., 76–77.

19. Ibid., 30.

20. Ibid.

21. Barry A. Kosmin, Egon Mayer, and Ariela Keysar, "American Religious Identification Survey, 2001," The Graduate Center of the City University of New York, 8.

22. The figure for evangelicals is from Michael Luo, "Asian-American Churches Try Integration," Associated Press, *The Tribune* (Ames, Iowa), February 1, 2002, p. A2. Other figures are from the respective denominations, except for the Episcopal Church, which is estimated. In contrast to the 4.6 million who are Christian, estimates of the number who are Buddhist are as high as 3 million. See Pyong Gap Min and Jung Ha Kim, eds., *Religions in Asian America: Building Faith Communities* (Walnut Creek, Calif.: Alta Mira Press, 2002), 4.

23. Raymond Brady Williams, "Asian Indian and Pakistani Religions in the United States," in *Americans and Religions in the Twenty-First Century,* edited by Wade Clark Roof, The Annals of the American Academy of Political and Social Science 558 (July 1998): 186.

24. Ibid., 187. Also see Raymond Brady Williams, *Christian Pluralism in the United States: The Indian Immigrant Experience* (Cambridge: Cambridge University Press, 1996).

25. Thomas C. Fox, "Untold Story: New Pastoral on Asian- and Pacific-Americans Sheds Light on Overlooked Catholics," *National Catholic Reporter,* November 9, 2001, 13–16.

26. Examples of popular religion characteristic of both Mexican American and Filipino American Catholics are "Christmas novena prayers, a strong veneration of Mary, and worship filled with pageantry." See Leslie Wirpsa, "Filipinos Sing, Share Festive Foods, Teach Old Ways to Young," *National Catholic Reporter,* August 14, 1998, 3.

27. Luo, "Asian-American Churches." About 20 percent of Chinese immigrants are estimated to be Christian, most having converted in the United States.

28. For two excellent case studies see Fenggang Yang, "Chinese Gospel Church: The Sinicization of Christianity" and Victoria Hyonchu Kwon, "Houston Korean Ethnic Church: An Ethnic Enclave," in *Religion and the New Immigrants: Continuities and Adaptations in Immigrant Congregations* (eds. Helen Rose Ebaugh and Janet Saltzman Chafetz; Walnut Creek, Calif.: Alta Mira Press, 2000). Also see the introduction, 19.

29. Jung Young Lee, *Korean Preaching: An Interpretation* (Nashville: Abingdon Press), 138.

30. Ibid., 31.

31. David Ng, "A Path of Concentric Circles: Toward an Autobiographical Theology of Community," in *Journeys at the Margin: Toward an Autobiographical Theology in American-Asian Perspective* (eds. Peter C. Phan and Jung Young Lee; Collegeville, Minn.: The Liturgical Press, 1999), 85.

32. Heup Young Kim and David Ng, "The Central Issue of Community: An Example of Asian North American Theology on the Way," in *People on the Way: Asian North Americans Discovering Christ, Culture, and Community* (ed. David Ng; Valley Forge, Penn.: Judson Press, 1996), 30.

33. Ibid., 28.

34. Ibid., 27–28.

35. David Ng, ed., *People on the Way: Asian North Americans Discovering Christ, Culture, and Community* (Valley Forge, Penn.: Judson Press, 1996), 63.

36. Ibid., 105–6.

37. Ibid., 83, 86.

38. Eleazar S. Fernandez, "A Filipino Perspective: 'Unfinished Dream' in the Land of Promise," in *Preaching Justice: Ethnic and Cultural Perspectives* (ed. Christine Marie Smith; Cleveland: United Church Press, 1998), n.p.

39. Lee, *Korean Preaching,* 59.

40. Ibid., 58–59.

41. Andrew Sung Park, "Church and Theology: My Theological Journey," in *Journeys at the Margin: Toward an Autobiographical Theology in American-Asian Perspective* (eds. Peter C. Phan and Jung Young Lee; Collegeville, Minn.: The Liturgical Press), 166.

42. Ibid., 167–68.

43. Lee, Jung Young. *Marginality: The Key to Multicultural Theology* (Minneapolis: Fortress Press, 1995), 73.

44. Ibid., 104.

45. Ibid., 108.

46. Ibid., 109.

47. Ibid., 107, 105.

48. Ibid., 123.

49. Ibid., 121, 123.

—CHAPTER 8—
Women's Sacred Communities

In November of 2002, St. John's Lutheran Church in Des Moines, Iowa, hosted an ecumenical prayer service for peace. The speakers—five white men, six white women, and one African American man—included the bishops and head ministers of the local jurisdictions of many denominations: Catholic, Episcopalian, Lutheran (ELCA), Presbyterian, United Methodist, United Church of Christ, American Baptist, Christian Church/Disciples, Community of Christ Church, and Friends Meeting. But the denominational affiliation was far less significant than the gender of the speakers.

The five white men spoke first. They talked about Christ the King and the Prince of Peace. They were followed by the six white women, who spoke of the people of Iraq; of God's wish for a reconciled creation; of harmony, understanding, and love. One woman dared to observe that it was her first time standing behind a pulpit that was shaped as an eagle—the symbol, she noted, of American power and strength. In short, a service that began as patriarchal-church transitioned into women-church, laying the groundwork for the main preacher—Bishop Gregory Palmer, an African American United Methodist who spoke passionately of the need for a worldwide war against poverty and hunger.

A mere thirty years earlier, this service in all likelihood would have consisted of twelve white men speaking in monarchical language, while women were silent in the pews. The stories of Christian women in the United States have been partially told in earlier chapters—the stories of women of color in the chapters on the respective ethnic minority groups; the stories of white women in the chapters on the Imperial Church, because they have been members and agents of that church. But Christian women have their own stories to tell: white women have also been oppressed in the Imperial Church, and women of color experience oppressions beyond that of racism, both in the society at large and within their own communities and churches.

Not all women would agree that they have a separate story. Legions of women in evangelical churches, both seeker churches and traditional fundamentalist churches, and in mainline churches, as well, continue to affirm a patriarchal configuration that they believe to be sanctioned biblically. To what extent their endorsement of this theology and sociology is freely made and to what extent it is but a residue of cultural habit and church socialization is difficult to determine. But the reality is that for many women traditionally defined roles and doctrines provide a sense of security and comfort. In their world, there is scant acknowledgment of systemic inequity and oppression, for gender roles are considered to be ordained of God, not of men. They are the inheritors of a tradition that has served church power structures well—though it has ill-served the people at whose expense the male-dominated structures are preserved.

At the same time, it is precisely the critique of patriarchy that has fueled and continues to fuel the dissent of women who, since the late 1960s, have either left the church or are working to transform it. Many of those who have left have formulated their own individual spiritual practices, often drawing on Eastern or Native American traditions. Others have turned to neo-pagan or nature-based practices that replace a patriarchal God with a feminine Goddess and that promote egalitarian community. Those who have opted to retain a Christian identity, both those who remain within the church institution and those who do not, likewise are intent on creating sacred communities distinguished by nonhierarchical theologies, liturgies, and rituals.

In focusing on community-building, women who name themselves as feminists are making a statement that patriarchal and hierarchical configurations are inherently anti-community. Furthermore, they make a statement regarding the absence of spirituality in established churches. Thus, community-building and a transcendent feminist spirituality that affirms the worth of women and serves to empower women operate in tandem both in Christian and non-Christian feminist circles.

Feminist women who have chosen to retain their Christian identity have responded to the specific imperative to live community as they perceive it to be portrayed in the gospel. Their experience of the absence of lived community in organized churches has compelled them to be intentional in creating community—to embrace community as a way of life and to model alternative ways of being in relationship. For feminist Christians, community is both liberating and a means to liberation. Christian community, in other words, is understood to involve far more than slipping in and out of church every other Sunday.

As women have created community among themselves, they have come more and more to understand church to be "community" and community to be "church." This insight is generally more of a revelation for white women than for women of color. African, Native, and Latina women who have retained their indigenous communal orientations are more prone to understand community as central in their cultures and in the living of Christianity. White women, on the other hand, were subject to the individualistic emphasis of the majority society and of white evangelical Christianity.

Not that community-building among white women is an entirely new phenomenon. White Protestant women experienced a shift in their roles and status beginning in the mid-1800s. In spite of their continuing subordination, they regularly and creatively carved out space where, under the guise of "women's work," they established moral standards, provided social services, and sought to reform society. Some of them even were empowered to act as change agents in a manner that was subversive of the status quo in church and society alike.

Women's Space

The creation of women's space is as ancient as religion itself. Throughout history, women's space has variously been self-defined and involuntarily imposed. In the latter circumstances—if they were not destroyed through the witch hunts of medieval Europe, the slave trade and the institutions of slavery and segregation, the forced migrations and confinements to reservations—if they survived these ordeals, women invariably brought their resourcefulness to bear to create community with one another.

Such was the case for Roman Catholic women in Europe who, beginning in medieval times, escaped the societal devaluing of women by joining Church-sanctioned religious communities. Living a vowed life of poverty, celibacy, and obedience removed these individuals from the stereotypical views of women as carnal temptresses who needed to be controlled so as not to cause the downfall of virtuous men. It also removed them from the obligation of marriage to tyrannical men, the socially sanctioned mode of exercising control.

Conversely, women who took these vows found space in which to develop their spiritual lives through prayer and contemplation, as well as through service to those in need. In the 1800s, when millions of Catholics from Ireland, Germany, Italy, and Eastern Europe migrated to the United States, they were accompanied by members of religious orders who not only founded new communities, but hospitals, schools, and orphanages designed to meet the needs of the new immigrants. Following the social customs of the larger society, however, black Catholic women, if they wished to take vows, joined a separate order, the Oblate Sisters of Providence or Sisters of the Blessed Sacrament.

Ultimately, these institutions, and the religious orders themselves, were under the oversight of the male hierarchy of the Church, and more immediately, under the oversight of women superiors who often times had internalized a masculine mode of keeping subordinates in line. The vows that sisters took meant going without material comforts, foregoing family, and being obedient to rules formulated and enforced by a patriarchal structure. To the extent that women's spirituality was expressed, it was carefully circumscribed.

There were no complete counterparts in mainstream Protestantism to Catholic women's communities. The voluntary societies formed by Protestant women in the early 1800s performed charitable work, distributed Bibles, and raised funds to educate male ministers and support male missionaries, but this work was done primarily by married women whose full-time vocation was that of homemaker.[1] The wives of some missionaries did perform unofficial missionary roles both overseas and in Indian nations; some women even were regarded as missionaries in their own right.[2] But there was no taking of vows and no lifelong commitment.

During the intense revivalism of the early decades of the 1800s, as many as one hundred women became itinerant, evangelical preachers. Those who were white generally spoke to lower-class white audiences as they pursued the common evangelical mission of "creating a Christian nation." They received considerable support from male ministers in the Methodist and Baptist sects from which most of them came. But they were harshly condemned by ministers in the established denominations and by both lay men and women in middle-class churches. It was understood by all concerned, and accepted by the women preachers, as well, that under no circumstances would they be officially ordained.[3]

Black women preachers—Sojourner Truth, Jarena Lee, and Maria Stewart among them—also aspired to a "Christian nation," but for them the phrase had quite a different meaning: Evangelism meant not just the saving of individual souls, but the saving of America's soul through the elimination of both slavery and women's subordination. Several black women preachers did push for ordination.

During the first half of the 1800s, both northern and southern women were active in ecumenical efforts such as the American Tract Society, the American Bible Society, and the American Sunday School Union. Beginning in the 1830s, women organized moral reform societies to oppose prostitution and to work for temperance. At the same time, white southern women, especially, were actively involved in maintaining the system of slavery.[4] Women who joined the anti-slavery movement were very much the exception, but for those who did, it was this activity more than anything that raised their consciousness with regard to their own oppression as women. The result, in the 1840s, was the beginning of the women's rights movement and the creation of single-focus organizations to work for women's suffrage.

From the beginning, the pursuit of political rights was grounded in religious understandings. When two of the leading women abolitionists, Quakers Sarah and Angelina Grimké, were attacked not only for the content of their stands on slavery and racial prejudice, but for their "defiance of the traditional role of women" in taking their stand publicly, they responded with biblical commentary on the book of Genesis and the New Testament. Their theology asserted the equality of women and men, the sin entailed in one group of humans dominating another, and the wrongfulness of separate social spheres and duties based on gender.[5]

Lucretia Mott, a prominent Quaker and a leader of the Female Anti-Slavery Society, defied social conventions in bringing together black and white women from their respective churches. Mott herself preached in black churches and organized white women to provide support for black women's service projects. She became a sophisticated student of the Bible and critic of Christian doctrine, formulating a theological foundation for her positions on abolitionism, women's rights, and pacifism. Rosemary Radford Ruether writes that, for Mott,

> All of [the] doctrines of inherited sin, vicarious atonement, an exclusive divinity of Christ, and biblical inerrancy, as well as various ceremonial forms, are tools of clerical domination by which a priestly caste set themselves up to lord over others, preventing ordinary people from thinking for themselves; blocking the real message of the gospel, which is the call to a real transformation of the self and society into living ways of love, justice, and peace. This creates a system of religious hierarchy that justifies other forms of domination, denying the truth that we are all equal in this process of experiencing God's revelation in ourselves and doing our own work of redemptive change to overcome the real and concrete evils in and around us. For Mott, at the top of the list of such evils were slavery, oppression of blacks and Indians, subjugation of women, intemperance, and war.[6]

In 1840, Mott met Elizabeth Cady Stanton, another abolitionist who was committed to women's rights. Three years later, Stanton in turn met Susan B. Anthony, a Quaker teacher, and these three became the backbone of the women's rights movement. Stanton, who grew up Presbyterian, had learned to read the Bible in Greek when she was eleven years old. Exposed to evangelical revivalism as a teenager, she quickly rejected its emotionalism and subsequently developed her own radical and feminist reading of the

Bible.[7] Although Anthony preferred to keep religion separate from political matters, Mott and Stanton did not, and when the first women's rights convention was held in Seneca Falls, New York, in 1848, many of the speakers, one of whom was Sojourner Truth, spoke in religious terms. A theme throughout the deliberations was that women were both religiously and politically equal to men. According to Catherine Brekus, "Since God intended women to be 'man's equal,' they declared, they had a 'sacred right to the elective franchise.' Although early feminists phrased many of their arguments in the abstract language of natural rights, they also claimed that God has specially 'anointed,' 'sanctified,' and 'baptized' them to fight for a 'sacred cause.' As one woman explained, God had called her 'to restore the divine order to the world.'"[8]

Ultimately, Stanton rejected Christianity altogether to become a Unitarian. She presented her most stringent critique of Christianity in the commentaries she and a committee of religiously informed women wrote in the 1890s and published as *The Women's Bible*. In essence, writes Ruether, this document "came down clearly on the side of a condemnation of the Bible as a purely 'man-made' book whose primary effect has been to justify women's subjugation. Stanton believed the Christian clergy were so wedded to these texts that the church could not be reformed to support women's emancipation. For her, the greatest evil effect of Christianity has been in convincing women that self-sacrifice is their particular duty and calling. Against this view, she asserts that the first duty of women (as of men) is to self-development, not self-sacrifice."[9]

Male ministers were outraged by Stanton's "Bible," calling it the "work of the Devil." Her views were rejected by most of her peers in women's rights organizations as well, including the National American Women's Suffrage Association (NAWSA) in which she herself played a prominent role. "For the majority of the women members of the NAWSA, the linking of women's suffrage with an attack on the Bible was personally offensive and threatened to retard their efforts to win middle-ground American opinion."[10] In addition, Stanton's positions clashed with the prevailing societal views about "women's nature." Most women in the suffrage movement "not only wished to argue that the Bible was the great charter of female emancipation; but they were also deeply wedded to a view of women as superior to men, innately altruistic and loving."[11]

A Limited Sisterhood

This latter view was also prevalent among middle-class church women who were engaged in mission and various types of reform work during the so-called "golden age" of separate women's organizations and institutions. The period between 1870 and 1920 began with the flourishing of women's denominational and interdenominational mission societies, which supported single women in lifelong careers of mission work.[12] In the early twentieth century, some of the women serving abroad as missionaries, as well as those serving at home as deaconesses, began living together communally. Both in their living arrangements and in their extensive social service activity, these groups represented the closest parallel to Catholic religious communities, albeit with significant differences.[13]

By 1910, forty-four women's mission societies were in existence, with a collective membership of two million. Together these societies, some of which were interracial, had established "some 2100 schools, 75 hospitals, and 78 dispensaries, as well as orphanages, leper asylums, nurses' homes, and other institutions."[14] Some of the societies remained under the general mission structure of their denomination, but most had independent status and as such controlled their own budgets, selected their own leadership, and provided their own training. However, while they placed more emphasis on education and health care than male missionaries, women missionaries generally imparted the same mission perspective as men.

> For women who were immersed in the evangelical cultures in which they had grown up, the cause of spreading Christ's Gospel throughout the nation and the world was the most pressing, exciting, and fulfilling activity in which any Christian woman could possibly be engaged. Closely connected with the theme of religious commitment was the idea that it was essential to spread Christian civilization throughout the world. The form in which activist American Protestant church women embraced this unity of religion and culture was their passionate belief that "heathen women" must be rescued from the degradations that they were suffering in their own non-Christian cultures. The concomitant belief that only Christianization of these cultures and their adoption of the middle-class American emphasis on domesticity could improve the lives of women in foreign lands gave an added sense of urgency to the women's societies.[15]

Out of misguided activity sometimes come positive results. For the middle-class women involved in mission work—not only the missionaries themselves but the members and officers of the societies and the denominational department heads—the positives included the development of organizing and communication skills, the opportunity to travel, experience in exercising power, and a degree of status otherwise unavailable to them. Perhaps most important, however, was the bonding with one another that they experienced.

In the missionary societies, the sense of sisterhood typical of nine-teenth-century women who participated in common endeavors developed in several ways. First of all, members of the local societies forged close bonds as they met to enrich their spiritual life ... and learn about missions. In addition, visits from missionaries on fur-lough brought women living in isolated areas and small towns the strong sense that they were part of a great collective sisterhood. Volunteer women who went on to become officers and department heads ... became part of a regional and church-wide sisterhood of women with a strong sense of group identity. At the same time, the missionaries and deaconesses who undertook a lifetime religious vocation experienced their own sisterhood as single women in reli-gious service.[16]

In 1874, a new organization was formed that, even more than women's missionary societies, functioned as "women's church." The Women's Christian Temperance Union (WCTU) was born out of frustration that churches were failing to take a strong enough stand against men's abuse of alcohol, a situation that compromised the economic and physical security of women and their families. At its founding convention, the WCTU was described as a "religious movement," as a gathering of "women of Galilee." "Ours," its founders said, "is a most solemn call. Our God is upon our side."[17] Three years later, one WCTU chapter reported that it was conduct-ing a "Woman's Church," which had been attended by fifty thousand people over the previous year, and which was presided over, not by a male minister, but by a "shepherdess": "It is emphatically a company of believers, whose spiritual and temporal interests are in the hands of seven women—dea-conesses they might well be called—members of the Woman's Temperance League, of Cleveland. In this spiritual home believers are baptized, the Lord's Supper is administered, and the dead have been buried. Pastors of the various churches cordially officiate on these occasions, but their sermons are with the 'Women's Kingdom.'"[18]

The WCTU did not actually establish a separate church; members con-tinued to be a part of Protestant churches in order to "criticize the patriarchy of the church from within." But according to WCTU's leader, Francis Willard, they practiced a "religion of compassionate action" that derived from their understanding of God's "mother-heart." In her book, *Woman in the Pulpit*, Willard's message was that "male clergy had perversely translated God's mes-sage of love, life, and compassion into dogma, creeds, formulas, exegesis, and martyrdom." God, she said, had "both a male and female nature"; therefore, it followed that there should be both male and female clergy in God's church.[19]

The WCTU had its own Evangelistic Department and hired evangelists, some of whom were ordained ministers, to preach both temperance and the gospel.[20] It also developed a broad agenda of social action, beyond the initial focus on temperance, which included advocating for women's suffrage and lobbying for the passage of local, state, and federal legislation. The organization resisted the notion that women should have to marry to obtain economic security and argued that "all occupations should be open to women on an equal basis." But at the same time it asserted the equality of men and women, its singular rationale—at least its *publicly* offered rationale—for women's involvement in the public sphere was to "protect the home." Women were represented as having "a special perspective to offer as nurturers especially concerned with issues affecting children and other women."[21] Both positions—that men and women were equal and that women were spiritually and morally superior to men—were invoked by WCTU members, "sometimes in the same breath," to argue for the inclusion of women in positions of authority.[22]

By the turn of the century, the WCTU was the largest women's organization in the country and had trained a generation of women in "the arts of political organization and action." But with the death of Frances Willard in 1898 the organization began a decline that continued over the next forty years, during which time its earlier focus on women's religious authority was abandoned and its legislative advocacy on behalf of social reform diminished.[23] Long before these changes took effect the WCTU was overshadowed by yet another group, the General Federation of Women's Clubs, organized in 1892. Soon after the General Federation came into being, the affiliated clubs shifted their focus from literary and cultural activities to involvement in civic affairs. But they held to the same rationale for women's public involvement as the WCTU.[24]

Through these varied involvements of the 1800s, many women developed a gender consciousness in terms of the contributions they could make to church and society. The goal of most middle-class white women, however, was to foster in the society as a whole the stereotypical qualities that society had assigned to them. This "social feminism," as it has been called,[25] stood in sharp contrast to the feminism of Mott and Stanton and Anthony, which demanded "the removal of legal disabilities affecting women as a matter of basic human rights"[26] and which extended concern for human rights to the entire human family.

It was the approach of social feminism that garnered the votes of men for passage of the Nineteenth Amendment in 1921.[27] But in the process, as Ruether points out, "The belief that civil rights for all are founded on the 'natural' or essential equality of all humans was surrendered by many of the new women's leaders. Instead, they argued that woman's moral superiority calls for her enfranchisement in order to uplift society."[28] "Moral superiority," however, was understood to be an attribute of white, middle-class women; their platform was fundamentally racist and classist, excluding, as it did, blacks, Indians, and immigrants.

Black, Feminist, and Christian

Needless to say, the feminist consciousness of black women was of a different order, inasmuch as it was concerned not only with the status of women but the status of black people in general in the United States. The church was an even more critical arena for empowerment of black women than for white. Indeed, with few exceptions, it was the one institution where black women *and* men had a degree of autonomy and could exercise authority. Because the Black Church adopted the patriarchal structure of white Christianity, women were excluded from ordained ministry, the one exception being the AME Zion Church. But in every other respect, women were the life-force of black churches.

From the 1860s to the mid-1950s—and even before, during the years of slavery—the Black Church was understood to be coterminous with the black community. Scarcely a distinction was made between church work and community work—"community work," as defined by Cheryl Gilkes, being all types of activity designed to alleviate the oppressive circumstances of black life in America.[29] Much of this activity was carried out by church women in black Methodist denominations and regional Baptist organizations. In 1895, a number of black Baptist groups were united to create the National Baptist Convention, making it the largest and most influential of the black denominations. In 1900, the National Baptist Women's Convention was established, creating a space where black women's self-worth was affirmed and their own sisterhood fostered.

In her study of this convention, Elizabeth Higginbotham finds that black women's feminist views were expressed in critiques of the patriarchal chauvinism of the Black Church and in interracial cooperation with the mission work of white Baptist women. Throughout the early decades of the twentieth century, the Women's Convention and its state and local counterparts were actively involved in urban reform movements. As individuals, the members also expressed their theological commitments to "racial uplift" and empowerment through the network of "secular" women's clubs known as the National Association of Colored Women. Furthermore, black Baptist women became religious-political missionaries to white America as their "practical Christianity" was conjoined with democratic ideals to contest white supremacy and to advocate for civil rights.[30]

One of the lasting contributions of the Women's Convention was the establishment of a national Women's Day, proposed by its prominent leader, Nannie Helen Burroughs, who had observed the tradition in Baptist women's state conventions. While this annually designated day was in part an occasion to raise funds for foreign missions, notably to Africa and the Caribbean, its primary function was to cultivate women's speaking and leadership abilities. It also assured, as Gilkes notes, that on at least one day of the year, every black congregation—ultimately in white denominations as well as black—would hear a woman speak from the pulpit with a voice of authority.[31]

The Church of God in Christ (COGIC), founded at the turn of the century, from the beginning appointed "organizers" of women's work, a reflection of the belief held by church leaders that "women should be led by women." This system, writes Gilkes, then "evolved into a separate women's convention whose jurisdiction and officers parallel precisely the authority of the elders and bishops of the church." Prominent among the early leaders of the convention was Mother Lillian Brooks Coffey ("mother" being a honorific title commonly given to older, highly respected women in black churches), whose advocacy of women's suffrage on religious grounds has been compared to Lucretia Mott's.[32] The "feminist biblical tradition" of black women, as Gilkes terms it, was uniquely apparent in the creation of a book by COGIC women in which all the anonymous women referenced in the Bible were given names and in which they "expanded upon the perspectives of women in the Bible."[33]

In contrast to black church women, beginning in the 1920s middle-class white women considered that there was no longer a need for separate women's organizations inasmuch as equality with men, it was presumed, would soon be secured. Accordingly, they opted for assimilation into gender-inclusive bodies. Within the churches, this decision was not always voluntary. Beginning in 1910 and continuing for several decades, autonomous women's missionary units were stripped of funding and integrated into general denominational mission structures, which is to say, into "male-governed agencies" that were taken to be the "*real* church organizations." Especially in the earlier decades of the century, these actions represented an intentional undermining of women's national leadership by men who were threatened by the demonstrated capability of women. The Presbyterian and Congregationalist women's mission societies were among those that succumbed to this turn of events.[34]

In later years, Theressa Hoover, the head of the United Methodist Women's Division, remarked that, "Despite varying degrees of resistance and expressed outrage, the women leaders were in most cases co-opted. The formalities were of course courteous," and professional churchwomen were assured of continuing significant roles in mission programs and on general boards. Laywomen, however, "soon discovered that they had lost the major, and in most cases the *only,* real female power base in their denominations."[35]

In the 1960s, the integration of women's units that had survived co-optation was a voluntary choice. Episcopal Church Women (ECW), for one, came to feel at this time that the power to control their own division was at the expense of being able to influence change in the denomination as a whole; accordingly, they recommended that ECW and the General Division of Women's Work be dismantled.[36] Women in other denominations, with the exception of United Methodists, took similar steps. But as Hoover observed in the early 1980s, "The integration of separate women's missionary boards ... has not in itself restructured the relations of women and men in the churches positively." On the contrary, the change had "a powerful negative effect." Not only did integration weaken women's previous commitment to missions, but it "lessened their sense of community with other women in the United States and around the world."[37]

The major black denominations retained auxiliary women's divisions that continue to carry out mission, evangelizing, and educational activities, though Baptist and Methodist auxiliaries have notably less autonomy than those of the Church of God in Christ.

A Change of Mission

At the same time that women in mainline white churches were relinquishing—or being relieved of—traditional mission work, they were assigning new meanings to the very term "mission." First, they began to acknowledge the arrogance in the assumptions of the past century, developing in their stead an appreciation of other cultures and a respect for self-determination. Second, church women began to consider the ways in which they had themselves been colonized in the church; how they themselves had participated, as members of the church, in the colonizing of others; and what was needed to accomplish their own liberation and the liberation of other marginalized people. "Mission" became less a condescending practice of the privileged and more an exploration of how to be in solidarity with people, both politically and spiritually, in their struggles for freedom.

The loss of traditional women's divisions did not mean that women in the affected denominations did not share in this new understanding of mission. Women's caucuses were organized both in mainline denominations and in the National Council of Churches; these caucuses provided forums for exploring feminist issues and developing agendas for action. But the transformations were especially evident in the mid-decades of the twentieth century in three arenas: the Women's Division of the United Methodist

Church, the ecumenical organization known as Church Women United, and the movement of Catholic lay women called the Grail.

The Methodist Woman's Division of Christian Service was formed in 1940 following the merger in 1939 of three smaller Methodist denominations, including the Methodist Episcopal Church, South, which had broken away over the issue of slavery in the 1850s. The union was accomplished only with a compromise that created a segregated black jurisdiction, thus assuring that no black bishops would be appointed to southern Methodist conferences. The Central Jurisdiction, as it was called, in turn created its own Woman's Society of Christian Service.[38] Not until 1968, when the Methodist Church merged with the Evangelical United Brethren Church to become the United Methodist Church, was the separate black jurisdiction abolished. Since that time, the United Methodist Church has had the largest African American membership of any of the mainline Protestant denominations, which has also meant a strong presence of African Americans in the Women's Division.

Among the several departments of the earlier Woman's Division of Christian Service was one called Christian Social Relations. For twenty-eight years, this unit was headed by one woman, Thelma Stevens, who worked diligently to bring about improved race relations. Her efforts laid the groundwork for the Women's Division of later years—at least for that portion of the division that survived the trend of gender integration. In 1964, the Methodist Church was restructured in a manner that removed both the Home Mission and Foreign Mission departments from the Woman's Division, as it was then called, leaving only the department of Christian Social Relations. The Woman's Division itself was preserved, however, with financial sovereignty; a portion of the funds the division raised were transferred to the relocated mission programs, but a significant portion remained with the division to be used at its discretion. The reduced Woman's Division was restructured at this time into three units: Finance, Program and Education for Christian Mission, and Christian Social Relations.

With the 1968 merger, the name was changed to the Women's Division and new leadership was appointed: Theressa Hoover as the head of the entire division and Peggy Billings as head of Christian Social Relations. Both served until the early 1980s; together, they made the Women's Division the cutting edge of the entire denomination, and to a large extent, of American Protestantism.

The years from 1968 to 1972 were especially volatile ones. Opposed by much of the church hierarchy as well as by secular women who were skeptical of organized religion, the challenge became, as Billings put it, "to rebuild the house we were living in without moving out! We were determined not to leave." At the same time, they were determined to embrace the theological paradigm shift that was taking place around the world as people of color challenged both imperialism and the normative claims of Western theology. Part of embracing the new paradigm of liberation theologies, including the emergent women's liberation theology, meant being "active in the places where changes were coming."[39]

Changes were coming from all directions: the black power movement, the United Farm Workers movement, the American Indian Movement, the National Welfare Rights Organization, the women's rights movement, the war against poverty, the anti-war movement against involvement in Viet Nam, even the family farm movement and the labor movement. In all these places representatives of the Women's Division could be found. They were also at the United Nations, the World Council of Churches, the National Council of Churches, Church Women United, and the Grail headquarters. And they were in Africa, China, the Middle East, and Central America.

Throughout the 1970s, the Women's Division conducted study missions, provided mediation teams in places of conflict, acted as intermediaries, funded other individuals and groups engaged in social justice efforts, worked collaboratively with other faith organizations, and proposed resolutions that were adopted by the denomination as a whole. Among these resolutions was one that led to the establishment of the Commission on the Status and Role of Women, which was charged with working for justice for women both in the church and outside it; another in support of the Equal Rights Amendment; one that called U.S. involvement in Viet Nam "a profound violation of the Christian faith;" and another that committed the denomination to the elimination of racism.[40]

In 1972, the Women's Division became the policy-making body for United Methodist Women, the network of local units that were to be found in nearly every United Methodist Church, all of which received program resources from the national office regarding women's concerns and other social justice issues. In this way, millions of women became conduits of the ideas and activism of the national body, whether they always agreed with the national staff or not. The Women's Division was especially attentive to facilitating the involvement of younger women, working women, and ethnic minority women. Theressa Hoover herself was African American.

Starting in 1972 and continuing until 1979, the Women's Division conducted a series of Ethnic Women's Seminars, five with Native American women, five with Hispanic women, four with Asian Americans, and two with African Americans, the smaller number with this last group reflecting its stronger presence in the Women's Division already. Some seminars were mono-cultural, which enabled women to affirm their own cultural heritages; others were cross-cultural, permitting them to learn from one another and discover common bonds. Through prayer, worship, song, and scriptural study, the seminars became, for the moment, small Christian communities. Many participants were subsequently elected to offices at various church levels, thus expanding the process of community-building.

Since the 1980s, the Women's Division, like most social justice groups, has become less vocal and less public. Nonetheless, its prophetic witness during a turbulent time stands as a model of "spirit-church."[41]

The closest parallel to the UMC Women's Division is the ecumenical organization Church Women United (CWU). Though CWU started as a Protestant group, Catholic women have participated since the Second Vatican Council, as have Orthodox women and women from other smaller Christian bodies. CWU has been a prophetic voice of Christian women in the United States for more than sixty years, and today is a presence in some 170 countries around the world. Founded in 1941, the national body quickly became a strong advocate of peace abroad and civil rights at home. Throughout that decade, CWU strongly supported the United Nations, while local integrated units in the Deep South met "behind closed doors" in violation of their communities' segregation codes.

During the McCarthyism of the 1950s, CWU prepared an alternative Christian declaration of loyalty that said, in part, "Many valiant defenders of God-given freedom are being wrongfully accused....We will uphold them.... We do our own thinking.... We dare to speak out." In appreciation for this stand, President Dwight D. Eisenhower spoke at their national assembly in 1953, by which time CWU was organized in eighteen hundred communities in all forty-eight states. In the 1960s, the national office provided teams of persons trained in civil rights to work with local units in advancing the civil rights agenda; joined in establishing the Farm Worker Ministry in California to support farm worker organizing; and sent delegates abroad to develop relations with women in other nations.

Church Women United, along with the United Methodist Women's Division, was one of the earliest church-related groups to respond to the issues being raised by the emerging women's liberation movement in the late 1960s. Its response took the form of organizing consciousness-raising groups, exploring strategies to address sexism in its respective church structures, and consulting with cutting-edge feminist thinkers.[42] These activities led in the early 1970s to multiple gatherings of "Women Doing Theology," some of them jointly sponsored with the Grail movement. In that decade, CWU also implemented a listening process that involved local units in all fifty states in the development of a "People's Platform for a Global Society," a document that called for nationwide attention to quality of life issues.

Following up on this theme, the focus of the 1980s was elimination of the root causes of poverty among women and children. Central to this effort were the training sessions CWU designed to cultivate an awareness on the part of local members of the difference between the traditional service work of church women and structural change. At the same time, an office was opened in Washington, D.C. to facilitate legislative advocacy. In the 1990s, some 30,000 women had input into a process of analyzing proposed legislative reforms around issues of health care. In addition, 150 women were trained to become community leaders in facilitating social and economic change at the local level.

Church Women United is best known for its annual celebration of World Day of Prayer, which was originated in 1887 by Ella James. Its intention, then as now, was that the prayers of this day be grounded in a spirit of contrition for the role of the U.S. government in contributing to the realities of suffering and pain in various places in the world. Through this event, as well as other special observances and study guides, members of local CWU units have been involved over the years in theological reflection and action. As the membership has aged, the local emphasis on peace and justice activism has been diluted; still, the agenda of educating members about the circumstances of women around the world remains strong and serves to cultivate a sense of connection with those who struggle for life and liberty.[43]

Among Catholics in the 1940s and 1950s, leavening was provided by a movement of lay women known as the Grail. The Grail movement, which started in Holland in 1921, was brought to the United States in 1940. Here, a small group of women established a community on an acreage known as Doddrige Farm that was owned by the archdiocese of Chicago. In 1944, the community relocated to land that residents had purchased near Cincinnati, Ohio, where they developed a village that became known as "Grailville."

The Grail movement was devoted to developing a lay women's apostolate, that is, to preparing young lay women to embrace Christianity as a complete way of life and to model that life through their work in the larger world. Grailville became the training base for young women as they learned of the movement from Grailville speakers who traveled around the country lecturing and meeting with small groups of interested individuals.

It was a radical proposition in the context of the times, when clericalism held sway and lay people as a whole were nonparticipants in matters of liturgy, theology, and governance. The Grail differed from traditional women's religious communities in several important respects. Participants in the movement neither wore habits nor lived in convents. The Grail community owned its own property and was not subject to the canonical laws of the Church. Both married and single women—whether committed to celibacy or not—were admitted to the variety of training sessions held at Grailville that ranged from weekend retreats to two-week seminars to summer-long or year-long (after 1968, semester-long) residencies. Those who resided at Grailville—for the year, or permanently—performed manual work that enabled the community to be self-sustaining. They also "lived the liturgy," meaning that daily life revolved around mass, prayer, music, and contemplation. The year-long residents—usually sixty-five in number—were divided into "family" units of eight to ten individuals who lived a communal lifestyle within the context of the larger community.

But the intention was that upon completing their training and community living experience, participants would venture out to organize new intentional communities of lay women who embraced the Grail vision. Some in fact did so. In addition, between 1949 and 1963, thirteen centers were established in urban areas around the country. These centers typically provided communal living space, liturgical space and meeting rooms, and an art and book store. Grail community members initiated ventures ranging from buying co-ops to family support services to cultural programs to basic adult education. In addition to these centers, Grail "graduates" were sent out in teams to work in high schools, on college campuses, in factories, or wherever opportunities for apostolic work could be generated. Their work also extended overseas, where Grail women early on rejected the patronizing connotations of mission work, instead insisting on integrated congregations, emphasizing the oneness of the Church and of the world, and involving themselves in locally defined community development efforts.

From the beginning, the Grail welcomed black and Hispanic women to its training programs and established groups and centers in black and Latina/o communities. Young lay women from both middle-class and working-class backgrounds were empowered to assume leadership roles that, while challenging to many priests and bishops, were welcomed by others. Catholics from all walks of life, laity as well as clerics, journeyed to Grailville to participate in lively discussions and explorations of new and controversial ideas. The overall result was that Grail women helped lay the groundwork for the expanded roles for women and laity as a whole that came out of the Second Vatican Council.

As it did with the Women's Division of the United Methodist Church, the whirlwind of the 1960s brought major change to the Grail movement. In affirming the ability and the right of women to be active players in Christian work, Grail participants had become theologically sophisticated.

Core members embraced the liberation theology emerging from Latin America, particularly the notion of being on the side of the oppressed and the use of radical social analysis. What was not embraced was the model of base Christian communities; ironically, as more opportunities became available to women, fewer of them opted for community living. Involvement shifted from the Grail centers and groups to justice work as individual members became active in the civil rights, farm workers, and peace movements.

Prompted in part by the example set by Church Women United, the Grail began developing an overtly feminist stance in the 1970s. It also became more ecumenical, welcoming first Protestant and then Jewish participants. In 1972, the Grail and Church Women United cosponsored a week-long conference at Grailville called "Women Exploring Theology" that brought together seventy-five theologians, seminarians, church staff people, and prominent lay women. The two organizations then cosponsored "Women Exploring Theology" meetings throughout that year and the following year, involving women from all around the country. Throughout the decade, Grailville provided space for women to gather and to develop feminist theology; among the participants were Rosemary Ruether and Elisabeth Fiorenza.[44] Individual members of the Grail also participated in emerging organizations of Catholic women that more overtly challenged societal and church configurations and assumptions, of which more will be said shortly.

Important as these groups were, in the early 1980s women remained subordinate to men in their organized church life—be they black churches, Catholic, Orthodox, or white Protestant. At the same time, vastly greater numbers of women were exploring alternative ways of being church as they engaged in the exhilarating process of reinterpreting Christianity.

Feminist Liberation Theology

"Reinterpreting" Christianity meant the development of new theological perspectives, or more accurately, the revival and extension of theological perspectives offered by nineteenth-century feminists, especially the Grimké sisters, Stanton, and Mott. Impetus for this renewed activity came in part from the secular women's rights movement, which was itself given impetus by the civil rights and student movements of the 1960s, as well as the publication of Betty Friedan's book, *The Feminine Mystique,* in 1963. The National Organization for Women was organized in 1966, providing a formal structure for supporting the agenda of middle-class white women as they focused on expanded career opportunities and "equal pay for equal work."

Throughout the 1970s, Latina, black, and Asian American activist women also developed a feminist consciousness. Their challenge was to address sexism in their own communities, while at the same time confronting racism and exclusion in the white feminist movement. Chicana feminists, especially, took up the issues of poor and working-class women, including welfare rights, child care, reproductive rights, and domestic abuse—an experience shared by women of all colors and classes. Notwithstanding this commonality, white women did occupy positions of privilege and as they came to understand what that meant, some individuals made a commitment to work on white racism and to be in solidarity with women of color.

Because women were in the unique situation of living with the oppressor (that is, with men who, if they did not embody male oppression, at least symbolized it), separate space—women's space—became an imperative. Thus, a hallmark of the new feminist movement was the phenomenon of consciousness-raising groups in which women came together to share their common life experiences. Here, they discussed their personal relationships, cultivated a deeper awareness of inequities based on gender, and developed strategies for confronting both individual and systemic sexism, including the sexism of religious institutions.

As the stories of the Women's Division and CWU demonstrate, the activities of feminist church women were from the very beginning in dialectical relationship with the work of feminist theologians and biblical scholars in the academy. Among the groundbreakers was Mary Daly, whose critique of the manner in which the gender roles of women had been socially constructed and then sanctioned by the religious systems of both Judaism and Christianity became a central tenet of feminist theology as a whole. Rosemary Radford Ruether, who began writing at the same time as Daly, went a step further to draw parallels between the way patriarchal Christianity had subordinated women and the way it had exploited the planet earth. Ruether was also attuned to other people's experiences of oppression as a result of her involvements in the civil rights movement and her experiences teaching at a black seminary, the Howard University School of Religion.

In contrast to Ruether and Daly, who were Catholic, Letty Russell was a Presbyterian minister, one of the first to be ordained in her denomination; but like Ruether, she was influenced by her civil rights involvements, by the liberation theologies of Latin America and black Americans, and by her pastoral work in impoverished black communities. Hers was explicitly a feminist theology of *liberation*. A fourth pioneer was Beverly Wildung Harrison, professor of Christian ethics at Union Theological Seminary. Harrison's theological emphasis was the imperative of mutual relations, as over against unequal and exploitative power relations. Biblical scholars Phyllis Trible and Elisabeth Schüssler Fiorenza made major contributions as they researched early Christianity and the roles of women in the Bible.

Initially dismissed by other seminary professors and rejected by church officials, these early thinkers created community with their students, who eagerly embraced their critiques of imperial Christianity. Among the second-generation theologians were Carter Heyward, Sheila Collins, Carol Christ, Mary Hunt, Sharon Welch, and Rita Nakashima Brock. Brock speaks out of her experiences both as a woman and as an Asian American. These women and others were prolific in the 1980s and 1990s and the body of feminist theological writing continues to expand.

While the theology of each individual has its particular emphases, they start from common premises. Theology should come out of the experiences that are shared by women in their daily lives. Theology can be expressed not only in a scholarly mode, but in stories, art, and poetry. Basic assumptions such as dualistic and hierarchical views of reality, which are so prominent in Christianity, should be challenged. Theology should contribute to liberation through the ongoing praxis of experience and reflection on experience.[45] As Schüssler Fiorenza puts it, "To affirm that Christian faith and theology are not inherently patriarchal and sexist and to maintain, at the same time, that Christian theology and the Christian churches are guilty of the sin of sexism is the task of … Christian feminist theology."[46] Or in Ruether's words, "The critical principle of feminist theology is the promotion of the full humanity of women. Whatever denies, diminishes, or distorts the full humanity of women is, therefore, appraised as not redemptive." Conversely, "What does promote the full humanity of women is of the Holy, it does reflect true relation to the divine, it is the true nature of things, the authentic message of redemption and the mission of redemptive community."[47]

The understanding that not only gender roles of humans, but gender identities of deities were socially constructed led feminist theologians to entertain other images and other names. Among them are Mother/Father, Mother, Goddess, Sophia/Wisdom, and She Who Is.[48] Some rejected the traditional conceptualization of a theistic God, a God "out there" in the universe, altogether. Some found the idea of the immanence of God in relationships and/or creation meaningful, while others moved to panentheism, conceptualizing God as both permeating the world and encompassing the world. Concomitantly, traditional Christian doctrines of redemption and sacrificial atonement were challenged.[49]

As these ideas developed, women responded in various ways. Some concluded that Christianity was hopelessly patriarchal and rejected the religion altogether. Others determined to claim the faith as their own and to change their churches. Yet others, namely African American women, declared both feminist liberation theology and the black liberation theology that had been developed by African American men to be inadequate. Feminist theology, they said, did not address racism; black theology did not address sexism; neither addressed classism—but all three oppressions were a part of their life experiences. Borrowing a term from Alice Walker's *In Search of Our Mothers' Gardens,* black feminist theologians and ethicists developed "womanist theology," which spoke to liberation of the entire black community. Among those involved in the development of this theology are Jacqueline Grant, Delores Williams, Katie Geneva Cannon, Emilie Townes, Toinette Eugene, Kelly Brown Douglas, and Diana Hayes.[50]

Not that womanist theologians dismissed the issues that had been raised by white feminist theologians. They, too, were committed to church reform and, in practical terms, reform efforts centered around two issues: the ordination of women and the use of inclusive language.

Restructuring the Church

Recognizing that power resided in ordination and that disempowerment was fostered by the exclusive use of masculine language and symbols in liturgy and preaching, feminist Christians moved these aspects of Christian tradition to the forefront of their agenda for change.

For women, the privileging of male imagery and male pronouns was central to the imperial character of the church. God had always been imaged as "father"; the phraseology of beloved hymns was held sacred; the traditional language of the sacraments, especially, was deemed inviolable. What women sought was a transformation of church culture that would enable them to feel included in worship services and in the church community—a transformation, indeed, that would lead their church communities to become inclusive Christian communities. Over time, mainline Protestant churches have instituted significant changes. Hymnals have been revised; preachers are more careful in their choice of words; God is occasionally Father/Mother, though usually not in the Lord's Prayer or in baptismal and communion rituals. In the official Catholic Church, the use of inclusive language has been emphatically rejected, though a few progressive local parishes have made accommodations.

Likewise, systemic change with regard to ordination has occurred only in Protestant denominations. The history of women's ordination is extremely convoluted due to the schisms and mergers that have occurred in all the major Protestant families over the past two centuries. The AME Zion Church first ordained a woman in 1848, Congregationalists in 1853, and

Unitarians in 1863. Many Holiness and Pentecostal churches that were formed from the 1860s to the early 1900s ordained women, although as the century progressed, the practice was discouraged. Some Methodist groups allowed ordination during this period as well. Other Methodist and Presbyterian denominations approved ordination in the late 1940s and 1950s when churches were experiencing unusual growth.

The more liberal Lutheran denominations approved ordination in the 1970s. After a protracted and very public controversy, so did the Episcopal Church. American Baptists ordain women, but Southern Baptists, who at one time did so, determined in 2000 that they no longer would; nor do most black Baptist churches ordain women, although that is a decision that is made at the local level.[51]

But the legal provision for ordination did not mean that ordination of women was encouraged. As of 1960, fewer than 4,400 women were ordained. By 1977, the number had increased to some 10,000. By 1986, that number had doubled and as of 1990, more than 30,000 were ordained.[52] Thus, between the 1950s and the mid-1990s, the proportion of clergy who were women increased only from 2.1 percent to barely 9 percent.[53]

Ordination in and of itself, however, was not the end of the struggle. Not all who are ordained then have the opportunity to serve as pastors in local churches. Overcoming the opposition of not only men but women to a female pastor has been an arduous process that continues today. Those who are given appointments often are assigned to small, less prestigious churches in rural areas or as associate or assistant pastors in multi-staffed urban congregations. Nonetheless, the door was opened and as women's feminist consciousness was raised, more and more women walked through. Seminaries of all the mainstream Protestant denominations found the demographics of their student bodies radically altered; by the mid-1990s, women had achieved parity both in numbers enrolled and as voices in the conversation. Even Catholic seminaries were admitting women, though for them, the doorway to the priesthood remained blocked.

Hopes for change were raised among Catholic women by the emphases of the Second Vatican Council on the Church as "the people of God," on enhanced roles of lay members and more collaborative decision making, and on Pope John XXIII's affirmation of the dignity and worth of women. The council's statement entitled "The Church in the Modern World" affirmed the right of women to be free from discrimination and to "acquire an education or cultural benefits equal to those recognized for men." But these rights applied in the secular world, not in the Church.[54]

Rejecting this distinction, Catholic women began addressing the ordination issue in a serious way in the early 1970s. In 1972, the Leadership

Conference of Women Religious (LCWR), the coordinating body of most of the women's religious communities in the United States, raised the issue of ordination at its national assembly. At its 1974 assembly, a resolution was passed stating that "LCWR supports the principle that all ministries in the Church be open to women and men as the Spirit calls them." LCWR proceeded to prepare study packets for their member congregations "to educate them in feminist consciousness as women and to point them toward feminist praxis in society."[55] Summarizing the position of LCWR, Ruether wrote,

> Scripture has a special place because it is the original written witness to Christ, but it … only partly appropriated (in the life of the early Church) his liberation message. Tradition too is an earthen vessel, both bearing and betraying Christ's message. Personal experience always remains as the primary forum to which one must turn to test the meaning of the Gospel for one's own life. But over all stands Christ, who calls us to overcome every form of oppression, including sexism. No tradition which enshrines such oppression, therefore, can be "of him," but must stand under judgement by the liberation to which the Gospel beckons us.[56]

With this stance, Ruether claimed, "The sisters gain full confidence to be loyal dissenters, calling the Church (and themselves as Church, first of all) to true loyalty to the liberation of all persons, which is the Gospel."[57]

Out of this activity came an organization called Women's Ordination Conference (WOC), which convened its first conference in 1975. The event was attended by more than twelve hundred people, over 80 percent of whom were Catholic sisters, and a number of whom were Grail women or theologians who had been involved in Grail activities.[58] However, because lay women as a whole were underrepresented, so, too, were Latinas, despite their being such a large proportion of Catholic women. This meeting in turn gave rise to a number of other groups, including the Catholic Women's Seminary Fund and Priests for Equality. In 1977, the Vatican issued a "Declaration on the Question of the Admission of Women to the Ministerial Priesthood," which stated emphatically that "the exclusion of women was founded on Christ's intent and is basic to the Church's understanding of priesthood, and that therefore, it cannot be changed."[59] WOC responded by convening a second conference in 1978, which was attended by more than two thousand people, the majority of whom were lay men and women.[60]

Following years of activism, including protests of papal visits, WOC celebrated its twentieth anniversary with a third conference in 1995. The stated purpose and mission of WOC as of 2002 was, "1) to reclaim the church's early tradition of a discipleship of equals, 2) to recognize a variety of ministries in the Roman Catholic Church, 3) to promote inclusive spiritualities which are liberating and feminist, 4) to support ministries that meet the spiritual needs of the People of God, and 5) to celebrate our diversity of gender, race, ethnicity, sexuality, language and symbol."[61]

Confronted with the reality that ordination for women would not be approved any time soon, in the early 2000s a few Catholic women determined to initiate the change through time-honored methods: doing what they have been forbidden to do, as Episcopal women did in 1974. When seven women, including one American, were ordained in Europe in 2002 by two bishops outside of the Roman Church, representatives of the Women's Ordination Conference were present to provide support. Upon declaring themselves Catholic priests, the seven were promptly excommunicated. Indications are, however, that the act may be replicated in the United States at some future time.[62]

Many more women, including those who had come to question whether the office of ordination as it currently existed was worthy of pursuit, turned to the creation of alternative "churches" in the form of women's small Christian communities.

Women-Church

In 1983, Catholic theologian Mary Hunt and her partner Diann Neu founded an organization called Women's Alliance for Theology, Ethics, and Ritual, or WATER. Both had been involved in the earlier WOC conferences and Hunt had spent time working with women in Latin America. WATER was designed to be a "think-and-do tank" to work on women's social justice issues from a feminist, religious perspective and to develop alternative feminist liturgies.[63] That same year, WATER joined with women from WOC, the National Coalition of American Nuns, LAS HERMANAS, and other smaller organizations to convene a conference called "Woman Church Speaks." Out of this meeting came a new organization called Women-Church Convergence, which quickly became ecumenical and ethnically diverse.

Women-Church Convergence held a second conference in 1987 and a third in 1993. But its primary expression is a network of grassroots women's groups that are called "Women-Church." The term "Women-Church" was derived from a phrase contributed by Schüssler Fiorenza, "the *Ekklesia* of Women." Rosemary Ruether, who with Mary Hunt was among the theologians centrally involved in Women-Church Convergence, proposed in her 1983 book, *Sexism and God-talk*, "the creation of autonomous feminist base communities as the vehicle for developing a community of liberation from sexism."

> A feminist base community is an autonomous, self-gathered community that takes responsibility for reflecting on, celebrating, and

acting on the understanding of redemption as liberation from patriarchy. Such a community might take on as many or as few of the functions of Church as they choose. They might range from consciousness-raising groups that primarily share experiences, to groups who engage in study and analysis as well, to groups that also worship together. From a study, teaching, and worshiping group, such a community might also choose to share means of livelihood with one another. They might further choose to make their shared spiritual and social life together the base of political action.[64]

For Ruether, creation of women's community did not mean complete separation from the institutional Church. Rather, she envisioned that people might participate in both and that the "transformed liturgies, theological reflection, and social action developed in base groups could then be brought to bear on the institutionalized Church." Speaking of the "exodus out of the institutional Church into the feminist base community," Ruether anticipated not schism, but "a creative dialectic between the two" that would "transform the historical Church." She was clear, however, that transformation meant dismantling clericalism and embracing a style of ministry that "transforms leadership from power over others to empowerment of others." It also entailed the creation of new rites of passage and new understandings of mission as the pursuit of a transformed world "without the alienating isms of exploitation and oppression."[65] These ideas were further developed in Ruether's book, *Women-Church: Theology and Practice* (1986), which constitutes a veritable manual for creating Women-Church groups.

Drawing on her Latin American experience, Mary Hunt also understood Women-Church as "women's base communities, small groups that gather in the homes of the members for worship, social change, and community building." Women-Church, for her, meant a "theological commitment" to Schüssler Fiorenza's idea of a "discipleship of equals," as existed in the early church. "Historical encrustations of patriarchy," writes Hunt, "robbed women of the self-understanding and men of the women-identification necessary to embody [community] in contemporary churches. Only by calling attention to it, making the place of women (and by inference other marginalized people as well) explicitly equal to that of men, can there be any hope of fulfilling the potential of the Jesus movement."[66]

The first conference of Women-Church Convergence benefited from the contributions of members of LAS HERMANAS, the organization of Latina religious sisters and lay women who were in the forefront of activism in the Latina/o community in the 1970s. In addition, low-income women from migrant labor communities and urban barrios who were present participated by virtue of the conference being fully bilingual. Members of LAS

HERMANAS who had worked in Texas with the Mexican American
Cultural Center, especially, were familiar with Latin American liberation
theology and with the attendant base Christian communities being formed
in the Southwest, in which women had important leadership roles.

In 1988, the first book of Hispanic women's theology appeared. *Hispanic
Women: Prophetic Voice in the Church*, by Ada María Isasi-Díaz and Yolanda
Tarango, C.C.V.I., at that time the national coordinator of LAS HER-
MANAS, launched the development in the United States of what came to be
called Mujerista theology. In the prologue of the book, the authors write,
"Doing theology is a communal process. We do theology because of, for, and
with other Hispanic Women with whom we participate in the struggle for
liberation.... Our goal, our hope, is the creation of the community of struggle: that is what the 'kin-dom' of God is all about. The common good of the
community is one of our main preoccupations, a common good that cannot fall under ideological control and is always being understood anew."[67]

Literally, the methodology of Mujerista theology is communal, arising
out of story-telling and reflections on the religious and life experiences of
women gathered together. This is less the case for Womanist theology,
although individual theologians affirm the importance of "sharing womanist perspectives with our sisters who are not ensconced in the academy or as
seminary-trained clergy."[68] Like Womanist theology, Mujerista theology is
concerned with the intersections of racism, sexism, and classism in Hispanic
communities and in the larger world. Unlike Womanist theology, Mujerista
theology was not so much sequential to the work of male liberation theologians as concomitant. Like other liberation theologies, it utilizes the praxis
model of action/reflection to address issues of injustice. In addition, it draws
on the "women-church" experience that has been part of the tradition of
popular religiosity for centuries.

To an extent, Ruether's dialectic of Women-Church and institutional
Church is enacted by the many Catholic women, some twenty thousand as
of 1997, a fourth of whom are vowed religious sisters—who serve as pastoral
associates or parish administrators. Those assigned to parishes in which
there is no priest perform most of the functions of priests, save for celebrating the sacraments. While they cannot consecrate the elements for
Eucharist, they do preside over "word and communion" services.[69]

Outside the parish, however, the situation of an increasing number of
women is quite different. For some women, both Catholic and Protestant,
their small communities are not supplementary to parish churches, but
rather constitute their *only* church. Thus, the concept of "Women-Church"
has been appropriated to refer to the entire phenomenon of women forming their own spirituality and liturgical groups, either completely outside of

churches or tangential to them. Members of some of these communities explicitly identify themselves as "Women-Church," while others do not.

Some have embraced the term "WomenEucharist." For Catholic women, especially, celebration of the Eucharist (Communion or the Lord's Supper, for Protestants) is undoubtedly the most critical issue next to that of ordination. WomenEucharist is an umbrella term for the various informal groups of women that gather to celebrate the Eucharist without the presence of a priest. As of 1997, Sheila Durkin Dierks has identified more than one hundred such groups nationwide. Her research indicates that the majority of participants are "cradle Catholics." Many are, or have been, members of women's religious communities. Although the history of discrimination against women in the church was cited as a common incentive to join these gatherings, other participants considered their new ways of celebrating Eucharist as a natural extension of Vatican II, which is understood to have returned the Eucharist to the people. Both women and men "grew to understand that it is not only our right, but also our duty in good conscience, to return authority to its intended place, centered in community."[70]

Not surprisingly, since religious sisters have been among the key participants in the creation of Women-Church as a whole, canonical religious communities themselves have undergone dramatic change. Some of these changes were instigated by the "Decree on the Renewal of Religious Life" that came out of the Second Vatican Council. Women, both lay and religious, were allowed to have roles in the mass and to serve on newly mandated parish councils. Sisters had the choice of continuing to wear habits or wearing ordinary clothes. Housing arrangements were no longer restricted to convents; occupations were encouraged beyond the traditional roles of teacher or social worker. Religious communities were encouraged to return to the charism, the primary focus or mission, that brought their particular community into being in the first place.

At the time, many sisters, like many priests, opted to leave religious life altogether. Of those who remained, it was primarily the younger sisters who became active participants in the movements and small communities that were free of Church oversight and that developed their feminist consciousness. Most religious communities have been in a process of change ever since. Writing in 1994, Elizabeth Johnson observed that "religious orders in this country ... are in the midst of a transformative process so profound that it will lead to the demise of some, the revitalizing of others, and the birth of new forms of the evangelical life as yet unimagined."[71]

Vatican II encouraged sisters to live in the world and be a part of it. This they have done, taking on issues of racism, violence against women and children, poverty and hunger, destruction of the environment, militarism, and labor exploitation, among others. But then Pope John Paul II, early in his reign, expressed concern that the religious orders were becoming "too secularized, too preoccupied with social concerns, and not sufficiently involved in the service of the Church." In 1992, an outline for a worldwide synod of bishops revived the premise that religious life is superior to lay life, totally reversing the proclamation of Vatican II, and asserted that those in religious life needed to have strict obedience to the hierarchy and devotion to the pope.[72]

The ambiguity of roles, along with their diminishing numbers, have many asking what the future of women's religious orders might be. While some argue that the traditional, communal living of women religious is a thing of the past, others are persuaded that religious life has tremendous growth potential. Part of the way growth is occurring is through the development of "associate" programs, which variously allow men and women, single and married, lay and clerical, to affiliate with a religious community while continuing a secular lifestyle.

If there is a Protestant counterpart to the cutting edge of the Catholic Women-Church movement, it is the Re-Imagining movement that began in Minneapolis, Minnesota, in 1993. That year, in conjunction with the Ecumenical Decade of Churches in Solidarity, women were called together to "re-imagine" creation, family, sexuality, models of church and ministry, language, the arts, and ethics. More than two thousand participants attended this first Re-Imagining conference, which, because of its use of feminist rituals and language, generated a firestorm of protest from mainline Protestant churches. Nonetheless, imaginative women returned for a number of years to participate in subsequent conferences and to explore the formation of sacred community. Out of this movement came the organization called Re-Imagining Community, which defines itself as a space where "exploration, discussion, study, and practice of the Christian faith are carried out freely and responsibly to seek justice, honor creation, and call the church into solidarity with all people of God."[73]

The words might well serve as a statement of the mission of feminist Christian women throughout the past forty years of wandering in the wilderness—and, undoubtedly, for the forty years to come. The Promised Land lies far on the horizon.

For Further Reading

Brock, Rita Nakashima, and Rebecca Ann Parker. *Proverbs of Ashes: Violence, Redemptive Suffering, and the Search for What Saves Us.* Boston: Beacon Press, 2001.

Clifford, Anne M. *Introducing Feminist Theology.* Maryknoll, N.Y.: Orbis Books, 2001.

Gilkes, Cheryl Townsend. *"If It Wasn't for the Women …": Black Women's Experience and Womanist Culture in Church and Community.* Maryknoll, N.Y.: Orbis Books, 2001.

Isasi-Díaz, Ada María. *Mujerista Theology.* Maryknoll, N.Y.: Orbis Books, 1996.

Lindley, Susan Hill. *"You Have Stept out of Your Place": A History of Women and Religion in America.* Louisville: Westminster John Knox Press, 1996.

Moessner, Jeanne Stevenson. *Through the Eyes of Women: Insights for Pastoral Care.* Minneapolis: Fortress Press, 1996.

Ruether, Rosemary Radford. *Women and Redemption: A Theological History.* Minneapolis: Fortress Press, 1998.

Ruether, Rosemary Radford, and Rosemary Skinner Keller, eds. *In Our Own Voices: Four Centuries of American Women's Religious Writing.* San Francisco: HarperSanFrancisco, 1995.

Schneider, Laurel C. *Re-Imagining the Divine: Confronting the Backlash against Feminist Theology.* Cleveland: The Pilgrim Press, 1998.

Townes, Emilie M., ed. *Embracing the Spirit: Womanist Perspectives on Hope, Salvation, and Transformation.* Maryknoll, N.Y.: Orbis Books, 1997.

Welch, Sharon D. *Communities of Resistance and Solidarity: A Feminist Theology of Liberation.* Maryknoll, N.Y.: Orbis Books, 1985.

Wittberg, Patricia, S.C., *Pathways to Re-Creating Religious Communities.* New York: Paulist Press, 1996.

NOTES

1. Ann Fagan, *This Is Our Song: Employed Women in the United Methodist Tradition* (The Women's Division of the General Board of Global Ministries, The United Methodist Church, 1986), 3, 8.

2. Catherine A. Brekus, "The Revolution in the Churches: Women's Religious Activism in the Early American Republic," in *Religion and the New Republic: Faith in the Founding of America* (ed. James H. Hutson; Lanham, Md.: Rowman & Littlefield, 2000), 127.

3. Ibid., 128.

4. See Barbara Hilkert Andolsen, *"Daughters of Jefferson, Daughters of Bootblacks": Racism and American Feminism* (Macon, Ga.: Mercer University Press, 1986), 114–15.

5. Rosemary Radford Ruether, *Women and Redemption: A Theological History* (Minneapolis: Fortress Press, 1998), 162–65.

6. Ibid., 171.

7. Jeanne Stevenson-Moessner, "Elizabeth Cady Stanton, Reformer to Revolutionary: A Theological Trajectory," *Journal of the American Academy of Religion* 62, no. 3 (fall 1964): 673, 684.

8. Brekus, "The Revolution in the Churches," 130. The internal quotes are from Elizabeth Cady Stanton, Susan B. Anthony, and Matilda Joslyn Gage, *History of Woman Suffrage,* vol. 1, 1848–1861(1881; repr., New York: Arno Press, 1969), 383, 523.

9. Ruether, *Women and Redemption,* 175–76.

10. Ibid., 174.

11. Ibid., 176.

12. Fagan, *This Is Our Song,* 1.

13. Theressa Hoover, *With Unveiled Face: Centennial Reflections on Women and Men in the Community of the Church* (New York: Women's Division, General Board of Global Ministries, The United Methodist Church, 1983), 14.

14. Fagan, *This Is Our Song,* 5.

15. Ibid., 6.

16. Ibid., 7–9.

17. Nancy G. Garner, "The Woman's Christian Temperance Union: A Woman's Branch of American Protestantism," in *Re-forming the Center: American Protestantism, 1900 to the Present* (eds. Douglas Jacobsen and Wm. Vance Trollinger, Jr.; Grand Rapids, Mich.: Eerdmans, 1998), 273. The quotes cited by Garner are from the WTCU Minutes, 1874 Convention, 6.

18. Ibid., 274. The quotes here are from the WCTU Minutes, 1877 Convention, 196.

19. Ibid., 275.

20. Ibid., 277.

21. Fagan, *This Is Our Song*, 9–10.

22. Garner, "The Woman's Christian Temperance Union," 274.

23. Ibid., 279.

24. Fagan, *This Is Our Song*, 10–11.

25. Ibid., 11, 176 n. 43. Fagan credits William L. O'Neill as the first to use this term in *Everyone Was Brave: A History of Feminism in America* (Chicago: Quadrange Books, n.d.), 51.

26. Fagan, *This Is Our Song*, 3.

27. Ibid, 11.

28. Ruether, *Women and Redemption*, 175. For an in-depth discussion of the racism in the nineteenth-century women's rights movement, see Andolsen in note 4, above.

29. Cheryl Townsend Gilkes, *"If It Wasn't for the Women …": Black Women's Experience and Womanist Culture in Church and Community* (Maryknoll, N.Y.: Orbis Books, 2001), 17.

30. See Evelyn Brooks Higginbotham, *Righteous Discontent: The Women's Movement in the Black Baptist Church, 1880–1920* (Cambridge, Mass.: Harvard University Press), 1993.

31. Gilkes, *"If It Wasn't for the Women,"* 114–15.

32. Ibid., 69.

33. Ibid., 113–14.

34. Hoover, *With Unveiled Face*, 16.

35. Ibid., 17.

36. Mary Sudman Donovan, "The Cost of Integrating," *The Witness* 77, no. 4 (July 1994): 32.

37. Hoover, *With Unveiled Face*, 20.

38. See *To a Higher Glory: The Growth and Development of Black Women Organized for Mission in The Methodist Church, 1940–1968*, prepared by the Task Group on the History of the Central Jurisdiction Women's Organization, The United Methodist Church (The Education and Cultivation Division for the Women's Division, Board of Global Ministries, The United Methodist Church, n.d.).

39. Peggy Billings, *Speaking Out in the Public Space: An Account of the Section of Christian Social Relations: Women's Division, The United Methodist Church, 1968–1984* (New York: The Mission Education and Cultivation Program Department for the Women's Division, General Board of Global Ministries, The United Methodist Church, 1995), 2–3, 15.

40. The story of these involvements is told in Billings' book, *Speaking Out in the Public Space.*

41. I am indebted to Elaine Gasser for the loan of her books on the Women's Division of the United Methodist Church, which proved vital in writing this section.

42. These consultations were convened by Claire Randall, program director of CWU. Participants included Janet Kalven, one of the founders of the Grail; theologian Nelle Morton; feminist writer Charlotte Brunch; *Cross Currents* editor Sally Cuneen; civil rights

activist Pauli Murray; and philosopher/theologian Mary Daly. See Janet Kalven, *Women Breaking Boundaries: A Grail Journey, 1940–1995* (Albany: SUNY Press, 1999), 224.

43. I am indebted to Nancy Warner, a long-time activist in Church Women United, for her assistance with this historical overview.

44. The foregoing discussion of the Grail in the United States is based on Kalven, *Women Breaking Boundaries.* The specific references to cooperative efforts with Church Women United are found on pages 224, 226–27, and 232. For a more condensed discussion of the Grail, see chapter 2 in Mary Jo Weaver, *Springs of Water in a Dry Land: Spiritual Survival for Catholic Women Today* (Boston: Beacon Press, 1993).

45. Barbara J. MacHaffie, *Her Story: Women in Christian Tradition* (Philadelphia: Fortress Press, 1986), 148–49.

46. Elisabeth Schüssler Fiorenza, *Discipleship of Equals* (New York: Crossroad, 1993), 101.

47. Rosemary Radford Ruether, *Sexism and God-Talk: Toward a Feminist Theology* (Boston: Beacon Press, 1983), 18–19.

48. See Elizabeth A. Johnson, *She Who Is: The Mystery of God in Feminist Theological Discourse* (New York: Crossroad, 1992).

49. Among those who challenged traditional doctrines were Carter Heyward, Sharon Welch, and Rita Nakashima Brock. See Laurel C. Schneider, *Re-Imagining the Divine: Confronting the Backlash against Feminist Theology* (Cleveland: The Pilgrim Press, 1998), 50.

50. See chapter 4 of Kelly Brown Douglas, *The Black Christ* (Maryknoll, N.Y.: Orbis Books, 1994) for an overview of the emergence of womanist theology. The first essay on black theology and black women, written by Jacquelyn Grant, appeared in 1979. Grant's first book, entitled *White Women's Christ and Black Women's Jesus: Feminist Christology and Womanist Response* (Atlanta: Scholar's Press) was published in 1989.

51. For a more complete presentation of the ordination histories of both white and black Protestants, see Anne M. Clifford, *Introducing Feminist Theology* (Maryknoll, N.Y.: Orbis Books, 2001), 153–55, 160.

52. Ibid., 155.

53. See Paula Nesbitt, *Feminization of the Clergy in America* (New York: Oxford University Press, 1997), 25.

54. Clifford, *Introducing Feminist Theology,* 142.

55. Rosemary Ruether, "The Roman Catholic Story," in *Women of Spirit: Female Leadership in the Jewish and Catholic Traditions* (eds. Rosemary Radford Ruether and Eleanor McLaughlin; New York: Simon and Schuster, 1979), 375–77.

56. Ibid., 376–77.

57. Ibid., 377.

58. Kalven, *Women Breaking Boundaries,* 231. Prominent among the theologians were Rosemary Ruether and Elisabeth Schüssler Fiorenza.

59. Ibid., 379–80. For a discussion of the Church's position on the ordination of women, see Clifford, *Introducing Feminist Theology,* 142–48.

60. For an account of the "preconference process," which involved discussions by more than fifty local groups, see chapter 10 of Schüssler Fiorenza, *Discipleship of Equals.*

61. See <www.womensordination.org/pages/intro.html>.

62. John L. Allen, Jr., "Ordinations Ignite Debate over Tactics," *National Catholic Reporter* (July 19, 2002): 7. "Vatican Excommunicates Women Ordained in June," *National Catholic Reporter* (August 16, 2002): 13.

63. Rose Solari, "In Her Own Image," *Common Boundary* (July/August 1995): 24.

64. Ruether, *Sexism and God-Talk*, 205.

65. Ibid., 205–6, 211–12.

66. Mary E. Hunt, *Fierce Tenderness: A Feminist Theology of Friendship* (New York: Crossroad, 1992).

67. Ada María Isasi-Díaz and Yolanda Tarango, *Hispanic Women: Prophetic Voice in the Church* (San Francicso: Harper & Row, 1988), ix, xvii.

68. Teresa L. Fry Brown, "Avoiding Asphyxiation," in *Embracing the Spirit: Womanist Perspectives on Hope, Salvation, and Transformation* (ed. Emilie Townes; Maryknoll, N.Y., 1997), 73. Brown describes a program and model for forming small communities of black women, called S.W.E.E.T., Sisters Working Encouraging Empowering Together, that involved several hundred women in Denver over a period of several years.

69. Clifford, *Introducing Feminist Theology*, 149.

70. Sheila Durkin Dierks, *WomenEucharist* (Boulder, Colo.: WovenWord Press, 1997), 77–78.

71. Elizabeth A. Johnson, "Between the Times: Religious Life and the Postmodern Experience of God," *Review for Religious* (January–February 1994): 7.

72. Patricia Wittberg, *The Rise and Fall of Catholic Religious Orders* (New York: SUNY Press, 1994).

73. Re-Imagining Community brochure.

−CHAPTER 9−
GLBT Gifts and Grievances

An Affirmation of Faith

I believe in a loving God, creator of love and peace
who shows grace in times of sorrow and is present during deepest
    loneliness.
I believe in Jesus Christ, who lived a life of justice
and dreamed a vision of inclusivity,
who spoke words that were ignored
and showed compassion to people who were ignored,
who gave the gift of his life,
allowing us to live abundantly.
I believe in the Holy Spirit,
a force so magical and mystical
yet undeniably working in our hearts and minds and souls.
I believe in the relationships between self and God and self and
    others
as a way to fulfill Jesus' prophetic words.
I believe in holy communion, the life given by the breaking of bread
and the blessings flowing from the cup
whenever two or more are gathered at table
in loving Christian community.
I believe in singing songs of praise,
the lifting of many voices
blending to spread messages of love, forgiveness, understanding,
    and joy.
I believe in the power of the church
when it allows all of God's children
to find a home where each is nourished, challenged, encouraged,
    and comforted.

—Anna Blaedel

This affirmation of faith was written by Anna Blaedel in the summer of 2002 when she was between her sophomore and junior years in college. It was composed through her tears as she was attending the Iowa Annual Conference of the United Methodist Church. Anna loves her church. She plans to attend seminary to pursue a master of divinity degree. She hopes to be ordained. Her local congregation is personally supportive of her. But unless her denomination changes its policy, she will have to go elsewhere to be ordained. Thus the tears. In addition to being intellectually astute, spiritually grounded, theologically mature, and deeply committed to social justice, Anna is lesbian.

A statement made by a Protestant bishop in casual conversation is representative of the attitudes of many church leaders: "Oh, we know they're there," he said. "They're in the choir and in the pew and in the pulpit. We all know that. And that's fine, as long as they don't bring it up, as long as they don't make an issue of it." It is the military's version of "don't ask, don't tell."

These terms are not "fine" to those who are silenced. More gays and lesbians in the pews and in the pulpits have committed suicide because of this silencing than church officials would ever acknowledge, or even want to know. Most often, when seemingly contented pastors take their own lives, their congregations never learn the truth of what transpired or why. They do not know their own culpability.

Probably no institution has done more to impose "otherness" on the gay and lesbian population than the Church, which has historically condemned individuals whose orientation was other than convincingly heterosexual. In recent decades, spokespersons of the Religious Right have elevated this condemnation to the level of public, political discourse, even as they offer the rhetorical admonition that one should "hate the sin but not the sinner." The more moderate churches on the Christian continuum still struggle with the homophobia and heterosexism[1] that are deeply engrained in both the church culture and the secular culture of America. Even churches that historically have been on the liberal and progressive end of the spectrum are unable to come to resolution because their denominations are now divided into quarreling factions and their leaders find it less than profitable to take a prophetic stance.

Only two denominations, as a matter of official policy, ordain individuals who are openly gay, lesbian, or transgender: the United Church of Christ and the Unitarian-Universalist Association. In the Episcopal Church, decisions regarding ordination are left to individual bishops, some of whom have ordained openly gay candidates for the priesthood. Lutherans of the ELCA branch permit ordination of gay and lesbian candidates only when those candidates take vows of celibacy. Of course, all denominations that ordain women as well as men also ordain both lesbian and gay individuals, albeit unknowingly. These ministers must then remain secretive and closeted; they lead double lives or they deny their sexuality, and thereby deny much of their personhood.

GLBT individuals who serve as ministers of music, organists and pianists, choir directors or choir members, and whose sexual orientation is known, are generally tolerated at best. GLBT Christians who share the pews on Sunday morning with unsuspecting fellow congregants find themselves cringing when the preacher condemns them, hurting when the litany of those who have been wronged fails to mention their community. But the greatest number of GLBT individuals never set foot inside a church, knowing that, were their identity known, they would likely find no welcome there, no comfort in their times of sorrow, no celebration in their times of joy.

In recent years, however, a growing number of gay, lesbian, bisexual, and transgender Christians have chosen not to be silenced and not to silence themselves. Anna is but one example. That they dare to speak their truth today, when for centuries they could not, is one measure of the impact of the gay rights movement that began late in the 1960s.

Gay Empowerment: Secular and Sacred

In June 1969, a gay bar in New York City, the Stonewall Inn, was raided by the police. The raid sparked a riot by gay men who patronized the bar; it also sparked a determination on the part of many gay and lesbian citizens to put an end to their historic malignment. Every year Stonewall is commemorated with gay pride parades in cities all around the country. The parades, however, are but the tip of the community infrastructure that has developed in the past few decades. Gay resource centers, gay newspapers, scholarly literature by and about GLBT people, political action committees, gay-friendly businesses, health care centers, women's collectives, men's choral groups— all these and more are both examples and vehicles of GLBT self-affirmation and empowerment.

Just as did the civil rights and women's movements, the gay rights movement has worked for equal treatment in housing, employment, and public accommodations. In addition, it has sought legal rights in such areas as parental custody, recognition of committed relationships, inheritance, medical care, and insurance coverage—rights that are already extended to the heterosexual population. Indeed, the movement has sought structural, societal changes that would lead to the complete elimination of institutionalized heterosexism, much as ethnic minority groups continue to work for the elimination of institutionalized racism and women of all colors work for the elimination of institutionalized sexism.

Ironically, even as the women's movement addressed sexism, it was challenged to come to terms with its heterosexism. Lesbians who regarded themselves as feminists found that they were not always welcome in feminist circles. Heterosexual women's concerns that their movement would be discredited by the presence of lesbians was a clear sign that they were still beholden to patriarchal judgments. Thus, lesbians have had the added task of consciousness raising among heterosexual women; in the process, many have arrived at new meanings of what it is to be lesbian. Mary Hunt, for example, writes,

> No longer is a lesbian defined as one who does not sleep with men, nor even as one who sleeps with women. Rather, a lesbian is understood as a woman who, in a heterosexist patriarchal context, with all its weight to the contrary, takes her relationships with other women radically seriously.... Her intimate companion may be a woman, but the burden of the definition does not rest on that information. Further, the word lesbian has come to include an orientation toward community, a community of women striving to live beyond patriarchal structures.... Lesbianism frees women to love whom they will in what I call the deepest mystery of the universe.[2]

Convictions about community, love, and freedom are at the center of GLBT spirituality, which has been an important aspect of the GLBT movement. If the expansion of interest in spirituality paralleled that of the general population from the 1960s to the 1980s, it was sparked by quite different circumstances.

A focus on spirituality was inevitable in light of the terrible devastation wrought on the communities of gay men and lesbians by the disease called AIDS. Beginning in the late 1970s and continuing throughout the 1980s and into the 1990s, thousands upon thousands of America's most creative and gifted young people suffered premature death. Not that America mourned the loss. For the most part, it was left to gay and lesbian communities to care for the sick, bury their dead, and grieve the loss of their loved ones.

The angst of community-wide tragedy was compounded by allegations that AIDS was a "gay disease," notwithstanding that the disease was also taking a toll in heterosexual populations in the United States and around the world. It was compounded even further by allegations of conservative Christians that the plague was punishment for the so-called "sins" of homosexuals. Those who were victims of the illness, as well as those who cared for them, became the victims as well of a hatefulness that made allowances for neither tenderness nor compassion. In its hour of greatest need, the gay community experienced its most severe rejection.

As gay and lesbian individuals were disowned by their nuclear families, denied counseling and support in their churches, and ostracized in the larger society, many turned inward or to one another, seeking meaning and purpose, seeking spiritual answers. The seeking has led along a diversity of religious paths,[3] some of which bespeak an extraordinary capacity for forgiveness.

In both Catholic and Protestant churches, gay and lesbian members have formed organizations designed to provide support to GLBT members and to function as change agents for transforming their respective denominations. Among the first was Dignity, an organization of gay and lesbian Catholics that was started in 1969 and by 1973 had became a national organization. In spite of being prohibited from meeting on property owned by the Catholic Church, more than seventy-five chapters have formed, providing worship opportunities for openly gay and lesbian Catholics and working for social change.

Throughout the 1970s, gay caucuses were organized in the United Church of Christ (Coalition for GLBT Concerns), American Baptist Churches (ABC Concerned), the Presbyterian Church (U.S.A.) (More Light), the Episcopal Church (Integrity), Disciples of Christ (GLAD, Gay, Lesbian, and Affirming Disciples Alliance), and the United Methodist Church (Affirmation). In the 1980s, similar organizations were formed by Mennonites and by members of the Evangelical Lutheran Church of America. Groups such as Seventh-Day Adventists, Christian Scientists, and Mormons established caucuses as well, while gay and lesbian evangelicals formed a group called Evangelicals Concerned and Pentecostals organized the National Gay Pentecostal Alliance.

Here, in the company of fellow Christians who experienced the same exclusion and rejection, gay men and lesbians found a place of security and safety, of real community and conviction, of hopefulness and assurance that they were indeed loved by God. This occurred even as the general memberships of mainline denominations were waging war, torn by dissension and divisiveness as they struggled to address what many continued to regard as a "problem" and others saw as a matter of justice. But while some GLBT members were determined to be a presence and a witness among the heterosexual majority, however unwelcome they might be, others sought sanctuary in denominations created expressly to serve them.

Gay and Lesbian Denominations

Aside from African Americans, the gay and lesbian population is alone among marginalized groups in organizing separate denominations. One of these, the Unity Fellowship Movement, which was incorporated in 1985 by its founder, Archbishop Carl Bean, is itself predominantly African American. Unity Fellowship Movement has twelve congregations, the two largest being the "Mother Church," Unity Fellowship of Christ Church, in Los Angeles, and Inner Light Unity Fellowship Church in Washington, D.C., which offers as its creed, "God is love and love is for every one."

A number of other small, separatist denominations have organized under the banners of Orthodoxy and Catholicism.[4] The largest denomination created to serve gays and lesbians, however, has roots in evangelicalism and Pentecostalism.

The Universal Fellowship of Metropolitan Community Churches (MCC) was founded in 1968 by Troy Perry. In his autobiography, Perry writes that he founded the church "so gays would have a place to worship God in dignity, and not as lepers or outcasts, but as His creation, as His children."[5] Perry's own family background was that of Southern, fundamentalist pentecostalism. Licensed to preach by a Baptist church at age fifteen, he subsequently served congregations of the Church of God and Church of God Prophecy, but was dismissed from each pastorate when his homosexuality became known. In 1968, he began organizing the Mother Church of MCC in Los Angeles and within five years MCC congregations were formed from coast to coast, with Perry serving as the general moderator of the new denomination.

As of 2000, MCC had more than three hundred congregations in sixteen different countries, with a total membership of some forty-four thousand individuals. While both the clergy and members are racially and ethnically diverse, white gay men constitute the majority of members in U.S. congregations. The denomination has several times applied for membership in the National Council of Churches (NCC) and each time been denied, even though MCC's statement of beliefs is in accord with traditional Christian creeds.[6]

Although MCC is ecumenical—its members include both mainline and conservative Protestant Christians, as well as Catholics and Mormons— many of its congregations' worship services retain an evangelical and even charismatic flavor and often evidence a theological conservatism. But it is conservatism in a different key. MCC's mission statement begins: "The Universal Fellowship of Metropolitan Community Churches is a Christian Church founded in and reaching beyond the Gay and Lesbian communities. We embody and proclaim Christian salvation and liberation, Christian inclusivity and community, and Christian social action and justice. We serve among those seeking and celebrating the integration of their spirituality and sexuality."[7] This statement contains the key elements of gay liberation theology: inclusive community, social justice for all people, and a revisioning of sexuality as something intrinsically good, something that is a gift from God.

Gay Liberation Theology

The challenge of gay and lesbian theologians has been to confront patriarchal church leaders (men) with their obsessive control of others' sexual behavior and, in the process, to expose the source of this controlling impulse: namely, their fear of sexuality in general and of homosexuality in particular. In short, churches have been afraid to address sexuality as an essential dimension of human life and so have become imperialistic at the most basic level of human relationality.[8]

Carter Heyward, who was among the initial group of women to be ordained in the Episcopal Church, has been on the cutting edge of gay liberation theology in focusing on the "erotic" as "power in right relation." In *Touching Our Strength: The Erotic as Power and the Love of God,* she writes:

> This book is not about either sex or God as these terms have denoted particular traditional points of reference: to male and female reproductive/pleasure organs and their manipulation, or to an anthropomorphized deity to whom we ascribe absolute power. I am reflecting on the erotic as our embodied yearning for mutuality. As such, I am interested not merely in a "theology of sexuality"— examining sexuality through theological lenses; but rather in probing the Sacred—exploring divine terrain—through sexual experience.
>
> Whether in the context of long-term monogamous mutual relationships or of sex play between occasional partners who are wrestling toward right relation, lovemaking is a form of justice-making. This is so not only because, in the context of mutuality, sex is an expression of a commitment to right relation; but also because such sexual expression generates more energy for passionate involvement in the movements for justice in the world. Lovemaking turns us simultaneously *into* ourselves and *beyond* ourselves. In experiencing the depths of our power in right relation as pleasurable and good, we catch a glimpse of the power of right relation in larger, more complicated configurations of our life together.[9]

Structures of "wrong relation" that generate sexual and gender injustice are, for Heyward, inextricably linked to patterns of racial and economic injustice. "It follows that the liberation of *anyone* depends on the tenacity of the connections and coalitions we are able to forge together." It follows, as well, that churches must undergo institutional transformation that affirms "womanpower as sacred" and "sexual pleasure as a delightful relational happening that needs no higher justification."[10]

Similar themes of transformation, relationship, and social justice are expressed in the writings of another Episcopal priest and theologian, Malcolm Boyd. "For gays," writes Boyd, "God's revelation is a continuing process in life; not locked inside, or restricted to, the pages of the Bible. It stands with feminist theology in invoking a new 'theology of the church.' This veers sharply away from institutional patriarchy. A monarchial, rigid type of church leadership needs to be supplanted by a collegial form which is more democratic and reflects an open community. The church has no right to place the perpetuation of its own power and machinery over the struggles and needs of people."[11] Boyd envisions "the Christian movement in the gay and lesbian world"[12] as a potential agent for bringing about such change, not only within the institutional church, but outside it:

> If the Christian movement in the gay and lesbian world can address a spiritual hunger that is universal, and focus on Christ's gospel instead of simply its own problems, it may exert a profound influence on the course of Christianity in America. It knows the meaning of persecution from experience. Can it proclaim the crucified and risen Christ in fresh, compelling ways to the whole church, the whole society? Can the movement find wide expression as a "moral minority" of genuine spiritual and witnessing power? ... Can an underground church of lesbian and gay Christians pursue a course of discipleship to honor Christ's cross and "convert" churchianity to true servanthood in Christ's name? Can this movement hear Christ's call in humility and move into the world to do foot-washing and healing?[13]

Boyd's questions constitute a clarion call for lesbian and gay Christians to evangelize the official Church. But the reality is that for gay, lesbian, bisexual, and transgender individuals, to be Christian remains an anomaly. Great are the numbers of former church members within the GLBT community in the United States who now abhor Christianity as the most historically virulent source of their oppression and dehumanization. Those who continue to claim Christianity as their own do so only as they are able to distinguish the essence of the faith from the institutional structures and religious thinkers and leaders who for centuries declared them beyond the boundaries of moral acceptability. For those who would reclaim their spiritual home, skepticism abounds as churches wrestle with their proverbial angels.

Protestant Dissension

Whereas the issue for churches with regard to women has been their proper role—namely, subordinate to men—the issue with regard to homosexuals, male and female, has been preeminently one of morality, that is, of the alleged "sinfulness" of their very being. As recently as 1993, the Southern Baptist Convention passed a resolution affirming "the biblical truth that homosexuality is a sin, as well as the biblical promise that all persons, including homosexuals, can receive abundant, new and eternal life by repenting of their sin...."[14]

Those who assert this "biblical truth" typically point to the few verses that appear to condemn homosexuality. With the development of biblical criticism and its admonition to read the Scriptures in the context of historical, cultural circumstances, the significance of these texts has been challenged. This latter position is succinctly stated by the Reverend David Ruhe, former national moderator of the United Church of Christ:

> Homosexuality as sexual orientation is not dealt with in the Bible. There is no discussion of a committed same-gender relationship between consenting adults. The only form in which homosexuality could be said to be discussed is with reference to behavior, and the behavior under discussion usually takes place within a greater context that is what the text is really addressing.
>
> What really jumps out at a person is how little the Bible has to say about homosexuality. Jesus has nothing at all to say. What appear to us to be references to homosexuality are found in Leviticus and in a couple of the Epistles. If this were an issue of great moral consequence to the biblical authors—or, by extension, to God—one would think it would get more ink.
>
> Old Testament references in Leviticus are a part of the Holiness Code, which details behaviors of Israel that are to set the covenant people apart from the rest of humankind, making Israel a people specially dedicated to God. In Leviticus, what appears to be homosexual activity is said to be an "abomination." That sounds like a very strong word, and clearly something to be avoided—except that other examples of "abominations" include things like eating shellfish.
>
> The New Testament also seems to discuss homosexuality. But usually it does so in the context of idolatry. In the ancient Greek world, the word commonly translated as "homosexuality" refers to the practice of men having sex with young male prostitutes as a part of pagan cultic religious practice. The primary objection is not

sexual, but religious: this is seen as a return of Christian converts to their earlier pagan practices.[15]

Ruhe adds, "None of these objections, of course, will be convincing to those who believe that the Bible must be taken literally. Even in that regard, though, we may ask why some elements of the law are given so much more weight than others; why are we supposed to cling to apparent condemnations of homosexuality while we abandon other elements of the law such as dietary restrictions" and while we ignore other Pauline injunctions, such as women remaining silent in the church?[16]

Ruhe's words are not totally convincing even for many who do not read the Bible literally. Christians in the progressive fold are able to juxtapose these few verses against the overarching scriptural commandments regarding love, justice, and inclusiveness. But in practice, this means that mainline denominations now make a distinction between sexual orientation and sexual behavior, a distinction that enables them to take a stance in favor of society's protecting the civil rights of gay persons and at the same time impose a requirement of celibacy on gay church leaders and members.[17]

The formation of GLBT caucuses did not signify acceptance by the respective denominations as a whole, although in the 1970s most mainline denominations developed task forces and study programs on the issue of homosexuality, with mixed results. The Unitarian Universalist Association, Society of Friends (Quakers), and United Church of Christ proved to be the most open and supportive. Many denominations that had never previously had official policies regarding homosexuality now felt compelled to formulate them. While some of these policies were affirming, more of them were negative, and not a few were contradictory. In the United Methodist Church, for example:

> In 1972, a statement was presented for inclusion in the Church's Social Principles, which affirmed that "homosexuals … are persons of sacred worth," and recommended the Church's support of gay civil rights. However, the statement also clarified that the Church does not "condone the practice of homosexuality" and considers its practice "incompatible with Christian teaching." Although attempts were later made at a 1976 General Conference [and at every General Conference thereafter] to repeal this negative language, they not only failed but further prohibitions were added, preventing the use of Church funds to promote in any way the acceptance of homosexuality. Furthermore, in 1984, the General Conference explicitly laid out a commitment to "fidelity in marriage and celibacy in singleness," thereby prohibiting the ordination of open, practicing homosexuals. In 1996, a sentence was added to the Church's Social

Principles section which read, "Ceremonies that celebrate homosexual unions shall not be conducted by our ministers and shall not
be conducted by our churches."[18]

It should not be thought that the resistance in mainline churches to
affirming gays and lesbians fully is entirely a product of internal deliberations. Several of these denominations have been targeted by the Institute on
Religion and Democracy (IRD), an arm of the Religious Right, which,
according to its self-description, "was founded in 1981 to combat the irre-
sponsible political lobbying of mainline churches."[19] In a working paper
entitled "Reforming America's Churches Project 2001–2004," the IRD
writes,

> Liberal theology failed America's mainline churches in the
> Twentieth Century. These diminished but still influential denomi-
> nations are now starting to acknowledge their mistakes. The IRD
> believes that the next four years offer a rare opportunity to redirect
> these churches away from their reflexive alliance with the political
> left and back towards classical Christianity. Conservatives have won
> surprising victories on key theological and sexuality issues at recent
> church conventions. Now is the time to translate those victories into
> real influence for conservatives within the permanent governing
> structures of these churches, so they can help renew the wider cul-
> ture of our nation.

The document asserts the importance of ecumenical alliances with "socially
conservative Roman Catholics and Evangelicals." But the primary focus is
on three mainline Protestant denominations: the United Methodist Church,
the Presbyterian Church (U.S.A.), and the Episcopal Church. Why these
three? Because, according to the IRD,

> Their influence is disproportionate to their numbers. Their respec-
> tive memberships include remarkably high numbers of leaders in
> politics, business, and culture. For example, over one-third of the
> members of the U.S. Senate belong to these three denominations.
> These denominations include a disproportionate number of higher
> income and educated Americans. They are affiliated with hundreds
> of colleges, universities, seminaries, academies and charitable out-
> reach centers.... These denominations are still flagship churches
> that directly or indirectly influence millions of Americans.[20]

The document goes on to detail a widespread media campaign; the issues to
be addressed, including "marriage initiatives," "hate crimes" legislation,
"federal social entitlements," and "national security"; and target dates for

influencing the governing church bodies, namely, the national conventions of each denomination from 2001 to 2004.

But even before this document was prepared, the IRD had already made major inroads. Wrote James Wall, editor of the *Christian Century*, in July of 2000,

> The United Methodist Church has made a sharp turn to the political and theological right, and it appears that it will continue to move in that direction. The particular battle is over, at least for the moment. The liberal dominance in United Methodism, the denomination that helped end the war in Vietnam and bring a halt to racial segregation in the church, has ended.

> The Good News movement, the United Methodist wing of the Institute on Religion and Democracy, and many of its bishops and tall-steeple pastors have taken over the church's governing body. That means, in the long run, that it will also take over the national and regional institutions. It is important to remember that the IRD came into being in the early 1980s with support from, and as part of, the conservative movement that elected Ronald Reagan president. Why this happened, and how long this trend will prevail, is a more complicated matter. But this much is clear: what started in the age of Reagan is now a reality in United Methodist power circles.[21]

The United Methodist Church is not alone in these developments. But not all church leaders are captive of them. To cite one example, in most Protestant churches sexual activity is condemned both for individuals who are gay and those who are straight but unmarried. Thus, the prohibition for gays and lesbians is absolute and lifelong since, in mainline as well as fundamentalist churches, ceremonial recognition of long-term committed relationships is denied, at least officially. Unofficially, many ministers are practicing what is not preached. Notes one observer, "Even as denominations try to maintain order in their ranks, pastors across the country are turning the most contentious argument in today's churches into a moot point by continuing to bless gay and lesbian relationships. It is, in effect, a classically Protestant behavior; the clergy are simply bypassing the churches' central authorities."[22] Or as Episcopal priest Susan Russell puts it, "It is my experience that the spirit of God continues to move ahead of the institutional church."[23] Not only Episcopal, but United Methodist, Presbyterian, and ELCA clergy—not just gay and lesbian clergy, but straight clergy as well—are performing these ceremonies. Not a few have paid the price of losing their jobs and even losing their ordination credentials.

Black Churches

Paradoxically, among the most recalcitrant of Protestant churches to affirm
the full humanity of gays and lesbians are the historic black churches—
Methodist, Baptist, and Pentecostal alike. Only in the past decade or so have
a few black religious leaders assumed a prophetic public stance on the issue
of homosexuality, calling black preachers and congregations to task for their
rejection of their gay brothers and sisters.[24]

The Reverend Dr. Alton B. Pollard III, director of Black Church Studies
at Candler Theological Seminary in Atlanta, issued this challenge in a sermon delivered at a conference on the Black Church and human sexuality
held at the Divinity School of Vanderbilt University:

> For persons whose stories and struggles have everything to do with
> matters of human sexuality, there is the terribly urgent ache to know
> why the Black Church born of struggle—that nurtured and empow-
> ered a people, and affirmed their absolute sense of worth; whose
> social legacy is community, solidarity, justice, and freedom—is a
> church that today cannot bring itself to accept sexual difference, sex-
> ual diversity, sexual identity, sexual equality, sexual love…. The
> Black Church is in trouble; the faith is in trouble; our society is in
> trouble; and our souls are in trouble. Today the Black Church in
> America stands at the crossroads once more. How will we respond?[25]

Pollard's own answer is to harken to the text of John 3:16: "For God so loved
the world, that he gave his only son, that *whosoever* believeth in him should
not perish but have eternal life."[26] "'Whosoever,' Jesus said. I am so glad for
that word. For it is the only answer I know for people who want to find out
whether or not God—and the Church of God—is indeed accepting of all. It
is a word without conditions, unrestricted, universal, and unreserved….
Jesus says *whosoever* is welcome here. All are accepted. All women and all
men, all gays and all straights, all children and all nations, all colors and all cultures, all conditions and all convictions, all creeds and all communities—for
all time. Whosoever. Come. Home."[27]

But for many African American GLBT Christians, the Black Church is not
a place to call home. Nor is the Catholic Church—which on matters of sexuality has historically resembled the Black Church—regarded as home by
many GLBT Christians, whether African American, Latina/o, Asian
American, Native American, or Euro-American. This, as noted earlier, is not
to say there are no gay individuals, both lay and clerical, in the Catholic
Church.

Catholic Contradictions

The presence of gay priests in the Catholic Church is not because of official neutrality with regard to sexual orientation or official sanctioning of the ordination of gay men. Rather, it is the Church's policy of requiring all priests to live a celibate lifestyle that has rendered sexual orientation of clergy, in practice, a matter of lesser consequence than in other segments of the universal Church.

While the Catholic Church has long "looked the other way" with regard to homosexuality in the priesthood, the scandal of sexual abuse that erupted in the early years of the twenty-first century has caused it to examine existing realities more overtly. The concern on the part of many clergy and parishioners is that gay priests will be singled out and that candidates for the priesthood will in the future be scrutinized more closely with regard to sexual orientation, notwithstanding that the sexual abuse of children by priests has been substantiated as the behavior of pedophiles, a behavior not defined by sexual orientation.

The priesthood aside, the official stance of the Catholic Church with regard to homosexuality turns on understandings of family and marriage. A 1990 document of the U.S. Catholic bishops called *Human Sexuality* states: "We believe that it is only within a heterosexual marital relationship that genital sexual activity is morally acceptable. Only within marriage does sexual intercourse fully symbolize the Creator's dual design, as an act of covenant love, with the potential of co-creating new human life."[28] This stance harkens back to the literal rendering of the admonition to the biblical figures of Adam and Eve to "be fruitful and multiply."[29] Given the contemporary situation of world overpopulation, some Catholic practitioners encourage putting more emphasis on sexual activity as "an act of covenant love" rather than on reproduction of the race.

The Church in Rome says otherwise, however. It continues to place prohibitions on the use of artificial means of birth control (so as not to impede procreation) and it characterizes homosexual genital acts as "intrinsically disordered." At the same time, it takes the position that "orientation" itself is not morally wrong because orientation is "not freely chosen." Furthermore, the Church has asserted that, "It is deplorable that homosexual persons have been and are the object of violent malice in speech, or in action. Such treatment deserves condemnation from the Church's pastors wherever it occurs."[30]

Concerned that the negative attitudes of the Church and of the society at large were providing fodder for the rejection and abuse of gay and lesbian individuals, in 1997 the U.S. Catholic bishops' Committee on

Marriage and Family issued a statement entitled "Always Our Children: A Pastoral Message to Parents of Homosexual Children and Suggestions for Pastoral Ministers." In this message, the bishops admonish Catholics to accept, love, and support gay and lesbian members of their families and enjoin Catholic parishes to do likewise.[31]

Even before this message was issued, 20 dioceses (out of 188 total in the United States) had official outreach ministries to gays and lesbians. Some of them had "welcoming parishes" programs, some sponsored educational and spiritual conferences and retreats, others held weekly liturgies for gays and lesbians.[32] In 2001, the Los Angeles archdiocese's Ministry with Gay and Lesbian Catholics, among the largest and most committed of such ministries, celebrated its fifteenth anniversary with a mass attended by some six hundred lesbian and gay Catholics and their family members, along with a bishop and two dozen priests.[33]

But two years earlier, in 1999, a nun and a priest, Sr. Jeannine Gramick and Fr. Robert Nugent, were "permanently prohibited from any pastoral work involving homosexual persons" and were declared "ineligible, for an undetermined period, for any office in their respective religious institutes."[34] The ban was issued by the Vatican's Congregation for the Doctrine of the Faith and it was directed at the work that Gramick and Nugent had been doing for more than twenty years through a program they founded called New Ways Ministry.

Among other activities, New Ways Ministry publishes *Bondings,* a periodic news report on issues related to the Church and to gay and lesbian Catholics, and *Womanjourney Weavings,* a newsletter for lesbian members of religious communities. The organization conducts regional workshops and seminars as well as national symposiums that bring together theologians, scholars, and church leaders to explore ministry to, for, and by gay and lesbian Catholics. Nugent and Gramick were banned for allegedly failing to represent accurately the "authentic teaching of the church."[35] Shortly after the banning, a petition was printed in the *National Catholic Reporter,* signed by some forty-five hundred individuals and supported by the leadership of fifty religious communities, calling on the National Conference of Bishops to "exercise their collegial right and ask the Vatican to reconsider this decision."[36]

The banning was not without precedent. In 1987, John J. McNeill, an ordained priest, practicing psychotherapist, and highly regarded theologian, was expelled from the Society of Jesus when he refused to cease ministering to gay men and lesbians. But McNeill continues to write and continues to provide spiritual support and nurture to those who struggle both to be the church and to change the institutional church.

So the dialectic continues, of affirmation and negation, of promise and betrayal, of progress and regression. Among church leaders, both Catholic and Protestant, are those who indulge their righteousness, those who wrestle with their consciences, and those who are committed to building inclusive Christian communities. The latter group, in partnership with GLBT Christians, are key players in the project of transforming the church.

A Church Transforming

In the year 2000, an extraordinary thing happened when a newly formed group called "United Methodists of Color for a Fully Inclusive Church" issued a statement declaring themselves to be in solidarity with gay and lesbian members. Signed by forty African American, Asian American, and Latina/o clergy and lay leaders, the statement reads in part:

> Remembering the voices who have told us to wait on justice, we dispute the notion that issues of race and nationality are so overwhelming that to fight for another issue of injustice is to water down the movement. For the storehouses of God's justice do not run low, and we must recognize the interconnectedness of all forms of oppression if we are ever to achieve the Kindom…. Inaction is impossible. For in the current climate, where difference is often answered with death, the church is either an instrument of peace, or an instrument of violence. The United Methodist Church must act boldly to end further injury to the Body of Christ.[37]

In another action that followed the United Methodist's 2000 national meeting, delegates to the New England Annual Conference signed the "New England Declaration" in which, in defiance of national policies, they vowed to ordain gay men and lesbians and to perform same-sex union ceremonies.[38]

In 2001, another United Methodist group called the Clergy Alliance committed itself to three actions: working within the church system to change the denomination's discriminatory policies and practices regarding sexual orientation and other identities; the nonviolent challenging of unjust policies and laws of the denomination; and the establishment of a Professing Church, a "church within a church" that "will be less focused on attempting to directly interact with the denomination than it will be committed to enabling faithful ministry by participating clergy and congregations."[39]

In a book published in 2000 called *The Loyal Opposition*, fourteen writers discuss their understandings of the appropriateness of resistance to discriminatory and oppressive practices regarding GLBT persons. One contributor speaks of resistance and human rights, another of ecclesial disobedience as a spiritual discipline, others of the very fact of *being* in the church constituting resistance.[40]

Nonviolent confrontation in fact has occurred numerous times at national meetings not only of the United Methodist Church, but of the Presbyterian Church (U.S.A.) and the Episcopal Church. Ecclesial disobedience, as earlier noted, is practiced by ministers who perform or witness to commitment ceremonies. In the early 2000s, Mel White formed an organization called Soulforce for the express purpose of conducting nonviolent resistance. Soulforce has been a presence at the trials of ministers charged with violating church laws; at the headquarters of Jerry Falwell in Lynchburg, Virginia; and at meetings of the Southern Baptist Convention. Hundreds of individuals have been arrested; hundreds more have been trained in the principles and tactics of nonviolent civil disobedience.[41]

Numerous other groups are functioning outside the institutional church in hopes of re-creating church. The Conference for Catholic Lesbians (CCL) works to promote Catholic lesbian community via the internet, to resist discrimination against gays and lesbians in Catholic institutions, including schools, and against Catholics and other Christians in the larger lesbian community.[42] Christian Lesbians Out (CLOUT) describes itself as "a movement of out Christian Lesbians making public witness to a radically inclusive, liberationist vision of the Gospel and its creative and revolutionary power in our lives."[43] CLOUT publishes a quarterly newsletter with the slogan, "proudly progressive, actively anti-racist, creatively spiritual, *milagro* bound."[44]

That All May Freely Serve is a movement that was founded by the Reverend Jane Spahr when, after coming out as a lesbian, she was forbidden by her denomination, the Presbyterian Church (U.S.A.), to preach. The organization functions at the national and regional levels to raise awareness of the status of GLBT people in the church, to "actively resist and transform … all structures of exploitation and oppression,"[45] and to "create a just and inclusive Presbyterian Church, a church in which all may freely serve."[46]

These movements and organizations and many others like them, together with the respective GLBT caucuses in the various denominations, have taken the overall name of the Welcoming Church movement. A primary focus of this movement is the extension of invitations to local congregations to become Welcoming churches. Each denomination has a program coordinator for this effort; many publish newsletters or convene annual convocations. Resource materials are provided to local congregations, which embark on an extended process of study and discussion before taking a vote. If affirmative, the congregation becomes "Open and Affirming" (UCC and Disciples of Christ), "Reconciling" (UMC), "Reconciled in Christ" (ELCA),

"More Light" (Presbyterian), "Welcoming and Affirming" (American Baptist), "Supportive Congregations" (Mennonite), or "Welcoming" (Unitarian Universalist).[47]

What this identification actually means varies widely. Most congregations print a public statement of inclusiveness in their church bulletins. Some develop programming or support groups specifically for GLBT members. Much depends on whether there is a critical mass of GLBT members as the congregation goes through the decision-making process, as this in turn typically determines whether new GLBT members are drawn to the church. Some congregations develop into vibrant, celebratory, justice-seeking congregations in which GLBT members assume key leadership roles; some become widely known as gay-oriented with a predominantly gay and lesbian membership.

In the year 2000, a national ecumenical conference of Christians of diverse sexual orientation and gender was convened under the sponsorship of the various denominational Welcoming programs. Witness Our Welcome 2000 (WOW 2000) was followed by a second conference, WOW 2003.[48] The implication is that the Welcoming movement is developing a community that moves it in the direction of truly being a "church within the church." As one minister puts it, "Whatever the difficulties the church at large has with the issue of gay and lesbian Christians, there are vibrant and affirming oases within it, missions and parishes that embrace and welcome gay and lesbian Christians, and both listen and respond to the growing confidence of men and women who refuse to believe that God abhors what God has created."[49]

Ultimately, the most important players in the Welcoming Church movement and in the overall process of transformation are GLBT Christians themselves. One of the players, M. R. Ritley, speaking of the mission of gay and lesbian Christians to the whole of the Church, sums up their role this way:

> The open reentry of gay and lesbian people into the public life of the Christian community is a healthy return to the vitality of the early church, in which the boundaries of the legalistic first-century Hebrew religion had to be enlarged to include the despised Gentiles as equals. This, at least in part, is what the stories of gay and lesbian Christians in the twenty-first century will be about: the enlarging of the tent's borders, the enriching of the community's fabric. It is also about vocally claiming a separate and legitimate identity in the church: not simply flawed heterosexuals, but God's gay people, God's gay tribe, bearing gifts the church truly needs, even when it least wants them.[50]

If the Kindom is not yet, the eschatological signs are at least coming out.

For Further Reading

Boyd, Malcolm, and Nancy L. Wilson, eds. *Amazing Grace: Stories of Lesbian and Gay Faith.* Freedom, Calif.: The Crossing Press, 1991.

Comstock, Gary David. *Unrepentant, Self-Affirming, Practicing: Lesbian/Bisexual/Gay People within Organized Religion.* New York: Continuum, 1996.

Countryman, L. William, and M. R. Ritley. *Gifted by Otherness: Gay and Lesbian Christians in the Church.* Harrisburg, Pa.: Morehouse Publishing, 2001.

Douglas, Kelly Brown. *Sexuality and the Black Church: A Womanist Perspective.* Maryknoll, N.Y.: Orbis Books, 1999.

Heyward, Carter. *Staying Power: Reflections on Gender, Justice, and Compassion.* Cleveland: The Pilgrim Press, 1995.

McNeill, John J. *Taking a Chance on God: Liberating Theology for Gays, Lesbians, and Their Lovers, Families, and Friends.* Boston: Beacon Press, 1996.

Morrison, Melanie. *The Grace of Coming Home: Spirituality, Sexuality, and the Struggle for Justice.* Cleveland: The Pilgrim Press, 1995.

Sample, Tex, and Amy E. DeLong. *The Loyal Opposition: Struggling with the Church on Homosexuality.* Nashville: Abingdon Press, 2000.

Tigert, Leanne McCall. *Coming Out While Staying In: Struggles and Celebrations of Lesbians, Gays, and Bisexuals in the Church.* Cleveland: United Church Press, 1996.

NOTES

1. "Homophobia" refers to a fear of homosexuals or homosexuality, while "heterosexism" is the assertion that this is the superior or exclusively acceptable life-style. In practice, heterosexism means discrimination against same-sex relationships.

2. Mary E. Hunt, "A Political Perspective," in *Women's Spirit Bonding* (eds. Janet Kalven and Mary I. Buckley; New York: Pilgrim Press, 1984), 253–54.

3. For a catalogue of the different spiritual paths gays and lesbians have taken, see Christian de la Huerta, *Coming Out Spiritually: The Next Step* (New York: Jeremy P. Tarcher/Putnam, 1999).

4. J. Gordon Melton, "Homosexually Oriented Churches," in *Encyclopedia of American Religions* (4th ed.; Detroit: Gale Research Inc., 1993), 1016–19.

5. Troy D. Perry, *The Lord Is My Shepherd and He Knows I'm Gay* (Los Angeles: NashsPublishing, 1972), 222.

6. See the religious movements homepage at <http://religiousmovements.lib.virginia.edu/nrms/ufmcc.html>.

7. See <www.ufmcc.com/perrybio.htm>.

8. For an inside discussion of these matters by a multi-racial, multi-ethnic group of feminist theologians, see chapter 6 of the Mudflower Collective's *God's Fierce Whimsy: Christian Feminism and Theological Education* (New York: The Pilgrim Press, 1985).

9. Carter Heyward, *Touching Our Strength: The Erotic as Power and the Love of God* (San Francisco: HarperSanFrancisco, 1989), 2–4, passim.

10. Ibid., 3–4.

11. Malcolm Boyd, "Underground Christians," *Amazing Grace: Stories of Lesbian and Gay Faith* (eds. Malcolm Boyd and Nancy L. Wilson; Freedom, Calif.: The Crossing Press, 1991), 2.

12. Ibid.

13. Ibid., 2–4, passim.

14. 1993 Southern Baptist Convention Proceedings, "Resolution No. 3—On Homosexuality, Military Service and Civil Rights," p. 99, cited in "Call to a Faithful Decision—Issue Paper Number One," The Interfaith Alliance Foundation, Washington D.C., n.d., 5. It bears mention that it was only in the mid-1990s that the Southern Baptist Convention acknowledged that racism was a sin and apologized for its participation in the system of slavery.

15. David Ruhe, unpublished statement made at the "Making Our Schools Safe for GLBT Youth" Forum, Ames, Iowa, February 5, 2003.

16. Ibid. Southern Baptists, it bears mentioning, in the 1990s adopted a formal policy that women could not speak from the pulpit, that they could not be ordained. This stance is not unique to the Southern Baptist Convention, although many Baptist groups, in accordance with congregational polity, provide for these decisions to be made at the local level.

17. Religious groups that have official policies supporting the legal protection of civil rights of persons regardless of sexual orientation include American Baptist Churches, U.S.A.; the Christian Church (Disciples of Christ); the Episcopal Church; the Evangelical Lutheran Church in America; Friends Committee on National Legislation; the Presbyterian Church (U.S.A.); the United Church of Christ; the United Methodist Church; and the Unitarian Universalist Association of Congregations. See the "Call to a Faithful Decision" issue paper cited above.

18. Christian de la Huerta, *Coming Out Spiritually*, 188–89. Appendices 1 and 2 in this book provide additional information on the GLBT caucuses and organizations in various religious groups.

19. Institute on Religion and Democracy, "Reforming America's Churches Project 2001–2004."

20. Ibid.

21. James M. Wall, "A Simple Solution," *Christian Century* (July 19–26): 2000, 739.

22. "Proceeding with Gay Unions," *Christian Century* (August 16–23): 2000, 823.

23. Ibid.

24. See Kelly Brown Douglas, *Sexuality and the Black Church: A Womanist Perspective* (Maryknoll, N.Y.: Orbis Books, 1999). Douglas locates her discussion in the historic context of white assault on black sexuality. Other African American theologians and ethicists who have called the Black Church to address matters of sexuality include Toinette Eugene, Emilie Townes, and Cornel West. Among those who have taken the lead among black pastors are the Reverend James Forbes, Riverside Church in New York City; the Reverend Cecil "Chip" Murray, First AME in Los Angeles; and the Reverend Phillip Lawson, Easter Hill United Methodist Church, Richmond, California.

25. Alton B. Pollard III, "Whosoever …," sermon preached at the Jefferson Street Missionary Baptist Church for the Kelly Miller Smith Institute and Carpenter Program in Religion, Gender, and Sexuality conference on the Black Church and human sexuality, Vanderbilt University Divinity School, Nashville, Tennessee, November 15, 2000.

26. John 3:16 (RSV).

27. Pollard, "Whosoever …".

28. *Human Sexuality*, #55, cited in Richard Sparks, C.S.P., "What the Church Teaches about Homosexuality," *Catholic Update*, published by St. Anthony Messenger Press, Cincinnati, Ohio, 1999.

29. Gen 1:28 (NRSV).

30. "Letter to the Bishops of the World on the Pastoral Care of Homosexual Persons, #10," Congregation for the Doctrine of the Faith, the Vatican, cited in Sparks, "What the Church Teaches about Homosexuality."

31. This message was revised and reissued in 1998, with the approval of the Vatican.

32. Catholic News Service, "Gay, Lesbian Ministry Growing," *National Catholic Reporter* (September 22, 1995): 7.

33. Arthur Jones, "Ministry with Gays and Lesbians Celebrates 15 Years," *National Catholic Reporter* (February 16, 2001): 5.

34. These excerpts from the ban are cited in a petition protesting the ban entitled "Jubilee Justice Begins at Home," which was subsequently published as a paid advertisement in the *National Catholic Reporter,* date and page unknown. For a discussion of the ban, see Teresa Malcolm, "Pair Dealt a Lifetime Ban on Ministry to Homosexuals," *National Catholic Reporter* (July 30, 2000): 3–4.

35. See Malcolm, "Pair Dealt a Lifetime Ban," 3.

36. "Jubilee Justice Begins at Home."

37. "UMC Policy Defied," *Christian Century* (June 21–28, 2000): 673.

38. Ibid.

39. "Clergy Alliance Formed," *Social Questions Bulletin*, Methodist Federation for Social Action 91:4 (September–October 2001).

40. Tex Sample and Amy E. DeLong, eds., *The Loyal Opposition: Struggling with the Church on Homosexuality* (Nashville: Abingdon Press, 2000).

41. See <www.soulforce.org>.

42. See <www.catholiclesbians.org/pages/aboutus.html>.

43. See <www.siteplace.com/clout>.

44. See CLOUT newsletter.

45. *That All May Freely Serve* newsletter, vol. 9.2 (September 2002): 4.

46. Ibid.

47. Leanne McCall Tigert, *Coming Out While Staying In: Struggles and Celebrations of Lesbians, Gays, and Bisexuals in the Church* (Cleveland: United Church Press, 1996), 40–41.

48. The Mission Statement of WOW 2000 read: "We will gather as members and friends of the Welcoming Church Movement to worship, study and play. We will gather in our human diversity to celebrate God's love for people of all sexual orientations. We will gather to experience the presence of Jesus Christ and participate in the Spirit's work to transform church and society." Program Booklet, Witness Our Welcome, August 3–6, 2000.

49. L. William Countryman and M. R. Ritley, *Gifted by Otherness: Gay and Lesbian Christians in the Church* (Harrisburg, Pa.: Morehouse Publishing, 2001), 15–16.

50. Ibid., 16.

PART 3:
Toward a Renewed and Transformed Church

D o not be conformed to this world, but be transformed by the renewing of your minds, so that you may discern what is the will of God...."

—Rom 12:2 (NRSV)

Christians of privilege who reject the paradigm of privilege—that is, who have themselves been transformed—discern the will of God to be the renewal and transformation of "church." This does not mean merely reforming the existing established church; it means embodying a vision of "church" that is loving, justice-seeking, and inclusive. The mandate translates as: Do not be conformed to the *institutional church as it is presently configured,* but transform "church" by the building of Christian community.

For Quakers, Mennonites, and Brethren, this is scarcely a novel insight. Since their initial appearance in this country, members of these groups have declined privilege in favor of living community. For the most part, they have stood apart from establishment churches and mainstream culture, except to model alternative lifestyles and values.

Since the 1960s, however, a different cadre of Christians, born into the privilege that accompanies whiteness and economic security, has elected to function as the loyal opposition in relation to the Christian establishment in the United States: loyal, because they believe in *ecclesia* as the essential expression of Christianity, but oppositional because they seek to avoid the imperial features of institutional churches. They are a part of what Malcolm Boyd, in 1967, called the "underground church"[1] and what Ched Myers, some thirty years later, refers to as the "radical Christian movement of the First World."[2]

For these Christians, much as for the Christians discussed in part 2, transformation or renewal of "church"—of what church looks like and how it acts—is not an end in itself, but rather the means to the end of transforming an oppressive, exploitative, dehumanizing (sin-full) world. Notwithstanding the privilege inherent in being white, members of this population experience various forms of oppression, sexism and heterosexism among them. Some are profoundly alienated by a capitalist economic system that mandates consumerism, pollutes the environment, and treats people like objects instead of human beings. Others feel keenly the oppressiveness of being a part of the oppressor class. Responding to the call to radical discipleship,[3] they struggle to change a system that generates multiple and interlocking forms of oppression for themselves and other populations.

Because white Christians of privilege can never totally escape the circumstances of their birth and all that that implies, those who are committed to transformation must be engaged in a perpetual process of self-examination and rededication. They must daily seek ways to be in solidarity with the poor and the oppressed—working for empowerment as opposed to merely offering charity—as they place their educational, technological, and economic resources in the service of building a more humane world. At the same time, they inevitably struggle with the same dilemma that has challenged prophetic, spirit-community Christians throughout history: maintaining a balance of inward spirituality and outward activism.

Myers offers reminders that communal renewal movements have been inspired in "each era of Christendom to attempt to dis-establish the church and to defect from its Constantinian [imperial] alliances." In the history of the United States, as in other times and places, such movements have invariably tended to one of two extremes: "One tendency was to seek refuge from the social and cultural alienation that characterizes modernity. The other tendency was to pursue specific tasks of outreach and service to the world. On the whole, focus on communal discipline has tended to come at the expense of socio-political withdrawal, while socio-political activism has tended to sacrifice coherent community life."[4]

The renewal movements that have emerged since the 1960s follow this same pattern.[5] Consequently, it is helpful to think of Transformative White Christians—TWCs, for short—as constituting a continuum. At one end are individuals and groups who are preeminently concerned with social activism. At the other end are spirituality groups that are devoid of a social justice component. In the center are communal, extra-church bodies, both inside and outside of established congregations/parishes and denominations, that practice a dialectic of theological reflection/spirituality and action.

Theological reflection, in this context, involves more than Bible study, more than witnessing or testifying to one's personal faith experience. It involves reading the Bible specifically in the light of the inequity, injustice, and disharmony of our world and discerning what responsibilities and actions for change the Scriptures call forth. Spirituality is not just a charismatic experience of the Spirit. It involves being attentive to the movement and instruction of the Spirit as a part of the process of discernment. Both theological reflection and spirituality require intentionality and location within a group context in order to confirm the veracity of the call.

Neither of the two extremes, activism or spirituality, provides for Christian community as defined in this book, though they potentially may make a contribution to the renewal and transformation of church and/or society. On the other hand, the center, which is the praxis model of Latin

American base Christian communities, represents an *ideal* model for Christian community. In the realities of the United States, examples generally fall to either side of the ideal. Thus, in between the ideal of the center and the activist individuals are extra-church organizations and movements that give relatively more emphasis to social activism, but activism that is informed by theological reflection. In between the ideal of the center and the spirituality groups are self-described "communities" that give relatively more emphasis to spirituality and to sustaining community structures, but also demonstrate a concern for social justice.

Real life examples of this middle range are the subject of part 3. These imperfect but embodied examples *are* the Church transformed and renewed, even as they strive to renew and transform the Church.

In recent decades the language of Christian community has perhaps been used even more by Euro-American Christians than it has by Christians of color. Most especially, TWCs speak of "intentional" communities. For white middle-class Christians to create genuine community amongst themselves requires a high degree of intentionality. By contrast, people of color do not so much speak of *creating* community as living it; it is their inheritance, although they are now having to heal the damage done to their respective inheritances by colonialism and its religious agents.

TWCs have their inheritance as well: monastic communities, utopian communities, independent Christian communities, socialist communities; indeed, they share, along with all other Christians, the inheritance of the house churches of the early Christians during the first three centuries of the faith. But these communities have always been *counter* to their members' culture; they are the exception, rather than the norm. So, too, contemporary movements and communities of TWCs are countercultural in character, going against the status quo of established churches and mainstream society alike.

Many members of these transformative movements, organizations, and intentional communities have a history with establishment churches, others with evangelical or Anabaptist (Mennonite and Brethren) churches. They include priests and ministers, bishops both Catholic and Protestant, involved lay church members, and believers in exile. Some communities function as subunits of church parishes and congregations; others as semi-autonomous, extra-church entities; and some are completely autonomous.

TWCs are not alone in using the language of "church renewal." However, not everyone who invokes this language has in mind the type of renewal that involves transformation. As Christian Smith puts it, "Some advocate miraculous signs and wonders as the key to renewal. Others think the answer is to return to traditional liturgy. One school of thought argues for intense evangelistic outreach. Another experiments with the formation of small groups. Yet another calls for a new focus on prayer." But these do not begin to address the fundamental issues. "Most churches today don't need mere revival or rejuvenation," Smith writes, "they need serious overhaul. It's not just a matter of slapping on a new coat of paint, but of structural renovations. Christians need to go to the root," which is to say, they need to be radical.[6]

> Radical church renewal requires basic changes both in our *consciousness* and our *structures*. A change in consciousness means an overturning of our common values, thoughts, and expectations. Unfortunately, to paraphrase an old adage, you can take some people out of an old, stale church, but you can't take the old, stale church out of some people. In other words, to be successful, renewal demands that we change how we *think* about church as well as how we practice church.

> Radical church renewal also means changing church structures. Renewal demands that we alter—and sometimes eliminate—many institutional practices, rules, roles, and programs.[7]

Chapter 10 profiles examples of activities that move in the direction of this *radical* renewal, as well as some that do not. Most of the examples cited come from the Episcopal, United Methodist, or Catholic Church, or represent ecumenical efforts. Other mainline Protestants have their stories of community-building and their share of TWCs as well. Whether in social change movements, extra-church organizations, or intentional communities, they have one common denominator: they have all been influenced, directly or indirectly, by the liberation theologies and social change movements of marginalized populations in the United States and around the world. They have been evangelized. And they have been converted. Accordingly, they have themselves become a marginalized people.

NOTES

1. Malcolm Boyd, ed., *The Underground Church* (Baltimore: Penguin Books, 1969). See Boyd's preface, in which he points out that the "underground church" was underground in its worship, but "radically out-in-the-open" with its involvement in social issues (xiii).

2. Ched Myers, *Who Will Roll Away the Stone? Discipleship Queries for First World Christians* (Maryknoll, N.Y.: Orbis Books, 1994), xv.

3. Ibid., xxiii.

4. Ibid., 179–80.

5. Ibid.

6. Christian Smith, *Going to the Root: Nine Proposals for Radical Church Renewal* (Scottdale, Pa.: Herald Press, 1992), 13–14.

7. Ibid., 15–16.

—CHAPTER 10—
Enclaves of Renewers and Transformers

In the early years of the 1960s, many northern white college students, as well as Protestant ministers and Catholic priests and sisters, journeyed South to join the civil rights movement. Some participated in the Freedom Rides organized by the Congress of Racial Equality (CORE), while others were involved in the voter registration drives of the Student Nonviolent Coordinating Committee (SNCC). Still other religious leaders and college youth were involved in northern expressions of the movement. It was a transforming experience for all participants.

Ministers and priests sometimes moved from these experiences to involvement in the United Farm Workers movement, the American Indian Movement, or the *La Raza* movement. Some of the students became leaders in the women's rights movement, while Catholic sisters encouraged their communities to become more socially aware. College activists and religious leaders alike became involved in the anti-Viet Nam War movement. Some of the youth emerged as leaders of the nation-wide student movement or joined the radical New Left spearheaded by Students for a Democratic Society (SDS), while others found a home in the social justice-oriented Student Christian Movement.

Among this group of activists were some who spent time in Latin America, where they were deeply influenced both by the grassroots practice and the scholarly expression of liberation theology. Black liberation theology emerged in the United States at roughly the same time as Latin American liberation theology, challenging the racism of American Christianity. Feminist theology, with its critique of hierarchy and patriarchy, followed in short order, as did Latino, Mujerista, and Womanist theologies. The churches of white Christians in America have not been the same since. Many of them have become more reactionary. Some few have rejected the old paradigm of imperial Christendom in favor of spirit-based Christian community. Vast numbers of them are still floundering, struggling to figure out what it is they want to be and how to get there.

Factors other than radical theology come into play in this turmoil. For Catholics, there was the Second Vatican Council; for mainline Protestants, declining church memberships and aging congregants. For both, there is the impact of the widespread interest in spirituality that emerged throughout the United States in the 1960s and 1970s at the same time as liberation theologies. The interest in spiritualities unrelated to organized churches eventually generated a demand for greater emphasis on spirituality inside the churches. In some quarters, this renewed emphasis on spirituality has opened the way to Christian community. In others, it has provided an escape route from Christian social responsibility. Undoubtedly, the majority of churches emphasizing spirituality, especially in the form of charismatic renewal, see this as an end in itself.

Catholics and Protestants alike are also challenged by pluralism. Within the Church itself, white Catholics are increasingly called upon to share power and decision making with Hispanics. Establishment Protestants find their hegemonic influence diminished both by the presence in American society of non-Christian religious groups and by Christian fundamentalists. Indeed, according to C. Kirk Hadaway and David Roozen, "Nearly everyone agrees that mainstream denominations are in the midst of an identity crisis, largely resulting from the 'disestablishment' of this stream of Protestantism from its status as the unofficial 'Church' of American society."[1]

The first step in revitalizing mainline Protestantism, they suggest, is to "stop trying to be the established church for the cultural center [because] the cultural center no longer exists." Instead, they recommend that mainline Protestants "take advantage of the pluralistic character of American society and withdraw from direct participation in America's liberal/conservative 'culture war'.... Perhaps as mainstreamers," they suggest, "we do not want to be dogmatic and intolerant, the charges we cast at fundamentalists. But we also do not need to be the antithesis of fundamentalists. We can be ... well, something different—not liberal, not conservative. We can ignore the continuum and be something else."[2]

That "something else" is a devolution of mainline churches into a "spiritual movement." Hadaway and Roozen envision this movement as "a decentralized partnership of churches, judicatories, denominational agencies, independent parachurch organizations, and individuals, connected through a nonhierarchical network of intersecting lines of relationships. The central element to a revitalized mainstream ... is the reclamation of religious experience and spirituality."[3]

Hadaway and Roozen point out that this decentralization is already in process, citing the mission network of "tall steeple churches" and the Leadership Network in which churches mentor one another. All that is needed is a unifying movement to join such networks and agencies together.[4] The intention, then, is that as members of this movement are engaged in the larger world, they will come to understand their involvements as "lay vocations," which is to say that "sacred" value will be restored to the performance of "secular" tasks. In broad outline, the plan sounds very much like the model of seeker/new paradigm evangelical churches. It differs partly in that denominations will still exist as keepers of the historical memory of the tradition. But they will no longer be engaged in "social activism" and "efforts to reform society."[5]

The envisioned movement will, however, create "communities." The code words for church renewal today are "small groups." Small groups are the "new paradigm" for evangelical seeker churches and megachurches as a whole. Small groups are the prescribed mode for renewing Catholic parishes. Small groups are even commended for mainline churches. Sometimes these small groups are called "communities;" sometimes they actually become Christian community. But not as a rule.

White Christians who assign a radical meaning to the project of renewal and transformation agree with Hadaway and Roozen on some points. Certainly all would agreed that mainline denominations should stop trying to be the established church. Many would agree that spirituality is an imperative. But an imperative for what? Toward what end? Transformative White Christians (TWCs), like so many other Christians on the margins, see that Christianity calls for so much more. And Christian community means something so very different.

Not that TWCs are a homogeneous lot. Over the past fifty years, the Catholic and Protestant and ecumenical enclaves scattered here and there throughout the country have each had their own focus, their own priorities. But they are all concerned in some fashion with systemic change that leads to more just and caring relationships among people and among peoples. Some attend more to creating the church/community forms out of which to engage in these efforts, while others attend more to the efforts themselves.

Among the latter are those who conjoin the emphasis in Latin American liberation theology on Marxist class analysis with the North American tradition of Christian socialism. In the United States of the 1970s, these individuals constituted the religious counterpart of the secular New Left. But their lineage could be traced back to nearly a century earlier.

Christian Socialism

In the 1880s, the organized labor movement had gained sufficient strength and momentum to begin capturing the imagination of certain church leaders. The Society of Christian Socialists, founded by an

Episcopal priest in 1889, ultimately organized chapters in a number of industrial cities. By the end of that century, both the Catholic Church and the Protestant social gospel movement were lending support to the rights of laborers, although support was confined to the rights of *white* laborers. Social gospel theologians, notably Walter Rauschenbusch, were influential in persuading mainline Protestant denominations of the necessity of social missions, toward the end of establishing a Christian social order—that is, the kingdom of God.

Initially, "Christian social order" was understood as a "'third way,' a vision that was neither capitalist nor socialist. In the interests of ethical purity, the church was unwilling to identify itself too closely with the goals of secular movements." But as the secular Socialist Party found increasing support among workers and farmers, "many Christians adopted the position that political parties rather than the church should be the primary agents of social change." The result was the organizing in 1911 of the Church Socialist League, with leadership provided by Episcopal ministers. In 1919, as the Socialist Party declined, the Church Socialist League was replaced with the Church League for Industrial Democracy (CLID).[6]

CLID was the vision of an Episcopal churchwoman named Vida Scudder who, while persuaded that church social action needed to be based in the middle class, also believed that the middle class would no longer support an explicitly socialist organization. "Her greatest fear following the First World War was that the middle class would support anti-left repression. Thus … she effectively argued for forming an organization with broad middle class support by uniting liberals and socialists who would work for civil liberties and industrial reform without explicitly favoring socialism." The use of the phrase "industrial democracy" indicated that "the conflict between labor and capital was the central issue of social concern." Racism and sexism were not deemed unimportant; members of CLID simply understood that "once the possibility that some can advance by dividing and exploiting others was eliminated, racism and sexism would fade away."[7]

Throughout the 1920s, CLID was primarily concerned with educating Episcopal church members about the injustices of capitalism and with defending Episcopal social activists who came under attack by the church or the federal government. During the years of the Great Depression, the organization worked cooperatively with groups similar to itself to support labor, combat fascism, and oppose racial discrimination. Among the other groups were the Fellowship of Christian Socialists, the Methodist Federation for Social Service, the Rauschenbusch Fellowship for Baptists, the Reformed Council for Social Reconstruction, and various Presbyterian and Congregationalist bodies. All of these groups, in turn, were members of a radical federation called the United Christian Council for Democracy (UCCD) organized in 1936 by Reinhold Niebuhr.[8]

In the 1940s, among other activities, CLID provided relief support to China and the Soviet Union and lobbied for "full employment and a guaranteed annual income along with opposition to the closed shop, the poll-tax, and legislation that deprived women of equal rights." The organization's name was changed to the Episcopal League for Social Action (ELSA) in order to reflect these broader concerns. But in the 1950s a confluence of factors—the turning away of the middle class from industrial issues, the push of McCarthyism, and the pull of other social issues—led to the demise of ELSA. In its place, progressive Episcopalians took up other causes, including "civil rights, pacifism and peace work, anti-imperialist politics, anti-sexism, and sexual liberation [gay rights]."[9]

Among the various progressive Christian organizations, the Methodist Federation for Social Service (MFSS) alone remained intact at the end of the 1950s. This extra-church group was born in 1907 as the Methodist voice of the social gospel. For some time the northern Methodist denomination recognized MFSS as the agency responsible for mobilizing the entire denomination on behalf of social reform. With the appointment of Harry F. Ward as executive secretary in 1911, the MFSS became a strong advocate of church community service programs, the labor movement, and the rights of conscientious objectors and political dissenters. The latter issue achieved such importance during World War I that Ward helped found the American Civil Liberties Union, serving as its president for twenty years.[10]

In the 1930s, the singular focus of MFSS was its unyielding critique of capitalism as a "pagan [un-Christian] economic order." George McClain, who became the executive director of the MFSA decades later, writes, "The Federation's entire energy was officially thrown into the struggle against the capitalist order. By vote of the [MFSS] general meeting and ratification by the membership in late 1933 and early 1934, the Federation was henceforth to be identified as 'an organization which seeks to abolish the profit system and to develop the classless society based upon the obligation of mutual service.'" In 1934, Ward put on yet another hat as president of the American League Against War and Facism, later known as the American League for Peace and Freedom. Although the MFSS was divided over joining the league on account of the fact that its membership included members of the Communist Party, it ultimately did join, becoming the only church group ever to do so.[11]

The stance taken by MFSS brought to the fore the growing conservatism in the denomination as a whole, which in turn led members of the MFSS to begin organizing independent units. By the late 1940s, local chapters had been formed in three dozen Methodist conferences and in numerous colleges and cities. Furthermore, MFSS was intentional in recruiting members from the racially segregated Central Jurisdiction that was created when the northern and southern branches of Methodism reunited in 1939; in 1948, a bishop of the all-black jurisdiction, Robert Brooks, was elected president of what that same year became the Methodist Federation of Social Action (MFSA).[12]

McClain writes that the organization was the "chief victim among all religious groups of the McCarthyite anti-Communist persecution which engulfed the country in the late 1940s and 1950s." The attack was so virulent that the Methodist Church officially disassociated itself from the federation, going so far as to eliminate from its social creed all references to "the subordination of the profit motive to the creative and cooperative spirit." The federation experienced a serious decline over the next several years, but survived with volunteer staff until 1960, when a new executive director, Lee Ball, began a rebuilding process and led the organization in opposing the war in Vietnam.

In the 1970s, MFSA, influenced by the liberation theology of Latin America, resumed its critique of capitalism. At the end of the decade, it was among the first groups publicly to point to the growth of the "New Far Right" within the United Methodist denomination.[13] Resisting this development, the MFSA in the 1980s and 1990s, under McClain's leadership, became a dedicated advocate of gay rights both within the church and in the larger society. In different parts of the country, local chapters functioned as Christian communities, engaging in theological reflection and taking action to address local, regional, and national issues of concern. The MFSA as a whole became a critical presence at conferences of the United Methodist Church and continues to serve as a rallying point for progressive ministers and laity working to transform the denomination.

Theological Reflection and Social Action

The Methodist Federation for Social Action stands as but one example of the influence of Latin American liberation theology on politically left, white North American Christians. In the 1970s, Christian socialism in the United States resurfaced with the organizing of "ACTS 4:32," an ecumenical branch of a movement called Christians for Socialism that began in Chile in 1972 and quickly spread around the world. By 1977, ACTS 4:32 (which also stood for American Christians Toward Socialism) consisted of ten chapters, each with several subgroups that functioned essentially as base Christian communities.[14] As one subgroup reported: "The locally-based programs of ACTS chapters are concerned with concrete practice, reflection, communication and celebration of faith in Christ, taking the actual daily experience of members as the point of departure and return. In taking up such tasks, we adopt the most valid and serviceable instruments of social, economic, political and cultural analysis, and we embrace the demands of Jesus' practice, recognizing in him the foundation of a new humanity."[15]

In 1978, ACTS 4:32 took the name of the parent movement, Christians for Socialism. In a brochure describing its objectives, the group spoke of "creating a new society":

> We believe that the best way to achieve this new society is to build a socialist society which reflects our democratic traditions. CFS is committed to working with other like-minded people toward this goal, especially within a religious context.
>
> Specifically, we want the resources of the churches used to bring social justice, especially for working people and the poor. This means that the churches' power, resources and property should be used to help people help themselves. The message of the churches should convey the biblical message of love and justice.
>
> Religion is sometimes used to make people accept suffering and exploitation. Instead it must be turned around to give people the hope and the courage to make new lives and a new society.[16]

The statement continues: "We work for a better economic system which is committed to meeting peoples' needs rather than to making profits for a few; we are committed to liberate the churches from the economic and cultural bonds of capitalism and authoritarianism." Furthermore, "we are opposed to racism and sexism" and "we support people of all sexual orientations."[17] CFS, in short, envisioned a transformed church and society, both of which would be fully inclusive.

Most members of the organization were clergy or lay members in the progressive wings of their respective denominations. Most of them were white, well educated, and economically stable, although exceptions could be found in California, where more of the members were Latin American and Mexican, some of them laborers and some of them priests and sisters in exile.[18] Ultimately, CFS in the United States succumbed to its dominant demographics and to what CFS itself described as the "problematic of the U.S. situation," that is, the deep resistance and obstacles in American society to a socialist agenda.[19]

While CFS was still functioning, its national executive director, Kathleen Schultz, joined with representatives from other groups—the MFSA; the editors of the left journal *Radical Religion;* the staff of the Episcopal magazine *The Witness;* and members of the Episcopal Church and Society Network, among others—to form the Inter-Religious Task Force for Social Analysis. In 1979, this group produced a document entitled "Must We Choose Sides? Christian Commitment for the '80s," which explored the contradictions of capitalism and Christianity and was widely used by church study groups.

Other members of the Inter-Religious Task Force for Social Analysis included individuals who were actively involved in the Theology in the Americas (TIA) project. TIA began in 1974 with the convening of sixty small action/reflection groups that for a year studied various liberation theologies and the systemic dimensions of different forms of oppression. These groups came together in 1975 at TIA's first conference, which was planned under the auspices of the Latin American Sections of the United States Catholic Conference and the National Council of Churches.[20] The conference was coordinated by Sergio Torres, an exiled Chilean priest. Participants included theologians, social activists, and church and community workers from both North and South America who were "Black, Hispanic, Asian, Native American, women, workers or marginalized whites."[21]

At this conference, delegates designed a five-year program that was "committed to a new theological methodology based on the grassroots experiences of those who are oppressed by society's racism, sexism, classism and imperialism, … a theology which both comes from and can serve the liberation process of today's poor and powerless."[22] Their official statement of purpose read,

> Theology in the Americas demands a commitment from its constituency to *praxis*—an ongoing process of action/reflection leading to an ever deepening political and life-style option. It combines both *social analysis* and *theological reflection* in an effort to relate the message of the Gospel to the structures of society in which we live. We envision the creation of a *contextualized U.S. theology* wherein our Lord's liberating action is experienced in our day:
>
> > The Spirit of the Lord is upon me,
> > For God has anointed me.
> > And has sent me to bring
> > The good news to the poor,
> > To proclaim liberty to the captives
> > And to the blind new sight;
> > To set the downtrodden free
> > To proclaim the Lord's year of favor.
> >
> > —Luke 4:18–19.[23]

Theology in the Americas formed a series of affinity groups to address the specific oppression of respective groups and the role that North American

white Christians might play. These groups then reconvened in a second conference in 1980.[24]

Apart from these more identifiable movements and organizations, Latin
American liberation theology had a profound impact on many individual
progressive Catholics. In the 1960s and 1970s, commitment to social transformation was expressed in the movement led by Philip and Daniel Berrigan,
Elizabeth McAlister, and other radically prophetic individuals who opposed
not only the Viet Nam War, but the armaments race as a whole, and who supported the freedom movements of colonized peoples both in the United
States and around the world. Around the country, formal and informal
action/reflection groups, many of them ecumenical, were formed, constituting what came to be referred to as the "underground church."[25]

In 1967, Malcolm Boyd described the "members" of the underground
this way: "Some go to church and some don't. Those who do are deeply frus-
trated by existing forms and attitudes, by the ungiving nature of the official
church. The movement is deeply concerned about human need. Its religious
questions are about poverty, race, sexuality, war and peace—but with
emphasis on doing, not talking." In referring to the underground church
itself, Boyd explained,

> I mean a condition of revolutionary change and surgical renewal in
> the church, and not simply a label or name. "Underground" ...
> reminds us that fundamental changes must take place at the bottom
> of the church instead of at the top; it speaks of a ferment presently
> taking place in the "basement" of the church, not its chanceries; it
> means (especially for many Protestant clergy) that social action and
> theological speculation must be undertaken under wraps, for these
> cut against the status quo norma of congregations and hierar-
> chies—by whatever name—which can fire and hire very quickly.[26]

The underground church movement generated a number of organizations committed to pursuing social change through governmental processes
but within a theological framework. Among those that have endured are
NETWORK, a Catholic social justice lobby, and Bread for the World, an
ecumenical lobby for the elimination of hunger. Other participants in the
underground church were drawn to what Ched Myers variously describes as
"communities of defection from the dominant culture" or "discipleship
communities," all of which shared the objectives of personal renewal and
mission, that is, spirituality and peace and justice work.[27]

Intentional Christian Communities

In the 1960s and 1970s,

> Christian intentional communities were "surfing" on the waves of a much broader cultural movement that included the birth of many secular communities as well. The manifest flaws of society—war in Vietnam, Watergate-style abuse of authority, denial of civil rights to minorities, ecological degradation, and the spiritual emptiness of many churches—all called for a new radical synthesis. The Post-American community [later named Sojourners] and its magazine [by the same name], under Jim Wallis's leadership, put a radical discipleship theology together with communal life and a prophetic critique of national policies. Theirs was a marching flag that many Christian communities kept in view.[28]

A 1978 census identified eighty-six communities or churches with communal components in the United States and Canada that were part of this Christian communities movement. Several of them belonged to an association called Community of Communities.[29] While each community was distinctive in its make-up and in the particular social issues it sought to address, they shared some common features. One observer offers this profile:

> Intentional Christian communities are faith-based families of people who recognize and respond to the existence of God in themselves, others, and the world. The men and women in them also belong to communities of resistance that refuse to accept injustice and dehumanization in the name of empire. They do not voice their criticism as irrational sectarians mouthing Jeremiads, or revolutionaries addicted to a self-indulgent, imaginary utopia. They are, rather, responsible people who understand what is wrong and want to transform the world in light of what it can be.... The members of intentional communities live modestly and often pool their resources. Convinced that race, culture, and gender are not barriers to human understanding as much as intriguing facets of our humanity, they do everything in their power to understand each other and people outside the community despite inevitable difficulties.... Finally, they insist that society is something that we are called to shape in new and imaginative ways.[30]

Writing some years later, David Janzen reflected that "this period of intense common life and spiritual renewal had a profound impact on tens of thousands who took part in it. Many will say today that they never lived more sacrificially, closer to the Lord, or were more meaningfully engaged in ministry."[31] Yet, by the mid-1990s, many of the communities that came into existence in the 1960s and 1970s had ceased to exist. "A variety of forces came together in the 1980s to disperse a movement that many expected to be a prime mover of church renewal," explained Janzen. "Some community members experienced exhaustion from years of activism and communal living arrangements that tried to make extroverts of everyone." Predictably, as they grew older, married, and had families, many members were drawn to a different life-style. And "countless wounded persons" who had found healing in the "family" of community also "experienced community as the 'parent' from whom they needed to individuate."[32]

> Cultural forces outside community life also had their impact. Idealism died in the younger generation, and pursuit of lucrative careers took over as a dominant motivation. Ronald Reagan entered the White House and the glorification of self-interest seemed to sweep all before it. None of these anti-community forces in the 1980s amounted to active persecution. Rather, communities found themselves in the belly of a beast whose stomach acids seemed to dissolve all support for a life of sacrifice to the common good.
>
> More overt persecution was not absent, however. Government surveillance and dirty tricks dogged activist communities like Sojourners and Jubilee Partners. The Reagan administration used the Internal Revenue Service to investigate nonprofit organizations, including many community groups....[33]

After hosting one last conference of Christian communities in 1984, the Community of Communities dissolved; most of its member communities vacated their communal covenants and abandoned the practice of pooling economic resources. Not all communities succumbed to the hostile climate of the 1980s or to the appeal of self-advancement, however. Some of those that endured had grown deep roots long before the advent of the 1960s.

The Bruderhof ("place of brothers") came to the United States after suffering persecution in Nazi Germany and now consists of six communities with some twenty-five hundred members in the states of New York, Pennsylvania, and Connecticut. As a result of new converts, the three largest have grown since the mid-1980s and have established three new subunits, or "hofs." Bruderhof members live community as depicted in the book of Acts, but with a strong social justice component. The radical discipleship of the Spring Valley Bruderhof in Pennsylvania, for example, has been expressed in members' nonviolent opposition to the U.S. invasion of Iraq, the embargo in Cuba, and the death penalty. The writings of the Bruderhof founder, Eberhard Arnold, continue to be an important resource for other intentional communities, while visitations to the Bruderhof communities provide inspiration to begin still other communities.[34]

The Hutterites, founded in the United States in 1874, continue to grow by virtue of a high birth rate. With four hundred communities and some thirty thousand members, they represent the largest "family" of intentional Christian communities anywhere in the world. Located in rural Canada and in the northern plains states, they are more insulated and biblically conservative than the Bruderhof.[35] Along with the Shakers and the Amana Colonies, the Hutterites are members of the National Historic Communal Societies Association.

The Catholic Worker movement is perhaps next in line numerically, so far as the United States is concerned, with some 130 "houses of hospitality." The Catholic Worker movement began in 1933 with the publication of a newspaper called *The Catholic Worker*, which promoted the biblical promises of justice and mercy. Six months later, the paper's two publishers, Dorothy Day and Peter Maurin, proposed to the U.S. bishops the establishment of a house of hospitality in every parish, "where the homeless, the hungry, and the forsaken would always be welcome."[36] Day and Maurin advanced the cause of voluntary poverty, believing that choosing this life-style would "give the movement insight into the inequitable social and economic forces at work in the world, insight that comes harder when mired in a position of economic privilege."[37] Over the years, at Day's insistence, the movement also embraced a commitment to nonviolence.

Today, after more than seventy years, *The Catholic Worker* is still being published and Catholic Worker communities retain their original commitments. In addition, "growing numbers of Worker communities are focusing on such varied vocations as ministering in prison, advocating for refugees, establishing land trusts and health cooperatives, building communities of resistance, providing legal and medical assistance, creating sustainable farms and cottage industries, and working with the developmentally disabled." The movement today is a "dynamic and organic tradition, centered in the grassroots experience of the laity trying to find meaning and purpose in today's consumeristic and commodified world, where the spiritual is so often subordinated to the material."[38]

Since the 1970s, L'Arche communities have flourished in the United States and Canada. Part of the International Federation of L'Arche, a movement founded in France by Jean Vanier, these Christian communities provide places of welcome for adults and children with physical and mental disabilities who live in community with their caretakers.

Highly educated young women and men, who could be making money in lucrative professions, prefer to spend their time holding and helping those broken in body and spirit. They live day in and day out with severely handicapped people and when they celebrate the Eucharist they do so as a united, believing community, healthy and sick, strong and weak together. They do so because they believe in the incarnation as the ultimate truth, rather than in wealth and power.... In the face of a seemingly all-powerful, dehumanizing system, uncanny grace abounds and people rediscover the joy of having a common identity as God's children.[39]

The impact of this movement extends beyond the individual communities, which have become an influential model for the entire Christian community movement.[40]

Unaffiliated Intentional Communities

In his census of intentional communities, Janzen identifies another forty communities that are not affiliated with any network or organizations. Among the better known of these is Koinonia, founded in 1942 near Americus, Georgia. One of the founders and the principal leader of this community until his death in 1969 was Clarence Jordan, a well-known proponent of racial reconciliation. Founded as an interracial community in the heart of the segregated South, members quickly felt the wrath both of the KKK and the local Baptist Church. In the mid-1950s, all of the black residents, about a quarter of the total membership, were compelled to leave. Over the years, the membership has waxed and waned, reaching its peak in 1979 with "36 adult full members, along with several dozen children and short- and long-term volunteers." That same year, three couples left to form another community, Jubilee Partners, whose primary mission is working with refugees.[41]

Since its initial founding, Koinonia's projects have ranged from teaching farming methods to tenant farmers, to a pecan-and-fruitcake mail order business, to building low-income housing. In 1976, the Koinonia members who started the community's Fund for Humanity left to establish Habitat for Humanity International. In the early years of the twenty-first century, the community still lives its original precepts of Christian pacifism, racial reconciliation, and simple living.[42]

The impact of these intentional communities extends beyond the resident members. Observes Jantzen:

> Every Christian intentional community is part of an extended community of friends, newsletter contacts, and affiliations that offer support to the community. Many people in the extended circle of support around a community have some sense of call to community themselves, but because of life circumstances, they are not able to live out this calling in full community. This longing for deeper

fellowship and spiritual nurture is often most acute, ironically, for pastors of congregations and service workers who feel isolated in their calling to a life fully dedicated to following Jesus.[43]

Among the independent communities are those spawned by a local church; in fact, local churches themselves may constitute an intentional community. The Church of the Savior, in Washington, D.C., is an exemplary example of both.

The Church of the Savior was started in 1947 by Gordon and Mary Cosby. Fifty-five years later, Gordon Cosby was still preaching every Sunday and Mary Cosby was still teaching in the church's Servant Leadership School, the in-house seminary that was modeled after the underground seminary created by the German Lutheran pastor, Dietrich Bonhoeffer, during the Second World War. Over the years, the Church of the Savior has given life to more than seventy-five independent ministries, many of them in the poorest areas of the nation's capital, and to twelve faith communities. The church itself has an expansive missions program, which includes low-income housing for more than eight hundred, an after-school mentoring and tutoring program, a job training and placement program, a small hospital for homeless people, a walk-in clinic for the poor, residential housing for people with AIDS, a home for the elderly poor, a major drug and alcohol rehabilitation program that has become a national model, and a retreat center called Dayspring.[44]

The membership of the Church of the Savior has deliberately been kept small, never exceeding 150, out of the founders' conviction that "the greatest impact on the world comes by small, highly committed and disciplined communities of people focused on outward mission, inward transformation, and loving, accountable community. Size," believes Gordon Crosby, "actually inhibits effectiveness, work[ing] against a community of people being truly counter-cultural, having depth, breaking addictions to the culture, and truly witnessing to the gospel."[45] Thus, when the membership becomes too large, they simply divide, creating a new community, a smaller church. Those who attend and become involved in the Church of the Savior, however, number in the hundreds at any given time.[46]

Actual membership in the church requires an intense period of study, serious practice of spiritual disciplines, participation in one of the church's mission groups, and an annual renewal of membership vows. The Church of the Savior, in short, is itself a community that integrates spirituality, service, and social action and demands the relinquishing of privilege.

> There's no way to hang onto the Christian faith without taking seriously God's longing for equality for the total human family. Lots of people have heard of God being just, but they don't even think about

attempting to literally embody that justice. What does that mean? How much privilege do I have a right to hang onto? How much privilege do I have a right to pass on to my children? Do I have a right to spend all my resources seeing that my children get a university education when other children don't get any education at all? That's privilege. People say, "Well, if I can educate my children, they are then going to use their education to work for compassion and justice." But that doesn't normally happen. That education is usually used for self-advancement and perpetuating the separation.[47]

Cosby speaks for many who commit themselves to radical discipleship in communal living when he says, "We're not just talking about a general command, 'Love one another'—we're talking about a particular, concrete group of people where that is actually happening."[48]

Not all intentional communities involve members living together or pooling economic resources. Especially in today's urban settings, members of intentional communities may live in the same neighborhood, or they may commute some distance to congregate periodically in a private home or in the basement of a church. The newer intentional communities of the 1980s and 1990s are identified by various names: house churches, the people's church, the popular church, base Christian or base ecclesial communities, small Christian communities, and Women-Church. "Despite the variety of labels," writes one participant/observer, "at the core of [this later] movement lies a dynamic vision of what the church can and should be. This vision weaves together the themes of community, participation, spiritual growth, celebration, service to the poor, discipleship, mutual accountability, and social transformation into a fresh experience of church."[49]

Not all communities that go by these names, however, embody all of these features. Terry Veling makes a distinction between "mainstream" communities and "marginal" communities. A key difference is that "one development finds its primary location within the mainstream ethos and institutional structures of church life, [while] the other adopts a critical distance from these structures."[50]

> Whereas "mainstream" communities retain a strong allegiance to the parish, with small communities being more like a "sub-set" of parish life, members of "marginal" communities see the intentional community to which they belong as their *primary* religious group, claiming their primary allegiance. Common to the self-understanding of marginal Christian communities is the awareness that when they gather, they are gathering as *church*. They do not consider themselves as "parts" or "pieces" of a larger entity we call "church," but as genuine church, as truly ecclesial expressions.[51]

Many of the "mainstream" communities have been formed, however, with the intent that they would serve to "renew" the church from within. This is particularly the case in the Catholic Church of the past twenty-five years or so.

Catholic Parish Renewal

The most prolific source of what Catholics term "small Christian communities" is the program called RENEW, which began in the archdiocese of Newark, New Jersey, in the late 1970s. In the years since, this program has generated thousands of small groups in more than seventy dioceses and hundreds of local parishes. Initially, the local parish groups are formed around the liturgical seasons of Advent and Lent and meet during these weeks, usually in members' homes, over a three-year cycle. Some of these evolve into long-term communities and participate in what is called the Post-RENEW process.

The progressive plan of the RENEW program starts with an emphasis on spiritual growth, moving from individual spirituality to spirituality of the group and ultimately to spirituality of the whole parish. Groups that continue beyond a season become involved in a parish ministry—for example, the liturgy committee, bereavement committee, parish council, social concerns, food pantry, and so forth. In meetings of community members, time is given not only to personal sharing, prayer, and Bible study, but to serious study of Catholic social teachings. Only in the final stage, when a group becomes involved in outreach toward social justice, is it officially regarded as a small Christian community.[52] As RENEW staff members put it,

> Small Christian communities are not truly Christian communities if they are only sharing, prayer, study or support groups. They are communities if they recognize that they are empowered by the Holy Spirit to proclaim and to live the good news of Jesus. Through the power of the Holy Spirit, Christians are continually in the process of conversion; the Spirit changes hearts and behaviors. We need only look to Jesus to see action and outreach that was completely generated by a total love for God. While love is a feeling and a desire, it is also an action.[53]

Few RENEW groups achieve this goal, however. In their emphasis on access to the Scriptures, the communal character of Catholicism, the church as the people, and the roles of laity, these groups do represent a change from the clerical, authoritarian church of the pre–Vatican II years. But insofar as they lack a commitment to radical transformation either of church or society, they are more appropriately described as faith-sharing groups than as Christian communities.

Pointing to some of the political realities of trying to transform the church from within, Allan Deck comments,

RENEW appears to be a nuanced and balanced effort to promote renewal gradually, with a balanced pedagogy. The highly developed organizational aspects of the program seem inspired on a very North American sense of what is practical, efficient, and orderly. A strenuous effort is made to win the explicit backing of the bishops and the local pastors. In this way RENEW avoids the suspicion and fear that all movements coming from outside the parish and diocese can often generate.... The RENEW process defuses fears about small faith-sharing groups becoming parallel or underground churches.[54]

Similarly, older renewal programs such as Cursillo, Marriage Encounter, and the Christian Family Movement provide little challenge to the established church. Upon completing the spiritual retreat that is central in each of these programs, participants sometimes form follow-up communities. They are generally short-lived, however, and their focus most often is renewal of personal and family relationships, not of the larger church or society.

In their study of Catholic small Christian communities (SCCs), Bernard Lee, S.M. and William V. D'Antonio identify some 37,000 groups, around 14,000 of which are products of RENEW. Some of the oldest communities included in this survey have roots in the underground church. Others are the product of a program developed in the early 1980s by Father Art Baranowski called the National Alliance for Parishes Restructuring into Communities, or a similar program initiated by the staff of several dioceses called the National Forum for Small Christian Communities. Other communities in the survey were started independently by local parish staff or lay leaders and a number of these are affiliated with Buena Vista, a national network of SCCs that was formed in the late 1980s.[55]

Buena Vista, especially, is intentional in including Latina/o community members. It also emphasizes social action as an essential component of authentic Christian community. Each of these networks, the National Alliance for Parishes Restructuring into Communities, the National Forum, and Buena Vista, regularly holds regional and/or national meetings. Since 1993, they have held three joint conferences in order to solidify and support the small Christian community movement as a whole.

The communities in these three networks, together with the RENEW groups, constitute about two-thirds of the total 37,000 surveyed. Hispanic/Latino communities account for 20 percent of the total. About 12 percent are charismatic communities, which, not surprisingly, are "the most traditional in beliefs and church allegiance."[56]

This survey does not include the 100 or so WomenEucharist communities identified by Sheila Durkin Dierks or the many other communities and spirituality groups of the Women-Church movement. Nor does it include the associates affiliated with women's religious communities. The North American Conference of Associates and Religious, as of 1995, identified more than 14,000 associates, many of whom gather in small communities at the local level.[57] It does include communities that go by the name of "Call to Action," of which more will be said later. The latter, however, represent less than 1 percent of the total.

Lee and D'Antonio found that "SCC members do not differ much with the general Catholic population in identifying themselves as conservative, moderate, or liberal in both church and civil matters." Except for Hispanic/Latino communities, however, "SCC Catholics are better educated and more affluent than the average U.S. Catholic." Most are middle-aged and above, that is, over forty years of age. About 75 percent of the communities are connected with a local parish.[58]

Their findings confirm that the most common activities of SCCs overall are prayer, faith sharing, and reading Scripture. Prayer and family emerge as the two items of greatest importance to members. Actively addressing social issues is far down the scale, though it is higher for Hispanic communities than others. Thus, the researchers conclude that "*gathering* is the most rewarding part of SCC experience, and that *being sent*—that is, social outreach—is a problematic dimension of the ecclesial reality of SCCs."[59]

Still, Catholics and Protestants alike keep searching for models of small communities that integrate spirituality and social justice, not only in theory but in practice. Few are as encompassing of an entire denomination as RENEW; more often, individual congregations go in search of resources that enable them to devise their own plan of renewal.

Congregational Renewal

One such resource is a program called *Just*Faith, initially developed in 1989 in a Kentucky parish by Jack Jezreel. Since 1996, with sponsorship from Catholic Charities U.S.A., Jezreel has been training local parish personnel around the country to replicate the process. *Just*Faith is an education/immersion program designed to create communities that embrace the mission to "bring justice to a broken world." Participants meet weekly for twenty-five weeks to share "books, videos, lectures, discussion, prayer, retreats, and hands-on experience. The intent is to provide a tapestry of learning opportunities that emphasize and enliven the remarkable justice tradition of the Church." This "conversion-based process" is intended to make "advocates for justice" of participants, and to "strengthen the commitment of Catholic parishes to be tools of social transformation."[60] Although started as a Catholic program, *Just*Faith is now garnering interest from Protestant congregations as well.

Another resource is the workshops offered by Ched Myers, whose concept of "distributive economic justice" constitutes the heart of his approach to transform First World Christians into radical disciples. In *Who Will Roll Away the Stone: Discipleship Queries for First World Christians*, Myers writes:

> This book is at its core a theology of repentance because that is the central theme of Mark's story of Jesus. But in the biblical tradition, the demand for change arises from compassion, not contempt. *Jesus looked at the rich man and loved him* (10:21). It is my conviction that we of the First World must come to terms with the social architecture of our privilege and our legacy as oppressors. This does *not* mean I believe our story as a people is a seamless tale of duplicity and betrayal, however. Demonizing is, after all, merely the flip side of idealizing. In fact there is much to be redeemed and preserved from the social ideas, experiments, and institutions of European America. The invitation ... is to deconstruct what is wrong about our way of life and to reconstruct one that is more characterized by justice and dignity.[61]

One cluster of radical disciples is to be found in the movement of United Methodists called Church within a Church, which started in 2002. Housed at Broadway United Methodist Church in Chicago, this initiative is partnering with another group of disciples, United Methodists of Color for a Fully Inclusive Church, which functions as an advocate of gay, lesbian, bisexual, and transgendered United Methodists. The focus of Church within a Church is the revitalization of existing local congregations or the creation of new congregations that are intentionally diverse—multiracial and inclusive of GLBT individuals—both in their outreach and in their own memberships. The theological statement of the movement reads:

> At this critical juncture in our common history as United Methodists, we are called to hold our church accountable to be an inclusive community. The sin of exclusion manifests itself as white privilege, male privilege, heterosexual privilege, economic privilege and other privileges through imperialism, domination, arrogance and violence. We stand for the celebration of the sacred worth of all persons and of the rest of creation. We witness to God's work of breaking down the dividing walls of hostility and will co-operate with God in creating a new humanity in the image and likeness of Christ Jesus.[62]

Broadway UMC is itself exemplary of the transformed and transforming congregations to be found in every mainline denomination today.

In a study conducted in the late 1990s, Paul Wilkes identified a series of what he defined as "excellent" congregations. Key characteristics of these churches were the ability to develop programs and outreach appropriate to different groups within the congregation; being welcoming, accessible, and open, and manifesting a "joyful spirit"; possessing a collaborative, nonauthoritative style; fostering an understanding that members have "a unique role collectively as a Christian community"; and "reaching beyond their walls to the larger community." The results of Wilkes's research were published in two volumes, *Excellent Catholic Parishes* and *Excellent Protestant Congregations.* One of the significant trends he found was a "cross-fertilization" between Catholic and Protestant churches. "Catholic parishes," Wilkes writes, "are taking on a model that has been successful for Protestant megachurches" and "Protestant congregations, in turn, are adopting Catholic forms of spirituality."[63]

For the most part, the congregations in this study, which represent a geographical and ethnic mix, were identified by various specialists and consultants in church renewal. Among the better known and longest established organizations providing such expertise is the nonprofit Alban Institute, an ecumenical think tank established in 1974 whose membership of eight thousand includes ordained clergy, professional church staff, church executives, and active lay members. The institute's purpose is "to encourage vigorous, faithful congregations that can equip the people of God to minister within their faith communities and in the world," while its mission is "to gather, generate, and provide practical knowledge across denominational lines through action research, consulting and training services, publications, and continuing education for all those involved with congregations."[64]

The literature generated by the institute addresses all dimensions of church life, including, predictably, the creation of small groups or communities. One publication that also speaks to the imperative of social ministry is *Basic Steps toward Community Ministry,* by Carl S. Dudley, which includes a useful discussion of the differences between service ministries, "acting with Christian compassion," and justice ministries, "challenging dysfunctional systems."[65] Throughout the book, Dudley provides examples of both service and justice ministries from nearly forty congregations, all of which are described briefly in an appendix.

In a book entitled *The Once and Future Church: Reinventing the Congregation for a New Mission Frontier,* Loren B. Mead, the founder of the Alban Institute, refers to the old paradigm of Christendom that first emerged in the fourth century and that, notwithstanding the permutations it has gone through, still survives today. Indeed, this paradigm of Christendom is enjoying new vitality through the conservative, evangelical movement, even as it has become less and less functional for establishment Protestants who for much of their history in the United States were the primary bearers of the paradigm. Mead points out that this is the paradigm in which most church leaders today were conditioned and most church structures and institutions built.[66]

A large amount of discomfort is being generated, Mead observes, as a new paradigm begins to reveal itself. Part of the discomfort is that in the emergent new paradigm, the mission field shifts "from the far-off edge of Empire to the doors of the local congregation." In Mead's vision of the "reinvented church," conversion will lose its "religious and military imperialism" and servanthood will consist not just of "good intentions" but a genuine "call to serve." It will preserve the best of both parish and congregation: in the one instance, indissoluble engagement in the world, in the other, "an intensity of faith-commitment that can result in personal, moral, and spiritual growth at the same time it impels individuals to minister to social ills." Furthermore, "the new church demands a new locus of theology, a change from the library and university to the place where the baptized person encounters the world, the place I have called the missionary frontier."[67]

One example of working at the doors of the local church is the Center for New Community founded by David Ostendorf and located in Oak Park, Illinois. The Center for New Community uses an organizing methodology rooted in Bible study and theological reflection to "revitalize congregations and community for genuine social, economic and political democracy."[68] The Center for New Community has been centrally involved in working with clusters of rural churches to counter the rise of far-right, white supremacist, militia groups in the Midwest.

In its coalition-building approach, the Center has an affinity with the congregation-based community organizing movement that was inspired by the methodology of social change artisan Saul Alinsky and the values and principles of Martin Luther King Jr. In this movement, "Dr. King is viewed as God-sent, as a prophet whose vision and charisma mobilized tens of thousands into the courageous struggles of the civil rights movement. Dr. King's consistent summons to nonviolence, to conscience, to the kingdom values of Jesus, to passionate prayer joined to civil disobedience, speaks directly to the hearts of believers. The historic success of the civil rights movement encourages those who still hope that the church can signify the kingdom of God in an oppressive society."[69]

As of 2000, four national networks of congregationally based community organizations were active in the United States: the Gamaliel Foundation

(Chicago), the Industrial Areas Foundation (also in Chicago), the Pacific Institute for Community Organization (Oakland), and the Direct Action and Research Training Center (Miami).[70] Each of the networks works with local congregations in much the same way.

> Usually a few visionary clergy or bishops invite a network to their city to explore the possibility of organizing. An organizer is sent to meet with interested leaders. A presentation by the organizer covers the basic principles and methodology of organizing. If the conversation gets serious, a relationship between local congregations and the network begins to develop. A sponsoring committee is formed with three specific tasks: raising money (normally $150,000), recruitment of dues-paying congregations (usually at least twenty), and training (sending significant numbers of leaders to the national weeklong or ten-day training of the network). At the outset, these tasks seem daunting. But networks know better than to respond to half-hearted commitments that will result in faltering, weak organizations. The point is to build power organizations, and this goal requires organized money and organized people.[71]

These steps represent only the beginning of what is a prolonged and involved process of pursuing systemic change in local communities. But this style of congregation-based community organizing, when successful, produces not only secular transformation, but a shared sense of Christian community among the ecumenical participants.

Many white Christians, however, have despaired of bringing about transformation of the church from the inside of institutional structures, or of institutional churches bringing about transformation of the larger society. Some among them turn to extra-church movements and organizations as forums for theological reflection, mouthpieces for prophetic utterances to both church and civic officials, and venues of resistance to dehumanizing policies and practices.

Catholic Extra-Church Organizations and Movements

Among the Catholic extra-church organizations, Call to Action has emerged as one of the most important. In 1971, Pope Paul VI went a step further than the Second Vatican Council in declaring that it was the church laity who had received the primary "call to action" to create a more just world. Responding to the pope's mandate, some eight hundred thousand American Catholics participated in a "creative consultation process," which culminated in the convening of a Call to Action Conference by U.S. bishops in 1976. At the end of three days of discussion and debate, the assembly declared that "the church must stand up to the chronic racism, sexism, militarism and poverty in modern society. And to do so in a credible way, the church must reevaluate its positions on issues like celibacy for priests, the male-only clergy, homosexuality, [and] birth control" with "the involvement of every level of the church in important decisions."[72]

Fairly quickly, the leadership of the Conference of Catholic Bishops distanced themselves from this event. Two years later, however, a second conference was convened in Chicago that was attended by more than four hundred sisters, priests, teachers, and concerned laity, and Call to Action (CTA) was launched as a regional organization. Following a decade and more of such conferences, the Call to Action governing board developed a "Call for Reform in the Catholic Church" that sought greater responsiveness on the part of the Church to the issues of justice, equality, and participation. This statement was printed as a full-page ad in the *New York Times* in 1990. Within a few months, the document had twenty-five thousand signers and CTA had become a national entity. In part, the "Call for Reform" reads as follows:

> We appeal to the institutional church to reform and renew its structures. We also appeal to the people of God to witness to the Spirit who lives within us and to seek ways to serve the vision of God in human society. We call upon church officials to incorporate women at all levels of ministry and decision-making. We call upon the church to discard the medieval discipline of mandatory priestly celibacy.... We claim our responsibility as committed laity, religious and clergy to participate in the selection of our local bishops.... We call for a fundamental change so that young people will see and hear God living in and through the church as a participatory community of believers who practice what they preach.[73]

This "Call for Reform" remains the organization's basic platform. As of 2002, Call to Action claimed a membership of more than twenty-five thousand with some forty local chapters, many of which consider themselves small Christian communities. Since 1990, national and regional conferences of Call to Action have provided forums for theological education related to such issues as poverty, gender equity, and racial diversity and as important sources of inspiration and personal renewal for individual attendees. In the early 2000s, Call to Action was in the forefront of the movement for church reform around the issue of clergy sexual abuse.

In 1990 the Resurrection parish council in Solon, Ohio adopted a resolution calling on U.S. bishops to "look beyond substituting communion services for the Mass in priestless parishes and to consider opening ordination to all the Baptized." This resolution was then endorsed by other Cleveland area parish councils, which came together to form the Future Church coalition. The coalition describes itself as "parish-based Catholics who are committed to preserving the Eucharist as the core of our Catholic worship." Along with urging the bishops to move toward opening priestly ordination to women and permitting priests to marry, FutureChurch is also concerned with inclusive language, democratic decision making in the Church, the rights of Church members, optional celibacy, and grass roots education about the reforms and spirit of Vatican II.[74]

We Are Church is part of an international coalition of Catholic groups by the same name that is "working for a church which is inclusive, egalitarian, affirming and democratic." In 1995 and 1996, this coalition sponsored the "Referendum of the People of God," which states in part: "We believe in a loving church where the equality of all the faithful is respected ... with equal rights for women ... where priests may choose either a celibate or non-celibate way of life.... We believe in a church which affirms the goodness of sexuality ... [and] the human rights of all persons regardless of sexual orientation.... We believe in a church which affirms people rather than condemns them." This referendum was signed by more than two million people worldwide and was presented to an official representative of the Vatican in 1997.[75]

The Voice of the Faithful is a new group of Roman Catholic laity formed in the early 2000s amid the clerical sex abuse scandals in the Boston archdiocese. The organization's initial rally, held in July 2002, was attended by more than four thousand people representing thirty-six states and seven countries. The organization styles itself as a centrist group promoting governance reform, not ideological change, with its central premise being that "the hierarchy that failed to protect our children cannot be trusted to exercise sole control of the property, money, and fate of our Church." Accordingly, its three-pronged focus is the monitoring of bishops' compliance with their own Charter for the Protection of Children and Young People, the maintenance of a data bank that identifies abusive priests, and the development of a "Voice of Compassion Fund" for those who choose not to contribute money to church entities but wish to support worthy programs.[76] Whether this organization will endure, and whether it will develop communal and transformative dimensions remains to be seen.

In the 1960s, Eileen Egan, who had worked with both Mother Teresa and Dorothy Day, co-founded the American Pax Association, which in 1972 became Pax Christi, USA, the American branch of the international Catholic peace movement.[77] Today, the statement of purpose of this organization reads: "Pax Christi USA strives to create a world that reflects the Peace of Christ by exploring, articulating, and witnessing to the call of Christian nonviolence. This work begins in personal life and extends to communities of reflection and action to transform structures of society. Pax

Christi USA rejects war, preparations for war, and every form of violence and domination. It advocates primacy of conscience, economic and social justice, and respect for creation."[78]

The membership of Pax Christi USA includes more than 14,000 individual members, 140 Catholic bishops, and various parishes, universities, and religious communities. More than 200 local and regional groups across the country meet on a regular basis to pray, study, and act for peace with justice. The organization is a major source of peace education literature for nonmember individuals and groups throughout the country as well.[79]

Protestant and Ecumenical Movements

The growth of the Religious Right since the 1970s has served as a wake-up call to progressive Christians. Recognizing that their liberal politics of the past are no longer adequate, they have also seen that inaction in public affairs creates a vacuum quickly filled by a strain of Christianity that represents the antithesis of their prophetic tradition. These realizations and the concerns they generate have given impetus to any number of organizations and movements that are devoted to countering the agenda of conservative evangelicals and fundamentalists.

An example is the Call to Renewal movement, which began in 1995 with the public issuance of a statement signed by more than one hundred Christian leaders from various faith communities. This "Cry to Renewal," as it was called, was based on a book written by Jim Wallis, head of the Sojourners community in Washington, D.C., which describes itself as a radical evangelical body. Wallis's book, *The Soul of Politics*, detailed an alternative both to the conservative Christian Coalition and to political liberalism. Since the initial Call to Renewal conference held in 1986, the movement has grown as a "network of networks committed to creating a new spiritual politics."[80] Call to Renewal consists of a coalition of evangelical, mainline Protestant, and Catholic social service and social justice groups that focuses on returning the issue of poverty to the national agenda. Following a roundtable conversation of these groups, the *National Catholic Reporter* remarked, "Our hope is that such efforts would reclaim the word *Christian* from the extreme religious right, which is trying to copyright it, and put it back at its starting place—with Jesus' call to walk with the poor and marginalized."[81]

The Interfaith Alliance was formed in 1994 as a nonpartisan, grass roots organization to "promote the positive and healing role of religion in public life through encouraging civic participation, facilitating community activism, and challenging religious political extremism." The organization is devoted to protecting religious liberty and civil rights for all, strengthening public education, eliminating poverty, and working for a clean environment.

In each of these areas, the Alliance opposes the agenda of the Religious Right. As of 2002, the Alliance claimed some 130,000 members representing fifty different faith traditions, and had organized affiliates in thirty-eight states.[82]

Another organization formed in the mid-1990s is the Center for Progressive Christianity. The Center's mission is to "reach out to those for whom organized religion has proved ineffectual, irrelevant, or repressive, as well as to those who have given up on or are unacquainted with it; to uphold evangelism as an agent of justice and peace; to give a strong voice both in the churches and the public arena to the advocates of progressive Christianity; to support those who embrace search, not certainty." The Center for Progressive Christianity, perhaps more than any other group, constitutes a home for "believers in exile," a phrase made popular by one of the Center's advisers, retired Episcopal bishop John Spong. One of the Center's goals is to create "open and welcoming communities of faith" that "do not assume the absolute superiority of Christianity so that we do not contribute to the world's tragic divisions."[83]

Progressive Religious Partnership is a project of People for the American Way, a secular organization that opposes the Religious Right. The partnership is a "network of people and congregations working in and through communities of faith to bring about a nation and world that more reflects the 'beloved community.'" The project challenges the "hypocrisy of the Religious Right," opposes racism and sexism, works for economic justice for all, and promotes "a healing sexuality."[84]

Mobilization for the Human Family, based in California, works for "the inclusion of and justice for all God's children," focusing particularly on injustices related to welfare reform, the criminal justice system, sweat-shop labor, and civil rights. The group publishes a newsletter called *Progressive Christianity* and works with local congregations in neighbor-hoods of change through its Life and Faith Academy, utilizing a methodol-ogy of reflection and action.[85]

Equal Partners in Faith is "a multi-racial national network of religious leaders and people of faith committed to equality and diversity" that is head-quartered in Washington, D.C. Its mission statement reads: "Our diverse faith traditions and shared religious values lead us to affirm and defend the equal-ity of all people, regardless of religion, race, ability, gender, sexual orientation or gender identity. As people of faith, we actively oppose the manipulation of religion to promote inequality and exclusion." Equal Partners in Faith spon-sors four major projects: the People of Color of Faith Initiative—Countering the Religious Right in Communities of Color; Faith and Feminism—Promoting the Equality of Women and Men in Religion and Society; Proclaiming Our Values—A Faith-Based Response to the Leaders of the

Promise Keepers and Their Religious Right Allies; and the National Religious Leadership Roundtable—Promoting Civil and Religious Equality for Lesbian, Gay, Bisexual and Transgender Persons (co-convened with the National Gay and Lesbian Task Force Foundation).[86]

In 1999, representatives of various networks of Christian activists connected to mainline denominations but without official status initiated a conversation with one another. Included were the Methodist Federation for Social Action, UCC Christians for Justice Action, Disciples Justice Action Network, the Witherspoon Society in the Presbyterian Church, the Lutheran Human Relations Association, the Baptist Peace Fellowship, and individuals within the Episcopal Church. Originally called Oxbow and subsequently renamed Protestant Justice Action (PJA), members of this coalition speak as a progressive voice on matters of public policy, as well as a progressive voice *to* their respective denominations. Though racially and ethnically diverse, the coalition also represents one of the largest assemblages of transformative white Protestants.

Exactly what role these various organizations and movements will play in the future of mainline churches remains to be seen. More and more local congregations may be genuinely transformed. Step by step, the denominations themselves may change. Whether they become relics of the past, or vehicles of escapist spirituality, or deconstructed fragments of their former selves, they will never be what they once were. A possible scenario is that, until the tide of religious conservatism is turned, traditionally liberal churches will increasingly be consigned to the margins, where they will be challenged to learn how to live Christian community from the very Christians that their churches historically helped to marginalize. In that process, they will be aided by the transformative white Christians who even now are living and working on the margins, striving to be "church."

Indeed, it may be not only the churches, but the politics of the Religious Right that precipitate this turn of events. If for the time being the United States is the hegemonic force in the world, the twenty-first century brings no assurance that this will continue to be the case. Empires come, and empires go. In such an event, Christianity would no longer have a role as sustainer of Western dominance. Less incentive would exist for preserving the imperial features of Christian churches that even now, in today's changing world, appear as such anachronisms.

Instead, the spirit-community tradition might prevail as the more authentic expression of a religion that was never meant to serve imperialism in the first place. With the ascendancy of this tradition, the different peoples of the United States might even learn to live in community with one another, and with their neighbors around the globe.

For Further Reading

Everist, Norma Cook, ed. *The Difficult but Indispensable Church.* Minneapolis: Fortress Press, 2002.

Forster, Patricia M., O.S.F., and Thomas P. Sweetser, S.J. *Transforming the Parish: Models for the Future.* Kansas City, Mo.: Sheed & Ward, 1993.

Holland, Joe, and Peter Henriot, S.J. *Social Analysis: Linking Faith and Justice.* Rev. and enl. ed.; Maryknoll, N.Y.: Orbis Books in cooperation with the Center for Concern, Washington, D.C., 1983.

Jacobsen, Dennis A. *Doing Justice: Congregations and Community Organizing.* Minneapolis: Fortress Press, 2001.

Janzen, David et al. *Fire, Salt, and Peace: Intentional Christian Communities Alive in North America.* Evanston, Ill.: Shalom Mission Communities, 1996.

Lee, Bernard J., and Michael A. Cowan. *Gathered and Sent: The Mission of Small Church Communities Today.* New York: Paulist Press, 2003.

Myers, Ched. *Who Will Roll Away the Stone? Discipleship Queries for First World Christians.* Maryknoll, N.Y.: Orbis Books, 1994.

Smith, Christian. *Going to the Root: Nine Proposals for Radical Church Renewal.* Scottdale, Pa.: Herald Press, 1992.

Whitehead, Evelyn Eaton, and James D. Whitehead. *Community of Faith: Crafting Christian Communities Today.* Mystic, Conn.: Twenty-Third Publications, 1992.

Wink, Walter. *Engaging the Powers: Discernment and Resistance in a World of Domination.* Minneapolis: Fortress Press, 1992.

NOTES

1. C. Kirk Hadaway and David A. Roozen, *Rerouting the Protestant Mainstream: Sources of Growth and Opportunities for Change* (Nashville: Abingdon Press, 1995), 109.

2. Ibid., 112–13.

3. Ibid., 121, 113.

4. Ibid., 122–23.

5. Ibid., 115.

6. Gordon Greathouse, "The Church League for Industrial Democracy," in *Struggling with the System: Probing Alternatives,* a study-action guide prepared by the Church and Society Network and *Witness* Magazine, 1976, 38.

7. Ibid.

8. Ibid., 39–40.

9. Ibid., 41.

10. George D. McClain, "Pioneering Social Gospel Radicalism: An Overview of the History of the Methodist Federation for Social Action," *Radical Religion* 5, no. 1 (1980): 10–11.

11. Ibid., 12–13.

12. Ibid., 17.

13. Ibid., 19–20.

14. Kathleen Schultz, "CFS/USA: History and Perspectives of Our Movement," *Radical Religion,* 4, no. 3–4 (1979): 11.

15. Ibid.

16. CFS brochure, circa 1978.

17. Ibid.

18. The author is here speaking from personal experience.

19. Schultz, "CFS/USA," 11.

20. Sheila Collins, "Liberation Theology in the Making: Part II," *Social Questions Bulletin.* Part 1 of this two-part article was published in volume 65, no. 5 (September–October 1975). It is probable that part 2, cited here, was published in volume 65, no. 6 (November–December 1975). This article provides an excellent overview of the initial TIA Conference. *Social Questions Bulletin* is the newsletter of the Methodist Federation for Social Action and is still published today.

21. TIA brochure, "Theology in the Americas: A Process, A Program, A Network," circa 1975.

22. Ibid.

23. Ibid.

24. These included The Black Project; The Hispanic Project; The Women's Project; Quest for Liberation in the White Church; The Task Force of Professional Theologians; Labor and Church Dialogue; Asian Americans in the U.S. Context; and Land, Native Americans, and Red Theology. In 1978, TIA published a document entitled "Is Liberation Theology for North America? The Response of First World Christians." This document contained a series of articles responding to challenges issued by "Third World" theologians, including Torres, James Cone, Vine Deloria Jr., Beverly Harrison (feminist, but not Third World), and Gustavo Gutierrez. Among the respondents were a number of the more prominent white theologians and social scientists working in the mode of liberation during this period of time and continuing into the following decades: Robert McAfee Brown, Rosemary Radford Ruether, Joe Holland, William Tabb, Robert T. Handy, Kathleen Schultz, Marie Augusta Neal, M. Douglas Meeks, and Jim Wallis.

25. Malcolm Boyd, ed., *The Underground Church* (New York: Penguin Books, 1969).

26. Ibid., viii.

27. Ched Myers, *Who Will Roll Away the Stone?: Discipleship Queries for First World Christians* (Maryknoll, N.Y.: Orbis Books, 1994), 180–81.

28. David Janzen, *Fire, Salt, and Peace: Intentional Christian Communities Alive in North America* (Evanston, Ill.: Shalom Mission Communities, 1996), 172–73.

29. Ibid., 173.

30. Curt Cadorette, "Legion and the Believing Community: Discipleship in an Imperial Age," in *The Church as Counterculture* (eds. Michael L. Budde and Robert W. Brimlow; Albany, N.Y.: SUNY Press, 2000), 165.

31. Janzen, *Fire, Salt, and Peace,* 173.

32. Ibid.

33. Ibid., 174.

34. See Lee Van Ham and Juanita Mangan-Van Ham, "A Freeing Idea: Living in Community Is Impossible," *Faith @ Work* 113, no. 1 (spring 2000): 12–13.

35. Ibid., 177.

36. See <www.catholicworker.org>.

37. Patrick G. Coy, "Introduction," in *Revolution of the Heart: Essays on the Catholic Worker* (ed. Patrick Coy; Philadelphia: New Society Publishers, 1988), 5.

38. Ibid., 7.

39. Cadorette, "Legion," 165.

40. Janzen, *Fire, Salt, and Peace,* 177. See Jean Vanier, *Community and Growth: Our Pilgrimage Together* (New York: Paulist Press, 1979). Among the other "families" of independent communities are "Plain People" (four communities), REMAR International (five

communities), Shalom Mission (three communities), and Sword of the Spirit (ten communities). Pages 193–99 of Janzen constitute an appendix of names, addresses, and phone numbers of the identified communities.

41. This discussion is based on Andrew S. Chancey, "Koinonia in the '90s," *Christian Century* (October 14, 1992): 892–94.

42. Ibid.

43. Janzen, *Fire, Salt, and Peace,* 188.

44. "Journey Inward, Outward, and Forward: The Radical Vision of the Church of the Savior," booklet of the Church of the Savior, 3–6. This booklet is a reprint of an article by Jeff Bailey that appeared in *Cutting Edge,* a publication of the U.S. Association of Vineyard Churches, in the Fall 2001 issue.

45. Ibid, 6.

46. Ibid.

47. Ibid., 13.

48. Ibid., 12.

49. Christian Smith, *Going to the Root: Nine Proposals for Radical Church Renewal* (Scottdale, Pa: Herald Press,1992), 16. Questions have been raised as to whether white, North American, middle-class Christians can legitimately lay claim to the Latin American model of base Christian communities. Margaret Hebblethwaite is among those who argue, in *Basic Is Beautiful: Basic Ecclesial Communities from Third World to First World* (New York: Harper Collins, 1993), that the praxis model of reflection and action can indeed be adapted to the very different circumstances of middle-class, white Americans. The essential criterion is that the community, by whatever name, conjoins theological reflection and social justice activism. Others make the case that while the name and the dynamic may be the same, differences in political and economic circumstances introduce profound qualitative differences in the process and the product.

50. Terry Veling, "Living in the Margins: The Interpretive Edge of Intentional Christian Communities," *International Papers in Pastoral Ministry* 6, no. 1 (February–March 1995): 3. *International Papers* is published by Latin America/North American Church Concerns, The University of Notre Dame. This article is a summary of Veling's doctoral dissertation, which was subsequently published as *Living in the Margins: Intentional Communities and the Art of Interpretation* (New York: Crossroad, 1996).

51. Ibid.

52. See Thomas A. Kiessler, Margo A. LeBert, and Mary C. McGuinness, *Small Christian Communities: A Vision of Hope* (Mahwah, N.J.: Paulist Press, 1991). Kiessler is the person primarily responsible for the development and implementation of the RENEW process, both in the United States and internationally.

53. Ibid., 235–36.

54. Allan Figueroa Deck, S.J., *The Second Wave: Hispanic Ministry and the Evangelization of Cultures* (New York: Paulist Press, 1989), 74.

55. Bernard J. Lee, S.M., with William V. D'Antonio, et al, *The Catholic Experience of Small Christian Communities* (New York: Paulist Press, 2000), 10–13. For an extended discussion of these networks, see chapter 5 of John Paul Vandenakker, *Small Christian Communities and the Parish: An Ecclesiological Analysis of the North American Experience* (Kansas City, Mo.: Sheed & Ward, 1994).

56. Lee with D'Antonio, *The Catholic Experience,* 75.

57. Ibid., 31.

58. Ibid., 75–76.

59. Ibid., 93–95.

60. "What Is *Just*Faith," information sheet from the Office of *Just*Faith, Louisville, Kentucky, n.d.

61. Myers, *Who Will Roll Away the Stone?*, xvi.

62. "Church within a Church Update," newsletter of Broadway United Methodist Church, Chicago, Illinois, November 2002, 6–7.

63. "Finding Great Churches," *Initiatives in Religion* 9, no. 1 (spring 2001), 7–8, newsletter of Lilly Endowment, Inc.

64. The Alban Institute, "Publications Catalogue" (July–December 1997): 2.

65. Carl S. Dudley, *Basic Steps toward Community Ministry* (Washington, D.C.: The Alban Institute, 1991), 104.

66. Loren B. Mead, *The Once and Future Church: Reinventing the Congregation for a New Mission Frontier* (Washington, D.C.: The Alban Institute, 1991), 13–20, 41.

67. Ibid., 44–56, passim.

68. "The Center for New Community," information sheet from the Center for New Community, Oak Park, Illinois.

69. Dennis A. Jacobsen, *Doing Justice: Congregations and Community Organizing* (Minneapolis: Fortress Press, 2001), 24.

70. Ibid., 24–25.

71. Ibid., 26.

72. See <www.cta-usa.org/whohistory.html>.

73. Ibid.

74. From the FutureChurch brochure.

75. See <www.we-are-church.org/us>.

76. Chuck Colber, "Growing Movement Grapples with Sex Abuse Crisis and a Future Church," *National Catholic Reporter* (August 2, 2002): n.p. Also, see Richard N. Ostling, "Catholic Group Faces a Tough Road Ahead," *Tribune* (Ames, Iowa) (July 31, 2002): n.p.

77. Antonia S. Malone, "Eileen Egan, Pacifist, Helped Start Pax Christi," *National Catholic Reporter* (October 20, 2000): 7.

78. "Gathered in Peace: Forming Pax Christi Communities," a publication of Pax Christi USA, revised in 1984, 11.

79. See <paxchristiusa.org>.

80. Invitation to the Call to Renewal National Conference, 1996.

81. "Group May Bring Us Closer to Being Christian," *National Catholic Reporter* (May 9, 1997): 28.

82. See <www.interfaithalliance.org>.

83. See <www.tcpc.org>.

84. See <www. religiousprogressives.org>.

85. See <www.mfhf.org>.

86. See <www.us.net/epf.html>.

–APPENDIX 1–
Ethnic Minority Memberships of Selected Denominations

No precise statistics on ethnic membership in denominations exist. Three sources provide partial information, but each has its limitations. The General Social Survey 2000, conducted by the National Opinion Research Center and made available by the American Religion Data Archive, provides data on religious identification and race and ethnicity, but only for adults and only for the English-speaking population. Furthermore, interviewees were asked to indicate their first, second, and third racial/ethnic identities, and many Native Americans and Hispanics listed white as the first identity. Non-Hispanic whites are not separated out, which means the data has limited utility. In fact, except for African Americans, this survey shows zero ethnic members in almost every denomination cited, which may be attributable to the small size of the sample.

The American Religious Identification Survey 2001, conducted by the Graduate Center of the City University of New York, involves a much larger sample, but it, too, was limited to adults who spoke English. Questions about religious adherence were open-ended. That is, participants were not asked about membership in specific denominations. Thus, respondents might volunteer that they were Christian, or Protestant or Catholic, or they might name a specific denomination, or they might say they were born-again. The response, even if a denomination was named after some prompting, did not necessarily signify formal membership or active participation. In addition, the survey involved the forty-eight states of the continental United States, but not Alaska or Hawaii.

The third source, from which the following data comes, is the denominations themselves. Accurate membership statistics are difficult to ascertain for denominations, which tend to report different figures depending on the use to which they will be put. Comparisons of ethnic minority memberships especially must be made cautiously, as different denominations have different methods of counting and estimating.

The Catholic Church, with nearly 64 million registered members, is the largest Christian group in the United States, accounting for nearly 42 percent of all reported church members.[1] Adjusting this official number for some 14 million estimated Hispanic Catholics who are not registered in local parishes results in an estimated total of 78 million, or nearly 28 percent of the U.S. population.[2] The Catholic Church is the second most diverse church (next to American Baptist Churches). As of 2000, the Catholic ethnic minority membership was approximately 37 percent. (See table 1.) The numbers of Hispanic and Asian American members are growing at the fastest rates and it is probable that in the not too distant future, non-Hispanic whites will be in the minority while peoples of color will be in the majority. Indeed, the 2002 *Catholic Almanac* projects that by the year 2050, the U.S. Catholic population will be 86 percent Hispanic.

Table 1. Estimated Catholic Church Membership by Percentage, 2000 (78 million total)

1.0	Native American
2.2	Asian American
2.6	African American
31.4	Hispanic
63.0	Non-Hispanic Caucasian

Source: *Yearbook of American and Canadian Churches, 2000;* United States Conference of Catholic Bishops, Secretariat for Hispanic Affairs

Except for the number of Latina/o members, predominantly white Protestant denominations are comparable in their diversity to the Catholic Church. The exception is the American Baptist Churches in the U.S.A., which has a total membership of 1.4 million. This denomination has no census of individual members by race and ethnicity, but 41 percent of its members are in congregations that are majority black and another 5 percent are in congregations that are majority Latina/o.

Figures for the five largest predominantly white Protestant denominations—the Southern Baptist Convention (15.9 million), United Methodist Church (8.3 million), Evangelical Lutheran Church in America (5.1 million), Presbyterian Church (U.S.A.) (3.5 million), and Assemblies of God (2.6 million)—are far more modest in terms of ethnic minority representation. Like the American Baptist Churches, the Southern Baptist Convention and the Assemblies of God count all members of respective local congregations as being part of the dominant racial/ethnic group of that congregation. (For example, a congregation that is 10 percent black and 90 percent white would be reported as 100 percent white.) In terms of their categories of reporting (number of members by predominant racial identity of the congregation), the combined ethnic minority figure for the Southern Baptist Convention is 5.3 percent. The Assemblies of God statistics by race and ethnicity differ even further in that they are for *average attendance* rather than for memberships. The average attendance of ethnic minorities (by predominant racial identity of the congregation) is 16.3 percent (with 12 percent being Hispanic and 2.2 percent Asian American).[3]

The combined membership of African Americans, Latinas/os, Asian and Pacific Islanders, and Native Americans is 6.8 percent for the United Methodist Church (with 5.1 percent being African American), 6.8 percent for the United Church of Christ (with 4.6 percent being African American), 5.8 percent for the Presbyterian Church (U.S.A.), and 2.3 percent for the Evangelical Lutheran Church of America (ELCA).

Table 2. Racial/Ethnic Memberships of Selected Mainline Protestant Denominations by Percentage

	African American	Hispanic	Asian/ Pacific Isl.	Native American	Total
United Methodist (8.3 m)	5.06	.59	.92	.24	6.81
ELCA (5.1 m)	1.03	.73	.44	.15	2.35
Presbyterian (U.S.A.) (3.5 m)	2.70	1.00	1.90	.20	5.80
Episcopal (2.3 m)	N.A.	N.A.	N.A.	N.A.	N.A.
American Baptist* (1.4 m)	40.93	5.34	.69	.14	47.10
United Church of Christ* (1.4 m)	4.63	.45	1.70	.07	6.85

Source: Membership totals are from the *Yearbook of American and Canadian Churches, 2000*, while ethnic minority percentages are from the respective denomination's offices.

*Both UCC and American Baptists base their figures on predominant racial/ethnic membership of local congregations.

Estimates of the percentage of local churches in the United States altogether that are racially/ethnically mixed (i.e., integrated), defined as a congregation in which at least 20 percent of its members provide racial or ethnic diversity, range from 7 to 11 percent. Various studies of mixed congregations agree that there are more such congregations to be found in the newer, theologically conservative, nondenominational churches than in mainline churches—from 2 to 4 percent of mainline Protestant churches and nearly 25 percent of independent, nondenominational churches.[4]

Several explanations are offered for these differences. According to Nancy Ammerman, a sociologist of religion with the Hartford Institute for Religious Research,

> One [reason] surely is the disproportionately upper-middle class, highly educated character of traditional Anglo mainline congregations. Another barrier to integration, in many instances, is a "high church" style of worship steeped in European literary and musical culture. [Furthermore,] their members are older and perhaps on average less inclined toward multicultural experiences. This cluster of factors has made integration difficult for mainline churches and easier for conservatives and Pentecostals whose demographics and history situate them better for the task.[5]

Scott Thumma, also with the Hartford Institute, adds that "a plausible explanation is that denominational labels create a cultural expectation of whether they are 'white' or 'black churches,'" Reporting the views of a parish priest in the Los Angeles Episcopal Diocese, Floyd "Butch" Gamarra, John Dart writes that "'in a lot of mainline churches the issues are race and class.' Liberal churches present the theological idea that 'the world is supposed to be a rainbow,' but the upper-middle-class church members 'want to be cerebral' about it. The Pentecostal and independent churches 'tend to attract more working-class people who are in the same social, economic class. The mix is a lot easier.'"[6]

Aside from the racially integrated congregations, both mainline and conservative denominations have congregations that are totally or predominantly African American or Hispanic or Asian American or Native American. And, as noted in chapter 3, all of the mainline denominations have within them caucuses or councils of their respective ethnic minority group members. Furthermore, most African Americans, as discussed in chapter 4, are members of the historic black denominations.

Notes

1. Eileen W. Lindner, ed., *Yearbook of American and Canadian Churches, 2002*, National Council of Churches of Christ in the U.S.A. (Nashville, Tenn.: Abingdon Press, 2002). The membership statistics reported are for the year 2000.

2. Different studies estimate that anywhere from 70 to 78 percent of the 35 million Hispanics in the United States are Catholic. Using the more conservative figure of 70 percent results in 24.5 million Hispanic Catholics, which is 14 million more than the official figures of CARA, the research source for the United States Catholic Conference of Bishops (USCCB).

3. Membership totals are from the *Yearbook of American and Canadian Churches*, with ethnic minority breakdowns based on data obtained from the respective denominations. It is significant to note that the ten largest religious bodies include not only the Catholic Church and these six predominantly white Protestant denominations, but the Church of

Jesus Christ of Latter Day Saints (5.2 million) and three traditional black denominations: The National Baptist Convention, U.S.A., Inc. (5.0 million), the Church of God in Christ (5.5 million), and the National Baptist Convention of America, Inc. (3.5 million). For further discussion of these denominations, see chapter 4.

4. John Dart, "Hues in the Pews," *Christian Century* (February 28, 2001). The studies cited include the Organizing Religious Work (ORW) project of the Hartford Institute, directed by Nancy Ammerman, and the Congregations Project conducted by sociologist Michael Emerson at Rice University. The reference here is to the generation of nondenominational (or independent or post-denominational) churches that have appeared since the mid-1970s.

5. Ibid.

6. Ibid.

−APPENDIX 2−
Stories of
Christian Community
by John L. Kater Jr.
The Church Divinity School of the Pacific, 1994

"Ahead of Our Time:" Liberation Theology in Iowa

Small-town Iowa would seem to be an unlikely outpost for a committed community of Christian socialists inspired by the experience of Latin American Christians. And a Methodist Church in the American heartland would seem to be an unlikely crucible for its emergence. Nevertheless, both are true.

Clinton, Iowa is a somewhat typical midwestern town, with a population of about 28,000. Over the years, its growth has extended toward the nearby community of Comanche. While in some ways they have become a single urban organism, Comanche still reflects the look and feel of its rural past.

More than twenty-five years ago, St. Mark's United Methodist Church in Comanche was shaken by the appointment of its young new pastor. Gilbert Dawes had returned to the United States from a brief ministry in Argentina, where he had been much impressed by the efforts of local church leaders to take seriously the plight of the poor. News of his interests had preceded him; on his first Sunday in Comanche, several longtime members of the church accused him of being a communist and left the congregation.

Dawes' impact was immediate and profound. Putting into practice techniques learned from Latin American base communities, he preached not from the pulpit but among the worshippers, and encouraged dialogue not only in discussions but during the service itself. In the words of Paul Schaaf, an insurance adjuster who came to admire Dawes, "He wanted to teach the congregation so that when he left we would be able to carry on. He took himself off a pedestal and said, 'I am one of you; just because I have the theology, I am not above you.'"

Many of the conservative members of St. Mark's Church were appalled at the direction they perceived it to be moving under Dawes' leadership;

membership dwindled from nearly 125 to less than half that number. But those who remained were transformed by his style. "He brought the Bible into living history," says Schaaf. Myrna Weller, a secretary at the local community college, considers that Dawes' insight was prophetic in his ability to understand the reality of their world and to make politics and history come alive.

As some of the faithful members of St. Mark's Church began to respond to Dawes' preaching and teaching, they searched for ways to put their new commitments into practice. Many worked with an activist Franciscan nun and other local residents to organize protests against the Vietnam War, by now in its last stages; others joined Citizens for Safe Energy, begun by a group of farmers whose land had been purchased as a site for a nuclear power plant. Many were attracted to the Methodist Federation for Social Action, an unofficial organization within the United Methodist Church that has served as an advocate for many progressive causes.

"It wasn't easy for some of us at the beginning," Myrna Weller admits. "For me it was hard when we were assisting strikers at a local corn processing company; that was totally against my background." Sue Miller, assistant to a local orthodontist, recalls that hard feelings lasted for a long time after the strike; but members of the congregation believed that since the strike affected the entire community, they had a right and an obligation to intervene.

By 1980, when the pastor invited Angela Davis, president of the American Communist Party, to give a lecture, the church and its remaining members were seriously alienated from their denomination. Former members, some of whom had left even before Dawes' arrival, were demanding his ouster. The bishop and his cabinet, made up of Iowa's thirteen district superintendents, began to address the situation, and one of them revealed those conversations to the press, much to the parish leadership's dismay.

By 1981, it was clear that Dawes' departure from the congregation was inevitable. After a brief and conflicted interim pastorate, the United Methodist Church assigned the Reverend Charles Klink as St. Mark's new pastor.

"We knew we wouldn't get another pastor with an emphasis on liberation theology," Sue Miller recalls. "The church was clear that we wanted a pastor who was open-minded." Concretely, the congregation asked that the custom of open discussions after the sermon continue; Klink reluctantly agreed. But the hopes for some kind of *modus vivendi* between the congregation and their new pastor seemed doomed.

On one hand, Klink worked hard to persuade disaffected members of the congregation to return; on the other, he urged the leadership to be less rigid in its approach to social and political issues. The matter came to a head when Klink preached a Labor Day sermon interpreted as endorsing the economic status quo; in the heated conversation that followed, he told the administrative board that only he had sufficient theological training to interpret scriptures appropriately. A few weeks later, the pastor refused to open the floor for dialogue after his sermon and announced the closing hymn. The organist, who sided with the church's lay leaders, refused to play the hymn. After a few feeble efforts to sing without the organ, the pastor walked out of the church. The organist began playing "We Shall Overcome" and the congregation closed the service with "Solidarity Forever."

In the face of the situation, an appeal was sent to the executive secretary of the Methodist Federation for Social Action (MFSA) for support for the beleaguered congregation. In December, the Social Witness Group wrote to the bishop asking, "Is there a place under the umbrella of the United Methodist Church for a church which understands its Christian Mission to be social witness?" They went on to list the requirements for their study and worship: free dialogue, including the worship service; an atmosphere where mutual growth would be encouraged and marked by trust and respect; and a sermon "with a concrete message that isn't planned to appease the majority." None of these requirements, the letter stated, were being met. Furthermore, the denomination was requiring that at least half the administrative board be comprised of returning members in order for the church's slate of officers to be ratified.

The next day, the twenty-two members of the administrative board submitted their resignations. They announced their intention to "remain members of St. Mark's United Methodist Church," and to "continue to struggle for God's Kingdom in our community." But soon, about fifty members decided that they could no longer identify themselves with the congregation. Those who did so wanted to maintain some affiliation with the church and with a national organization; the Methodist Federation for Social Action welcomed them as a "subgroup" of its Iowa chapter, and the group remains identified in this way.

The group now faced the challenge to be the church in a way that its members had studied but never experienced. Not surprisingly, in the beginning they considered the possibility of calling their own pastor; indeed, Dawes recommended several clergy who were interested in working with them. But some were opposed in principle, while others realized that hiring a pastor would have depleted their slim financial resources. "In effect, we had learned from Gil Dawes that the strength of the church is in the dialogue," commented Bill March, a retired social worker. Meeting weekly, they began taking turns as officiants at the service. "As we shared leadership, we developed more than we would had we been able to get a minister," he said.

They also considered, and rejected, their own church building for the same reasons. "We thought that the building was important to us," observed Myrna Weller, "but we found out the people were what was important."

In the years since its exodus from Comanche's United Methodist Church, the group has crafted its own community and ministry. It has never had a home of its own; at different times Clinton Community College, the local YMCA, and a Roman Catholic college have provided space.

"We felt it was important to identify a direction and we unanimously chose a social justice ministry," recalls Bob Miller, manager of the plant at the local community college. "We wanted to continue to do community education on issues and we also wanted to make a significant financial contribution to the progressive movement."

In the early years, the community continued to pledge financial contributions, which now supported projects identified by its members rather than to support a pastor or maintain a building. At first, the group provided Christian education for its children, but they are now grown and such classes are no longer needed.

The community now rents meeting space in the basement of the local Unitarian Church and meets twice monthly for Sunday worship, and gathers three times a month for Wednesday study sessions. Its budget reaches $5000, with between 80 and 85 percent earmarked for progressive causes.

"We take turns doing all the work," said Sue Miller, the group's convener. "People research and prepare the message, someone else volunteers to take charge of the service, including the bulletin, music, and everything." "One Sunday a month," added Judy Schaaf, a clerk in Clinton's City Hall, "we do our own communion; the leader is responsible for that part of the service too."

"Now we understand communion as sharing the experience and remembering," added Bill March. "In performing the functions of a minister, we have learned a lot more." Bob Miller recalls that people were accustomed to counseling and other activities that they missed at first, but "now we rely on each other to provide those skills." "We have supported each other," added Myrna Weller, "because we feel like family."

Over the years, the group has developed a perspective that stretches far beyond its immediate neighborhood. "At the beginning," Bob Miller remembers, "we worked almost entirely outside the community and we felt ostracized." "It took us a long time to get over the feeling that we were branded as 'communists that they were able to kick out of the church,' " added Sue Miller. Some admit that they have still not entirely lost the feeling of being "branded."

"Since then," said Bob Miller, "we have generally been bringing ourselves back into the community." Indeed, the group has made a local impact far beyond its numbers. It assisted in serving refugees from Latin America, and in programs to address the issue of nuclear power. It helped form the Gateway Peace Council and the local chapter of the National Association for the Advancement of Colored People (NAACP). Recently, it voted to become a "reconciling church" of the United Methodist denomination, publicly announcing its willingness to accept gay and lesbian people as active members of its community.

While the group never advertised for members and has not grown, Sue Miller noted that "we are reaching out to the black community and are now a 'reconciling church.' We are much more visible in the community and now is our chance to grow."

Explained Bill Miller, "We consider ourselves a church but we visualize that differently than many." "We are part of what is going on globally," said Bill March, "the democratization of religious identities." "I see us as a unique group," said Sue Miller, "but I don't know that there is anything special about us except that what we are doing is a little ahead of our time."

"New People"

The MacArthur Park neighborhood of Los Angeles is one of the most densely populated areas in the United States. It is home to thousands of immigrants, many of them from Latin America and a large number in the United States illegally. The conditions that surround the neighborhood are all too predictable in the presence of chronic unemployment and poverty: crime, violence, drug and alcohol addiction, over-crowded and substandard housing, and family crises.

MacArthur Park is also the site of Pueblo Nuevo, "New People," a ministry undertaken by the Reverend Philip Lance precisely because the neighborhood *is* so scarred by poverty. Lance, who is an experienced community organizer as well as an Episcopal priest, received his training from the Industrial Areas Foundation, established many years ago by Saul Alinsky to organize and train victims of poverty to demand and create solutions to their situation. A series of visits throughout the neighborhood in the spring of 1992 convinced him that there were many who would welcome a church-sponsored presence in their community, already home to both the hotel workers' and janitors' unions.

In June of 1992, the congregation of Pueblo Nuevo was born, in MacArthur Park itself, since there was no building. For seven months, the park was the church's "home." Lance describes their services as "radically inclusive," since they attracted not only the fledgling congregation's members but street people and families who happened to be enjoying the park. There was no sermon, but those present read and commented on Bible passages together and shared a simple Eucharist and potluck meal.

By the beginning of 1993, Pueblo Nuevo had rented a storefront in its neighborhood and launched its first economic project, a thrift shop. The congregation has a long-term relationship with All Saints' Church in Beverly Hills, which provides one thousand dollars a month as well as clothing and furniture to be sold in the shop. The Episcopal Diocese of Los Angeles and other congregations also offer some financial support.

Although the thrift shop had as its goal both generating income for the church and providing employment in the neighborhood, the shop was staffed by church volunteers for three months, with Father Lance serving as the manager. As Lance observes, "The Christianity of the church community was work as well as worship."

After several months, the congregation organized a cooperative, Pueblo Nuevo Enterprises, now owned by its six employees, each of whom earns between one thousand and fifteen hundred dollars a month. Lance continues to serve as manager as part of his duties as the congregation's pastor.

Pueblo Nuevo Enterprises now also runs a property-maintenance service that employs nine members of the congregation and has a monthly income of about twelve thousand dollars. Negotiations are underway with the city for permission to establish another project, called a "Business Incubator," in the store adjacent to the building that houses the church and thrift shop. This will be a space where cottage industries can be housed, and neighbors can sell wares made in their homes.

Lance, who himself speaks fluent Spanish, is assisted by Hector Jeréz, a priest born in Guatemala. The Sunday afternoon worship at Pueblo Nuevo is at the heart of the congregation's life. Latin American cultures are deeply religious, and many of the people in the neighborhood were alienated from the church; the congregation has provided a place for reconciliation and spiritual development. Its overtly Christian perspective has also "enabled us to develop a common vision and common values," says Lance

But, he insists, "the relationship between worship and work is a symbiotic one." In a neighborhood as poor as MacArthur Park, "economic development requires sacrifice. People had to donate months of free labor. The maintenance people worked for months before they had enough work to go full-time. This led to tensions and conflicts. The aspect of the church gives us a center—a vision behind everything we're doing. People aren't employees but part of a community that has a vision for this neighborhood.

I don't know if the economic development would have been possible without the worship."

Certainly few if any of the people at Pueblo Nuevo were experienced leaders when the mission began; some did, however, exhibit the gifts from which community leadership can spring—as Lance describes them, "passion, anger, willingness to work with others on problems"—the raw material from which visionaries are formed. Pueblo Nuevo has formed a community and provided a center where those gifts can be put to work, trained and directed in ways that bear fruit. "We're working now on moving people from being leaders to leader-organizers."

Lance is clear about the need for organization if the poverty of neighborhoods like MacArthur Park is ever to be overcome. "I believe in organizing for power," he says. "It is the best hope for narrowing the gap between rich and poor. The poor need power to change things around—union organizing, political power through neighborhood organizations." At Pueblo Nuevo, it is its people—the "New People"—who set the agenda and decide what kind of community they want to be.

A Visit to the Church of the Four Winds

It is not always easy to be a Native American in urban America.

A century and more after the uprooting of Indian peoples across the continent and their relocation to reservations far from their historic homelands, generations after the efforts of the Indian schools to erase every trace of tribal identity, the tragic consequences remain. To be an urban Indian is to be removed from the reservation and the traditions of its members; to find oneself subject to countless pressures to ignore or forget the past and to conform to the culture that shapes city living in the United States. To be a Native American in the urban context means accepting the status of a small minority in a place that your ancestors may once have assumed was theirs to call home. Indian Christians often feel considerable loyalty to the church they knew on the reservation, but do not always feel at home in its big-city congregations. Like many other Native people who are Christian, they wonder about the relationship between the spirituality of their Indian past and the practices of the church of their birth. And they cannot forget the sad fact that American churches are implicated in many of the events that devastated Native people in the past.

Native Americans number some fourteen thousand in the greater Portland area, less than 5 percent of the population. Many have lived there since the Second World War; others have arrived much more recently from reservations, in Oregon or elsewhere. The population is diverse, tribally, educationally, and culturally. The area offices of the Bureau of Indian

Affairs and the Indian Health Office employ numbers of Native persons with professional training; Portland is also home to a number of regional organizations, including the Affiliated Tribes of Northwest Indians.

The Church of the Four Winds came into being in the mid-1980s under the impetus of a number of people, some of them belonging to tribes with historic ties to the Episcopal Church in South Dakota and Navajoland. Episcopal funding helped establish the congregation, but it was never conceived as a denominational church. Rather, it was seen as a place where Indians of any church, or no church, could be nurtured. For five years it has also been receiving funding from the Evangelical Lutheran Church, and recently received a grant from the Presbyterian Church for its community ministry.

The church's members differ among themselves about what the church is, and ought to be. Some consider the church to be primarily an *Indian* group, which should therefore remain open to non-Christian spirituality; some see no need for an ordained minister from the outside. Others, while affirming the place of Indian elements in its worship, see it as a *church*, proclaiming the Christian gospel through word and sacrament. Still others consider it an important but secondary loyalty; their first is to another congregation. The congregation copes with this difference of opinion by alternating the emphasis of its twice-monthly services. Worship on the first Sunday of each month is a celebration of the Eucharist, while the gathering on the third Sunday may draw from the longhouse tradition, the Native American Church, or provide a forum for speakers on issues of concern to the Indian community.

Ramona Rank, who is studying for the Lutheran Church's ordained ministry and has been a member of the Church of the Four Winds nearly from the beginning, considers it indeed to be a church, but the primary identities its people share are their Indian heritage and their Christian faith, *not* their denominational allegiance. Although she has chief responsibility for worship, other members of the congregation now share in its planning. By incorporating Indian music and other traditional elements into their services, "we are trying," she says, "to use the foundation of our Christianity to shape and build an experience of worship that is *ours:* worship that will have the same elements, but done in our own way."

Members of the Church of the Four Winds have worshipped in three different churches, all of them Episcopal, since the congregation was organized. Most of the clergy who have provided the services for which an ordained minister is required have also been Episcopalians, but for as long as three years the church maintained itself without a regular pastor, and has never had the services of full-time clergy. The current clergyperson, the Reverend Edward Wilson, undertook the responsibility while still rector of another parish. Aside from officiating at the sacraments, his chief duties are hospital and home visits. Native spirituality is accustomed to ascribing holiness to its spiritual leaders; the congregation does not see its clergy as *administrators* but as *holy people.*

Members find echoes of their congregation's life and character in the description of the churches in the book of Acts. Like the early Christian community, Native Americans have great respect for their elders and it is the lay members of the Church of the Four Winds, not the clergy, who set its direction. Program, worship, and communication are the responsibility of an eight-member board of directors, most of them women. Women also predominate in the congregation. This is partly a reflection of the important leadership role women played among Northwest Indians before the Conquest. But it is also surely a reflection of the tragic social toll inflicted upon Native men by American society. Unemployment, an affront to Indian tradition and sense of worth, and the consequent loss of self-esteem, are a principal cause of the alcoholism that has decimated the Native population, and especially its men.

The Church of the Four Winds is not large; its core group numbers some forty people, although it is not unusual for two hundred people to be present for a special service or event. All its gatherings include a potluck meal, in keeping with Indian traditions of hospitality and also to assure that spiritual and community needs are both addressed.

In such a setting, the gospel comes as good news to a people for whom exile from their homeland is both a memory and a present fact of life. For Indian people, the gospel is only partly fulfilled when individuals learn of their acceptance by God. Like Israel, Indians suffered exile as members of a *people* or *nation,* and the gospel must address them as peoples and nations. The fundamental issue for Indians in the United States is *sovereignty:* their right to exist, permanently and unencumbered, as the free peoples the American government always claimed it recognized them to be. Sovereignty does not mean *ownership* of the land, but the right to its *use.*

Ministry in the Native context cannot avoid addressing the struggle for sovereignty, because for Indian Christians sovereignty is part of the very fabric of the gospel. Advocacy of Indian rights and prerogatives is not peripheral to ministry in such a setting; it is at its heart. Interest in the issue of sovereignty is one of the unifying factors for the Church of the Four Winds.

The congregation has recently begun working with other institutions to provide education and training for Indians in Portland. Young people are learning Indian dance and arts. The church has formed a partnership with a Title V entitlement program to address education needs. And the church's women's ministry is teaching women how to make traditional quilts, not only as a way of preserving arts and skills but to generate income.

One of the tasks of the Church of the Four Winds, says Ramona Rank, is to "affirm Indian people in finding out who they are." That mission is two-sided. It means proclaiming the gospel in ways that address Native Americans as they are; but it also means resisting the voices that would have them deny the importance of their Indian identity. For the Church of the Four Winds, *resistance* is not peripheral to Christian ministry; it is at its heart.

The Gospel in the High Country

Grand County is at the heart of Colorado's high country, draped across the Rocky Mountains at an altitude that carries the risk of snow long after spring flowers have already transformed the valleys below. It is enormous, encompassing ten thousand square miles, home to no more than ten thousand permanent residents, gathered in a few small towns and isolated on ranches or in scattered mountain cabins. For several months of the year, the roads to the outside world are risky and often impassable. People with medical emergencies are evacuated by helicopter. Two of the communities are seasonal; one flourishes as a ski resort, the other fills up with summer residents. There is only one traffic light in all of Grand County.

The Episcopal Church in Grand County is more a presence than a site; indeed, the church gathers in four different places, depending on the season of the year. Only two of the towns have permanent congregations.

The Reverend Kelsey Hogue is the vicar who provides pastoral leadership for the scattered members of the Episcopal Church in Grand County. He and his family live in Granby, down the street from St. John the Baptist Church, the larger of two permanent congregations.

But while the mountain scenery of the high country is often breathtaking, all is not well in these mountains. Betty Jo Woods, who worked as a librarian and teacher in Granby, points out that "independence penetrates every aspect of people's lives. People came here because they want to be alone. Organized religion never had a major impact in this county; it has never been a foregone conclusion that people would go to church."

In this sparsely settled area, independence, isolation, and loneliness are interrelated. Families often guard their privacy, yet the incidence of alcoholism, child abuse, and family violence is many times the national norm.

Hogue and his wife are not strangers to the area; they came from an hour down the road from Granby and are, he says, "the closest thing to home-grown leaders these churches could have." Grand County is home, he explains, to "a number of people who are retired from management positions in other parts of the country and are comfortably off, and another group who were raised here and have accumulated wealth, usually land. But one of the problems is that there are also people who moved here because they thought it was paradise. There are plenty of jobs in the county for maids, groundskeepers, and resort sales positions. But they are all low-pay, seasonal, and have no benefits at all. Both parents have to work two jobs to make ends meet, because they may make only five dollars an hour. If you don't work for the railroad, the county, the schools, or one of the towns, or reach middle management in the ski areas, you don't have a decent-paying job in this county. Families are having problems, and alcohol makes them worse."

That is certainly true. One in four adults in Granby County is alcoholic; in an eighteen-month period, eighty-seven cases of child sexual abuse were filed in a county with only ten thousand people. Since the local newspaper publishes court proceedings, everyone is aware of these tragic events. Debbie Hogue, who teaches eighth grade in the local school, observes that it is the schools that must pick up the pieces. "In my eighth grade alone, I could probably identify twenty to twenty-five out of eighty children with whom we openly discuss the alcoholism of one or both parents. The children talk about it among themselves. They all know, and they know who suffers the same difficulties they do. Out of ten children in our Sunday School, only two are not going through a divorce or family crisis. We provide a safe haven." And, adds Kelsey Hogue, when a couple goes through a divorce, the whole town takes sides.

St. John's Church is very much aware of its identity in the community and its responsibilities to its town. Many of the church's members recall when there was only one church in Granby, and to outsiders it often appeared cliquish and judgmental. One determined Episcopalian was convinced that what the community needed was an Episcopal church, and she convinced others that her dream was possible. Raising money for its construction occupied the little congregation's attention for years; one member describes St. John's as "the church that bake sales built."

Perhaps because that project was a costly and taxing one, its members enjoy a feeling of closeness that many describe as a sense of "family." Indeed, says Betty Clark, a retired school nurse who has committed herself to baking and delivering a loaf of bread to every newcomer who appears at St. John's, "St. John's is a real family. That's the biggest thing about this congregation." Recently arrived members agree. It has approximately sixty active adult members, "a congregation," in Hogue's words, "where you can't show up on Sunday morning and be left alone." And Mavis Tuten, in charge of the local emergency room and active at St. John's, points out that "it's hard to be anonymous in a small town. If you step into a church, you are making a 'statement.'"

That "statement" is made in many ways; after the "official" coffee hour that follows the service on Sunday morning, many of the members adjourn to a local coffee shop for breakfast. "Somehow," says Hogue, "people must make the connection between the group that shows up on Sunday morning and the people they are during the week." He himself spends time every day in the same setting. As Betty Jo Woods comments, "We asked for a long time for the kind of ministry Kelsey Hogue is doing—time downtown with people who 'express themselves in the vernacular.' People were surprised that religion comes up in normal conversation."

When summer comes, the population of the resort community of Grand Lake soars. A Roman Catholic family that owns a marina makes boats available for a Sunday evening service, and musicians from St. John's go to the lake for Evening Prayer.

Then, as summer fades into the fall season, large numbers of young people arrive to staff the ski areas around Winter Park. Kelsey Hogue and the local Baptist minister joined forces to work with a small group of lay volunteers to provide weekly meals for young people. Some eventually volunteered their services as musicians at local churches.

In the early days of the parish's life, many of those attracted to St. John's Church were people in search of spiritual support for their own work in the helping professions. In recent years, however, many of the newcomers are victims of alcoholism and abuse. "Some of the people coming into St. John's now," says Hogue, "are very needy. We have the capacity to bring in two or three people every six months. If we were to grow much faster than that, I don't think we could absorb them."

Kelsey Hogue is clear about how his role is related to the congregation's ministry in Grand County. "My role," he says, "is to empower people to go out and minister, not to leave them behind while I go out and do it." But, he adds, many clergy act as if the church were already comfortable with that new paradigm. "The task is to move people into the new paradigm. We are to be agents of change." Nancy Shaffer, St. John's senior warden, adds, "One thing about us is that we know what our ministry is."

Hogue's perspective shook Trinity Church in Kremmling, on the other side of Grand County, when he arrived on the scene. Smaller than the congregation in Granby, its members had grown used to a rapid turnover in clergy; they knew they often served as a "first assignment" for newly ordained priests who soon moved on to larger parishes.

"When Kelsey first came to Kremmling, he asked us what we wanted to be," says Janet Ohri. "We are all busy people. We said we didn't want more meetings and more things to take care of. We were going to use the church as a refuge and a place to come and draw from."

Troubled by what he perceived as their passivity and lack of commitment to the church and its mission, Hogue called a congregational potluck supper and parish meeting. "I had warned the bishop that if the people weren't going to be the Body of Christ I was going to close [the church] down. I told the congregation they had not responded when I opened my heart to them. They were horrified!" They had not been challenged to consider that their own faithfulness was an issue. "It had never occurred to them," says Hogue, "that things had changed. They have really responded. As soon as that happened, we began adding families."

"Remodeling the kitchen was another big milestone," adds Debbie Hogue. "The kitchen was dingy and Kelsey suggested making it a pleasant place to be. After we had covered the kitchen with sheetrock, the warden remarked, "Other priests have come with their Bible in their hand and told us what to do. You are the first priest who showed up with a tool belt and showed us how to do it."

On a typical spring Sunday, only four people in Trinity's congregation of about thirty are lifelong or even longtime Episcopalians. Many are refugees from denominations that stress the demands of membership, and are perceived as fostering a judgmental or critical attitude toward those inside and outside their number. Nancy Abbott, whose roots are in the Midwest but has lived in Grand County for nearly twenty years, remarked, "I think we serve a group of people and mindset, a group who would not feel as comfortable in other churches. We are more accepting of life's realities. It's not because we say that everything is all right, but I've never felt [more of] Christ's love and less of the judgment than I do here."

Amy Lichthardt, a newcomer to Kremmling, agrees. "It's God's job to decide who is and who isn't Christian." Nancy Peterson, who drives with her family from Yampa, an eighty-mile round trip, notes that "tolerance is the hallmark of the Episcopal Church, and our service proclaims the joy and love of God over and over again. I think we are here to bridge the factionalism between groups."

Mona Blandford, one of the few whose membership in Trinity Church stretches back more than thirty years, commented, "I am never sure what the phrase 'extended family' means; my idea of it is my family here. All the people here are part of my family. I know that outside of sharing Christ on Sunday morning, if there is something I need help with, I can call on any of my church family. There is a real feeling of closeness to Christ when I come here with these people. I could probably do something absolutely ridiculous and my church family would say, 'That's OK, we still love you.' That is the blessing of the small church. When we activate our prayer chain everybody is genuinely concerned. A few years ago a friend from a large Denver church came to visit. We had our normal congregation, and after church she said, 'It's been a long time since I really knew what the Eucharist meant.'"

Mindful of the eighty-mile round trip she and her family make weekly, Nancy Peterson remarked, "A church family is more than seeing each other in church or in the grocery store. It is vital to us as a family to make the trek. We carry your presence with us back over the mountain."

"Most people don't wear their sainthood visibly," commented Mona Blandford. "They don't boast about being Christian, but they do work in the community. The Lord says, 'Whom shall I send?' We say, 'Here I am, send me.' But we don't put on the label, we just go out and do it."

"Everybody has the same enthusiasm as the people did the day we built this church," added her husband Bob. "That harmony and love were present then; that is what brought us together in the first place. That bonding has remained."

In the Battle Zone

In 1944, the German theologian Dietrich Bonhoeffer doubted if the churches possessed the possibility to make the changes necessary to bring the Nazi terror to an end. All Christians could do, he suggested, was to wait, and pray, and struggle to be faithful.

Perhaps it is not surprising that John Meyer, in charge of St. Peter's Episcopal Church in downtown Detroit for fifteen years, finds great wisdom in Bonhoeffer's stance. For there is something eerily familiar about the center of Detroit; it looks for all the world like the aftermath of a gruesome war.

In many ways, St. Peter's Church is caught up in a war: a struggle between life and death. John Meyer speaks often of the "signs of death" that surround the church. In a paper reflecting upon a murder that occurred in the church's soup kitchen, he wrote, "We remain, as ever, in the place of risk, careening on the edge of non-being, blood and bean soup on the floor."

It is precisely this nearness to death that places the church at the side of the poor: to be poor means to be vulnerable to death. Of course, all mortals are vulnerable as such. In the mainstream society, however, everything is organized to keep death back. Death, as it were, has to wait in line. Not so among the poor; death is free to rage like a storm.

For John Meyer and the congregation of St. Peter's Church, the most potent signs of death are not the shells of blackened buildings that dot the nearby landscape, but the people they encounter daily. Just across the street from the Detroit Tigers' stadium, the church is also within easy walking distance of several blocks noted for prostitution. People at St. Peter's have been struck not only by the numbers of women working "the street," but by their increasing youth. Many are nearly children, and all too often they are suffering from addiction or AIDS or both. Meyer describes one young woman who came in a frantic search for help: "She was so thin, so diminutive in her features. In proportion, her eyes seemed larger than her body. She may not have weighed more than eighty pounds. Her arm, which I touched through her coat, seemed to be bone with only a little flesh. 'I feel as if I want to die,' she said."

St. Peter's was not always an outpost in a battle zone. It began as a flourishing Anglo-Irish congregation in the section of Detroit known as "Corktown." Its present church was planned as part of a massive building project in the 1920s but the 1929 crash left an unfinished shell. Only ten years later did a single wealthy family pay for the building to be nearly completed (some details still remain unfinished), and it has never regained its pre-Depression strength.

St. Peter's Church has a history of hospitality stretching back to the Second World War. At one point it ran a boys' home, then provided space for a halfway house for ex-prisoners until 1982. For three years it housed a homeless shelter, now the principal shelter in Detroit. When a crisis in 1987 stranded large numbers of refugees on their way to Canada, St. Peter's Home for Refugees opened its doors and remained open for nearly a year.

But it is the girls and young women who walk the streets of Corktown that have become the focus of the church's ministry. In 1988, a parish program known as Alternatives for Girls began, says Meyer, "with no funds and few staff or volunteers." In 1993, the program, now housed in the church's parish house but independent of the church, had a staff of forty-five and a yearly budget of more than a million dollars.

St. Peter's Inn houses 10 to 15 young women at a given time, offers drug and alcohol treatment, and an after-care program that provides training for independent living. There is also a program that reaches 150 girls at risk through clubs staffed by an ecumenical corps of volunteers. As many as 700 women are in regular contact with Alternatives for Girls through its street outreach. A soup kitchen staffed by Catholic Worker volunteers serves 500 meals daily.

The community around St. Peter's Church has been defined as an area of "100 percent abuse," meaning that *all* its children are at risk of physical, emotional, and sexual abuse. Indeed, Meyer wonders if perhaps abuse, and especially the sexual abuse of children, is the root cause of the culture of poverty he sees everywhere. "The core of what it means to be poor in this society," he says, "is a sense of curse. The effects of child abuse are not sloughed off—they are as lasting as any Vietnam experience. It determines your life course, your life chance."

This endemic abuse, says Meyer, "sets the tone for parish life." At least half the members of the vestry have been directly affected by it in some way. Certainly the Alternatives for Girls program, and the congregation's commitment to it, is a direct outcome of the reality that touches them. And just as the life of the congregation is shaped by it, so its understanding of Christian faith responds to it. "Theologically," says Meyer, "what we are dealing with is death. The gospel is that life wins, but the struggle remains."

The congregation of St. Peter's Church numbers only about a hundred, and on most Sundays the worshippers can fit into the choir stalls in front of the pews. Meyer and the assisting priest, David Lillvis, divide the duties of presiding and preaching between them, and sermons often take the form of a dialogue with those present.

The congregation, which John Meyer considers "the most important thing" about St. Peter's, has been ethnically diverse since the 1950s. An Oneida Indian group was once a significant component of the congregation, but has now dispersed. Today the congregation is made up mostly of African Americans and poor whites, with some people from Jamaica and a few Hispanic members as well. "It takes a lot of energy," Meyer observes, "to keep diversity together."

For the people of St. Peter's Church, their own congregation is the focus of their experience of the church and Christian faith. Brenda MacLean, who has worked for years as a community organizer in Detroit, finds that the parish and its people are a constant source of energy for struggling with the pervasive death she encounters daily in her work, as well as support in the concrete situations that arise with staggering frequency.

Some of the people at St. Peter's with a sense of the church's history and tradition identify themselves with the religious orders in the early church. Like those ancient Christians, they live without formal rule but consider their community, focused in the church, as a place of spiritual warfare against the powers of death around them. And like the desert fathers and mothers, they find reciting the Psalter at Morning and Evening Prayer a powerful weapon in that battle. On many days, some of the young women housed at St. Peter's Inn next door join in Evening Prayer.

And the people of St. Peter's have a strongly focused sense of *place* as part of the Christian calling. Their church itself serves them and others as a sanctuary in the midst of death, a place where prayer may be the most powerful witness to life it is possible to give. Meyer points out how often the figures in the Bible are called, not to a particular ministry but to a specific *place.* Certainly the people who form St. Peter's community consider themselves rooted in that congregation and the community it seeks to serve.

More and more, the people of St. Peter's Church focus on *baptism* as the key to their identity and a sign of life over against the signs of death that surround them. Meyer wonders if the traditional view of baptism that defines it as Christian initiation is enough. "What does it mean," he asks, "when the baptismal font is warmed up and ready to go?" The challenge is to find ways to emphasize the meaning of baptism as the key to understanding the nature of Christian faith and life. For the people of St. Peter's, "baptism is a breaking with culture—we are struggling with signs of death."

Indeed, for John Meyer and the congregation of St. Peter's Church, the sign of baptism is nothing less than "a lightning flash" in a world where there is too much death.

Index